Cultures of Anyone

Contemporary Hispanic and Lusophone Cultures

This series aims to provide a forum for new research on modern and contemporary hispanic and lusophone cultures and writing. The volumes published in Contemporary Hispanic and Lusophone Cultures reflect a wide variety of critical practices and theoretical approaches, in harmony with the intellectual, cultural and social developments that have taken place over the past few decades. All manifestations of contemporary hispanic and lusophone culture and expression are considered, including literature, cinema, popular culture, theory. The volumes in the series will participate in the wider debate on key aspects of contemporary culture.

Cultures of Anyone

Studies on Cultural Democratization in the Spanish Neoliberal Crisis

LUIS MORENO-CABALLUD

Translated by Linda Grabner

LIVERPOOL UNIVERSITY PRESS

First published 2015 by
Liverpool University Press
4 Cambridge Street
Liverpool
L69 7ZU

British Library Cataloguing-in-Publication data
A British Library CIP record is available

ISBN 978-1-78138-193-9 cased
ISBN 978-1-78694-184-8 softback

Typeset in Borges by
Carnegie Book Production, Lancaster

Contents

Part II. Cultural Democratizations

Acknowledgments

This book has been possible thanks to the direct or indirect contribution of a great variety of people who desire and experiment with collaborative and egalitarian—and, sometimes, non-capitalist and non-patriarchal—ways of life. You will find many of them quoted in the following pages. But a lot of them don't usually write or at least don't publish articles or books. I want to express my gratitude to them. I hope that they may find this book interesting, despite all its shortcomings, and that they find it a good tool to resist the excess of cultural authority that is usually granted on those of us who do write. I would like to thank particularly the people from the political collectives in which I have worked and learned in the last years: Democracia Real Ya NY, the General Assembly of NYC, Occupy Wall Street's Empowerment and Education working group, Making Worlds, 16 Beaver, Marea Granate NY, Círculo Podemos EEUU, and the NYC to Spain delegation. I thank my friends and colleagues in the universities where I studied and worked. I thank my dear friends and 'compas' in Madrid, New York and everywhere else. I could have never survived without your love. And I deeply and lovingly thank my sister, Ana Moreno, my parents, Merche Caballud and Ramiro Moreno, my partner Begonia Santa-Cecilia, and our son, Max Santa-Cecilia.

Introduction

The Spanish state, 2008–May 2015: unemployment rates approach 25%, and 50% among young people. Eight million living in poverty, according to official figures. The second highest rate of childhood malnutrition in Europe. The highest rise in economic inequality of all states in the OECD. Some 3 million empty homes and about 184 families evicted from their homes every day.

Despite changes in the governing party, the public policies that have attempted to address this situation have not changed since the beginning of what has come to be called the 'economic crisis:' obedience to the 'experts' of the Troika (the International Monetary Fund, the European Commission, the European Central Bank), bailouts of financial entities, prioritizing payment of the public debt over social spending, and cuts to basic public services like health, education, and disability benefits.

Regardless of whether or not these policies work, what my research seeks to emphasize is that such measures are not only *executed* by political authorities, but are also *normalized* by a certain form of cultural authority: the authority of the 'experts.' This authority is based on a long, complex tradition in every society that tends to establish a group of people 'in the know,' and another group 'in the dark.' In its most flexible manifestation, this tradition allows for those 'in the dark' to be able to move up to the group 'in the know,' if they fulfill an entire series of pedagogical prerequisites supervised by the latter group. But in any case, the decisions about important things, like the social organization of housing, work, food, health, and education, will be made made on the basis of the specialized technical opinion of those 'in the know' at any given moment.

Given this cultural tradition, those who implement political measures enabling situations as difficult for the majority of a population as those currently experienced in Spain can justify their policies based on the technical knowledge of the 'experts' who recommend them. There are also, of course, others who oppose them by putting forward the authority of

their own 'experts,' who—based on their respective technical knowledge—
recommend very different policies. In the midst of this confrontation between
differing groups of 'those in the know,' those who are supposedly 'in the
dark' are sometimes called upon to offer an opinion—primarily through
the election of political parties every four years. But again, according to this
cultural tradition, the opinion of 'just anyone'—of someone who does not
belong to the group of 'those in the know'—can never be equal to that of
those who bear the titles of established knowledge. In the capitalist version
of this tradition, those 'in the know' guarantee a way of life for everyone else
which, in addition to voting, they can use money as a measure of all social
value and channel their individual desires by consuming and competing
among themselves.[1]

1 The cultural authority of those 'in the know' is never isolated; on the contrary,
it is part of wider 'ways of life,' which reproduce complex structures of domination
operating at different levels. Thus, in its capitalist version, the segregation between
those 'in the know' and those 'in the dark' works together with, among other factors,
the crucial function of money as a measure of all social value, which reinforces
and reproduces social inequality (see Harvey 1989). In this sense, when I say that
public policies responding to the 'crisis' are *naturalized* by this system of cultural
authority, I don't exactly mean that many people really believe they are adequate
because a series of 'experts' say so. Moreover, and as I hope the following pages
will make clear, I mean that these policies are supported by a whole 'way of life'
through which we tend to internalize hierarchical and competitive divisions of value
that exclude many of us from the position of 'having a say' about the value of said
policies. In the words of French sociologist Pierre Bourdieu, this internalization is
a key aspect of domination, which consists in the limitation of the 'possibilities of
thought and action in the oppressed' (Bourdieu 2001, 41). Fortunately, we—people
of the twenty-first century—have inherited many tools to understand domination
and its 'cultural' aspect. In a world swamped by publicity, propaganda, spectacle,
and therapy, it seems increasingly clear that, as writer Ricardo Piglia (2000) likes to
say, quoting from Valery, 'physical repression alone is not enough to impose order;
fictional forces are required *as well.*' There have, of course, been very important
contributions to this understanding from intellectual and activist traditions.
Antonio Gramsci's concept of hegemony (1999) was instrumental in bringing to the
fore the power of education, religion, intellectuals, and the media in constructing
a worldview for the dominated to accept their condition. After Gramsci, there have
been many ways of qualifying the nature of this 'acceptance,' displacing simplistic
ideas of 'rational consensus.' To quote just some of them, we could remember the
aforementioned Bourdieu's work on the internalization of domination, Laclau and
Mouffe's Lacanian re-reading of Gramscian hegemony (2004), Beasley-Murray's
concept of 'posthegemony' (2010), Rancière's notion of the 'distribution of the
sensible' (2004), and Deleuze and Guattari's concepts of segmentation and molarity,
as well as their whole method of 'schizoanalysis' or 'cartography of desire' (1987).
In this book, the two last theoretical frames (Rancière's and Deleuze and Guattari's)

In recent years, however, something important has happened in the Spanish state. The economic disaster has generated such a huge drop in the credibility of political institutions that it has begun to affect this hierarchical cultural system, thus compromising the very authority of those 'in the know.' This has driven many people 'in the dark' to trust in their own abilities to collaboratively construct the knowledge they need in any given situation and to generate effective answers to the problems that confront them. In the process, they avoid having to weigh down their ways of knowing with the monopolistic, exclusive, hierarchical ambitions that accompany the tradition of the 'experts.'

This book studies some signs that seem to point towards a crisis of that tradition, along with others that announce the emergence of something I call 'cultures of anyone.' These cultures do not suggest a rejection of specialized fields of knowledge, but rather a rejection of the *uses* of such knowledge to monopolize cultural authority. They avoid creating divisions between those 'in the know' and those 'in the dark,' asserting that we all know something, nobody knows everything, and our abilities are developed better when we learn together than when we live in hierarchical relationships.[2]

are preferred for understanding domination (although not quoted extensively). This is because they seem more apt to investigating cultural processes that, instead of following Bourdieu's interest in the restriction of the 'possibilities of action and thought of the dominated,' strive to flee the hegemonic division of people into 'those who know and can' and those who 'don't know and can't,' by betting on the empowerment of the intelligence and abilities of anyone. This bet certainly has its risks, but as I will try to show, it cannot be considered simple wishful thinking, or a blind negation of the harsh and complex realities of domination.

2 This, of course, will always run the risk of not paying enough attention to the deep determinations that all sorts of hierarchical relationships have imprinted upon our lives. By opening a space for the 'anyone,' these cultures certainly are in danger of encouraging superficial understandings of such determinations, which would be doomed to return in conflictive ways. On the other side of the argument, however, there is always the risk of placing so much emphasis on those social determinations that one ends up reinforcing them. For instance: by victimizing and patronizing those who are 'suffering the most,' or by assigning them stereotypes that deprive them of the possibility of self-representation and value creation. Beyond categorical and universal judgments about the outcomes of 'cultures of anyone,' I propose to study certain concrete cultural processes that in the context of the neoliberal crisis in Spain have preferred to run the first of those two risks. I believe this is an important task not only because of the increasing social relevance of this type of process (which, as a cultural historian, I think I should investigate), but also because tactically—being aware of the ethical and political dimensions of all research work—I would like my own study to also be a contribution to the empowerment of the abilities of anyone attempted by these processes.

These 'cultures of anyone' have arisen mostly around grassroots social movements and in collaborative spaces fostered by digital technology, but they are spreading to many other social milieus, including those traditionally reserved for institutional 'culture' and 'politics.' They tend to promote the idea that the people affected by or involved in a situation should be the ones to participate in changing it, but not from a perspective of 'anything goes.' Rather, they promote processes of empowerment and collaborative learning that allow the development of anyone's abilities and knowledge base. The 'cultures of anyone' create 'collective intelligence.' They believe that what 'goes,' what works, what's worth doing, is better elucidated when everyone's diverse abilities are combined, as opposed to when the knowledge monopolies of a select few are imposed.

They are, in short, 'cultures of anyone' because within them it is understood that culture, the constant collective discussion—be it explicit or implicit—in which decisions are made about what has value, what constitutes a 'decent life,' is something that anyone should be able to participate in. From the point of view of this emergent culture, it is inexcusable that anyone should be excluded from the construction of the meaning of her or his dignity. For this reason, I propose to define 'cultures of anyone' as forms of *cultural democratization*—not so much in terms of allowing access to a body of already established knowledge and values (as understood in the habitual sense of the phrase), but in the sense of opening the construction of knowledge and of values to participation by anyone.

*

April 26, 2014, Madrid, Malasaña district: seven women—one pregnant—and eight children—the sons and daughters of those women—entered an apartment building that had been empty for 17 years, with the intention of making it their home. These women were neither in hiding nor alone. Signs are unfurled from the windows reading 'Together we can,' and 'Safe housing for everyone.' Down in the street, they are supported by a group of people, one of whom has a megaphone she uses to announce:

> We are a group of women fighting for the well-being of our children, who are in this situation right along with us. We are tired of being invisible to the public powers, we condemn the lack of recognition of the kind of work we do: domestic work and caring for our families. ... Being able to pamper our kids and raising them in the security of a home is not a luxury, it is our right.

The right to raise a child in a good home seems, in principle, eminently reasonable according to that ever-vague amalgam called 'common sense.' It is much less 'commonsensical,' at least in societies strongly based on a capitalist economy, to think that this right makes it okay for you to enter someone else's property to set up house and raise your children there. But these women have concluded that, given their uncertain situation and the way the public powers and their experts have interpreted the 'right to a good home' as guaranteed by the Spanish Constitution, it is legitimate to accord priority to their dignity and the dignity of their children over the validity of a deed of property.

This decision—and this is what I want to emphasize—was not made individually, but in the bosom of a social movement that is open to anyone and which collects and cultivates diverse abilities and ways of knowing— such as solidarity, legal knowledge, public policy analysis, diffusion, etc.—to collectively confront housing problems.

So, these women are among the 1,180 homeless or evicted individuals who have already 'recuperated' at least 20 empty buildings through the 'Social Work' campaign of the People Affected by the Mortgage Platform (Plataforma de Afectados por la Hipoteca, or PAH). It would be difficult to dispute that the PAH is one of the institutions most recognized for its legitimacy in Spanish society today, thanks to its work of mutual support during the 'housing emergency' currently taking place in Spain. Its legitimacy has not been gained through the authority of 'experts,' but earned through the democratic processes of a 'culture of anyone.'

Furthermore, it would be disingenuous to claim that this legitimacy was generated illegally or 'behind the backs' of the powers that be. The change of priorities proposed by the PAH has already begun to be translated into laws and precedents. Institutions like the Strasbourg Human Rights Commission have supported its rejection of evictions, and several judges have conceded 'non-recourse debt' (e.g., accepting the deed to a home as payment in full, instead of foreclosing) and even 'social rents' proposed by the PAH. In any case, all of the Platform's activities have always been supported by Article 47 of the Constitution: 'every person has the right to a decent home.'[3]

Laws are never unambiguous; they are designed to be interpreted. The same is true, although with greater flexibility, of legitimacy and 'common

3 The story of the People Affected by Mortgages Platform (PAH) and its achievements and social and institutional recognitions has been narrated by two of its founders and best-known members, activists Ada Colau and Adrià Alemany, in the book *Vidas hipotecadas* (2013). Also of interest on this subject are the documentaries *La Plataforma* (2013) and *7 Days with PAH Barcelona* (2014).

sense.' Both spheres, legality and legitimacy, depend on the cultural process through which the meanings and values of reality are constantly debated, whether tacitly or explicitly. Thus the 'culture of anyone,' the type of democratization of knowledge bases and value production cultivated by initiatives like those of the PAH, is liable to have crucial consequences in all areas of social life.

*

This book studies the tensions between historically established—although at times foundering—forms of cultural authority, and those 'cultures of anyone' that have reappeared time and again during Spain's 'economic crisis.' Regarding the former, the first part of the book proposes two interconnected genealogies. On one hand, the cultural authority prevailing at the onset of the 'economic crisis' partakes of the long 'modern' technocratic tradition (de Certeau 2010) that grants legitimacy in meaning production only to those who participate in certain disciplines and institutions (what Bauman calls 'the modern power/knowledge complex' (1987)), and only if they access it by acknowledging their inferiority to and dependence on those who already hold it (according to the hierarchical functioning of what Rancière called 'the pedagogical society' (2003)).

On the other hand, over the course of Spain's parliamentary monarchy (1978 to present), a new layer of particularly powerful disciplines and institutions has been deposited over this long tradition of cultural authoritarianism. These disciplines and institutions are extremely flexible devices, capable of invading daily life, imposing a way of producing meaning, or a 'way of the world,' as Dardot and Laval say, that essentially consists of generalized competition and turning life into a business (2014; see also Garcés Mascareñas 2013). This 'way of the world'—neoliberalism—is enshrined in the traditional ambitions of certain 'educated' elites to monopolize the production of meaning. These are the ones who have endorsed neoliberalism as 'the best possible system' so consistently that the general public has accepted it as inevitable even if they weren't quite ready to wholeheartedly embrace it.

This last becomes most obvious at times when a large part of that public begins to question the efficacy of neoliberal logic, because they are suffering economic insecurity and social inequality generated by its competitive principle. It is then, as we see every day, that those who hold political and cultural power brandish appeals to 'normality' and 'modernity,' to equality with 'more advanced countries,' and to the recommendations of 'experts,' to reinforce the discredited neoliberal 'way of the world.'

In the second part of the book, I study some emerging cultural logics that interrupt, to a certain degree, both the hierarchical, monopolistic authority of 'those in the know' and the neoliberal 'way of the world.' They do this by promoting ways of collaborating that tend to create favorable conditions for anyone's empowerment and the development of anyone's abilities. I suggest that these ways of collaborating have, so far, been much more able to offer meanings, languages, symbols, and sociability than to insure food, housing, and care. But I also believe that the former elements are just as necessary for human life as the latter. With support from feminist theories of social reproduction (such as those of Antonella Picchio (2009), Silvia Federici (2010), and Amaia Orozco (2014)), I show that in the constant collective process through which human life—always constituted by interdependent individuals—is sustained, it is also decided, tacitly or explicitly, what constitutes a life with dignity. For that decision, 'culture'—meaning, languages, symbols, sociability—is indispensable. In this sense, 'culture' plays an important part in maintaining human life, and being able to maintain a nonhierarchical, noncompetitive culture is a way of sustaining lives with a certain amount of autonomy—cultural autonomy—with respect to neoliberal reason.

I analyze the aspects of that 'cultural autonomy' relative to knowledge monopolies and the competitive mechanisms of neoliberalism by studying digital cultures, social movements emerging in the cycle opened by the 15M (or *Indignados*), and some examples of cultural institutions, both public and self-managed. Thus I propose a route that begins with the massive expansion of the ability to create cultural value collectively through information technologies and communication (about which Margarita Padilla (2013), Mayo Fuster Morell (2012), Manuel Castells (2009), and many others have written at length). At the same time, it suggests the constant difficulty for communities to self-manage the value they produce, because of the multiplicity of appropriation and precarization mechanisms at the disposal of more powerful agents in the game of widespread neoliberal competition (Harvey 2013; Harney 2010b; Rowan 2010).

I continue with an analysis of the 15M movement and other similar ones, like the Mareas (the Tides) and the PAH, which develop protocols for collaboration and the composition of diverse knowledge bases and abilities in closed physical environments, as Amador Fernández-Savater, one of the most interesting observers of these movements, has made clear (2008; 2011a; 2013). With these protocols they manage to provide support mechanisms for the bodies that participate in them. Based on the model of the 15M encampments as spaces where participants attempted to sustain a life completely devoid of competitiveness and open to anyone, I note the difficulties inherent in maintaining this type of experience, betting so heavily on the transformation of daily life, as well as its clashes with 'cultural authorities.'

Finally, I examine the existence of self-managed cultural institutions, like those participating in Fundación de los Comunes (the Commons Foundation Network), and public ones, like Medialab-Prado in Madrid, which have a certain ability to 'decommodify' the cultural life of those who participate in them. I also note the limits in each case. I analyze the difficulties, caused by the strong commodification of the public culture sector, in creating stable cultural institutions that can function democratically and that the population might be inclined to defend as much as schools and public hospitals. And, lastly, I discuss the added difficulties that the necessarily experimental aspect of the cultural sphere presupposes for those possibilities of institutionalization.

*

This book does not attempt to be 'above' or 'beyond' the immense cultural problem it seeks to theorize through the disjunction between a 'culture of experts' and a 'culture of anyone.' On the contrary, it is an investigation of that problem which attempts to inscribe itself within the democratizing logics of the very 'cultures of anyone' that it studies, as well as contributing something that could be useful for them.

Therefore, I want to clarify that I think the 'cultures of anyone' I am writing about are the most appropriate ones to study themselves and their context. My contribution attempts to respect this fact by bringing together numerous voices that emerge from them, and by recognizing that my own voice exists here due to that 'collective intelligence.' I attempt to show my indebtedness to these cultures explicitly through quotes, the frequency of which serves to belie the fiction of a strong authorial function. Such a dominant authorial voice would tend to obscure the collective sources of its knowledge in an effort to individually capitalize on their value. In any case, some of the lines of inquiry with which I dialogue will become more explicit in the rather more detailed summary of my argument, outlined chapter by chapter, that I offer to the reader below.[4]

In chapter one I first present some distinctive characteristics of the

---

4 I also want to clarify that most of the specific references to the cultures I am studying come from the Madrid area. This is not due to a deliberate choice, but because I have not, unfortunately, been able to extend the affinity and first-hand knowledge that has helped me carry out this investigation to all parts of the Spanish state to the extent I would have liked. For that I beg your pardon, and I hope to be able to correct these limitations in future works.

forms of cultural authority prevailing in a Spain in crisis, and then I begin to trace key lines of their genealogy. Starting with the ways in which big communications media, experts, politicians and intellectuals have presented the crisis, I discuss their capacity to 'establish a reality' (as Michel de Certeau says) that tends to imagine society as a collection of individuals competing among themselves for a market of diverse goods and possibilities. I note that this competitive, individualistic way of life, which constitutes the heart of neoliberalism (according to Laval and Dardot), has suffered a certain decline. Likewise, those agencies of cultural authority that 'establish' this way of life have seen their credibility suffer due to the economic collapse.

I trace the genealogy of the cultural model in crisis by starting from the structural division between the people responsible for sustaining life and the people responsible for managing the production of meaning. The anthropologist Paul Radin observed this division in precapitalist societies, but the sociologist Zygmunt Bauman also considers it a defining characteristic of modernity. The 'modern power/knowledge complex' is defined, according to Bauman, by the particularly virulent practice of monopolizing the production of meaning. During the Enlightenment, this led to the establishment of the 'garden societies' model through which the elites attempted not only to dominate everyone else, but to transform those other lives and cultures to be 'productive.' In other words, the elites tried to make the rest of the population adapt to the capitalist mode of production and distribution of value.

In accord with the historians Sánchez León (2010) and Jesús Izquierdo (2002), I argue that the widespread implantation of this capitalist way of life occurred during the second phase of Francoism, enshrined through the technoscientific legitimacy of certain expert elites who claimed to be 'modernizing' the country. To achieve this, the rural peasant culture(s) of some two-thirds of the population had to be discredited, which generated a whole series of significant collective inferiority complexes. But in addition, during that transformation, the foundations were laid for Spain's future participation in the European neoliberal economic model, as explained by the Observatorio Metropolitano de Madrid (López Hernández and Rodríguez López 2010). This participation was legitimized by the heirs to a long tradition of 'modernizing, pro-European' intellectual elites, who considered incorporation into neoliberal Europe the only possible path to democratic 'normalization.'

The second chapter comprises a more detailed analysis of the 'standardizing' operation carried out by the cultural authorities of the so-called 'Cultura de la Transición' or 'CT' (Transition Culture). It begins with a reminder of the well-known arguments regarding the exceptional nature of the situation experienced by everyone at the end of the dictatorship, and how this served as a justification for some less than democratic (opaque, nonrepresentative, elitist) ways of ushering in 'democracy.' I relate those well-known arguments to the added authority the political elites of the transition gained through their proximity to the cultural elites. I propose that not only is it true, as Guillem Martínez (creator of the idea of a 'Culture of Transition' (2012)) claimed, that the cultural world would deactivate its critical capacity, but also that a majority of its members opted for a depoliticized, individualist conception of aesthetic modernity, which I analyze drawing on Reinaldo Laddaga's work (2006).

Unlike in other cultural environments that were surely also 'modern' (such as the transitional underground culture studied by Germán Labrador (2008)), the official culture of post-dictatorial Spain would view aesthetic style as something separate from politics, reinforcing through that supposed neutrality the political value of a neoliberal status quo that was always presented as the 'only path to modernity.' The journalistic columnism of progressive intellectuals would turn out to be essential in this regard for consolidating a model of individual cultural authority based on the supposed apolitical exceptionality of the 'creator,' who has broken away from the communities from which he receives the cultural materials for his production. As a result, he is at constant risk of being manipulated in one way or another by the speculative mechanisms of neoliberalism.

The risk of manipulation becomes even more acute as widespread commodification increasingly spectacularizes the world of culture, transforming it into a 'brand' ready to be consumed. This 'culture brand' or 'culture bubble' model coexists with the intellectual's ambitions to constitute an independent, critical authority confronting the established powers. However, I argue that as long as he continues to be tacitly perceived as part of the elite that must lead everyone else to 'modernity,' the intellectual still participates in a structural inequality that turns him into an indirect guarantor of the very social order he criticizes.

The third chapter is a brief incursion into two possible counter-figures of the 'intellectual,' or simply, of the 'cultural agent.' These are characterized precisely by having maintained a fertile and generous dialogue with the communities of meaning production that have inspired and nourished their work. While I focus my argument primarily on writer Luis Mateo Díez's relationship with the peasant cultures of northwest Spain, and on Juan Marsé's with the working-class cultures of Barcelona, I also consider some other similar cases. I propose that the enthusiasm for regional autonomy during the Spanish transition generated a favorable breeding ground for experimentation with forms of political and aesthetic modernity that were capable of including aspects of traditional rural cultures. But I also note that perhaps the main difficulty for such operations was trying to reconcile cultures that prioritize the reproduction of a collective, interdependent life with the inevitably 'productivist,' individualistic drift of Spanish 'modernity.'

I finish by recuperating the odd cases of certain 'writer-workers,' like Marsé, Vázquez Montalbán, and Francisco Candel, who constructed their poetics inspired by the collective modes of creative consumption of an incipient postwar mass culture (cinema, music, comics, etc.). I argue that, as in the case of the writers inspired by 'peasant cultures,' these writer-workers also gravitated towards a separation from the traditional roots that inspire them, as the depoliticized, individualist model of the 'writer' imposed from outside weakens those precarious ties.

In the second part of the book, I move on to a study of some of the disagreements and alternatives that arose to confront the model of cultural authority during the neoliberal crisis. I begin in the fourth chapter by considering some collaborative modes of value production in digital cultures. I take as my starting point the cyberactivist campaigns begun in protest against the so-called Sinde Law (2009) that limited online sharing practices. I relate this mass defense of the Internet to the fact that increasing job insecurity drove many people, especially young people, to find a space online where they could collaboratively cultivate their abilities to create value, since there was no opportunity for them to do so in an increasingly competitive, exclusive job market.

Furthermore, I note the importance of the dual tradition of defense of freedom and defense of online equality (with its countercultural and academic origins) (Bollier 2008). Likewise, I examine the explosion of 'active publics' that have sprung up around the mass cultures of the digital age (Jenkins 2006) as breeding grounds for the appearance of a democratic, participative Web in the Spanish state—a Web that encountered its defining moment in the struggles against the Sinde Law. I highlight this culture as an important source for the creation of a 'subjectivity' (culturally constructed identity) unknown to the hierarchical, competitive cultural establishment.

In this respect, I show how the polemic about the Internet served to generate an increasingly elaborate self-representation by a new social group that perceived itself as different from the establishment, irrespective of how many and varied were the positions and discourses this new group espoused. Importantly, I also note the latent tensions and contradictions—expressed, for example, in the boycott campaign, 'No les votes,' against the parties that supported the Sinde Law—between a liberal, individualist conception of society, and the increasingly widespread reality of liberal institutions' inability to guarantee a true democracy.

In the fifth chapter, I analyze the drift of these new subjectivities and their contradictions into the 15M movement (also known as the *Indignados*). I argue that the creation of small 'tent cities' in the plazas at the start of the movement intensified the coordination of different abilities that was taking place online with the goal of collaboratively supporting the daily life of the protesters in the plazas. In other words, they avoided participation in the hierarchical, competitive logics of the neoliberal cultural authority that was being blamed for the economic crisis.

They thus strengthened a cultural model based on mutual empowerment and on the composition of diverse abilities and ways of knowing, from affective, daily, and experiential ones to specialized, technical ones. This model has become one of the main elements of a new political and cultural 'climate,' underpinning many other collective processes (Fernández-Savater 2012). Among these, of course, are those of the PAH and the civic Mareas (especially the Mareas in defense of public health and public education).

Opposition to this model by intellectuals and powerful media outlets has been staunch, and in this chapter I examine some of the ways these authorities have tried to discredit the 'cultures of anyone' arising from the '15M climate.' They attempt this through their reliance on a social model that requires a large part of the population to set limits on its intelligence and delegate its capacities to those responsible for 'establishing reality.' I show that the cultures of anyone have essentially confronted this cultural power in three ways. In the first place, they respond directly, as happens more and more often in public speeches defending their position as 'anyone.' Second, they sidestep classifications and representations emitted by the powers that be, often through the use of digital tools and humor. And third, they confront the power structure by constructing spaces where they can exercise their right to a truly democratic culture in a sustained way, such as the plazas of the 15M, despite their relative transience.

Finally, in the sixth chapter, I continue my inquiry into the modes of constructing alternatives to the tradition of cultural authoritarianism and neoliberalism. I turn to a study of institutions that try to offer permanent life spaces for the 'cultures of anyone.' I highlight the cultural and political project Traficantes de Sueños (TdS), which belongs to the Fundación de los Comunes network, as an example of the successes achieved by self-managed spaces that base their ability to decommodify and democratize meaning production on the daily support of the communities that nourish them and benefit from them. I compare this example to a public institution, like Medialab-Prado, which shares many of TdS's democratizing strategies, as well as contributing a few of its own. It suffers, however, from the widespread harassment aimed at the public sector by competitive, privatizing neoliberal logics.

I discuss how the growing civic interest in bringing the logics of democratic self-management to the public sphere runs up against that harassment. This is clearly exemplified in an offer of 'participation' extended by public institutions that doesn't include the possibility of truly confronting precarization or any of the means that neoliberalism has at its disposal of capturing and speculating with collectively produced values. Building on the work of other researchers of public cultural policies, such as Rubén Martínez (2013), Jaron Rowan (2013), and Adolfo Estalella (2012), I analyze these questions in relation to the recently proposed Plan Estratégico de la Cultura de Madrid (PECAM). But I also suggest that if there has not been a civic defense of public cultural institutions comparable to those of health care and education, it isn't just because the state has left those institutions to the mercy of neoliberal depredation. I think it's also because of the inevitable tension that arises in the cultural sphere between experimentation and institutionality. Thus I note, in agreement with Sánchez Criado (2014), the importance of experimentation in constructing truly democratic cultures. At the same time, I emphasize the difficulty of conceiving of institutions that are sufficiently open to be able to sustain such experimentation.

I conclude my tour by recuperating some aesthetic projects that have brought democratic experimentation into the sphere of languages, symbols, and forms of representation in general. These include the poetics seminar Euraca, the readers' network #Bookcamping, the musical platform Fundación Robo (and its 'literary faction,' Asalto), and the chronicle blog 'Al final de la asamblea.' Finally, I end by mentioning something I consider fundamental for the maintenance of the 'cultures of anyone': their ability not only to suggest answers to specific political and social problems, but also to question the authoritarian, competitive cultural lenses that condition our way of understanding those very problems, and to replace them with other, more democratic filters.

PART I

Cultural Authority and Neoliberal 'Modernization'

CHAPTER 1

Cultural Aspects of the Neoliberal Crisis: Genealogies of a Fractured Legitimacy

'... guiada verás de la pura ley
la mano del que sabe'

1.1. Crisis of a Hierarchical, Individualistic Cultural Model

1.1.1. Circuit of voices about crisis

At first, the 'crisis' was just one more news story, one more piece of information, one more topic of conversation in a world of news, information, and topics of conversation. Couched in the language of economists, the crisis appeared in the spring of 2007 as nothing more than an 'expectation of a slowdown in economic growth.' It was noted, however, that 'the level of individual debt was very high due to mortgage rates' and that 'the real estate market had cooled.'[1] The following year, surveys and newspapers confirmed the bad news: '63% of Spaniards will have to limit their vacations to only one or two weeks, if that,' 'Spaniards Will Spend 15% Less on Seasonal Sales Due to the Economic Slowdown,' 'The Crisis Is Pushing Users Towards Buying Cheaper Drugs.'[2] Because, of course, at the beginning the crisis was already a threat to the fulfillment of individual desires in a world of individuals who seek to fulfill their desires.

From that implicit perspective on life, the media created stories that highlighted the crisis, adding information and showing its effects. They offered the life stories of young men and women who were affected by the crisis. The national newspaper *El País* quoted a number of them in their 2012 report '#Nimileuristas' ('not 1,000 euros') on twenty-somethings and

---

1 See http://www.elmundo.es/mundodinero/2007/05/24/economia/1179999308.html.

2 See http://www.que.es/actualidad/sociedad/vacaciones-light-para-tiempos-de-crisis.html; http://www.elmundo.es/mundodinero/2008/07/01/economia/1214920305.html; http://www.diarioya.es/content/la-crisis-potencia-el-consumo-de-drogas-m%C3%A1s-baratas.

thirty-somethings who earn less than €1,000 a month and are desperate for work: 'If nobody gives me a chance, how can I get experience?' 'I've written up a new resume that says I only have a high school diploma.' 'I work three hours a day and earn 200 euros.' 'I have never turned down any kind of work' (*El País* 2012).

In the wake of this growing adjustment to 'the crisis,' and thus to an ever more precarious job market, the big media outlets kept repeating, summer after summer, 'This year there will be less post-vacation depression because of the crisis.' And the three or four people interviewed on the daily news shows confirmed, 'Having a job these days is a luxury!'[3] Through all these years 'in crisis,' the social barometer readings of the Center for Sociological Research (CIS in Spanish) have accompanied these sound bites, consistently illustrating 'Spaniards' greatest worries': unemployment, always in first place and apparently insurmountable, followed by the economy, corruption, and politics jockeying fiercely for the succeeding positions. 'Corruption Unseats the Crisis, Pushing It to Second Place,' announced public television in 2013, sounding for all the world like an announcer trying to generate excitement at a horse race.[4]

But not everything has been numbers and surveys: from the start, the expert information has been accompanied, as is customary, by the less technical, more 'human' commentary of 'intellectuals' and 'opinion-makers' who dealt in the supposed language of 'the man on the street.' Columnists like Javier Marías were warning us as long ago as 2006 that 'from the perspective of *el hombre vulgar*,' with whom Marías claimed to be in agreement, 'Spain is being destroyed by the deceptions of real estate developers, mayors, sponsors of public works, and independent counselors' (Marías 2006). From the government, highly placed politicians like the President himself made statements designed to calm these kinds of fears, at the height of a 2007 that now seems so naïve: 'Since Spanish financial entities are international models of solvency, they are much less exposed to risks like those faced by the mortgage market in the United States.'[5]

In harmony with the government's reassuring and almost proud response to the threat of the crisis, there were other declarations of the legitimacy of the status quo, occasionally from the 'cultural world.' A case in point is an academic book published shortly thereafter with the euphoric title of *Más es*

---

3 See   http://www.abc.es/videos-espana/20130902/crisis-atenua-sindrome-postvacacional-2644909004001.html.

4 See http://www.rtve.es/noticias/20130306/corrupcion-se-dispara-ya-segundo-problema-para-espanoles/613609.shtml.

5 Zapatero in an appearance with banker Emilio Botín in September 2007.

más: sociedad y cultura en la España democrática, 1986–2008 (Gracia and Ródenas 2009), which was still, in 2009, celebrating the recent transformation of Spain into 'an ultramodern, post-capitalist society which above all has lost a good part of the collective inferiority complexes that defined part of its image and its very reality.' Although, to be fair, in weighing the pros and cons, the book simultaneously lamented society's excessive confidence in 'a sector like construction, which is so prone to speculation' (14).

Undoubtedly there were also many other voices that are more difficult to recover now: we well know that at the same time, in private or semi-private circles, infinite daily conversations repeated, translated, countered, and reworked those news stories, pieces of information, and comments. In homes, in workplaces, at cinemas, museums and other entertainments, in cooperatives and activist milieus, and increasingly in the public-private sphere of digital networks, many people (placed by the words of those like Marías in the position of *'common man'*) were anticipating or already suffering difficulties, and blaming culprits. They tried to understand the technical language of economics by referring—often with total incredulity or suspicion—to that new reality of information still in formation: 'the crisis.'

1.1.2. Establishing and consuming reality

This whole cycle (formed by the media, experts, intellectuals, politicians, academics, and 'the people') was heavily influenced by the generalized custom in contemporary Western societies of accepting as 'reality' whatever is shown, explained, commented, and made visible with facts, images and stories. We could call this the 'habit of visible reality.' It is an indirect heir of the great transformation that occurred at the beginning of so-called Western 'modernity,' which was the cause, as Michel de Certeau notes, of a progressive change in the way people viewed reality. Little by little, they stopped believing that reality was an invisible nucleus surrounded by deceptive appearances. In its place, they began to accept the opposite perspective that reality was visible, but needed to be studied empirically to discredit unfounded beliefs. A big gap was also opened through which a large part of that reality was illuminated by what would be the great legitimized method of observation: science. The rest was left in the dark, waiting to be studied by means of authorized scientific procedures that would replace traditional knowledge now considered deficient ('primitive' or 'popular') by the new cultural elites.[6]

---

6 Lafuente and Rodríguez, in their book *¡Todos sabios!* (2013), propose a lucid historical explanation for the birth of this scientific paradigm, emphasizing its long

In a later (and more extreme) spin on this new paradigm, a new type of belief would spread: simply put, if something could be shown, made visible, it must be considered real. This is what de Certeau calls the 'creation of reality,' and this is how the mass media makes it work: representations, or simply visible 'fictions' or 'simulations,' are constructed which are assumed to be realistic, and which, by their very ability to make something visible, are taken as referents of reality.

Oddly, says de Certeau, this does not necessarily mean we believe that these fictions *are* reality. We know they are constructions, representations, and simulations. We don't believe in them 'directly'—what's more, we often believe they are pure manipulation—but at the same time, we give them the status of reality, because we think they are 'what everyone believes.' It becomes a vicious circle, because 'everyone' believes that '*everyone*' believes the media. Quoting 'everyone' thus becomes, according to de Certeau, the most sophisticated weapon for making people believe (or at least to get people to act *as if* they believe):

> since it plays on what others supposedly believe, [the quote] becomes the means through which reality is established ... 'Opinion surveys' have become the most basic and passive form of this kind of quote. This perpetual self-citation—the multiplicity of surveys—is the fiction through which the country is led to believe *what the country itself is*. (189)

'The Crisis Makes Us More Miserable: Spain Shows Sixth Greatest Decline in Happiness.' This was the finding of a UN study, later repeated on the journal *20 Minutes* in September 2013.[7]

On the other hand, this establishment of reality by the media takes place, as de Certeau also suggests, within the framework of an organizational system of commercialized, production- and consumer-oriented practices. This means that the media not only 'establish' reality, but also organize its reception by giving it the form of a market of products consumed by individuals. This organization thus reinforces another central custom of our contemporary Western societies: relating to reality as if it were a market of diverse possibilities to fulfill individual desires. And that, it seems to me, could be a good extended definition of what we sometimes call 'consumerism.'

In a documentary entitled '¿Generación perdida?' (Lost Generation?), which garnered a record audience for the public television program *Documentos TV* (746,000 viewers on October 9, 2011), an analysis of the crisis

---

duration and, thus, the impossibility of establishing clear limits between what is considered science and what is not.

7 See http://www.20minutos.es/noticia/1915941/0/felicidad/espana/crisis/.

was presented that was very much in line with this type of organization of reality. The story revolved around seven young people who were not acquainted, and who represented very different 'personal' options in the face of the crisis. Thus, while one young woman left to live in the country, one of the men emigrated, a second woman protested at the university, another man spent his days at home on the sofa, and yet another man exerted himself to become a successful entrepreneur, and so on. The story centered much more on all those apparently individual responses to the crisis than on what the crisis itself might have meant for the family, social, local, or institutional environments in which these young people lived—never mind the possible collective responses generated from within those environments, the existence of which was obscure at best.

This type of reading—facing the crisis by focusing on some supposed individual decisions that led people to suffer through the crisis or face it according to their personal preferences (we could almost call it a kind of 'crisis consumerism')—has dominated media representations. Significantly, it is reproduced, for example, in an array of reports about young people in crisis, like the aforementioned report in *El País*, '#Nimileuristas.' This was a sequel to material the newspaper had already published seven years previously about the 'mileuristas' ('1,000 euroists') (*El País* 2005): earning 1,000 euros a month only lasted a short time as a symbol of financial insecurity. In fact, in the seven years between 2005 and 2012, it became a coveted and unreachable goal for many. In both cases, the individual point of view was always given narrative pre-eminence. Furthermore, it was supported by basic assumptions, such as that society consists of a set of autonomous (in principal) individuals who form instrumental relationships among themselves, basically looking for work to gain access to the money that will allow them to fulfill their desires. The very labels 'mileuristas' and 'nimileuristas,' like the earlier and sadly famous 'Ni-Nis' (young people who 'neither [*ni*] studied, nor [*ni*] worked'), are especially apt for this type of individualist and consumerist interpretation of reality (in the broader sense that I have proposed), since they attempt to name anomalies in a paradigm that views society as a group of autonomous individuals who work for money to be able to satisfy their individual desires.

1.1.3. The individualist fallacy
But as the geographer David Harvey explained in *The Urban Experience* (1989), understanding social reality as though it were essentially a supermarket of goods that individuals can acquire tends to disguise the material constitutive interdependence of human beings, and to exacerbate the competition between them. The philosopher Marina Garcés recently published her reflections

on this constitutive human interdependence in her book *Un mundo común* (2013). She understands all existence as a radically unfinished, vulnerable, and relational process, asserting, 'To exist is to depend ... Our bodies, as thinking, desiring bodies, are imbricated in a network of interdependencies on multiple scales' (67). This becomes increasingly obvious, in other respects, in our present globalized world: 'The experience of global union is, in truth, the real but risky interdependence of the fundamental aspects of human life: reproduction, communication, and survival' (21). Based on this experience, it is becoming increasingly difficult to believe in what Garcés calls the 'fantasy of individual self-sufficiency,' a fantasy that has dominated Western experience since liberalism invented the 'individual owner,' who would only enter into relations with others of his own free will and to exchange property.[8]

No one is an island however. The necessary network of resources (cultural and 'natural'), care, and mutual help that makes human life possible is an essential common heritage. This heritage, however, becomes hidden behind a veil of commercial transactions between individuals when social life is represented in the form of a market. Apart from that, to expect human subsistence to be based solely on these commercial transactions is extremely risky because, as the Spanish philosopher César Rendueles (2013) says, 'commerce is a type of competitive interaction in which we try to take advantage of our opponent.' He goes on to say:

> Precapitalist societies thought it was crazy to base their material survival on the uncertainty of competition. For the same reason, we think a person who bets his or her only house at poker or plays Russian roulette is doing something not only risky but wrong: the imbalance between the risks and the benefits is too high. People always need food, clothing, care, and a place to lay their heads. Is it reasonable to subject these constant necessities to the whim of the market? (22)

8 With respect to the close connection between the paradigm of liberalism's legal individualism and commercialism, Garcés asserts, 'In the modern world, the relation of each individual to the abstract field of law guarantees the articulation of society ... the abstract subjectivity of the juridical, egalitarian, universal order is what allows us to think of society by assuming the premise of the individual freed of all community ties ... It is precisely the abstraction of that subjectivity, as guardian of equality and universality, that allows us to maintain human relations and concrete cooperation in terms of reciprocal indifference. Thus, juridical universalism is governed by the reduction of interpersonal relations to economic relations. "It is the universalism of businessmen," Barcellona clearly states. It is the form of togetherness that capitalism needs to develop and to function. We might add: together in the abstract, diverse and detached in the concrete' (26).

The relative commercialization of life that is inevitable in all societies that use some form of money is extended and multiplied in the capitalist West, where money is effectively coming to be used as 'the measure of all social value.' Consequently, we also find more prevalent in the West the establishment of what Harvey called 'the money community,' a form of social relationship that substitutes 'objective' dependency structures for personal ties.[9] Likewise, according to the anthropologist David Graeber (2011), this type of commercialization of social relationships allows us to delude ourselves that we can settle our ethical obligations to others by paying our monetary debts.

When the crisis hit the Spanish state about 2008, it was inevitably mediated through this paradigm of establishing and organizing reality as a market of products for individuals who relate to one another according to the laws of the 'money community,' reproducing a consumerist 'subjectivity'—a culturally constructed lifestyle.[10]

The crisis erupts, in fact, in a country integrated into a Western capitalism that tends to make money the measure of all social value. Moreover, the country has integrated an evolved, extreme form of capitalism that has been developing since the 1970s: neoliberalism. As Christian Laval and Pierre Dardot have noted, neoliberalism should be understood not only as an 'ideology' or an 'economic policy,' but as a true 'way of life' that would

---

9 Following Marx, Harvey states, 'Money arises out of concrete social practices of commodity exchange and the division of labor. The grand diversity of actual labor processes given over to the production of all manner of goods of specific qualities (concrete labor applied to produce use values) gets averaged out and represented in the single abstract magnitude of money (exchange value). Bonds of personal dependency are thereby broken and replaced by "objective dependency relations" between individuals who relate to each other through market prices and money and commodity transactions' (167). Money becomes the mediator and regulator of all economic relations between individuals; it becomes the abstract and universal measure of social wealth and the concrete means of expression of social power. Money, Marx (1973, 224-25) goes on to observe, dissolves the community and in so doing 'becomes the *real community*' (168).

10 Thus, concludes Rendueles, in our societies, consumerism becomes a way of making sense of all the facets of life in general: '[Consumerism] is a type of activity in which the ends are given and there is no room for discussion. It consists simply of choosing the means that I consider to be best suited to satisfying my desires. Adidas or Nike? Windows or Mac? In itself it is not such a bad thing. Our daily life would be impossible if we subjected all our preferences to constant critique. The problem is when this type of activity takes on a heavy symbolic load and becomes a privileged source of meaning, when it becomes how we forge our personal identity. ... In the market our interactions are simple, bounded, and easily conceptualized. Why not explain the rest of our life with the same precision and simplicity?' (185).

carry capitalism's individualistic logic to extremes: 'it has as a primary characteristic the generalization of competition as behavioral norm, and of business as a model for subjectivity.' Or even as a 'standard of life' that 'obligates everyone to live in a universe of generalized competition, commands both the employed and the unemployed, subjects relationships to the ways of the market, impels the justification of ever-greater inequalities, and also transforms the individual, who from then on is called on to perceive himself and conduct himself as a business' (14).[11]

1.1.4. Neoliberalism as the new way of the world

'Germans are all work, they don't take the time to chat as much as in Spain.' Javier, a Spaniard who emigrated due to the crisis, offered this opinion in the 'Expatriate' section of the *Huffington Post* ('Huyo de la realidad española' 2014). He continues, 'The important thing is to create a plan that lets you get to where you want to be in the future, and then follow it through.' Irene, another immigrant to Berlin, is also looking to the future: 'It hurts to leave my family, my boyfriend, my friends … But I think it's what's best for me.' The vice president of the Youth Council, however, is not so optimistic about emigration. 'It is obvious that this process will imply, first of all, a substantial loss of human capital for the country,' he laments.[12]

The neoliberal conversion of 'life' to 'human capital' clearly has a counterpart in all the rest of humanity which does not seem so 'capitalizable,' and which frequently encounters many more obstacles to emigration. This other mass of humanity is spoken of in other sections of the newspapers, and with very different metaphors—such as the recently much-overused one of 'attack': 'Massive Attack of Immigrants on Spanish Borders' (*Euronews*), 'Around 1,000 Immigrants Attempt Another Unsuccessful Attack on the

---

11 Laval and Dardot take as their point of departure Michel Foucault's analysis of neoliberalism in his 1979 courses published under the title *The Birth of Biopolitics* (2010). In these courses, Foucault opens the door to understanding neoliberalism as a compound of technologies of power and technologies of subjectivation. His concept of governmentality is key here, because it expands the analysis of neoliberalism beyond the role (or lack of a role) of states, shifting the focus to a wider spectrum of ways in which people 'conduct the conduct' of others. He also clarifies the relations between classic liberalism and neoliberalism, notably revealing, as Laval and Dardot themselves recently underscored (Fernández-Savater, Malo, and Ávila 2014), that the 'homo economicus' of neoliberalism is not the same as the 'entrepreneur of himself' of neoliberalism, this second becoming not so much someone who seeks a balance between his efforts and his compensation, but, moreover, somewhat constantly looking for more, constantly trying to 'go beyond himself.'

12 See http://www.huffingtonpost.es/2012/10/13/jovenes-espanoles-emigran_n_1963468.html.

Ceuta Border Fence' (*El Mundo*), 'One Civil Guard for Every 64 Immigrants Waiting for the Attack' (*La Razón*).[13]

Neoliberalism permeates everything, from the microbusiness that is me to giant transnational businesses and their flow of cheap labor. Exacerbating these competitive tendencies, which only increase as they move from monetarized societies to capitalist ones, neoliberalism's success is immense, and it ended up becoming the real 'reason for the world' towards the end of the twentieth century, according to Laval and Dardot:

> For more than 30 years, this rule of existence has dominated public policies, ruled global economic relations, and remodeled subjectivity. The circumstances of this normative success have been described frequently, be they the political aspect (the conquest of power by neoliberal forces), the economic aspect (the rise of globalized financial capitalism), the social aspect (individualization of social relations at the expense of collective solidarities, with extreme polarization between rich and poor), or the subjective aspect (appearance of a new subject and development of new psychological pathologies). (14)[14]

13 See   http://www.elmundo.es/espana/2014/03/04/53158197e2704e52238b456a. html; http://www.larazon.es/detalle_movil/noticias/5757689/espana/un-guardia-por-cada-64-inmigrantes-para-vigilar-la-frontera-de-ceuta-y-melilla#.UysNK43TYgc; http://es.euronews.com/2013/09/17/asalto-masivo-de-inmigrantes-a-las-fronteras-espanolas-en-el-norte-de-africa/.

14 As the Observatorio Metropolitano of Madrid—and in particular its member Emmanuel Rodríguez—notes in *Hipótesis democracia* (37–45), neoliberalism historically arises in parallel with the progressive financiarization of global capitalism. This financiarization, in turn, was the response to industrial capitalism's profit crisis, which emerged in the 1970s. Rodríguez asserts, after a quick history that covers the dollar's abandonment of the gold standard, the creation of big international financial markets, and the massive deregulation in that sector starting in the 1990s, that 'practically all social production is currently determined and negotiated through some type of financial instrument or value.' Thus, 'both the means of social security (such as pensions, access to higher education and, in some ways, to healthcare) and consumption itself (reduced because of salary stagnation) have become increasingly dependent on mechanisms of financiarized provisions' (41). This dependence has disastrous results, because financiarization in and of itself constitutes an unsustainable economic practice. Financiarization needs constantly to expand, but it always does so unsustainably, in the form of 'bubbles': 'As might be suspected, the increase in financial profit requires and forces financial expansion—in other words, a growing concentration of liquidity in certain financial assets, a noticeable increase in the creation of credit, and a price increase on those very assets. The convergence of this tendency with the basic structure of any financial bubble is total. The problem lies in the fact that these periods of financial expansion are always temporary' (42). With all regulation suppressed, and in trying

In twenty-first-century Spain, marked by the spread of neoliberal logic into all these areas (political, economic, social, or subjective), the crisis that began in 2008 was constructed as a media referent that filtered through a neoliberal lens the very real, prolonged, and increasing suffering of people who lost their homes, their jobs, and their hopes of finding a job; people impacted by cutbacks in basic public services for healthcare, addiction, or education, forced to emigrate in search of work, and a long and painful etcetera. As this media referent, the crisis was, again, primarily the story of an irritating situation that interrupted the 'normal' course of life, an obstacle to the possible satisfaction of individual desires in the reality market. It was constantly kept in the public eye through more surveys, more news stories, more facts and rumors that 'the public' could later use as fodder for conversations about 'the state of the country.' The crisis, we were told by the huge media corporations, keeps us from realizing our dreams, it makes life harder for us, it even causes 'human drama' (such as, notably, the 'drama of the evictions,' as the well-known journalistic formula goes).

1.1.5. Crisis of the system as crisis of a way of life

Regarding the causes of the crisis, the media presented two main hegemonic narratives, which were hinted at from the beginning. On one hand, it was suggested that the crisis was a technical problem, and as such, it had to be solved by experts ('Experts Ask the EU to "Intervene" in the Spanish Economy,' 2010; 'An Expert Affirms that the Crisis Will Not End this Legislature,' 2011; 'World Bank Expert: Spain Has No Solution without Credit to the SMEs,' 2013).[15] On the other hand, ethical and political responsibilities were pointed out. For the most part, these were seen as responsibilities of the elites and of professional groups like those construction firms and mayors Marías called 'the villains of the nation.' But sometimes, the finger was

---

to overcome its constant 'crises,' financiarization expands until it causes families and businesses to go into debt, but it is forced to find a limit to that indebtedness: 'The main limit to financiarization lies here in the limits on its expansion. With all legal restrictions eliminated, these limits rest on certain thresholds of family and business indebtedness, which are made especially patent at times, like the present, of collapse of equity bubbles and asset deflation' (42). Financiarization is therefore a dead end at the heart of neoliberalism. Or, as Rodríguez says, '[F]inanciarization today is the social and economic form of capitalism and also an unviable solution to its medium-term contradictions' (37). For an analysis that reaches similar conclusions from the perspective of feminist economics, see Pérez Orozco (2014).

15 See http://www.abc.es/20100122/economia-economia/piden-intervencion-europea-espana-201001220845.html; http://www.20minutos.es/noticia/977971/0/; http://www.invertia.com/noticias/experto-banco-mundial-espana-no-tiene-solucion-credito-pymes-2910077.htm.

pointed more generally at society as a whole, for 'living beyond its means' ('Fátima Báñez: Spain Has Lived beyond its Means,' 'Rajoy: We've Bought Trips to the Caribbean on Credit,' 'Urkullu Claims the Basques Have Lived beyond their Means').[16]

The crisis appeared, then, as a technical matter explained in the language of experts or as a moral question that the voices of authority should denounce, within that constant flow of stories channeled by the media. But the passage of time and the growing brutality of events they hoped to pass off as 'economic crisis' inevitably weakened the first narrative (crisis as 'technical failure' to be solved by experts). It also clearly showed that the accusation against the common citizens in general was perverse, and strengthened the version that pointed towards the guilty elites. The financial experts who were supposed to have solved the problem were not able to, so the crisis was probably something more than a 'technical' problem. For their part, the politicians in power in the halls of government had bet—and ultimately lost—almost all their credibility on those very same experts who supposedly had created a Spain 'without an inferiority complex' and with 'international models of solvency.' The citizens may have played a role in the disaster, but their actions were guided by the leadership of experts and politicians.

It is difficult to determine at what point the crisis of legitimacy that affected politicians and financial experts alike began to intensify, crossing a point of no return. The repeated corruption scandals in the political sphere were probably the last straw. A new incarnation of the 'crisis' phenomenon appeared. It was no longer merely a financial crisis, nor even a crisis caused by the moral irresponsibility of some social actors; now it was a 'system crisis.' Or perhaps we should say 'system error,' echoing the computer science language sometimes used by the 15M movement, which was one of the main defenders, but by no means the only one, of this 'systemic' reading of the crisis.

'They call it democracy, but it's not' and 'We're not anti-system, the system is anti-us' are slogans widely used by the political movement the mass media called *Indignados* (the outraged ones), but who generally called themselves '15M.' Both slogans refer to an intensification of the crisis of legitimacy of something, generally known as 'Spanish democracy,' that is perceived as a

16 See http://www.periodistadigital.com/politica/gobierno/2012/05/22/fatima-banez-espana-ha-vivido-por-encima-de-sus-posibilidades-muchos-anos-.shtml; http://www.eldiario.es/lacrispacion/Rajoy-comprado-credito-viajes-Caribe_6_75652449.html; http://www.elcorreo.com/vizcaya/20130713/mas-actualidad/politica/acuerdo-fiscal-entre-pnv-201307130008.html.

'system.' This 'system' has imprecise contours, but it undoubtedly includes experts and politicians as prominent movers and shakers who make it work. It also has temporal dimensions: it includes all currently existing official institutions, and also reaches into the recent past of its own development (generally back to the 'transition to democracy,' which becomes a polemical process that requires reinterpretation).

There are various assessments that could be made of the 15M movement and its immediate legacy. Nevertheless, its attenuation or transformation into other processes does not seem to have dispelled the narrative that vaguely declares the crisis to be one of 'the system.' This being the case, the 'system' could not be saved simply by replacing the people who fill its structures. Rather, a transformation of the very 'rules of the game' is required.

But the real question is, What game are we talking about? Is it merely a game of institutional powers, or one of the experts themselves? Does it exclude from 'social games,' to continue the metaphor, those players who do not hold institutional or expert positions, but participate actively or passively both in the 'system of reality creation' to which I have referred and in the 'neoliberal reason' that articulates that reality commercially and individually?

I think it is more interesting to question whether the tough economic situation has produced an important erosion in the ways of thinking and living that also facilitate those social games that permeate life beyond institutional power. That is, has the 'crisis of the system' affected the very 'system of reality creation and consumption' that was presented as the hegemonic frame of the crisis? In this sense, I want to explore sociocultural processes in which it seems that what is shaky is not only institutional prestige or the validity of explicit political and social consensus, but rather a kind of life experience (a kind of 'subjectivity') that tacitly accepts the organization of reality as a market by the mass media, experts, politicians, intellectuals, and opinion-makers. At the same time, of course, this 'subjectivity' fiercely demands individual freedom to choose between the competitive options offered in the world created by those external instances.

In other words, I think it is legitimate (and even necessary) to recognize and explore in what sense, since 2008, is not only the Spanish 'economy' that is in crisis, but also a very entrenched way of life, one in which political and economic experts, together with other experts and 'intellectuals' in general, are expected to shoulder the responsibility for guaranteeing the means for each and every person to be able to follow his or her individual desires. That is, we need to acknowledge that what has entered into crisis—up to a point that makes it necessary to investigate—has been a culture that is technocratic and hierarchical, because it understands the establishment of the social 'rules of the game' (politics and the economy) as technical or 'profound' matters to be resolved by experts and intellectuals. On the other hand, it is also a consumerist culture because it understands daily life as an individual's election and attainment of a series of desired objects, in a process that is eerily similar to a business transaction.

These are the cultural dimensions of the 'economic crisis' that I want to explore. I should clarify that they are frequently isolated and considered contradictory: some people believe the cultural authority or hierarchy of experts, intellectuals, and the media clashes with consumerist individualism, which no longer believes in any authority. Those commentators say the great modern paradigms of the former have lost power in the face of the selfish postmodern nihilism of the latter.

There seems to be a certain truth to these proposals, and no doubt the technocracy or the prestige of the intellectuals are very different phenomena from individualist consumerism. Nevertheless, I note a certain convergence between these cultural models in neoliberal Spain, as well as a common genealogy, and later a crisis that is equally shared by both. The apparent centrality of the consumerist individual, as Laval and Dardot indicate, goes hand in hand with a 'reason for the world' that imposes competitive means of existence. I would add that it is also supported by forms of authority, hierarchy, and cultural inequality—especially those established by the modern technoscientific divide, including its heirs in the media world. Therefore, I do not think that the desire to understand together these diverse ways of organizing the meaning of life should be understood *a priori* as reductionism. That is, I would hope that we could at least concede the possibility of asking whether it is relevant to do so to understand a series of concrete historical moments.

1.1.6. The cultural dimension of the economy and its technification

To begin this broad genealogical contextualization, I first turn to a central tenet of the feminist economics tradition regarding the technification of the field—one that has had so many consequences for neoliberalism and its glorification of 'financial experts' and 'markets.' This central tenet will also allow me to clarify what I mean by 'cultural impact of the economic crisis,' since it articulates precisely the necessary interdependence of the economic and the cultural.

The feminist Italian economist Antonella Picchio reminds us that the so-called classical political economics of Smith, Ricardo, and Marx always kept very clearly in mind the cultural—ethical and political—dimension of economics, beyond its technical, quantitative, or specialized aspects. And that the field was originally presented as being in the service of the common good or happiness, with the understanding that such happiness did not mean mere physical subsistence, but the possibility of a life worth living, a life that has value and meaning; in short, a 'decent life,' which included culture and sociability. Picchio shows that classicalists like Adam Smith never understood the 'wealth of nations' as something separate from happiness, customs, or social tastes, and definitely not separate from *how* those nations wanted to live. Smith says, in *Lectures on Jurisprudence and Wealth* (1776), 'The whole industry of human life is employed not in procuring the supply of our three humble necessities, food, clothes, and lodging, but in procuring the conveniences of it according to the nicety and delicacy of our taste' (2013, 160).

Thus, classical political economics proposed as necessary the pursuit of a life with dignity, firmly melding culture and economics as two sides of the same coin. There can be no material sustainability without a cultural understanding and elucidation of what we consider to be worth keeping in each case. (Of course, classical economics continued to reserve for itself the authority to answer from a privileged place the question of what is a life with dignity, since it was a field of knowledge authorized by its 'modern'—read 'scientific'—genealogy.) Only later, in a transformational process studied by Picchio, did the heirs of this field, specifically those who belonged to the so-called 'neoclassical' school, try to erase from economics that pursuit of a life with dignity. They argued the existence of purely economic matters that needed to be separated from cultural ones, adding that each individual should decide for him or herself how they wanted to be happy.

Picchio notes a key moment in this transformation: the appearance of the famous *Essay on the Nature and Significance of Economic Science*, written in 1932 by the British economist Lionel Robbins (1935). In it, asserts Picchio, 'with the purpose of reaching his goal of redefining economics, he trades the analytical object of wellbeing—understood as effective living conditions—for the more general, abstract idea of utility as optimization of individual choices, under the bonds of scarcity' (35). Robbins offers, in this sense, a definition of economics that has become famous: 'Economics is the science of analyzing human behavior as the relationship between some specific ends and some scarce means that have a range of possible uses' (16).

In proposing this definition, the British economist strengthened the belief—still hegemonic in the field today—that economics is a technical matter that supposedly asks about the means and not the ends. His proposal actually gave, implicitly, the following response to the great ethical and political question about a life with dignity: a life with dignity is whatever each individual wants to pursue within the rules given by the economic experts. What Robbins and the heirs of his definition of economics intended, therefore, was twofold: that all collective cultural work necessary to constantly respond to the question about what is worth sustaining socially be broken down to individual desires; and furthermore, that it be subject to their decisions as supposed economic experts.

This refusal by the field of economics to consider the goals of a life with dignity has spread throughout the entire capitalist world. Determining a 'decent life' has become a simple mathematical calculation that attempts— unsuccessfully, as César Rendueles graphically demonstrates—to explain all human activity as instrumental behavior (98). But, as I will shortly try to show in greater detail, that same technoscientific aura had already involved, for some considerable time, a key element to bring the field of economics to the highest circles of power in capitalist societies. In Spain's case, two historical moments to which I will return in this chapter are essential in this regard.

I refer, in the first place, to the famous rise of the Opus Dei technocrats to power during Francoism, who configured a first 'liberalization' of the Spanish economy; in other words, an opening for the entry of foreign capital following Franco's autarchy. This opening was essentially a bet on tourism as a privileged sector. Sánchez León notes that it was during this time that an important perception of Spanish society as 'middle class' became established. This included the acritical acceptance of the power of 'experts' as part of a great process of civic depoliticization, perhaps uninterrupted on a large scale until the current crisis.

Second, hidden within that depoliticization and inheriting a primacy from the tourism/real estate economic sector they will never really be able to change—as López and the collective known as the Observatorio Metropolitano de Madrid explain—in the 1980s, the protagonists of that other great moment of legitimacy and the triumph of the economic technocracy appear. The Partido Socialista Obrero Español (PSOE)—which was called upon to complete the long-awaited 'modernization' and 'standardization' of the country after the dictatorship—institutes the Spanish version of neoliberalism (industrial reconversion, job insecurity, privatization, etc.), always with the leitmotif of being necessary adjustments for Spain to enter the European Economic Community (EEC 1986).

1.1.7. Collective elucidation of 'a life with dignity'

If there was ever a society inclined not only to accept but to enshrine the technocratic power of 'economics' and its experts, it was Spain's neoliberal society of the last three decades. In that time, according to Harvey, the transition from industrial to financial capitalism has occurred on a global scale. In the name of those famous 'markets' to which the financing of global capitalism has given an almost limitless power, Spanish neoliberalism has built huge speculative bubbles like the one that initiated the economic crisis that recently left the country with almost 6 million people unemployed (some 26.7% of the active population), 8 million in poverty, and a loss of 700,000 to emigration since the crisis began. The cultural impact of the economic crisis in Spain has been so profound that it has affected this great assumption, the touchstone of neoliberalism: this confidence in the experts as organizers of the economy, and in essence, as authorities who decide what a life with dignity should be.

To give a well-known example, recently Spain's austerity policies, justified with technocratic plans, have recommended taking away a threshold of dignity considered necessary by many: free health care for everyone. Javier Fernández-Lasquetty, the Health Minister for Madrid, had to step down in 2014 in the face of massive protests because of his attempt to privatize the city's hospitals. He always tried to justify his policies with an economicist discourse, appealing to 'sustainability,' 'cost-cutting,' etc. That technical language, however, has not prevented the legitimacy of politicians like Fernández-Lasquetty from plummeting just like house prices in Spain (something experts always said would never happen). Politicians had relied on the expert words of economists to decide what has value, what Spanish society ought to take care of, support, and reproduce. With the crisis of confidence in experts, inevitably, collective processes of creating social value that are not based on technocratic estimates become visible or gain importance.

The feminist tradition, with thinkers like Picchio and another Italian, Silvia Federici, has also shown how domestic work and physical and emotional caregiving, despite being central to and indispensable for the social reproduction of a life with dignity, are made invisible and undervalued in neoliberal technocracies. Something similar happens with the cultural work performed daily by multitudes of nonexperts to collectively elucidate and propose the values and meanings of a life worth living. Collective cultural processes like the recent protests in defense of Internet freedom, the 15M movement and its subsequent mutations, have perhaps been, among other things, attempts to give value to all that unrecognized daily work and to intensify its democratic potential in the face of what the movements sometimes call 'the dictatorship of the markets.' In this sense, I will propose that they can be understood as processes of opening and support of spaces where people can meet as a community to pose anew the question about a life with dignity that classical political economics put on the table.

But before that, in this first part I want to study precisely that hierarchical, technocratic, consumerist culture characterized by presupposing the impossibility of collectively defining, with input from all walks of life, what a life with dignity is. This impossibility is articulated in two apparently incompatible, but actually complementary, ways. On one hand, we have the necessity that it be experts—or those 'in the know' in general—who have the responsibility for making a life with dignity possible by making decisions about our social organization. On the other, we have an insistence on the individual as the supposed protagonist of human life, and therefore as the necessary author and 'free agent' of the decisions that affect his or her life.

Together with the contradiction implicit in turning over to experts matters that clearly pertain to that supposed sacred space of our individual liberty, these two approaches also exhibit a fundamental convergence: the tacit acceptance of a profound inequality in society. That is, the acceptance that first of all, we define ourselves as unequal individuals who either belong to the group 'in the know,' or to the group 'in the dark,' as it were, and who ultimately respond to an individuality that reproduces that fundamental inequality on a smaller scale. To wit: an individual is someone who knows about 'what is good for me,' without having to worry about the interests of others, while an expert is someone who knows about 'what is good for all of society,' in the face of the inevitable ignorance of the uninformed masses. It seems to me that studying the cultural impact of the Spanish neoliberal crisis must involve an examination of the validity, and at the same time, the weakening of the deep beliefs and practices founded on that radical conception of human inequality.

1.2. Enlightened Gardeners, or, the Power of Knowledge

1.2.1. Ordinary people and people who think

The clear weakening of the authority of technoscientific experts, specifically economists, together with the weakening of the credibility of politicians that has occurred during the years of the Spanish neoliberal crisis, does not necessarily imply the twilight of what we might call 'cultures of inequality.' This is because these cultures are the underlying foundation of the intellectual hierarchies of technocracy and consumerism. Neoliberal economists and politicians are not the only figures to embody the divide between those 'in the know' and those 'in the dark.' Nor are they the only ones responsible for the continuing reproduction of the individualist, consumerist model of life. Assuming a broad historical perspective, if we trace the specific genealogy of their expert authority beyond the origins of the field of economics and of the neoliberalism that empowers it, we can illuminate a broader context for that 'culture of inequality' to which they belong.

Going very far back in that genealogy, one could even recover the American anthropologist Paul Radin (1883–1959), as Zygmunt Bauman did in his book *Legislators and Interpreters*. Bauman used Radin's work to research the existence of 'cultures of inequality' in premodern, precapitalist societies, and, of course, to investigate what might remain of them in the 'modern' (and 'postmodern') world. Without taking too seriously this American ethnographer and his studies of the cultures not only he, but modern science in general, considered 'primitive,' it is nonetheless interesting to consider a basic observation he made: the existence in all of those 'primitive tribes' of a division between 'religious' people, responsible for thinking, and other 'secular' people, responsible for doing. Bauman gives his own take on this universal division of labor described by Radin: 'In the beginning, there is an opposition between the great majority of ordinary people, preoccupied with their daily business of survival, "action" in the sense of the routine reproduction of their conditions of existence, and a small group of those who could not but reflect upon "action"' (10).

Of course, that minority with the privilege of thinking also needs to have the necessary conditions for its life (and its thinking) reproduced, and in this sense, it holds a parasitic position relative to the rest of the tribe, who guarantee that reproduction. But why would the majority accept this unfair situation? Why would they not only support those 'thinkers,' but also grant them the monopoly on an activity that is so basic and so important for human beings?

According to Radin, the answer is that these philosopher-priests serve the majority by confronting humanity's 'primary source of fear': uncertainty. The philosopher-priest postulates a privileged space from which he can supposedly confront uncertainty better than the rest of his people. This purported privileged space is often justified by a special familiarity the philosopher has with uncertainty itself (with chaos, fate, mystery). A familiarity that is 'shown' through rituals and periods of isolation, purification, and obsession, which, Bauman indicates, are not so different from those that grant legitimacy to the figure of the intellectual as he is understood by Western modernity.

And beyond the enormous differences between the shamans of precapitalist societies and modern intellectuals, what interests Bauman most among the lessons to be gleaned from Radin is simply the importance of the monopoly on intelligence and knowledge as a tool of domination. This is why he says that the mere appearance on the scene of a caste that attempts to specialize in the ability to reason produces at that moment a crucial segregation and social asymmetry: 'the doers now become dependent upon thinkers; the ordinary people cannot conduct their life business without asking for, and receiving, the religious formulators' assistance. As members of society, the ordinary people are now incomplete, imperfect, wanting' (12).

The dependence and the supposed 'incompleteness' of 'ordinary folk'—of 'just anyone'—would be intensified again and again, as new forms of domination were perfected and instituted, integrating and emphasizing that 'intellectual' element. Another crucial thing also happens: that particular intellectual element, and not the entire structure of domination, is charged with conceptualizing and naming the supposed weaknesses of the oppressed group. This is why it is not at all strange that the absence of intelligence becomes a classic attribute of this group:

> Whether the oppressed are constructed as primitive, traditional, or uncivilized; whether the category construed is that of non-European cultures, non-white races, the lower classes, women, the insane, the sick, or the criminal—inferiority of mental capability in general, and inferior grasp of moral principles or the absence of self-reflection and rational self-analysis in particular, are almost invariably salient in the definition. (18)

1.2.2. Enlightened modernity as monopoly of meaning production
We offer now some words written by one of the most celebrated Enlightenment thinkers of Spain, Father Benito Feijoo (2014), from his essay 'Honor and Benefits of Agriculture' (1739):

> Peasants are not people of reflection, nor of observation; from their betters they accept the bad and the good, and they insist on it, if no enlightenment comes to them from without. This is seen in several adages, which they obstinately retain; even if, however little reflection they might engage in, experience were to clearly demonstrate the falseness of these sayings. (XII, XVIII, 34)

How can we not see in this characterization of peasants a reworking of the classic construction of the oppressed as lacking in intelligence?—a construction performed, no less, by a member of the very group that reserves for themselves the right to use their intelligence.[17] In this case, the

---

17 In the same text, Feijoo repeats one of the classic representations of the Republic as a human body in which this cultural hierarchy is made very clear: the peasants are the feet and the Prince is the head. 'I cannot better represent to Your Eminence the importance of the application of Agriculture, than by taking advantage of an elegant and highly detailed allusion by the famous Englishman Juan Sarisberiense [John of Salisbury]. This wise Prelate compares the Body of the Republic to that of men, describing its parts thus. Religion, he says, is the soul, the Prince is the head, the Council the heart, the Viceroys the eyes, the Military the arms, the Administrators the stomach and intestines, and the Farmers the feet. Then he adds that the head

operation is articulated from that 'modernity' that is based on legitimizing observation as the source of truth and an antidote to unfounded beliefs ('experience ... put before their very eyes the falseness of these maxims'), instead of using the theological legitimation. But the mechanism is the same: the negation of intelligence in those who are dedicated to ensuring the reproduction of material life, and the construction of a monopoly on authorized knowledge.

As de Certeau explains, oppressed groups, or those not otherwise 'legitimized' by the divide opened by the paradigm of modern knowledge, always develop tactics that allow them to survive and make sense of their life from the position in which they find themselves. In Feijoo's words, that intelligence of the oppressed is glimpsed in those 'adages' used by peasants that he considers 'obstinate'; likewise, his disciple, the Count of Campomanes, father of classical economics in Spain, considered that 'the way their grandfathers taught them to work the land' kept workers from learning the scientific advances of modern agriculture.

More than a discussion of the greater or lesser value of traditional knowledge versus scientific, erudite knowledge, what I want to highlight is how that traditional knowledge is denied the very status of *being* knowledge, since it is expected that those who inherit and cultivate it have a supposed inability to 'reflect' and 'observe.' I obtained the previous quotes from the work of the historian Jesús Izquierdo, who has analyzed how citizen status has been repeatedly denied to rural peasants by the Spanish cultural and political elites. They are also excluded from that other great phenomenon of modernity, what we could consider the distant origin of consumerist individualism to which I referred earlier: 'the growth of an increasingly individualistic understanding of human nature that was considered to be embodied only in those who dwelled inside the symbolic walls of the city' (2007, 632). From that individualist perspective, Izquierdo reminds us, the notion of the 'modern citizen' is created, and from it, he says,

> We agree on (we experience together) a way of conceiving of ourselves— and of proceeding—as sovereign individuals in the determination of our personal interests, as entities whose moral compasses are autonomous, as subjects gifted with a *reflectivity* beyond compare that enables us to decide our identity and distance ourselves from the collective traditions and conventions that ensnared those who came

must be especially vigilant with regard to the feet; whether because they might stumble over many obstacles that may do them harm, or because they support and give movement to the whole body' (XII, IX, 38–39).

before us. We experience our society as an aggregate of individual wills from which, when the moment comes, one can voluntarily back away. In short, we theorize our subjectivity based on our identification with an individual 'I' that we consider part of the natural order of things. However, despite this anthropologically ahistorical appearance, this identity and its attributes are discursive and historical constructions that operate by giving us the necessary certainty about ourselves—a personal identity in space and time—to act rationally in the world in which we live. (2007, 629)

Izquierdo shows that it was not only the men of the Enlightenment, but also later generations of learned 'progressive' elites who naturalized this individualist ideology as if it were the only one possible, thus denying the possibility of intelligence and citizenship to the rural peasants because they did not share this anthropology. Thus, we can trace this theme through time: Jovellanos wrote in the eighteenth century of the 'barbaric customs' of the 'crude and simple peasant'; then in the nineteenth century, we find the regenerationist Joaquín Costa characterizing farmers as a 'backward, imaginative, and presumptuous race' or a 'sick, juvenile people.' In fact, Costa tends towards an even stronger naturalization of these negative characteristics as inherent to the people, while the Enlightenment intellectuals considered them more a question of circumstances, the result of a 'corruption of customs.' Even in the writings of the Republicans, who would launch (ultimately aborted) Agrarian Reforms, observations about the 'childish mentality of the peasant' can be found.

In any case, I am most interested in the especially violent inflection that intellectual domination seems to be developing in modern times. This could be because we are living in a time when those who reserve to themselves the monopoly of meaning production seek, perhaps more than ever before, to be able to more than merely attenuate that 'uncertainty' that always stalks us. Rather, they want the power to defeat it once and for all, returning to a state of *tabula rasa* all of the knowledge and traditions that do not meet their needs.

For Bauman, one of the keys to the appearance of what he calls the 'modern power/knowledge syndrome' is 'the emergence of a type of state power'—i.e., absolutist—'with the resources and will necessary to give form to and manage the social system according to a preconceived model of order' (26). The emergence of this type of absolutist power capable of imposing a 'preconceived order' is certainly an extremely complex and enduring historical phenomenon, which marches in parallel with the entire process of disarticulation of the feudal forms of power that would open the way to Foucault's 'disciplinary institutions' and 'bio-power.'[18] But Bauman graphically summarizes this complexity with the metaphor of 'savage' societies and garden societies. The former are equated with feudalism, in which the rich and powerful did not intervene directly in the lives of their subjects, except to regularly extract most of the wealth generated by their processes of reproduction (like a hunter who takes his prey from a fertile forest). The latter are equated with modern societies: the power players are gardeners who want to directly arrange and organize every aspect of the lives of the dominated, to be able to extract their wealth more efficiently, and, of course, to insure that the production of wealth that they themselves can appropriate drives every aspect of the lives of everyone beneath them.

For the 'gardening' work or, rather, 'social engineering' required by the new absolutist states, bearers of the new scientific legitimacy would be needed. Thus, the enlightened men or *philosophes* like Feijoo and Campomanes (with less luck than their peers in other countries, which were more inclined towards experimentation) would become the managers of the new version of a pastoral and proselytizing power (heir of the Christian paradigm, as Foucault explained) that would define the modern social order. After them, says Bauman, a whole new tradition of 'expert administrators, teachers, and social scientists specializing in converting and cultivating human souls and bodies' were to continue their task as the 'gardeners,' consolidating a 'new structure of domination—the rule of the knowledgeable and knowledge as a ruling force' (67).

1.2.3. The origin of capitalism as dispossession of the cultures of survival

Bauman's explanation of the emergence of this power/knowledge syndrome resonates with Silvia Federici's analysis of the origin of capitalism in *Calibán y*

---

18 In his *History of Sexuality* (1990), Foucault explains how, since the seventeenth century, power in the Western world is exerted not so much through the threat of taking people's lives (or the grace of letting them live), but as 'a positive influence on life, that endeavors to administer, optimize, and multiply it, subjecting it to precise controls and comprehensive regulations' (137). He goes on to explain that this 'administration of life' is conducted in two different forms: the first is 'centered on the body as a machine: its disciplining, the optimization of its capabilities ... the parallel increases of its usefulness and its docility, [and] its integration into systems of efficient and economic control' (139). The second form is 'focused on the species body, the body imbued with the mechanics of life and serving as the basis of the biological processes: propagation, births, and mortality ... life expectancy and longevity' (139). Thus, Foucault talks about a 'great bipolar technology—anatomic and biological,' which characterizes the way (bio)power works in Western modernity (139).

la bruja. For her, the central element of this process was denying the peasants access to the resources—i.e., that 'fertile forest' the feudal elites raided only occasionally—which would allow them to support and reproduce their lives with any degree of autonomy. This denial typically equates principally to the infamous enclosures of 'common lands' built at the beginning of agrarian capitalism—and to which Baumann also alludes. But Federici explains it in a much broader context: the appearance of capitalism implies the devaluation of all reproductive domestic work—caregiving, rearing, feeding, everything indispensable for subsistence and typically done by women—which is not directly compensated in the new wage system, and therefore becomes invisible and endangered.[19]

Together with all this reproductive work and caregiving, of course, much of the symbolic and intellectual wealth of the traditions and ways of life that nurtured what John Berger (1991) called 'cultures of [rural] survival'

---

19 This emphasis on the crisis of reproductive work under capitalism (and its gendered consequences) is actually the basis of Federici's criticism of Foucault's theory of 'biopower,' which, in turn, is very important for Bauman's own reading of the emergence of the modern 'power/knowledge syndrome.' Federici regrets the 'mysterious' quality of the emergence of biopower in Foucault's account. For her, it is clearly the capitalist process of 'primitive accumulation' (which in Federici's reading of Marx is actually not 'primitive' but perennial), and its need for the reproduction of the labor force, that motivates the appearance of biopower's 'fostering of life.' We can find a similar argument in George Caffentzis's (2013) criticism of Foucault's understanding of the crises of social reproduction: Caffentzis claims that the role attributed to capitalism in Foucault's explanation of modern societies is too vague, which prevents him from giving a satisfactory account of the crucial issue of social reproduction and its crises. For Foucault, the crisis of social reproduction seems to be a permanent condition of human history rather than a concrete effect of capitalism. But then, Caffentzis asks, 'how did the regime of bio-power begin to reproduce itself?' With Foucault's shift to a sort of metaphysics of 'biopower,' 'we are reminded,' says Caffentzis, 'of the Heracliteans of old, who, forced to explain the large-scale features of the universe, reverted to "harmonies in tension" and the Logos' (286). On the other hand, Caffentzis states that the most convincing explanation of the crises of social reproduction is the one elaborated by Marxist feminists since the '70s (including Federici). For them, the crisis is endogenous to capitalism because of 'the conflict between the needs of capitalist production and the demands of those whose work is centered in the arena of the social reproduction of labor power. This conflict can lead to major crises of reproduction appearing as dramatically falling (or rising) birth rates, urban riots, or agrarian revolts' (271). Despite this differences between Foucault's theory of biopower and the Marxist feminist theory of social reproduction under capitalism, I still think that one can very fruitfully combine Bauman's analysis of the modern 'power/knowledge syndrome' with Federici's account of the origins of capitalism. I think they complement each other, because the latter adds historical specificity to the former.

also became invisible and endangered. Among these traditions and ways of life, as Federici notes, were those that would become stigmatized as 'witchcraft.' In this sense, we could recall those 'adages' Feijoo denigrated, now understood as representative of all the heritage of oral, practical knowledge—for example, natural 'remedies' for birth control—that was heavily devalued with the advent of capitalism, since they neither contributed to nor adjusted to the new domain of wage relations as the main source of survival. The capitalist system, therefore, puts the production of wealth that can be converted to money (especially through paid work) at the center, thus threatening the material and cultural reproduction of large sectors of the population that do not have easy access to that type of wealth. This also effectively separates these populations from the traditional resources and knowledges that previously guaranteed their survival.

Of course, as Berger himself said, keeping this transformation in mind does not mean glorifying the 'cultures of survival,' which undoubtedly had their own conditions of misery and exploitation, as well as their own cultural hierarchies, which were just as hard as, or even harder than, those that arose under capitalism: 'Nobody can reasonably argue for the preservation and maintenance of the traditional peasant way of life. To do so is to argue that peasants should continue to be exploited, and that they should lead lives in which the burden of physical work is often devastating and always oppressive' (xxvii). Even so, I think it's important to remember the process of dispossessing feudal peons of the resources that allowed them to manage their own subsistence at least in some degree, and relate it to their transformation into 'biopolitical' objects of a social engineering focused on maximizing the production of goods under capitalism. This connection becomes crucial for understanding the series of complex, interrelated, long-term historical processes known as 'modernization,' and in particular, the role the educated elite played in them by attempting to monopolize the intellectual dimension (or at least, the cultural hierarchization they have created).

In considering the monopolistic role of the elites, we might think that 'modernization' includes using a version of the human intellectual domain as a form of domination that denies, in a particularly virulent way, the ability of 'ordinary folk' (as Bauman called them), of those 'nobodies' dedicated to the reproduction of life, to produce meaning. In that sense, 'modernization' would perhaps imply a particular disconnect between the activity of thinking and that of supporting life (which includes thinking itself, although that is disavowed).

1.3. 'Transplanting People':
Capitalist Modernization and Francoist Technocracy

1.3.1. Francoist implantation of a capitalism of 'experts'

In their seminal introduction to the collection of essays *Spanish Cultural Studies* (1995), Jo Labanyi and Helen Graham state that 'modernizing' processes include both the bourgeois political revolution and the economic implementation of capitalism. From these processes emerges the very notion of 'culture' that will go on to function as a form of legitimation and of exclusion in the service of those same historical processes: '"culture" takes on its modern sense in order to define who does or does not "have culture," and to discriminate between the different forms of culture possessed by different strata of the population' (7). *Bourgeois capitalist* modernization—which, with the help of those modifiers, could perhaps leave behind those quotation marks that remind us not to take its meaning for granted—postulates the privileged point of view of those who promote political liberalism and economic capitalism. That point of view is called 'culture.' Everyone else is allowed to have second-class cultures: 'folklore,' which does not participate in modernization and which therefore is mere decoration or something to inspire nostalgia or feed the souvenir business.

Labanyi and Graham also point out a crucial fact: it was not until the Franco years that the Spanish state fully achieved the second of the two essential pillars of that two-pronged modernizing process: the implementation of capitalism. Francoism would leave the first pillar, the rise to power of political liberalism with its system of parliament and political parties, unconstructed. But it would develop more than any of its preceding regimes the necessary elements for the implementation of capitalism, such as urbanization, specialization and division of labor, and the creation of a consumer society. Graham and Labanyi add that, despite these changes, a third parallel process of transformation, 'cultural modernization,' together with incomplete political liberalism, was hindered. They are thinking in particular, and quite aptly, of the Modernist movement and the avant-garde in the arts; that is, 'aesthetic modernity.' But it is important to add nuance here: within the broad meaning of 'culture' (production and circulation of meaning, ways of life, creation of subjectivity), the capitalist implementation instigated by Francoism undoubtedly implies a complete economic revolution—but it also implies a cultural one.[20]

---

20 There had, obviously, been previous important developments in the complex processes of change that we usually call 'modernization,' and that Graham and Labanyi define as 'a recognizable process of capital-driven social, economic, political

In the vanguard of this revolution, which we cannot help but qualify as partially 'modern,' of course we will see neither avant-garde artists nor progressive intellectuals, as in other countries. After the first few years, when fascist rhetoric (which included clearly anti-capitalist positions) held sway, Francoism would exert its 'gardening' power; that is, its desire to design a pre-established order that it would then impose biopolitically on society, in the hands of the Francoist technocrats of Opus Dei.

and cultural change occurring at differential rates over the past 200 years across Europe and the US' (10). There is an extended bibliography about pre-Francoist 'modernization' in Spain. An important part of it deals in one way or another with issues of 'backwardness,' 'insufficiency,' or 'underdevelopment.' The subject of the implantation of capitalism has traditionally been discussed in relation to problems of dependency on foreign capital and failed industrialization (see for example Costa 1983 and Nadal Oller 1978). Perhaps more pertinent to my argument here are the studies which attempt to map the cultural changes associated with the advent of national state power and capitalism in Spain in the passage from the nineteenth to the twentieth century. Particularly fruitful is, for example, the contribution of Álvarez Junco (1995) in relation to the difficulties of the frail liberal state in the 'Restauración' period trying to reach the countryside, because besides lack of infrastructure, problems of education, and cultural differences, it also had to confront the semi-feudal reality of *caciquismo* (chieftainship). Álvarez Junco points out that the disconnect between state and rural areas, however, diminished at the beginning of the twentieth century, with an intensification of fiscal and military recruitment campaigns in the countryside. The colonial wars of Cuba (1895–98) and Morocco (1911–27) were key moments in the configuration of what could be deemed, following Federici's and Harvey's perspectives, the Spanish version of the machine of accumulation by dispossession that is modern capitalism. Catalan historian Josep M. Fradera (2005) has also used the colonial vector to interpret the main conflicts of Spanish modernity, explaining how the 'loss' of the Cuban and Philippine colonies marks a fundamental shift from a liberal state that had created space for assimilating Catholicism and cultural diversity, to a nationalist refounding of the state based in Castilian identity, which would exacerbate all those differences, finally leading to the civil war. In parallel to these processes of rural assimilation and colonial nationalism, there is of course a wide arrange of subjective transformations, such as those studied in collections by Larson and Woods and, once more, Graham and Labanyi—notably changes in representations of the modern and a progressive shift towards mass culture. Jorge Uría (2003) has presented a particularly useful account of this shift, which for him characterizes Spanish culture from 1875 to 1939, to the extent that, he claims, the failure of the Republic of 1931 can be attributed to the increasing right-wing influence that mass forms such as *cuplé*, sensationalist press, and cinema exerted upon its 'social base.' The continuation of this reasoning in the postwar period is presented by Jesús Izquierdo, whom I follow directly in his claim that Francoism was the only regime capable of completing the task of dismantling rural traditional cultures and substituting them with consumerism and 'middle-class' values.

Actually, this was happening even before the famous 'Opus Dei technocrats' appropriated the Franco administration with their motto 'God and money,' towards the end of the '50s. From its very early days, Francoism had hoped to be an openly 'technocratic' regime as a way of avoiding the thorny question of 'ideology,' while at the same time maintaining a very strong theological component. In explaining the prominence of engineers during Franco's regime, the historians Pires Jimenez and Ramos Gorostiza (2005) assert that 'the "technical" was elevated to the level of an unquestionable social value. Thus, politics in the classic sense was replaced by the administration of public affairs by technicians and experts, in a supposedly objective and aseptic way, and without unnecessary delays or party or ideological biases' (92).[21]

1.3.2. Colonization of the peasant world

The tradition of those 'technicians and experts' who would implement capitalist 'modernization' in Spain could be none other than that of the technoscience that makes its way into the West by trying to erase all other knowledges, which it considers 'primitive.' In this sense, Izquierdo (2005) believes that only Francoism had the ability to complete the program of transforming the traditional rural community-based peasant cultures that the intellectuals of the Enlightenment had wanted to achieve, to turn those beings of 'barbaric customs' (Jovellanos) into citizens adapted to liberal individualist ideology and its capitalist subjectivization. The great social penetration achieved by Francoism in a rural Spain ravaged by the civil war and its consequences allowed the regime to fulfill that modern dream, formulated under Francoism as 'colonization,' as the conversion of the rural peasant to 'agricultural entrepreneur,' and also, of course, as 'modernization.' Izquierdo explains:

21 This technocratic element was always combined with a strong permanence of religion as a source of authority. Foucault and Bauman, with their noted emphasis on the 'pastoral' character of modern biopower, provide an apt theoretical frame for understanding this somewhat contradictory combination of technoscientific authority and theological rule. We can find an extended account of the macro-politics of this paradigm in studies such as Botti's *Cielo y dinero. El nacionalcatolicismo en España (1881–1975)* (2002), and the more specific characteristics of its educative model in works like those of Ferrándiz (2002) and García (1993). But perhaps, as in many other instances, the experiential, everyday life dimension of this paradigm of cultural authority can be best understood through the non-fiction works of writers such as Vázquez Montalbán in his *Crónica sentimental de España* (1986), Carmen Martín Gaite in her *Usos amorosos de la postguerra española* (1987), and also in the less well-known work by José María Arguedas, *Las comunidades de España y del Perú* (1968), to which I will come back in chapter 3.

Once the formally pro-peasant stage was over, Francoism began an agrarian policy that became synonymous with social standardization and with the assimilation of rural culture to the values represented by the city. Every means must converge to a single end: the transformation of the peasantry into rational individuals capable of speaking up on behalf of their own political interests—those of the Fatherland—without the mediation of third parties that might put them on a dangerous path. Furthermore, these peasants must also become entrepreneurs, true maximizers trained to contribute to the common interest of Spain's modernization. (2005, 20)

In this task, Francoism also had its own 'enlightened men,' such as the engineers of the National Institute of Colonization (INC in Spanish) or the sociologists of the Agricultural Extension Service. These men were likewise in charge of highlighting the peasants' lack of intelligence and their inability to learn through personal experience due to their 'habitual' adherence to traditions that could not be considered true knowledge. Izquierdo exemplifies this in the following quote from an engineer of the INC (Tudela de la Orden 1966):

[T]he peasant's concept of the land, of natural forces, of animals and plants, is not a concept he developed or acquired from his own experience. Rather, it has come down to him developed and proven through centuries in that same place where he lives, making it comfortably habitual. (10)

For Izquierdo, Francoist 'modernization' was extended to both external practices and subjectivities, and thus he considers the social change carried out by the regime in the rural world to be *'marginicidio,'* an assassination of the cultures of the marginalized. Perhaps one of the most spectacular examples of this type of totalizing transformation was the one that formed the so-called 'colonization towns,' those rural settlements built on newly irrigated land, thanks to the numerous hydraulic engineering works typical of Francoism. These towns were filled with 'colonists,' often brought from the very towns flooded by the reservoirs.[22] The 'colonization towns' were one of the preferred

22 Of course, as Barciela and López Ortiz (Nadal Oller 1978) have studied in detail, 'colonization' was the perverted leftover of the Agrarian Reform undertaken by the Second Republic that Francoism itself had overthrown. As such, it was one more tool in the service of the policies that repressed the impoverished, rural peasants and defended to the death the rights of the large landowners who were the core of the Francoist agrarian system. It is no surprise, then, that of the newly irrigated lands created by the National Institute of Colonization (INC in Spanish), an average of 72%

objects of the propagandistic display of Francoist 'modernization,' as reflected in a typical example of a euphoric NO-DO (Noticiarios y Documentales) documentary entitled 'La Provincia resurge. El Plan Badajoz' (Macasoli and Martín 1957). In it, Badajoz is presented as a province that suffered the stigma of backwardness, but would be modernized quickly thanks to a new irrigation and colonization plan that would bring 'progress' and 'economic expansion,' according to the NO-DO's characteristic voiceover, 'with some of the most modern machines and equipment in Europe.'

The result was towns with an inevitable coldness and artificiality, with houses that shared similar floor plans and facades, and were, moreover, arranged in a geometric urban pattern. These towns were sometimes simply called 'New Town,' although local toponyms were also common, with the ending *del caudillo* (of the commander) tacked on. (Some of these towns still use that ending, despite the passage of the so-called Historical Memory Law in 2007.)[23] The colonists arrived from different places and maintained the identity of their places of origin for generations. This was just one more of the irregularities and habits developed over time that Francoism seemed to want to erase from those settlements with 'cleanly designed streets, and dawns, and tidy houses' (as the NO-DO says), and in the middle of which sat the house of the INC engineers, who controlled every aspect of the town's productive life.

The 'colonization towns' are particularly interesting as an extreme example of the Francoist desire for biopolitical 'leveling,' which of course did not fail to encounter all manner of 'accidents.' Thus, oral testimonies recently gathered in Sodeto, one of the towns created by the INC in the Monegros Desert in Aragón, reveal a long-held local memory of disaster rather than success: when the engineers terraced and leveled the land, it caused saltpeter to rise to the surface, making the land all but sterile. This chance occurrence does not fail to have a powerful metaphorical reach: within the intended cultural erasure of this modernizing colonization, there revolved hidden layers that made any new 'rooting' impossible. One of those towns in particular, Puilato, had to be abandoned because of the sterility of the disturbed earth.

(and sometimes as high as 80%) remained in the hands of those landowners, while the limited remainder was given to new 'colonists,' who were chosen by Francoist authorities. Barciela also recalls how ridiculously small were the economic resources received by the INC considering the titanic task of 'solving the problems in the country' with which the Francoist state had charged it (8).

23 On February 18, 2010, Félix Población commented in the daily newspaper *Público* on the continued existence of at least nine Spanish towns that still kept the controversial suffix 'del Caudillo' in their names.

And that case was not unique. Hundreds of towns were drowned under Francoism's reservoirs, and others were deserted due to massive emigration. Despite being used by Francoist propaganda to symbolize Spain's roots, hundreds of thousands of rural peasants had to be 'transplanted' to the cities, and faced serious problems in trying to adapt. This whole story, the other face of Francoist 'modernization,' has yet to be told in all its depth and complexity. A particularly sensitive chapter of it is the massive spreading of the *paleto* (essentially a country bumpkin) stigma, which, as Izquierdo and Sánchez León remind us, took place right around the 1950s to become one of the main counter-models of the modern Spanish imaginary, and probably remains so even today.[24]

1.3.3. Hypothesis of a 'middle-class' continuity

But how is that technocratic Francoism still generating the paleto stigma even today? Since I am trying to offer a general outline of how cultural authority is formed—that habit of dividing the world into 'those in the know' and 'those in the dark'—to help consolidate the neoliberal world that would be hit by the crisis in 2008, and which I have characterized (with Laval and Dardot) as an exacerbation of capitalism, it seems appropriate to connect that present to the moment of the big push to implement capitalism in Spain.

In this sense, again I agree with the historians Izquierdo and Sánchez León regarding the so-called 'second phase of Francoism': it was a key moment in the configuration of the society that would later make the institutional transition to a parliamentary system, but which had already been substantially changed during the years of the dictatorship. At the risk of oversimplifying, this change could be summarized as the effect of three lines of Francoist action: the marginalization and disarticulation of community-based rural cultures; the implementation of a middle-class, individualist, urban, consumerist social model; and finally, a significant part of that implementation, the launch of a whole series of liberal economic policies (opening to global capital, prioritizing the service sector, financialization, etc.) that will establish the foundations of the neoliberal model still to come.

Undoubtedly, these lines bring together extraordinarily rich, complex, contradictory, and protracted historical processes that it is truly a shame to have to summarize so generically. On the other hand, it seems to me that we

---

24 Sánchez León says, 'cultural expropriation ... turned the country dweller into an increasingly exaggerated stereotype of "the country bumpkin" who was increasingly more excluded from the new civil status of middle class, [which] became one of the markers identified with backwardness and ignorance' (2010, 8).

are also dealing with barely told, considered, or studied pieces of a recent past that continues to affect the present of too many people to ignore it. Within the limited scope of this study, I want to contribute to the enormous task of making those connections explicit with my own small input related to the main theme of my study in this first part: the question about the genealogy of the type of cultural authority that leads from the creation of the modern power/knowledge complex to neoliberalism. In this sense, my intention is not to try to evaluate the extent to which it is or isn't appropriate to focus on those three grand lines to theorize Francoist developmentalism and its legacy to post-dictatorial society. Rather, I want to add some possible nuances to that broad outline.

If we accept the previously explained ideas of De Certeau, Bauman, Federici, and Labanyi and Graham, to help us understand capitalist 'modernization,' we could characterize the period of Francoist 'developmentalism' as the climax of a process of social engineering in which some elites, legitimized by their supposed monopoly on knowledge and intelligence, led the rest of society into adopting the standards of the 'money community' as the only possible form of social reproduction, depriving them of other forms that had previously guaranteed them a certain degree of self-management and self-sufficiency.[25]

In bringing the entire population into the 'money community' and the culture of progress and modernization that legitimizes it, as Sánchez León says in 'Encerrados con un sólo juguete,' Francoism left 'off the map of protagonists of the traumatic twentieth century at least two-thirds of the people who lived it' (2010, 5). He further indicates that the other side of this

25 In this sense, the recurrent phenomenon of *enclosure* about which the philosopher George Caffentzis speaks is not at all foreign to the Spanish state. Today in Spain, what Caffentzis notes can still be seen especially clearly: 'Most people can find in their genealogy or in their own lives some point when their ancestors or they themselves were forced from lands and associated relations that provided subsistence without having to sell either one's products or oneself, i.e., they suffered *enclosure*. Without these moments of force, money would have remained a marginal aspect of human history' (2013, 218). A key moment in the history of *enclosure* for the Spanish subaltern classes was, of course, the civil war. An interesting account of this process of dispossession and its effects is provided by Antonio Cazorla Sánchez (2009), who uses oral and archival testimonies to document the everyday dimension of terror, hunger, poverty, displacement, capitalist 'modernization,' and migration— all processes that lead, in his words, to a collective 'exchange of freedom for some form of peace' (4). Cazorla provides significant data revealing the crisis of social reproduction that was provoked by the ruling classes during the civil war and the postwar years. He says, for example, that 200,000 people starved to death in Spain between 1939 and 1945.

operation of expropriation and cultural stigmatization is the construction of a new common feeling that acts as a kind of 'single toy' bequeathed by Francoist developmentalism with which Spaniards would be 'locked up' at moments of self-representation from then on. He talks about the model of

> an individualist middle class, although with a dose of collective morality (even of solidarity) that was never excessively classist; an acquisitive and consumerist middle class, with the justification of being that way to contribute to development, institutionally well supported with social policies to guarantee its status and its mobility, essentially 'civil' and with an interest in politics basically limited to whether the administration will solve their problems adequately. (2010, 6)

The individualism, consumerism, depoliticization, and the 'developmentalism' of that urban 'middle class' consolidated under Francoism are, says Sánchez León, what will reproduce 'the policies of the great socialist majorities of the eighties,' thus establishing a fundamental continuity between Francoist society and that of 'democracy.' In other words, it would establish what we could call 'the Francoist roots of the Transition Culture,' taking up the concept coined by Guillem Martínez.

The cultural historian Germán Labrador recently suggested some illuminating qualifications to the hypothesis of the 'mesocratic' continuity proposed by Izquierdo and Sánchez León, pointing out the risk of falling into 'sociological abstractions.' Labrador asserts that this story of continuity leaves out a whole series of 'alternative subjectivities' that gained strength in the seventies and were never integrated into the paradigm of the depoliticized, urban middle class. To illustrate, Labrador brings to the scene what he calls the 'transitional culture,' which he has studied in depth in several exhaustive works that are essential for understanding Spain's recent past. In his article '¿Lo llamaban democracia?' (2014), Labrador explains:

> That ['transitional'] culture implicates the *realist* film of the transition, but this culture is not only filmic: it is constituted by other aesthetic forms already cited (documentary, counterculture magazines, political satire, urban art, graffiti, alternative theater, etc.) and other possible forms also characteristic of the time (graphic narrative, underground poetry, realist literature, and so on). These genres of the transition offer a look at an era of immense plasticity and great complexity. They show a world of subjectivities in formation and in a struggle that has nothing to do with the emptiness of the political scene or with the naturalization of its sociology. (28)

Nevertheless, it seems to me that the verification of this subjective plasticity during the seventies isn't incompatible with the observation of the continuity of a certain 'middle-class' cultural rigidity that comes and goes between the sixties and the eighties, and lasts even beyond that. Labrador himself effectively summarizes the area of the argument that most interests me to characterize this persistence of the imaginary and the practices of the 'middle class':

> Sánchez León explores the interest of anti-Francoist political engineering in *homo mesocraticus* as a potential mitigator of class struggle, demonstrating how, from the social sciences, a utopia is configured for a future democratic society of middle classes. This political imagination becomes inscribed on the social body by producing a classless subject, split in half in the unsalvageable distance between what Marxists called *class itself* (sociological class) and *class for itself* (the sociological imagination of social class or social identity). (26)

In this sense, whether or not we run the risk of falling into a sociological abstraction in saying Francoist developmentalism creates a middle-class culture that will be—even with many counter-examples, breaks, and tears— the foundation of a later democratic society, I think it is important to emphasize the perspective that this middle-class culture is, precisely, a projection that comes from the social sciences—and from other positions of legitimized knowledge—to be 'inscribed on the social body.' In other words, middle-class culture itself is introduced into Spanish society more as the desire or the biopolitical project of certain elites than of the self-representation of the rest of society. Sánchez León (2014) finds that middle-class imaginary not only in the anti-Francoist social sciences, but also in the discourse of the Francoist bureaucracy (specifically of the Vertical Union), in the tradition of liberalism that understands property as a social goal (the origin of the 'society of property owners' that will reach all the way to the boom of the real estate bubble). He also sees that imaginary in the 'progressive' sociologists who, after Francoism, still consider the middle class as an essential key to the success of 'democracy.'

Just as in the case of the Enlightenment intellectuals who projected their images and desires of 'progress' onto the peasants, I again find it useful to understand that projection of social imaginaries onto large populations as a form of domination that hopes to monopolize the ability to think and to know. Enlightened men wanted the peasants to progress because 'they didn't know what they were doing.' Similarly, the Francoist technocrats and the anti-Francoist sociologists wanted Spaniards to be 'middle class,' without worrying too much about Spaniards' opinion on the matter, and the technocrats and sociologists were willing to guide the population towards that goal with their authorized knowledges. It is the power/knowledge complex itself that incurs 'sociological abstractions,' projecting a 'preconceived order' that later tries to shape society. In the face of the cultural authority of that power/knowledge complex, those who are relegated to occupying the position of 'those in the dark' can either rebel—the garden is, in fact, a forest, and so there is always a multitude of things that don't fit, such as those found by Labrador—or they can accept the standards set by the elites.

1.3.4. 'Modernity' and inferiority complexes

What happens in any case—and here we borrow Picchio's economic terminology—is that most of the population is prohibited by the elites from participating in the collective process of elucidating the necessary conditions for a life with dignity. Obviously precapitalist cultures, or more specifically, those villages where Francoism would come in with its steamrollers, engineers, and sociologists, already had their own cultural hierarchies; that is, their own elites of people authorized to think for the rest—including leaders and representatives of the all-powerful Catholic Church. But again, perhaps what distinguishes capitalist technocratic ('modern') reasoning from other forms of cultural authority is the very small space the former leaves for any other intelligence or production of meaning, especially for one that makes collective subsistence its central tenet. So its ambition (which it deploys through its enormous disciplinary capacity) is to change everything, make every activity 'productive' in the sense of generation of private property and goods measurable by money. It works through substitution: it isn't enough, as with Catholicism, to demand compliance with a series of rites that may complement the labors and knowledges of the traditional, community-based cultures of survival. On the contrary, it wants to replace those labors and knowledges with its 'productivism' and its commercial individualism, which it considers to be the only possible form of a life with dignity.

In this sense, the understanding of the modern genealogy of Francoist cultural power can help us construct the question of how developmentalism creates a 'middle class,' calling attention to its especially devastating distribution of society between those 'in the know' and those 'in the dark.' Perhaps, moreover, in focusing only on implementing capitalism and slowing down the liberal transformation and 'aesthetic' modernity, Francoist 'modernization' was especially cruel to 'premodern' knowledges and traditions, which that aesthetic modernity could have helped to 'dignify'—as the avant-garde in the arts had already begun to do before the civil war (Lorca's case is paradigmatic in this regard)—and as some of the countercultures of that 'transitional' world studied by Labrador were also going to attempt again.[26]

The question is open in all its complexity. To illustrate the Francoist technocracy's perception of the special 'unworthiness' of unauthorized knowledges, we could show the numerous cultural manifestations of the *paleto* stigma during Francoism and the democracy. For instance, it has appeared in graphic humor (studied by Cristina Peñamarín (2002)) and in commercial and art-house films (analyzed by Nathan Richardson (2002)). And of course its presence in the television humor of recent decades has been almost constant: from 'Macario' by José Luis and his puppets, to the jokes of Marianico el Corto; from José Mota's rural characters to those of Muchachada Nui, they can almost always be interpreted as 'a way of representing what we didn't want to be, and at the same time, of differentiating it from ourselves' (Peñamarín 2002, 361).

We could even recall details like the fact that right up to 2014 the Dictionary of the Royal Academy of the Spanish Language (DRAE) offered 'uncouth, rough, attached to local things' as a second definition for 'rural.' And so, we could go on constructing the hypothesis of the existence of a 'neurotic' subjectivity, of the extension of a kind of collective inferiority complex caused by an enormous and particularly rapid process of replacing 'the old' with 'the new.' This is in line with what Ángel Loureiro (1998), in his critique of exaggerated modernizing pride, called 'manic Spain,' or with Agustín Sánchez Vidal's (1990) fabulous account of the 'modernization' of daily life in Spain in his essay *Sol y sombra*.[27]

In this last work, we also find numerous examples of how that subjectivity made 'neurotic' by technocratic modernization redirects its desire towards the world of consumption, in which the subject must make his way the best he can. Even Franco himself, claims Sánchez Vidal, liked yogurt with Nescafé and Fanta brand soft drinks, in a country that proudly showed its first toilets to visitors, and whose school books still counseled students not to make 'the regrettable mistake of getting into debt' even at the height of the sixties, when buying on credit and the SEAT 600 car were very popular.

The 'assumption at all costs of a mask of modernity' that comes from a 'sense of inferiority and shame' (Loureiro 1998, 17) is also confirmed by the

---

26 In my doctoral dissertation, 'Topos, vecinos y carnavales: derivas de lo rural en la transición española' (Moreno-Caballud 2010), I also had occasion to study some of the revisions, appropriations, and 'translations' of rural culture made not only by underground or avant-garde cultures, but also anti-Francoist, regionalist, and even 'mainstream' ones.

27 Víctor Pérez Díaz (1987) also offers an analysis of the dismantling of Spanish agricultural cultures in the book *El retorno de la sociedad civil*.

data provided by historians Pere Ysàs and Carme Molinero (Martínez et al. 1999). They claim that Spain didn't actually become a true consumer society until the seventies, when nonessential expenses rose to meet essential ones (housing, food, clothing) (182). On the other hand, the illusion of the 'middle class' began to soar long before this, thanks to TV advertising. By the end of the dictatorship, 70% of homes had television, but even as late as 1970, say Ysàs and Molinero, only 2% of the population had a college degree; in 1973, only 20% could afford to take a vacation (and half of these visited their home towns); even in 1975, 80% of those born into working-class or peasant families remained in the same social stratum. The 'centrality of private consumption,' according to Ysàs and Molinero, had become an 'illusion of social homogenization' (207).

Meanwhile, as Cazorla Sánchez says, the realities of exclusion and strong social stratification persisted. The so-called 'Spanish miracle' of the '60s cannot be explained without remembering that Spain offered 'an excellent package to capital investment, comprising low taxes, a disciplined and inexpensive workforce, and a captive consumer market' (15). Amidst general conditions of exploitation of waged-work (not to mention the even harsher realities of reproductive work, which had been rendered invisible) and a very deficient 'welfare-state,' Cazorla concludes, 'the price of Spain's 'miracle' was mostly paid by those who went hungry, those who did not receive adequate social or educational services, those who had to migrate to survive, those who worked hard and consumed little, and those who were forced to buy whatever the protected economy put in front of them. They were the poor, and they were the majority of the Spanish population; they were, by definition, the 'ordinary' Spaniards' (16).

At the end of the dictatorship, as John Hooper (2006) has pointed out, these poor Spaniards may had been comparatively better off than in the postwar 'years of hunger,' but economic inequality persisted: 4% of Spanish families retained 30% of the national wealth. Departing from this extremely unequal situation, they had to face the economic crisis of the '70s, which brought, for example, a 17% increase in the cost of living in 1974. In this same year, Molinero and Ysàs explain (179), 51 families controlled half of the management boards of the most important Spanish companies. Around 1,000 executives could be pinpointed as the true oligarchy of the nation, participating in the management of the seven most important banks and many related businesses, all of them consolidated under the wing of the Francoist dictatorship.

Again, without wishing to eliminate all the complexity surrounding these questions, I believe that analyzing the Francoist technocracy's totalizing will, which was heir to the modern power/knowledge complex, can throw light on the creation of the middle-class illusion, in which the stakes are not only what society is, but also who has the right to construct its representation. Along these lines, I would now like to highlight the importance of another type of cultural elite, beyond that of the Francoist technocracy: the intellectual elites responsible for the construction of a 'normalizing' 'middle-class' paradigm that became the hegemonic representation of Spanish society after the end of the dictatorship.

1.4. Pedagogy of 'Normalization' and Cultural Elites

1.4.1. Francoist roots of neoliberalism

To do this, I must first recall that together with the marginalization of rural cultures and the imposition of productivist, 'mesocratic,' consumerist values, the Franco regime also launched, as mentioned above, an economic liberalization that laid the 'unquestionable economic foundations' that would later form the backbone of the Transition Culture.

This has been explained very well by Isidro López and his colleague from the Observatorio Metropolitano, Emmanuel Rodríguez, both in the article 'The Spanish Model' (2011) and in their essential book *Fin de ciclo: financiarización, territorio y sociedad de propietarios en la onda larga del capitalismo hispano (1959—2010)* (2010). In these works, López and Rodríguez tell the story of the continuity between the 'modernization' of Francoism in the fifties and sixties and the neoliberal project of democracy from a macroeconomic and sociological perspective. They point out that with the arrival to power of the Francoist technocrats, Spain approached the Fordism of other countries, importing capital assets and equipment (machines, transportation equipment) without ever managing to make their industry self-sufficient, always subsidiary to foreign ones. The alternative that appeared to alleviate this problem was tourism (together with the money sent home by emigrants and foreign investment, but tourism brought in more than twice the income of the other two combined).

Tourism thus produced a rapid tertiarization (a growth in the importance of the service sector) of the economy. It also gave rise to the first real estate boom between 1970 and 1973, during which period 400,000 new homes were built every year. That same pattern would be reproduced later in the real estate bubble that preceded the 2008 crisis. This shouldn't be surprising, since Spain's entry into the EEC in 1986 simply served to confirm the guidelines created by Francoism: Europe didn't want Spain to have a strong industrial base, and so it was decided in Brussels (the headquarters of the EEC) that Spain would continue to specialize in tourism, in services, and as an experimental playground for new forms of financial speculation.

In an article in the essay collection on the Transition Culture, *CT o la cultura de la transición* edited by Guillem Martínez, López (2012) indicates that the project of radical economic and social transformation set in motion by neoliberalism basically consisted of 'recuperating the economic advantage of capitalist agents' by dismantling the mechanisms for the redistribution of wealth that had been created by Keynesianism (progressive taxes, welfare state, full employment, etc.) (82).[28] Specifically, following the stipulations of the Moncloa Accords (1977), the Spanish state carried out its project by suppressing regulation of the financial world and worsening conditions in the labor market. At the same time, as successive governments of the PSOE (1982–1996) decreed, industry was dismantled and large public companies were privatized to allow the entrance of international capital. In exchange, still according to López, the European Union assigned Spain a clear role within the 'international division of labor' that had been being organized since the beginning of capitalist globalization:

> a gigantic real estate and consumer market, through the promotion of financial and stock-market activities and of tourism, that bizarre activity that saved Francoism from the industrial crisis of the seventies, and through extremely heavy investment in transportation infrastructure. Banks, construction companies, privatized monopolies, the big mass media conglomerations, and the real estate developers would be the new leading sectors of Spanish capitalism, and they would be introduced in the new transnational order nourished by very generous doses of public spending. Meanwhile, in the rest of Europe a whole institutional framework was being constructed to prepare for the monetary union, which raised the doctrines of Atlantic neoliberalism to the status of laws. (86)

But López also points out something else, which is especially important for understanding the role played by the cultural elites in these processes. In the Anglo-Saxon countries that had had a welfare state, the redistribution of wealth towards the rich that neoliberalism implies was accompanied by an

---

28 In this definition of neoliberalism, López follows the foundational work of David Harvey in *A Brief History of Neoliberalism*. Harvey works with notions like 'accumulation through dispossession' and 'production of scarcity,' which are key to understanding the way wealth is redistributed under neoliberalism. The latter idea had previously appeared in his classic *Social Justice and the City*: 'If it is accepted that the maintenance of scarcity is essential for the functioning of the market system, then it follows that deprivation, appropriation, and exploitation are also necessary concomitants of the market system' (114).

ideology of disdain for the poor, stigmatized as supposed 'freeloaders' on the welfare system. Differently, the ideology that had enabled Spain's neoliberal transformation was that of integration into European 'modernity' (among other things because the Spanish welfare state was too weak to pretend that someone might 'take advantage' of it). As such, a revolutionary economic doctrine that would bring the country to the brink of an economic bubble never before seen and then to the brink of a probably irreversible economic depression, was introduced together with an ideological paradigm strongly founded on Spanish cultural tradition: the progressive, 'modernizing' Europeanism of the intellectual elites that has been cultivated since the Enlightenment.

1.4.2. Pro-European 'standardization' from the elites

Sánchez León explains that the 'modernizing' discourse associated with these intellectual elites has been, of course, the source of meaning from which 'the dominant accounts of the transition to democracy' have been constructed. To illustrate this idea, he quotes a genealogy of educated, modernizing cultural elites offered by Manuel Vicent in a 2009 column in the newspaper *El País*, which relates the history of the newspaper itself to the Spanish transition as a moment when

> the most noble dreams of the Second Republic, destroyed by the war and all the aspirations of modernity that were floating about in the air during the dictatorship [finally came true]. Giner de los Ríos's regenerationism, the Free Institution of Education, Ortega y Gasset's theories, Azaña's policies, the laity, liberty, democracy, and Europeanism ... a historical heritage [to which] was added the disposition of an enlightened bourgeois minority and the most avant-garde creativity of the younger generations.

Essentially, what was called Spanish 'democratic normalization' can be considered the apotheosis of a system for establishing and organizing reality. This system is supported by the authority of experts and intellectuals who are heirs to the long tradition of cultural elites who pedagogically guide the people towards 'modern progress.' In a clear continuation of this tradition, such 'progress' has often been called 'Europe,' since, as noted above, to be 'progressive' is to be 'European.'

Let us take a more or less archetypal example of the discourse of 'democratic normalization,' prepared from the satisfied position of someone who thinks it has already been achieved: the article 'La normalization de España' by the sociologist Emilio Lamo de Espinosa, published in 2001 in

Claves de razón práctica.[29] We find that he uses characteristically totalizing language:

> 1998 was the year when Spaniards realized that we had completed a great national political project, that of Spain's modernization and entry into Europe, whose origins we must date back to the humiliating days of our defeat in Cuba and the Philippines. Faced with the romantic, derogatory idea of a different Spain, savage, orientalized, authentic, but amodern, we wanted a Spain that was fully European, and even in its vanguard. We wanted to stop being the ugly duckling of the European countries, stop being different and unique, and make Spain normal and equal [to the rest of Europe].
>
> As we saw, this was not a project for one political party or one social group, nor even a project for the elites. Everyone from all walks of life, from different social classes, different geographical regions, and different political ideologies threw themselves into this national effort. Bourgeois or proletariat; socialist or conservative; people from Cataluña, Madrid, Valencia. It was the national attempt to deal with modernity, the Enlightenment, and the reason from which we had been separated by the Napoleonic invasion and consequent schizophrenia between patriotism and modernity, between being Spanish or being enlightened, between nation and reason, a schizophrenia that was the inheritance the Napoleonic invasions left to half of Europe. (2001, 12–13)

Leaving aside for the moment all the other problems that could be laid on that vague national 'we' (and which even seems to include a certain colonialist pride), I would like to highlight the self-representation of a project originated by intellectual elites in those terms of 'national project,' of 'everyone from all walks of life and different social classes.' To explain the history of that supposedly inclusive project, Lamo de Espinosa himself essentially resorts to an inventory of a series of intellectual and political elites who were dedicated to promoting the 'modernizing pro-European dream': the Enlightenment scholars, the regenerationists, the Generation of '98, the Generation of '14, and finally, the parties and institutions that wove the transition to democracy. This important methodological decision to focus on an analysis of the elites helps to make clear that a project for everyone is

29 As an interesting side note, Emilio Lamo de Espinosa Enriquez de Navarra, father of this Emilio de Lamo, had been one of those 'experts' who, in the journal *Revista de Estudios Agrosociales*, talked about the necessary transformation of peasants into businessmen (1962, 103).

not the same as a project for some elites who obtain the acquiescence or the approval of most of the people, always within the boundaries of a society strongly affected by that 'gardening spirit' that characterizes the modern power/knowledge complex based, as Bauman says, on 'the new appreciation of the fact that human conduct could not be left to individual discretion if it was to lead to social order' (48).

Ever since the Enlightenment when, according to Lamo de Espinosa, the 'pro-European dream' began to be conceived, this appreciation for the necessity of not leaving human conduct to its fate made it appropriate, according to the cultural elites, to undertake the immense and essential development of the tool of 'education.' At the beginning of the modern period, asserts Bauman, education went much further than the institution of school itself, it permeated everything: 'in no way was education a separate area in the social division of labor; it was, on the contrary, a function of all social institutions, an aspect of daily life, a total effect of designing society according to the voice of Reason' (49).

Education had to penetrate every corner of life for most people, who were perceived to have been 'poisoned in the past by wrong, irrational laws and the superstitions they bred' (69). Therefore, education was constituted in modernity as that system of 'objectification of the imperfection of the human individual,' which Jacques Rancière called, in *Le Maître ignorant*, 'pedagogical society,' in terms very similar to Bauman's.

1.4.3. Pedagogy as perpetuation of inequality

It is worth pausing a moment on one of Rancière's seminal books to question the supposed unity of elites and masses in the 'modernizing' project laid out by Lamo de Espinosa. *Le Maître ignorant* is a study of Joseph Jacotot, one of those *philosophes* designated part of the new, modern 'power/knowledge' complex, to replace 'primitive' knowledges with those legitimized by scientific modernity, and thus to increase the ranks of teachers whose responsibility it was to alleviate human imperfection through 'the pedagogization of society.'

A strange *philosophe*, however, because in his later years, Jacotot renounced all of that, suddenly taking a surprising path. After the return of the Bourbons to post-revolutionary France, Joseph Jacotot (1770–1840) had exiled himself to Louvain to be a reader at the university, and there he expected to spend 'peaceful days.' But when a group of Dutch students asked him to teach them French, it occurred to him to initiate a small pedagogical experiment whose result would change the course of his life. Jacotot gave them a bilingual version of *Telemachus*, to see what they were capable of doing on their own. To his surprise, months later they gave him essays written in perfect French.

This anecdote led Rancière to follow Jacotot in a radical questioning of pedagogical principles, beginning with the very notion of the need for teachers. The teacher, says Rancière, is justified as someone who must 'explain' to someone else things the latter doesn't know, so that he or she can learn them; but in reality, no explanation at all is needed in order to learn. 'To understand,' according to the pedagogical myth, would be 'to give the reasons' for something, when actually, understanding is always something more like translating. Human intelligence always works by feeling its way, repeating and relating, as can be observed in children learning to speak, and as Jacotot's students demonstrated by learning French by themselves out of a book. 'What children learn best is what no teacher can explain to them: their mother tongue. It is spoken to them, and it is spoken all around them. They hear and retain, imitate and repeat, make mistakes and correct them' (Rancière 22).

However, the pedagogical myth negates the value of this way of learning, and claims that, when we are older, we can only learn if someone 'explains' to us what we don't know. This contradiction, asserts Rancière, caused Jacotot's great revelation:

> The revelation that rocked Joseph Jacotot focuses on this: it is necessary to invert the logic of the explanatory system. Explanation is not necessary to remedy an inability to comprehend. On the contrary, this inability is the fiction that structures the explanatory conception of the World. The explainer needs the unskilled person, not the other way around; it is the former who constitutes the latter as unskilled. To explain something to someone is to first show him that he cannot understand it on his own. Rather than being the act of a true teacher, explanation is the myth of pedagogy, the parable of a world divided into wise souls and ignorant ones, mature souls and immature ones, skilled and unskilled ones, intelligent and stupid ones. (23)

The pedagogical myth, according to Rancière, has important social repercussions that carry far beyond the four walls of a school. In reality, what it does is change society into a school where people are denied the ability to learn for themselves, where constitutive inequality is instituted between 'those in the know' and 'those in the dark.' Only by yielding to the authority of those in the know can the rest 'progress.' And so what Bauman predicted has come to pass: most of the population becomes dependent on the knowledge elites and sees itself as incomplete and unable to provide itself with the intellectual resources it needs to live.

Rancière calls this 'the circle of impotence': those who are considered ignorant by society cease to trust in their ability to learn for themselves (an ability in which we all necessarily believe when we are children: no one 'explains' language to us, we learn it for ourselves), and accept that they will always need the guidance of those who do know. The end result is that we essentially cultivate our own inability to a certain degree, and our own ignorance. Large social groups appear that consider themselves incapable or incomplete; they internalize the contempt. 'Those who are excluded from the world of intelligence endorse the verdict of their own exclusion' (Rancière 34). And it is precisely this self-exclusion that is so often used as a justification to assert that 'people are uncouth,' that 'the problem of society is the lack of education,' or even that 'human nature is barbaric,' etc. The belief in the intellectual superiority of a few has the corrosive effect of extending what Rancière calls 'the passion for inequality': a refusal to fully explore one's own abilities because one believes that one will never be able to attain the intelligence that is the exclusive patrimony of exceptional beings, and because, at the same time, one guarantees the prerogative of making one's own intelligence unattainable and exceptional for others too, who may be 'at a lower level than me.' In the words of Rancière:

> Unequal passion is the vertigo of equality, laziness in the face of the infinite work that this demands, fear in the face of that which a reasonable being owes to himself. It is more comfortable to compare oneself, establish social exchange as that barter between glory and disdain where each one receives superiority in counterpart to the inferiority that he confesses. (106)

The pedagogical myth and the passion for inequality it promotes are especially prone to spread in modern societies; they have replaced classicist and theological paradigms with that of progress. The ideology of progress, asserts Rancière, is a fiction of inequality more potent and more dangerous than the ideology of classicism, because it lends itself more to pedagogy, which is always progressive: 'you have to learn, you still don't know enough, you still don't understand, etc.' (150). The ideology of progress is, in fact, the ideology of pedagogy turned into a law of society.

The collective of historians known as *Contratiempo*, to which Sánchez León and Izquierdo both belong, has explained how this pedagogical myth is articulated in relation to Spanish 'modernization,' in what they call the 'meta-story of Spanish modernity.' They describe

> the assumption that the forces of progress in Spain have always been embodied by educated, cultured minorities that promote the projects of political citizenship and economic modernization, before whom are situated on one hand certain traditional powers, and on the other, an

immense, uncouth population that can thus be manipulated and is
only turned into a historical agent capable of promoting modernization
when its action is duly channeled by illustrious progressive minorities.
(Contratiempo, historia y memoria 2014)

1.4.4. The determinist story of 'democratic modernization'

From here it seems that we can construct a more convincing explanation
of how the 'unity' of Lamo de Espinosa's supposed pro-European 'project
of everyone' was articulated. It refers to a project that may have affected
everyone but in which, ultimately, in no way is everyone equal. In short, it is
a pedagogical project, strongly impregnated with the 'passion for inequality'
due to which a minority appears as the vanguard of a progress which the
majority would be unable to attain on its own.

The genealogies of the educated minorities whom we must thank for
that 'progress' are repeated over and over in texts that justify Spanish
'normalization' as the price of integration into European modernity. The
cultural critic Jordi Gracia, coeditor of the aforementioned *Más es más*, to
which I will return, explained 'normalization' in *Hijos de la razón: contraluces
de la libertad en las letras españolas de la democracia* (2001) as 'an unprecedented
and lasting reconciliation between the logic of reason and the tortured logic
of our contemporary history' that had its distant origins in 'a minority
sympathetic to Erasmism.' He then continued with that minority's historical
line of descent 'slowly and laboriously enlightened,' then later with 'the
exile of the Romantic liberals,' Krausism, positivism ('capable of liberating
Spaniards from their most harmful and sterilizing mental baggage'), and
modernism, which leads him to the tumultuous twentieth century in which,
after the 'eclipse of reason' that was Francoism, 'Spain intertwines itself
definitively, following the same harmonic melody, with the European theme.
A dream unfulfilled by successive generations of Spaniards throughout the
1800s and 1900s, and which has finally come to pass at the turn of both the
century and the millennium' (16).

It is interesting to note that Gracia uses language that borders on
determinism in introducing this small genealogy of generations of
'reasonable' Spaniards:

Reason as an instrument of civilization knew how to silently
reestablish its validity as an instrument of coexistence and of human
understanding, as well as of transformation, like the intermittent
forge of a time that, despite all regrets, had to come and would come
according to a very ancient historical hope. (16)

Without wishing to over-interpret what might otherwise be a somewhat disproportionate rhetorical emphasis, it seems to me that there is something significant in this reading of 'modernization' brought by educated elites as something that 'had to come and would come.' And the tradition that defends this 'modernizing' discourse doesn't seem overly inclined to consider the very possibility that things could have been different, that perhaps 'modernity' could have meant other things, that the relationship of the enlightened elites to the vast cultural territory not occupied by them could perhaps have been articulated another way, including, at the extreme, that those elites could have come to consider their culture not by definition superior to any others, or at least that there was no reason for it to be the only authorized one.[30]

30 It is important to at least mention the centrality of one particular intellectual in the configuration of not only the ideological components of this quasi-determinist and elitist intellectual Europeanism, but also the institutional, material conditions of its reproduction. I am referring, of course, to José Ortega y Gasset. About him, intellectual historian Gregorio Morán stated: 'There is no intellectual figure in the Spanish twentieth century that can compare to him. There may be different opinions about his stature as philosopher, as essayist, as cultural promoter, as writer, as politician, as journalist, etc., but he is the most influential figure ... He has been recognized as a master to generations.' In his book about Ortega, *El maestro en el erial* (1998), Morán explained the philosopher's connivance with Francoism, causing an intense controversy which was perhaps as interesting as the book itself, because it showed the persistence of the figure of Ortega as a model of the intellectual for many in Spain. Eduardo Subirats (1993) had already analyzed his symptomatic centrality as a link between the 'ancient regime' and the new cultural elites of the democracy: 'Ortega was, for many reasons, the ideal voice. First, politically speaking, he was in an ambiguous position. He appeared to be a thinker who was open to 'Europe,' to humanism, to modern philosophy. He appeared to be a liberal thinker. At the same time, however, he had adopted a radical distance from the Spanish exile and its more eloquent signs' (62). Besides the ethical and political responsibilities which Morán and Subirats point out, I think it's interesting to note Ortega's position as the perfect example of the subject 'in the know,' as the model of what a member of the ruling intellectual class should be in a 'modern' capitalist disciplinary and pedagogical society. Born into a family of the high bourgeoisie, the son of the director of an important newspaper, he inherited a vast cultural capital—including the job as director of his father's newspaper—which he was able to multiply exponentially, through his access to the highest circles of intellectual prestige, notably the German philosophical tradition and university. He became an essential figure whose influence in the intellectual Spanish field is still very much alive, reaching institutions like the university, journalism, scholarly journals, and the publishing world in general. To use Bourdieu's concept, he was not only a founder and transformer of visible institutions, but also a crucial creator of 'habitus': of 'systems of durable, transposable dispositions, structured structures predisposed to function as structuring structures, that is, as principles which generate and organize practices and representations that can be objectively adapted to their

Labanyi and Graham asserted that using the concept of 'modernization' 'is made particularly problematic—beyond frequent lack of precision in definition—by the unacceptable normative and determinist baggage loaded onto it' (10). I think it is very important to point out that the power of the extraordinarily useful concept of 'Transition Culture' depends on a not insignificant amount of that 'normative and deterministic baggage' carried by the discourses of 'modernization' and its close relative 'standardization.' In this sense, I think the acritical 'cultural consensus' that Martínez says is formed around the post-transitional state is justified not only because of the threat of possible social instability, but also (as hindsight shows us from the comfort of a Spain already distanced from those turbulent years surrounding the end of the dictatorship) by integrating the state within that normative and deterministic power of modernizing discourse.

Again, the prototypical victorious claim of 'normalization' proposed by Lamo de Espinosa is a perfect example:

> What was gained through the PSOE was that immense, historical national project of modernization and Europeanization that had first inspired Enlightenment intellectuals, then the regenerationists, and then the Generations of '98 and '14, only to be driven underground for 50 years. But then, at last, it had its historic opportunity. Spain voted in the socialists as executors of that grand project. Its very slogan, 'For change,' was its summary and its synthesis. For the voters and those elected in 1982, the change was to modernize and democratize; and to modernize was to become European. (13)

Of course, one of the keys of this linear and teleological retelling of history is its constant omission of the central role played by the capitalist project, and likewise, of the neoliberal derivation of this project. In Spain's case, this omission is particularly important, since it avoids the inconvenience of having to acknowledge that it was the Francoist technocrats who completed one of the three great tasks of 'modernization': the conversion of subsistence economies into capitalist economies. The elites who had

outcomes without presupposing a conscious aiming at ends or an express mastery of the operations necessary in order to attain them' (1990, 53). Below that conscious level to which Bourdieu alludes, I think it is Ortega's influence in the construction of 'habitus' for the intellectual Spanish class that explains his omnipresence in Spanish culture, his ability to thrive in different political regimes (both as living human being and as posthumous figure), as well as the fact that, as Morán mentioned, he had disciples on both sides of the Civil War, and, as Subirats points out, he was recovered as a model figure in the post-dictatorship period despite his ambiguous political past.

considered themselves the vanguard of the other two modernizations—the political and cultural (or aesthetic)—would have to accept the company of those Francoist technocrats in their privileged space if they acknowledged the centrality of capitalism in the modernizing project. But in addition to this, there is another problem, perhaps even more profound, as I have tried to explain: the hierarchical, naturalized structure of the elites' (both technocratic and 'pedagogical') very leadership itself.

Obviously, this is not a purely Spanish problem, since it has its roots in the necessarily hierarchical functioning of the modern power/knowledge complex, which is articulated through the development of 'modernization' plans preconceived by the elites. This leaves the rest of the population to either assume a passive role and accept these plans, or, at most, try to join the ranks of the elites who design them by submitting to the 'educational' processes the elites consider necessary. This means the loss of the experiential, egalitarian, and creative potential present in all human beings: the possibility that anyone can invent valued ways of life to which anyone else can add value.

In Spain's case, as I will try to show in the next chapter, the late arrival of political and cultural 'modernization' that has historically accompanied capitalist 'modernization' has perhaps made the latent elitism of the modern power/knowledge complex of the twentieth and twenty-first centuries especially virulent. The political and cultural post-Francoist 'vanguards' considered the heirs of that long tradition of 'modernizing' elites enjoyed a particularly solid legitimacy, which caused them to carry to extremes their inability to recognize other sources of knowledge and value, thus naturalizing their exercise of power as a necessary and desirable 'normalization.'[31]

---

31 There has been a recent and very important contribution to the analysis of this 'normalization': Luisa Elena Delgado's *La nación singular. Fantasías de la normalidad democrática española (1996–2011)* (2014). It uses tools from Lacanian psychoanalysis and theories of cultural hegemony to shed light on the collective internalizing of the paradigm of a 'normal,' 'consensus-based,' and 'united' democratic nation. Working with an extended and plural archive of cultural objects (ranging from op-ed articles to commercial campaigns, as well as literary and essayist production and cultural policies), this book illuminates some important links between cultural, economic, and political power in Spanish democracy. Unlike my line of work here, Delgado's investigation tends to focus more on the right-wing version of 'fantasies' of normalization (notably, Spanish unity), perhaps because of the period she chose for her analysis, while I veer more towards the study of the 'progressive' (Europeanist, allegedly social-democrat) foundations of the same 'normalized' society she studies.

CHAPTER 2

'Standardizing' from Above:
Experts, Intellectuals, and Culture Bubble

2.1. Experts in Something and Experts in Everything: The Two Pillars of the Culture of the Transition

2.1.1. A less than democratic way to construct a democracy

His first name appears alone on the screen: just 'José Luis,' with no last name. He speaks in the first person plural, clearly differentiating *we* ('we never managed to hear the conversations') from *they* ('they asked for coffee, they asked for water'). He narrates a scene of intrigue, one might almost say a secret meeting. The place: the Madrid restaurant that bears his name, 'José Luis'; the time: the night bridging May 23 and 24, 1978. 'It was here, in this booth,' gravely intones the voice-over, while the camera pans between tables that still seem to exude power, 'that Alfonso Guerra and Abril Martorell drafted and negotiated 25 key articles of the Constitution.'

Indeed, during five long hours that night, from 10 pm to 3 am, these two politicians, one from the PSOE and the other from the Unión de Centro Democrático, decided such fundamental things for the future of Spaniards as that their state would be defined as a 'parliamentary monarchy,' 'secular,' and composed of diverse 'nationalities'; that their representatives would be chosen by means of an electoral law that distributed them across 45 provincial subdivisions—thus favoring the majority political parties; that their education would not take place in a single public lay school; and finally, that the Constitution that arranged all this would make it difficult for the citizens themselves to have any influence on that very document.

To be fair, it should be noted that Guerra and Martorell did not in fact personally decide these things; rather, they negotiated them for later approval by a commission of 37 representatives. The Basque Group and the Popular Alliance protested at not being invited to this particular nocturnal meeting, but it wouldn't have mattered in any case. The commission always voted in favor of what was negotiated by Guerra and Martorell and a few others who often met with them *en petit comité* outside the halls of congress, to negotiate the constitution of the nascent Spanish democracy.

The so-called 'seven presenters of the Constitution' are traditionally known as 'the fathers of the Constitution,' and on more than one occasion—including in the very documentary featuring the aforementioned José Luis, *Memoria de un consenso* (*Documental Canal Historia sobre la constitución española* 2004)—it has also been said that Guerra and Martorell helped 'birth' it. Whether two or seven, the attraction of such low numbers seems irresistible for this type of laudatory, and often overly dramatic, audiovisual story of the Spanish transition to democracy. In fact, such stories already constitute very nearly a subgenre, beginning with Victoria Prego's famous series for Spanish television, 'La Transición' (1995): the fewer the actors involved in events that are decisive for 'the future of Spaniards' (as the expression usually goes), the more this type of news article seems to delight in the events.

The scenes behind closed doors, the departures from the 'official' script due to unusual circumstances, the small injustices, and the almost amusing anecdotes that are generated are all recurring motifs. 'It has been said that we were eating supper,' Guerra says of nocturnal meetings in congressional offices, 'but the truth is, we didn't have a single bite to eat, not a thing. Once, at the beginning, Arzallus wanted to go out for sandwiches, but there were journalists with cameras and such, and everybody decided not to leave. So we didn't eat anything, not sandwiches, not anything.' Guerra is right: cigarettes and coffee go better with the aesthetics of this type of story than food. Ashtrays piled high in the wee hours of the morning. Men, a handful of men, smoking and deciding the fate of the country while everyone else sleeps. Guerra recounts in his memoirs that even after the Constitution was approved, Martorell and he continued meeting regularly, late at night. 'We developed the habit of spending the night talking about Spain and her problems,' he says.

Santiago Carrillo narrated in audiovisual news article for *El País Semanal* on the attempted coup d'état of February 23, 1981, known as the 23F (*Qué pasó la noche del 23-F, según Carrillo* 2011), a particularly dramatic version of this type of scene. On that ill-fated night, the coup participants put him next to General Gutiérrez Mellado in one of the congressional rooms, where they had also sequestered Felipe González and Alfonso Guerra, whom they had placed in separate corners facing the wall. They didn't make Carrillo and Mellado face the wall, perhaps because of their seniority, but they did assign a Civil Guard with a rifle to each of them. They couldn't speak, but they could smoke. When they finished off the cigarettes, an 'usher friend' (another one of those 'generic,' almost nameless witnesses, like José Luis, who are in charge of providing for the needs of the men who think for everyone), brought them a 'cartridge' [*sic*] of tobacco. 'The things history has [to tell],' says Carrillo, in voice-over. 'Who would have ever thought that we would find ourselves together that night defending the same thing? Me, a member of the Defense Council, and Gutiérrez Mellado, head of the Fifth Column of Madrid, sharing cigarettes and, in that moment, sharing feelings. That's enough to give you historical optimism,' he concludes.

The two Spains could be reconciled because their leaders smoked together. But to do that they needed secret, and even bizarre, intrigues, sometimes orchestrated by characters who had no leadership or official position, but who crept from the shadows for a moment to take part in History. The journalist and lawyer José Mario Armero is a paradigmatic case. As Victoria Prego recounts in 'La Transición' (1995), he offered his private home for the clandestine meeting between Suárez and Carrillo in 1976 that would culminate in the crucial decision to legalize the Spanish Communist party.

Armero adjusts to the foibles of the genre, narrating the scene in the present tense for greater vividness: 'Both of them smoke a ton of cigarettes. My wife has prepared something to eat, but they don't eat anything, not a bite.' His wife is another one of those nameless figures that serve. And Armero himself is perhaps a hybrid figure between the leaders who think and decide everyone's fate, and the servers who make sure they lack for nothing. He was there that night for the entire seven-hour duration of the conversation between Suarez and Carrillo, until well past midnight. It was not the only time he found himself in the middle of matters of 'high politics.' In a series of Spanish news articles titled 'Españoles con poder desaparecidos' (Papell 2011), he was said to be 'a key figure of the Spanish Transition, although he was never active in politics: he did his work in the name of and on behalf of civil society, of which he was a distinguished member.' The report called him a hybrid figure between the distinction of the great men with whom he rubbed shoulders ('he was the support of the young king in the social circulation of the crown') and the solicitude, which he shared in some measure, of the 'common man.' He embodied the 'cooperative sentiment of helpfulness that infused citizens at that time, when there existed an awareness of the delicacy of the task of transitioning peacefully from a dictatorship to a democracy that had yet to be built.'

Figures like Armero emphasize that the boundary between the 'distinguished gentlemen' and 'the common citizens,' so insurmountable for the majority (and especially for those who barely managed, as explained in the previous chapter, to meet the requirements to be considered the latter), sometimes becomes malleable and porous. Powerful people like to be magnanimous and cheerful with those around them, to skip official protocol and to treat those who surround them like friends. ('Suárez greeted me as if he had known me all my life. He was very friendly!' says Carrillo). Power is demonstrated by the capacity to give it to others, to show oneself to be above what 'the script' demands. That is, in many respects, the essence of the so-called 'transition to democracy' in Spain: a big, conspiratorial pat on the back for the citizenry from those in power, so that the former would feel so flattered that they would agree to turn a blind eye to the opaque, elitist maneuvers supposedly required by the exceptionality of the moment—a less than democratic way, as everyone knows, to try to build a democracy.[1]

2.1.2. Of friends, good educations, and common sense

Afterwards, when the supposed exceptional moment is past, how do we stop playing that old game of 'the elites' who decide collective fates in closed offices while their discreet servers trust them and bring them coffee and cigarettes? It's a whole way of life. It is impossible to overestimate the inertia and the comfort of reading every situation based on the exceptionality and brilliance of a few capable, authorized individuals, close to each other despite their 'official' opposition, which, in any case, always facilitates the exercise of their power. Gregorio Peces Barba, one of those seven 'fathers of the Constitution' whom Guerra and Martorell had to attend like 'midwives,' affirmed the following about that group of seven, who held supposedly opposing political views:

> We were very good friends. After all, we all knew each other from before. That is, I knew Don Miguel Roca of the Court of Public Order, Miguel Herrero, José Pedro Pérez-Llorca, and 'Gabi' Cisneros from

---

1 There is already an entire tradition of studies that have shown this 'lack of democracy' in the very 'transition to democracy' itself. This tradition has been articulated through the voices of such intellectuals as Manuel Vázquez Montalbán, Rafael Sánchez Ferlosio, and Ignacio Echevarría. These and others took it upon themselves to point out, during the 1980s and '90s, the costs of a transition that aspired to be exemplary, but that, according to these critics, was actually little more than the exchange of certain power elites for others (Montalbán 1998), embraced a trivialization of public discourse and culture (Ferlosio), and preferred to hide recent history beneath a mantle of consensus that cancelled the critical ability of the intellectual media (Echeverría). Guillem Martínez has recuperated this tradition in his exploration of the concept of a Transition Culture. Martínez himself also mentions Gregorio Morán and Juan Aranzadi, who round out an already classic list, to which should be added the research of authors who work in North American academia, such as Teresa Vilarós, Eduardo Subirats, Cristina Moreiras, and Germán Labrador. The writer and essayist Rafael Chirbes deserves special mention, since throughout his career he has traced a rich panorama of possible lives woven around betrayals, resignations, and impossibilities that for these critics characterize the transition period (see especially in this regard his novel *La caída de Madrid*).

college, and anyway, some had even been very good friends of mine. And I knew Fraga from when he had sent me to a town in the province of Burgos, because I had somehow collaborated, as he said, as a government spokesman with the student subversion.

The documentary *Memoria de un consenso* quickly dispels doubts about the possible animosity between Peces Barba and Fraga (a central figure of the Franco regime). The journalist Soledad Gallego, charged by the newspaper *El País* with covering the 'birth' of the Constitution, explains: 'Manuel Fraga was quickly on good terms with Gregorio Peces Barba. ... In spite of the conflict between left and right, their interactions were cordial.' Curiously, something similar happened between Fraga and his other possible adversary—who was even further to the left than Peces Barba—among the presenters of the Constitution, then-communist Jordi Solé Tura. Fraga comments: 'Like me, he was a professor of political law,' and although 'in principle we didn't have very compatible [political] positions, it soon turned out that we agreed on many things.' For Fraga, the subject of the similar 'training' of the group was very important:

> It must be recognized that we were all people with similar backgrounds; there were two political law professors, [and] a philosophy of law professor, which was Peces Barba. In short, we had early training that didn't agree on the conclusions, but did on the working methods, and on the custom of using legal reasoning, and that was good.

The exceptional ability of those who are called to lead in exceptional times is unquestionably justified by their 'training.' Bauman explains that never in the history of the world has there been a caste more convinced of its role as the vanguard of humanity than the one that formed around the modern power/knowledge complex:

> From at least the seventh century and well into the twentieth, the writing elite of Western Europe and its footholds on other continents considered its own way of life as a radical break in universal history. Virtually unchallenged faith in the superiority of its own mode over all alternative forms of life—contemporary or past—allowed it to take itself as the reference point for the interpretation of the *telos* of history. (110)

Is it going too far to interpret from Bauman's affirmation the attitudes and the self-perception of the elites that orchestrated the Spanish transition from the dictatorial regime to the parliamentary monarchy? Perhaps it doesn't seem like much of an exaggeration after listening to Fraga—who had been Franco's minister for seven years—justify his participation in the writing of the democratic Constitution by saying that 'he had been prepared for it, he had written books,' and that he had created 'an institute for studies on democratic reform.' Questions like that of his responsibility, as the Minister of the Interior, for the death of at least five people during the 'Vitoria massacre,' just two years before Fraga was seated to write the Constitution, are put on hold: books are books, studies are studies, and a university professor is a university professor.[2]

The expert 'fathers of the Constitution' are legitimized because they write books and because they have 'training'; in other words, because they are fluent in the technical language of the law. But also, and this is different, because they know how to negotiate, 'they interact cordially,' 'they have known each other for years,' and even 'get along well.' If you think about it, these arguments are rather contradictory. It is as if these 'distinguished gentlemen' gained legitimacy both because of their specialized training and because they could rise above that same technical specialization. Gabriel Cisneros, another one of the seven 'com-padres' of the Constitution, echoes this tension when he recalls that some people said (despite the presence of eminent jurists among them), 'The fact that the great "midwives" of contemporary Spanish constitutionalism are an agricultural engineer and an industrial engineer never ceases to be amusing.' But again it is Alfonso Guerra who confronts the contradiction more directly, making it work in his favor, when he says that Martorell and he were two people who hadn't studied law but who had 'something that is essential for a lawyer: common sense.'

Again the work of de Certeau is an excellent source of ideas to help us understand such questions of cultural authority and its contradictions. As I indicated in the previous chapter, in *The Practice of Everyday Life*, de Certeau explains that at the same time that Western 'modernity' was born, when reality began to be considered something that must be understood empirically rather than as an invisible essence, a new structure of epistemological legitimization was formed. This means for de Certeau that since then the ability 'to speak in name of reality' has come to be considered as belonging mainly to two figures, supported in different ways by this new horizon of legitimacy: the Expert and the Philosopher.

The Expert, according to de Certeau, specializes in a specific area of technoscientific knowledge. Based on that specialization, he is granted an

---

2 Regarding the so-called 'Vitoria massacre' and the lack of reparation offered to its victims, see Muriel (2012).

authority that, in principle, would consist of communicating or making his specialized knowledge useful for the rest of society. But it always ends up extending beyond that particular mission, and becoming an authority not directly related to his area of expertise. Ultimately, in fact, the Expert is expected to have 'common sense.' Or rather, his personal opinions end up being perceived as 'common sense,' because he is recognized as an 'authority' in general, and everyone forgets that in the beginning his authority was based on a particular type of technical, specialized knowledge. Thus it is that the 'expert in something'—in a certain specific thing—magically ends up becoming an 'expert in everything.' That is, he becomes an authorized representative of that 'common sense' that Guerra considers the key to Martorell's and his own success as creators of the legal norm of social coexistence that has been at work in the Spanish state for almost 40 years.

What happens with de Certeau's other figure of modern cultural authority, the Philosopher, is actually very similar. The Philosopher is someone who, to a certain extent, would be introduced from the beginning as a kind of 'expert in everything.' The Philosopher, according to de Certeau, acquires his legitimacy through the very fact that he does not specialize in something in particular. On the contrary, he claims to speak in the name of universality, in a meta-language that would allow him to observe from outside both expert knowledges and, in general, the daily production of meaning in ordinary language. This prerogative has been shown by studies of language and 'ordinary' culture, such as those of de Certeau himself (which in this regard take Wittgenstein's work as a point of departure), to be impossible. This is in line, in other respects, with all the critical theory that has, in many different ways, laid to rest those pretensions to universality during the twentieth century.[3]

De Certeau would consider, then, that both figures, the Expert and the Philosopher, receive an 'excess of authority' based on fallacies. Both start from a position of illegitimate power that constitutes the source of their authority in society. Thus, the problem is not (only) that it is not possible for 'anyone' to easily access the cultural authority of these figures. Rather, it lies in these figures' very ambition to monopolize the power/knowledge

---

3 The breakdown of positivism provoked the abandonment of an ingenuous view of referentiality as a correspondence between words and things. In its place was embraced an understanding of reality (whether that be 'language' or 'world') as a series of processes of identification and differentiation that enable or hinder the production of meaning. Key texts that articulate this tradition are, to name just a few, 'On Truth and Lies in a Nonmoral Sense' by Nietzsche, 'Identity and Difference' by Heidegger, Wittgenstein's own *Philosophical Investigations*, and later, 'Differance' by Derrida, and Deleuze's *The Logic of Sense*.

complex, regardless of who they might be. The fact that Guerra reminds us that he rejected the offer of a noble title and of an honorary doctorate in law for his participation in the birth of the Constitution is of little importance. What matters is that the ways of constructing power and cultural authority in Spanish society during the transition made it possible for only two people (or seven, it doesn't matter) to perform the critical task of outlining for the public, in the form of the Constitution, what a life with dignity must consist of.[4]

2.1.3. The meritocratic version of elite exceptionality

Guerra uses the argument of 'social mobility' covertly when he says that upon being offered those honors, he responded to Martorell (who transmitted the message to him from Suárez), 'Look, Fernando, you have only recently left the plow' (i.e., he is from a farming family), and adds that he himself is 'of very humble extraction,' although 'it's true I did also study technical engineering.' Guerra's point is—I believe—that the 'distinctions' being offered were excessive for those who had played a crucial role by using 'common sense'; in other words, they were excessive for those whose origins are in the world of the 'commoner' and not that of 'distinguished gentlemen.' However, what is implicit is that in order to be able to rise to the point where their 'common sense' would serve to place them in a position to negotiate a Constitution *en petit comité*, something had to happen. This might be a way for his 'it's true I did also study technical engineering' to be seen as a recognition that actually, this 'commoner' has 'taught himself' and has earned other titles more appropriate to his humble origins, and perhaps it was these that brought him to his present position, that he does not wish to go to the extreme of trying to show off a noble title or an honorary doctorate.

César Rendueles indicated in a text published on his blog 'Contra la igualdad de oportunidades' (2013) that in recent decades the left has assimilated the discourse of 'social mobility' and 'meritocracy,' which actually has clearly conservative origins:

> If being conservative means anything, it means justifying the privileges of the elites because of their superior intellectual or moral achievements. That is the classic argument of Burke, Bonald, Maistre,

4 This type of opaque, elitist constituent process has become so naturalized that it can also come to seem like 'common sense.' Nevertheless, recent decades have contributed numerous examples of how things can be done in much more democratic ways: in recent decades, countries like Iceland, Colombia, Bolivia, and Ecuador have opened constituent processes very different from the Spanish one. See, for example, the dossier published by *Periódico Diagonal* on 'constituent processes' (2012).

and all the reactionaries of the nineteenth century. The new left confuses democracy with an expansion of the mechanics of selecting elites.

Again, the problem is not that there are few Martorells or Guerras who can 'leave the plow' to take up the pen that writes the Constitution, but that there is only space for a few hands to hold that pen. Rendueles specifies the critique of the idea of 'social mobility' by quoting these words of the sociologist Christopher Lasch (1996), from his book *The Revolt of the Elites and the Betrayal of Democracy*:

> Meritocracy is a parody of democracy. Theoretically, it offers possibilities for [social] ascent to whoever has the talent to take advantage of them. But social mobility doesn't undermine the influence of the elites. In fact it contributes to the intensification of their influence by supporting the illusion that it is strictly merit-based. It only makes it more probable that the elites will exert their power irresponsibly when they recognize few obligations with respect to their predecessors or to the communities that they claim to manage. (41)

Alfonso Guerra's discourse in *Memoria de un consenso* represents a meritocratic variation on the leitmotif of the need for exceptional individuals in exceptional situations which is the backbone of the 'official' narrative of the Spanish transition. The social democratic inflection of that transition clearly imprinted a different tone on the 'distinctions' that indicated cultural authority in Spanish society in the eighties and nineties, incorporating into them the 'popular' origin and the 'humble extraction' of many other 'commoners' who were able to ascend to those distinguished heights. But at the same time, the social democratic turn of the Culture of the Transition (to borrow once more the term coined by Guillem Martinez) also maintained, perhaps inevitably, the basic structures of legitimation and cultural authority that underpin the modern paradigm—technoscientific, liberal, capitalist— by which this social democracy was recognized and expressed.

If we were to look for technocratic figures equivalent to Franco's planning engineers, we would find them, as Isidro Lopez (2012) indicates, primarily among the economists who introduced neoliberalism with the PSOE, such as the ministers Miguel Boyer and Carlos Solchaga—although we could also add the profile of the 'eminent jurist' (who would be embodied by Manuel Fraga in his 'improved, democratic' version 2.0). Beyond these figures, however, the cultural authority that predominated in the eighties and nineties must be sought out in places that were especially propitious for the meritocratic, populist version of the modern power/knowledge complex, such as education and what is usually called 'the cultural world,' in reference to the fine arts and literature.

I have already mentioned in the previous chapter the critical importance of the long pro-European, pedagogical tradition of the Spanish intellectual elites for post-Franco 'standardization.' Now I would like to expand on this issue, giving some examples of how these elites exert their authority and their capacity for legitimation from the 'world of art and culture,' but in close proximity to the political and financial worlds. Through these examples, I hope to enrich the analysis of the different varieties of cultural authority (technocratic, intellectual, aesthetic) which nurture that cultural elite. I also hope to refine the study of their importance in the post-transition period, during which the forms of modern cultural authority (bourgeois, liberal) converge with the generalization of the way of neoliberal life, which is based on indiscriminate competition and the corporatization of the individual.

2.2. Men Who Smoke and Men Who Drink (or, Culture, that Modern Invention)

2.2.1. The expert, the intellectual, the artist, and their checks

Essentially, alongside those 'men who smoke' all night to save the nation, there are others who, more and more often as the 'democratic' era progresses, do more than smoke. They drink 'hectoliters' of 'free alcohol' at cultural openings and cocktails, paid for with public funds from the State Treasury, and against which Rafael Sanchez Ferlosio railed in his famous article 'La cultura, ese invento del gobierno' (1984). Although the former are characterized by their untiring vigil, and the latter by their inspired drunkenness, perhaps there isn't much difference between the 'men who smoke' and these other 'men who drink.' It must be kept in mind that, as Ignacio Echevarría asserted in his article on the Culture of the Transition, the state and the 'cultural world' got along well enough at the height of the PSOE's rise to power in 1982—when, says Echevarría, 'the ideals of change, liberalization, and cosmopolitanism assumed by the state in the political action plan were also assumed by a good part of the creators and intellectuals' (CT 31).

It is interesting to see the similarities in the 'approach to ideals' taken by both politicians and cultural elites, as well as those in their respective approaches to practices and languages. The letter inviting Ferlosio to contribute to an exhibition catalogue and which sorely tried his patience—and made him write that famous article—is an excellent referent for this. The letter also shows that habit so typical of the elites of treating each other with complicit familiarity ('If you don't know me, don't even think of addressing me with [the familiar, informal] '*tú*,'" says Ferlosio) and of assuming that all 'distinguished gentlemen' are friends: 'We have invited pre-eminent essayists and poets,' the letter explains, 'whose contributions we think could be very interesting, and among whom you [*tú*] will find many friends.' Ferlosio is outraged by the brazenness, but at the same time he considers it archetypical of 'the current uses of cultural exchange.'

'How many times lately,' he laments, 'have I had to put up with being told, "It's nothing, two or three pages about anything, whatever you want, whatever occurs to you ..." Come on, I know that when you sit down at the machine ...!' This is what Ferlosio calls 'unconditional loyalty to the name': this is all they want, because he is part of the cast of 'distinguished' characters who can help to legitimize any cultural enterprise. Ferlosio's article has often been read as a critique of the PSOE's subsidized, populist government culture, which it undoubtedly is. However, it also contains a critique of a much older cultural elitism—the supposed superiority of those who appropriate the monopoly on knowledge—which in this commercialized context turns the work of intellectuals and artists into purely superficial prestige.

And in any case, there is no contradiction between these two critiques. On the one hand, the PSOE's cultural, subsidized populism can be perfectly understood as an expanded version of the traditional authoritarianism of the modern cultural elites. On the other hand, what the social democratic government tried to do was incorporate elements of 'popular culture' into the existing structures of cultural authority—chaired professorships, museums, Ministries of Culture, big cultural industries, etc.,—instead of making space for other, more democratic ways of producing and maintaining cultural value.

'It is a showing of current painters, who instead of painting on canvas will do it on fans,' explained the invitation. But then it immediately clarified, 'However, it isn't an exhibition of "fans," but rather the background isn't canvas.' In other words, a fan can be put in the space where a canvas was (just as it is possible to put a 'deserter of the plow' where a jurist would normally be), but the space continues to be the same, as the 'head of a public organization' who invited Ferlosio knew very well. No matter how much they want to integrate colorful or folkloric elements—like fans—into these 'high' places, it is always about maintaining the legitimacy of the 'cultural' sphere as a privileged space that is adorned, certainly, with symbols that are much less austere than those that surround those 'men who smoke'—expert saviors of the nation—but always fulfills, as Ferlosio says, the 'clairvoyant prophecy' of the song: 'in Chicote a posh entertainment / with the cream of intellectual society.'

'Honorary boozers drinking on the government's dime, to lend prestige to events with the hollow sound of their names.' According to Ferlosio, that is what the so-called Spanish 'intellectuals' became in the eighties. Pierre Bourdieu (1995) explained, however, that the invention of the figure of the intellectual—which may be summed up in Emile Zola's famous 'J'Accuse' (1898, Dreyfus case)—involved a moment of affirmation for the autonomy of art in the face of politics. Since then, for Bourdieu, and according to the idea that became hegemonic, the intellectual's legitimacy was based precisely on his independence from political intrigue, which he could denounce from an impartial position.

Denouncements of the PSOE's wasteful spending on culture; mentions of Felipe González's and Carmen Romero's famous regular meetings with the 'cream of the intellectual society' in the *bodeguilla* of Moncloa Palace (the Spanish presidential home); allusions to the possible 'clientelism' of the cultural world with respect to the Spanish 'democratic' state—all these have occurred abundantly in connection with the notion of the Culture of the Transition. And it seems to me that when these things are done, perhaps what they have in mind is the ideal counter-image of that 'intellectual autonomy' that was instituted at the end of the nineteenth century with Zola's symbolic gesture. The Spanish intellectuals and artists of the post-dictatorship period would be exactly the opposite of that critical, independent figure. As Guillem Martinez said, 'basically, the relationship between the state and culture in the CT is the following: culture doesn't get involved in politics—except to acknowledge that the state is right—and the state doesn't get involved in culture—except to subsidize it, to award it, or to give it honors' (16).

There is undoubtedly a great deal of truth in all this. But it seems to me that there is a danger in exaggerating the explicit, deliberate complicity between the 'cultural world' and the state. This can end up blurring—even if only accidentally—a deeper type of structural complicity that has to do with the common root of both political and 'cultural' power in the modern power/knowledge complex I have been analyzing, and to which the figure of the intellectual is in no way a stranger, even when he maintains his autonomy towards political power and money. Again, it has to do with enormously complex questions that I can only partially illuminate; but I still want to attempt to do so without departing from the more or less flexible path of my reasoning. In this regard, I will try to expound briefly on the keys of that structural complementarity between political power and modern cultural power (including that of the 'intellectuals') by returning to the meat of Ferlosio's substantial article. It seems to me that the three basic pieces of the complicated puzzle of 'modern' cultural authority were indeed already present in the famous fan exhibition just as the CT inherited it: political-technocratic power, cultural prestige—with the added variant of the aesthetic aura, to which I will now turn—and the power of money.[5]

Thus, on one hand, we have the head of the 'public' institution who invites Ferlosio. This would be the representative of political power, and that power is always based/founded on the expert's technocratic legitimacy. It is assumed that this gentleman is there because he has been suitably 'trained' in something specific, that is, because he has some 'technical' expert knowledge necessary to do his job. At the same time, the representative of this power seems 'complicit,' a 'friend of his friends,' with 'common sense' that leads him to *tutear* (address informally) everybody, even if he doesn't know them, and to be magnanimous and friendly with his close friends.

On the other hand are those 'pre-eminent essayists and poets' whom the political power invites to write something for the exhibition catalogue. These people are nourished by another type of legitimation that is no longer

5 There are many valuable contributions to the study of the often endogamic relations of these three sectors (state, money, and art/culture) since the Spanish 'transition to democracy,' including some of the critical approaches to the transition in general, which I mentioned earlier (see note 35). This is actually a very vibrant field of study, energized not only by Guillem Martínez's crucial notion of Cultura de la Transición (and Fernández-Savater's later reworking of the concept), but also by the recent publication of important works in the field of contemporary intellectual and cultural history, such as Delgado's aforementioned *La nación singular* (2014) and the much-anticipated and controversial *El cura y los mandarines* by Gregorio Morán (2014). Although different in scope and methodology, these two books are somewhat complementary in terms of their chronology: Morán extends his study from 1966 to 1996, and Delgado seems to take off from where Morán left it, focusing on the years from 1996 to 2011. In these, as well as in other important contributions—like Eduardo Subirats' criticism of the authoritarian cultural elites of the transition *Después de la lluvia* (1993) or Joan Ramon Resina's challenge of Castilian centralism in 'Hispanismo' *Del Hispanismo a los Estudios Ibéricos* (2009)—we find very important analysis of the specific ways in which 'the Spanish cultural class' has negotiated its ties to money and state power. While Morán is particularly meticulous in his almost detectivesque reconstructions of the corruptions great and small involved in those ties, some other authors work with broader contexts or are more theoretically focused. Despite, or because of, their differences, these works provide a wealth of historical knowledge to which I would like to offer my own research as a humble addition. Perhaps what I am mainly able to contribute in this respect are two different lines of work: on one side, a wide contextualization of Spanish cultural power in processes of modern cultural 'segregation' (those described by Bauman, de Certeau, and Rancière), and, on the other, a renewed vision of cultural authority based on the experiences of collaboration and radical democracy which, despite all their shortcomings and contradictions, have been creating a new cultural space of relative autonomy during the years of the present crisis (2008–15).

specialized and technocratic, but rather that of their intellectual capacity to have an opinion 'on anything': 'It's nothing, two or three pages on anything, whatever you want, whatever occurs to you ...' These 'pre-eminent essayists and poets' are invited not to share their own philosophical or literary research, but rather to express their opinion on the cultural event of the day. And they might share with 'the men who smoke' the practices and languages of that deeply rooted elitism due to which the distinguished gentlemen 'are all friends,' although they don't know each other. Furthermore, crucially, they might trade on the empty prestige of their name in exchange for entitlements and alcoholic 'refreshments,' thus integrating themselves into that great organizational system of the value of things to which the technocrats also respond: that of 'the money community' (Harvey 1989).

But, in addition—and this seems to me very useful for nuancing the arguments on the complicity between power and culture in the CT—the letter that infuriated Ferlosio includes another fundamental element: those artists of the fan exhibition who, according to the head of the public institution, 'have absolute freedom to paint them, to break them, to play and whatever [else] occurs to them.' Ferlosio is angry, and he wonders how much those artists will earn 'to make asses of themselves' with the fans. But here I want to emphasize that, besides the name of the prestigious intellectual, the 'popular' flavor the fans give, and the check made out to the 'bearer' for the participants, what the organizer also needs for his event to be successful is the playful, transgressive freedom of the artist, who, like the intellectual, is requested to do 'whatever occurs to him.'

What appears in that requirement is, of course, the third great transformation that, together with the capitalist and liberal-bourgeois ones, gave rise to the foundations of modern Western cultural authority, and which, as Graham and Labanyi remind us, Francoism had interrupted in Spain at the height of the thirties: 'aesthetic modernization.'

2.2.2. The individualistic heart of the modern aesthetic
The Argentine critic Reinaldo Laddaga summarizes the basic characteristics of this 'aesthetic modernity' in his *Estética de la emergencia*. He interprets it as a reaction to capitalist modernization. This, in turn, implies abandoning ways of life based on the power of the past and on tradition, replacing them with new ways of life governed by a culture of experts who determine the necessary means (always ruled by capitalist logic) to exert control over nature, which, one assumes, will bring progress in the future.

This technocratic culture produces a void of meaning and a deficit of sociability that causes the aesthetic reaction of modernism and the avant-garde. But—and this is the interesting thing here—Laddaga adds that this void of meaning and deficit of sociability is basically due to a series of massive processes of 'specialization and abstraction' in the face of which aesthetic modernity has an ambiguous answer: although it often tries to construct a 'new unity' that gives meaning to so much dispersion, it simultaneously manages to put on an exhibition—and almost an exacerbation—of the alienating aspects of those 'automatizing' processes of life.

This second aspect is what interests me. Modernism undoubtedly introduces a distortion of languages, a relativization of conventions—thus accompanying the 'melting into the air' that characterizes capitalist, urban, industrial modernization. Perhaps that is the origin of the suggestion— which, on the face of it, there is no reason to take for granted—that what the artists might do with the fans is 'to break them, to play.' And the assertion that 'it's not an exhibition of fans' is the organizer's way of making the familiar unfamiliar, very like the typical move/aim of the avant-garde and modernism, which seek to make us look at ordinary objects in new ways, 'outside the box' of convention.

In essence, Laddaga explains that the modern aesthetic, understood as a cultural regime begun in the eighteenth century and based on the presentation of a work of art by an artist to a silent spectator, necessarily consists of an interruption of the conventional: it has to do, says Laddaga, with presenting 'something completely exterior to the situation in which it appears.' He adds, 'that exteriority is conceived as an occurrence that cancels the routine implementation of communications and actions, it separates them from themselves and surprises them: it is a moment of absolute interruption of the community that can simultaneously be a promise of particular fullness' (41).

This moment of irruption of the strange isn't all that different, in other respects, from the operation of traditional cultures, which also have their mechanisms for causing rupture, improvisation, or ecstasy. But what is peculiar in the modern aesthetic, according to Laddaga, is that it accompanies that strong emphasis placed on the irruption of exteriority—as opposed to the maintenance of tradition—with a characteristic centrality of the individual, in the function of both creator and spectator:

> [A]n artist, in a state of solitude where she focuses intensely on increasing her receptivity, composes—from the fragments of sensitivity that she isolates—an object where a different thought is produced, destined to be developed elsewhere, perhaps neutralized, where an unknown, silent spectator scrutinizes it closely, with the intention of discovering its structure. (41)

Surely it is in relation to this priority of the singular that we must understand the 'absolute freedom' the organizer of the fan exhibition demands, so that the artists can 'paint them, break them, play, and whatever [else] occurs to them.' Only from that freedom could those artists find 'the occurrence that cancels the routine implementation of communications and actions,' that moment of creating meaning by distorting the conventional as aesthetic modernity understands it. But then, what is it in that description of the artists' work on fans that is so humiliating and upsets Ferlosio so much? Is it only the implied matter of them earning too much?

What happens, it seems to me, is that, like the case of the 'unconditional loyalty to the name,' the irritating thing here is that the possible 'occurrence' of exteriority at the center of the modern aesthetic experience may become a mere 'whim' of the individual who holds the title of 'artist.' The 'whatever occurs to them' that Ferlosio repeats is a perversion of the moment of 'exacerbated receptivity' (Laddaga) that is demanded of the modern artist to facilitate the irruption of something external not only to her, but also to the common world to which, ever since Schiller formulated the paradigm in *Letters for the Aesthetic Education of Humanity*, she is understood to belong.

If art is important in modernity, says Laddaga, paraphrasing Schiller, it is because in it 'the exhibition of a certain general truth of individuals or communities occurs such that it can be produced in a singular way.' He adds, 'it is how it is distinguished with respect to the world in which it originates that artwork becomes capable of indicating the authentically common at the heart of the common' (33).

Only because Guernika is painted that way, with those uncertain, tangled lines, only because it includes each one of those unique figures and not others, does it manage to achieve the intensity that makes it a widely recognized symbol of human suffering and of war. Only because it wanders through those phrases with strange, drawn-out rhythms, only because it invents the unique, peculiar characters Albertine and Marcel, can *À la recherche de temps perdu* achieve 'the exposition of a certain general truth' about the common experience of mortality and the passage of time. In this connection of the unique with the common, a fundamental ambiguity is expressed about modern aesthetics in the face of capitalist modernization, which I have already mentioned: at the same time as it aggravates the processes of deterritorialization (as Deleuze and Guattari say) that moves capitalism, it still manages to try to establish new 'common senses.'

Perhaps the clearest, most extreme cases of this second function of aesthetic modernization should be sought in the famous 'bringing art to life' of the historic avant-garde. In the wake of the many interpretations of this motto, aesthetics would play a foundational role in community-wide political experiments. Of these, those of the early Soviet Russia come to mind. Also, and more relevant for this context, there are those of Lorca's La Barraca theater group and other similar initiatives that united the avant-garde with popular culture during the Spanish Second Republic.[6]

Going forward, I don't find it unreasonable to assert that one of the problems with the type of perverse adaptation to aesthetic modernity that Ferlosio criticizes—and which he considers recurrent in the Spain of democratic cultural 'normalization'—is precisely that it erases that 'common' component which resonates in the modern aesthetic experience, changing it into a mere individual 'notion' or 'whim.'

2.2.3. Putting culture in my name
But why? Why would anyone be interested in thus perverting aesthetic modernity?

In part, no doubt, because of the existence of that other central element which, together with expert power, intellectual prestige, and the aura of aesthetics, completes the puzzle Ferlosio has drawn: the famous 'check made out to bearer' that the government wrote every time it heard the word 'culture,' those '10,000 *duros*'[7] a head given to those who participated in the catalogue, the plain and simple 'price of your name' to which the intellectual finds himself reduced. To wit: money. But not money as a kind of scapegoat or as the mysterious embodiment of all the ills of humanity; money as a very specific, very real instrument used historically to reduce all social value to something quantifiable, instrumental, and subject to becoming exclusive individual property. Changing culture into something that can 'put a name' on supposedly exceptional individuals in whom all the value of aesthetic creation—and even, more generally, cultural creation—is concentrated, facilitates the monetarization of that cultural value. And this is something that the most individualist interpretations of modern tradition allow. This is better understood if we consider that the process of cultural privatization and commercialization entailed by this monetarization is much more difficult to carry out in societies—known as 'traditional'—that understand their culture as a common, collective, anonymous process of production and maintenance of meanings that are necessary for life.[8]

---

6 Regarding experimental convergences of the aesthetic avant-garde and projects of political change during the Second Republic, see Graham and Labanyi (1995).

7 A Spanish coin worth 5 pesetas, or roughly US 4c.

8 It would be ingenuous to think that there are cultures in which the shared, the common, is not in tension with the individual, or in which the use value ('what is necessary to sustain life') is not in tension with the exchange value. To avoid oversimplifications, I think David Graeber's classification of the 'moral foundations

As Ferlosio explains, in the world of money, intellectual work isn't appealing if it's not 'paid':

> Nobody ever appeals to the so-called intellectuals by taking them seriously, as would only be the case if somebody sought them out, not to pay them just for the use of their names, but to request some free, anonymous benefit of them. (And what Government could have dreamed up a better disposition towards collaborationism than what the present one had before it in October 1982!) But their possible usefulness—whatever it may be worth—is neither wanted nor needed; in fact, being useful might actually be a hindrance. Rather, it is only the decorative emptiness of their fame and their names that is desirable.

Intensifying the quantifying logic of money and the abandonment of the use value that are both implied by neoliberalism led to a progressive commercialization of the 'cultural world' in Spain. Fortunately, there are already numerous studies about this, such as those of Graham and Labanyi, Bértolo (2008), López de Abiada (2001), Acín (1990), Alonso (2003), Reig (2012), Rowan (2010), Ferlosio himself (2000), and others.[9] Now is not the

---

of economics' is very useful. He identifies three: exchange, hierarchy, and what he calls 'baseline communism,' which functions according to the tacit principle of 'from each according to his abilities, to each according to his needs.' Conversations among friends, music, dancing, parties, or games, says Graeber, are environments in which 'baseline communism' or 'communism of the senses,' in which the goal is sharing in and of itself rather than competition, are frequently practiced. In precapitalist European peasant societies, like those studied by John Berger, the ties of interdependence were often so evident that many of the activities of daily life, including work, cultural transmission, and decision-making, were managed from that 'baseline communism.' This doesn't mean that that was the only form of social organization, since this tendency always appeared together with the other two forms of human relationship identified by Graeber. He does note, however, that 'baseline communism' is a kind of 'foundation' for all sociality, even though it is never found in a 'pure' form: 'baseline communism might be considered the raw material of sociality, a recognition of our ultimate interdependence that is the ultimate substance of social peace' (99).

9 One of Ferlosio's own texts that seems to me particularly effective for describing these dynamics and which I have mentioned on other occasions (Moreno-Caballud 2012) is 'Las cajas vacías,' included in the book *El alma y la vergüenza* (Ferlosio 2000). In it Ferlosio talks about the proliferation of an 'intransitive' individual ethic (indifferent to the object of its action as it produces individual profit) that affected all of society, and particularly the world of culture. He detected this 'intransitive' ethic in the (literally) 50,000 'cultural acts'—whatever those might be—proposed in advance by the organizers of the Universal Exposition of Seville in 1992, and in the need felt by the mass media to fill the same number of pages every day, even

time for that kind of analysis, which is very well developed in these works. They all agree on the importance of the 'fame and name' paradigm to which Ferlosio refers, the 'proper nouns' with which the new cultural industries, designed for mass consumption and concentrated around a few big media groups, were creating a kind of cultural 'star-system' to stimulate sales.

I will return shortly to the type of 'culture bubble' to which that 'cultural world's' neoliberal decline leads. However, first I want to propose that there is something else that works together with the power of money to foster that perversion of aesthetic modernity, which tends to turn it into nothing more than a mere individual whim. That something is the appearance of a specific historical juncture at which a large part of the Spanish 'creative class' tended to hide the relationship between their aesthetic work and the historical and cultural communities from which they took the conventional materials they used (languages, traditions, collective imaginaries, etc.), and to which, inevitably, they returned those materials transformed into 'works of art.' In other words, I propose that the type of degraded individualism that facilitated the 'buying and selling' of artists (and intellectuals) by those in power during the so-called Culture of Transition derived in part from the artists themselves, in exacerbating the individualism that was latent in the tradition of aesthetic modernity (to the detriment of its civic potential).

2.3. The Engineer's Great Style: A Depoliticized Aesthetic Modernity

2.3.1. An itch for artistic modernity in the face of Francoism

This is not at all a new idea. There have been innumerable discussions about the famous 'modernizing' itch that afflicted Spanish culture perhaps more than other countries during the 1960s and '70s. This is due precisely to the fact that Spain had experienced such a long interruption in its aesthetic 'modernization' because of Francoism—an interruption that entailed, of course, a notable decrease in the 'openness to a perceivable exteriority' that constitutes modern aesthetics. Such openness was replaced, by both the regime and its opposition, with a more conservative formal paradigm. To synthesize and simplify the argument: the new 'moderns' at the end of

---

when there wasn't any news. In any case, I think it's important not to see this commodification of culture as an isolated phenomenon, but rather, as one more dimension derived from the widespread financiarization of global capitalism that occurs in neoliberalism (as explained by Dardot and Laval (2014); Harney (2010); Harvey (2005); López Hernández and Rodríguez López (2010)).

Francoism would have disapproved of anything that smacked of collectivity, of aesthetics in service to a community, or even, more generally, to 'politics,' and would identify these elements with the 'backwardness' that Francoism had imposed on aesthetic modernization.[10]

We know this wasn't always so, and shortly I will give some examples of important exceptions. But at the same time, a tendency was undeniably forged towards the end of Francoism, and continues today with different variations in the sphere of institutional culture. That tendency emphasizes the individual aspect of aesthetics over the collective, its transgressive capacity over its foundational aspect, the formal over the historical, the ephemeral over the sustainable. And finally, in Spain, the side of aesthetic modernity that carried the relativization of the conventional to extremes tended to be emphasized over the side that sought a new convention. This relativization was understood (perhaps simplistically) as an expression of overcoming Francoism, which was associated with the past and with tradition.

An archetypal example of this modernizing itch in the Spanish aesthetics of the 1960s and '70s is the figure and the work of the writer Juan Benet. Bringing him into the discussion is particularly useful because it also allows me to clarify my small contribution to the debate about the CT. As I noted earlier, this deals with illuminating the structural connections between politics and cultural power (including the aura of aesthetics) that appear beyond the explicit personal alliances or collusions in the world of the CT. Juan Benet (1982) wrote in his famous 1965 essay *La inspiration y el estilo*, that the latter, when it could be characterized as *grand style*, was 'the state of grace,' that is, the place in which to seek

> that region of the spirit which, after having evicted the gods who had dwelled there, needs to replace their functions to give the writer an obvious path of knowledge ... that prepares him for a full description of the world, and is ultimately able to supply any type of response to the questions the writer had previously raised to his god. (38)

By putting style in the place hitherto occupied by divine inspiration, Benet repeats the move of modern aesthetics, for which formal experimentation would be, as Laddaga says, a procedure without rules, increasingly different, always unlikely and unpredictable, which the artwork must carry out every time to find the singularity that reveals the whole.

At the same time, Benet's essay attacked the type of literature that seemed incompatible with the revelation of aesthetic singularity, by

---

10 See, for example, Mainer (1994, 113).

concentrating on a function that he called 'informative,' 'realist,' or 'social': 'The informative novel has ended ... Naturalism died and the realist social novel was exhausted because its information interests very few people and leaves little impression other than a brief moment of febrile interest and a sequel of fraudulent interruptions' (128). He goes on to add, 'literature is only interesting for its style, not for its substance' (135). Starting from these types of considerations and from the prolonged, intense elaboration of a fiction that tried to put them in practice, Benet concentrates on his surroundings much of that 'modernizing itch' which Francoism had caused in opposition circles—not without a certain amount of misunderstanding, it seems to me. His rejection of the 'informative,' 'realist,' or 'social' in literature was often understood as—or at least contributed in one way or another to—a disdain for anything that seemed to put a political twist on aesthetic things. This helped foster that 'perverted' interpretation of aesthetic modernity denounced by Ferlosio.

Benet's interpretation of aesthetic modernity—with its misunderstandings—would stand for three decades until it became a whole aesthetic-political canon (of which Benet was obviously not the only inspiration). His substantial identification with the irrefutable value of 'modernity' was clearly announced in *El País* (García Posada 1994) on the first anniversary of his death:

> The emergence of Juan Benet in 1967 with *Volverás a Región*, put a permanent end to that never, or almost never, achieved desire for modernity in the Spanish novel ... Juan Benet takes on and finishes off the enterprise of locating the Spanish novel in the very center of modernity. What the poets of [the Generation of] '27 did for poetry, Benet does all on his own in his novel. *Volverás a Región* channels Joyce, channels Proust, and above all, channels Faulkner. It also channels the impenetrability that Ortega noted as an essential characteristic of narrative fiction capable of being fully modern.

2.3.2. Political consequences of a depoliticized aesthetic

Ignacio Echevarría's aforementioned article, 'La CT: un cambio de paradigma,' quotes this same essay by Benet, *La inspiration y el estilo*, but not to investigate whether the author ascribes to aesthetic modernity and how. Rather, he wants to recuperate Benet's idea that intellectuals in Spain had always been apart from the state, something that, according to Echevarría, could only have changed with the advent of the CT. As a notable example of this change, besides those already cited of the meetings in the *bodeguilla* of Moncloa Palace, Echevarría recalls the outstanding participation of Juan Benet in the manifesto 'Yes to NATO' that the PSOE in government had requested of the citizens in the 1986 referendum (País 1986).

Indeed, one might be surprised, as Echevarría says, not only to find Benet among the signatories of that manifesto, but even more surprised to find so many other intellectuals. Right besides Benet was none other than Ferlosio, 'characterized by his heated anti-war and anti-military stance' (besides being a fundamental model for the 'CT hypothesis'), as well as many others like Julio Caro Baroja, Jaime Gil de Biedma, Jorge Semprún, Santos Juliá, Assumpta Serna, Sancho Gracia, Adolfo Domínguez, and Luis Antonio de Villena. And there are still more: Eduardo Chillida, Antonio López, Carlos Bousoño, Amancio Prada, Oriol Bohígas, Juan Cueto, Víctor Pérez Díaz, Juan Marsé, Luis Goytisolo, José María Guelbenzu, Álvaro Pombo, Eduardo Úrculo, Jaime de Armiñán, Blanca Andreu, Luis de Pablo, Francisco Calvo Serraller, Javier Pradera, and even Michi Panero (among yet others).

It is worth asking why so many artists and intellectuals would agree to support something when, in principle, it might have brought them more popularity among their respective audiences if they had rejected it—or at least not supported it publicly. What kind of pact of the elites, or what 'spirit of the times' brought them to this surprising agreement?

When it comes to explaining these phenomena, there are two important points, temporal and structural, that must be borne in mind. First, and perhaps more typical, is the 'setting aside of any overtly critical attitude in the interest of a conciliatory, universal spirit'—more temporal—that Echevarría talks about (borrowing from Vázquez Montalbán). Second, and perhaps more critical for my purposes, is the influence—more structural— of the traditions of cultural modernity that had been recuperated at the end of Francoism in a form that was particularly blind to the political and social potentialities of aesthetic modernity. These were potentialities that could assuredly have provided shared alternatives from which to offer consistency to intellectuals' and artists' criticisms of capitalist power, which at that time was entering its neoliberal globalization phase.

In fact, there were plenty of criticisms. A trip through the archives reveals that in reality there was no lack of 'critical spirit' among the intellectuals and artists of the CT. Echevarría himself acknowledges that in the 'Yes to NATO' manifesto Benet was 'very critical' with 'the evident contradictions and culpable errors of the socialist leaders.' And there are many other examples, many of which I will return to later.

What *was* lacking, however, was that constructive, community component which was latent in the tradition of modern aesthetics, that 'will to bring art to life' of the avant-garde. This had been erased from the map by those, like Benet, who would establish the depoliticized canon of the Spanish version of aesthetic modernity by understanding 'style' as a formal and individual matter. Given that, perhaps we can view Juan Benet's promotion of the 'Yes to NATO' manifesto as an effect derived from helplessness in the face of the capitalist version of economic and political modernization produced by his particular interpretation of aesthetic modernity. Furthermore, we can understand the fact that so many other artists and intellectuals also signed it as an effect derived from the general acceptance of Benet's interpretation.

All this, by the way, is in no way incompatible with the idea of the 'deactivation of culture' in the CT discussed by Guillem Martínez. It will, though, perhaps allow us to nuance it, above all in the sense that it would no longer be necessary to deny the existence of constant criticisms of power from intellectuals and artists. Rather, it seems that starting in the early eighties, the intellectuals of the CT assiduously and openly protested and criticized the government and power in general. However, their critiques were made from an understanding of the figures of the intellectual and the artist that annulled their political capacity to open alternative social worlds. They were limited in this regard to movement in an abstractly formal environment and, tacitly, to a hegemonic understanding—liberal and capitalist—of society: 'society as a pact of theoretically independent individuals who decide to associate to exchange property,' to recall the words of the philosopher Marina Garcés discussed in the first chapter. The 'style' of the individual artist or intellectual would be, then, perhaps simply one more of those 'properties.'

2.3.3. Counter-example: The politicized aesthetic of the transitional underground

In any case, perhaps the strongest argument to explain the importance of this 'depoliticization' is the confirmation of the existence of a very important counter-version of that same aesthetic modernity: the underground counterculture. This counterculture did cultivate its civic, community aspect, and moreover, it did it during those same years. As mentioned in the previous chapter, the historian Germán Labrador has studied this counterculture exhaustively and exceptionally lucidly, as part of what he calls 'transitional cultures.' These transitional cultures construct subjectivities that don't fit with Francoist mesocratic values. Labrador has unearthed a whole constellation of practices, identities, and forms that turn on the recuperation of aesthetic modernity by marginal youth cultures that understand art as something that must necessarily 'change life,' in the same way that Rimbaud and the avant-garde envisaged it.

This culture begins in the sixties with the emergence of some 'strange lives,' which accompany their aesthetic experimentation with experiments in ways of life that clash head-on both with Francoist norms and with the orthodoxy of the opposition—for example, the transvestite artist Ocaña, the singer-songwriter Chicho Sánchez-Ferlosio, and the poets Leopoldo María Panero and Eduardo Haro Ivars. Despite the strangeness and radical positions of these figures, the enormous relevance of Labrador's research (2008) is based precisely on demonstrating that they were pioneers of a whole 'politics of life' that would spread among the youth of the generation he (and Pablo Sánchez León (2004)) calls the generation of '77; that is, those who were no longer socialized in the anti-Francoism that understood politics more as a change of institutions than of daily life itself, but did not socialize in the democratic 'normalization' that depoliticized cultural practices either.

Among these 'youth of '77,' experimentation with drugs, sex, music, and poetry constituted a form of political life and an avant-garde aesthetic all in one. Labrador exemplifies this double dimension by analyzing groups of poets he describes as 'from the extreme wing of the *novísimos*.'[11] He finds in them a cosmovision that doesn't exclude politics, since they follow the romantic and avant-garde creed according to which 'the poet must supply aesthetic ideas that serve to change life and reality.' Surrounding these poets, and with respect to that generation of '77, Labrador studies an entire almost forgotten archive of what he calls an 'epochal culture':

> In very general terms, we would be talking about a nucleus of some 2,000 books (poetry, narrative, theater, academic essays, or overtly countercultural, revelatory texts, texts of current events, translations of theoretical works about the counterculture and similar topics, biographies, translations of marginal or unorthodox literary works, collage texts, photograph books ...), some 20 magazines, ten alternative publishers and a couple hundred by very active cultural agents, thinkers and intellectuals. All together, and taking productions from all artistic disciplines, we should be able to speak of a legacy of some few thousand cultural objects; not a huge number, but still significant enough to constitute an epochal culture. (2006, 93)[12]

11 The Novísimos—translated as the 'Newest Ones'—were a group of poets in Spain who took their name from an anthology in which the Catalan critic Josep Maria Castellet gathered the work of young experimental poets in the 1970s: *Nueve novísimos poetas españoles* [*Nine Very New Spanish Poets*] (1970).

12 Labrador goes on to specify, 'At a strictly descriptive level, we would be talking about the works and productions of publishers such as La Banda de Moebius, La Piqueta, and Star Books; magazines like *Ajoblanco*, *Bicicleta*, and *El Viejo Topo*; poets like Aníbal Núñez, Fernando Merlo, and Carlos Oroza; musical groups like Derribos Arias or Veneno; and filmmakers like Maenza or Zulueta; not to mention innumerable painters, artists, and comic book illustrators' (92).

The mostly tragic end of this epochal culture is perhaps what is best known about it decades later. The violent deaths, the suicides, and the drug overdoses have contributed to feeding the individual legend of some of its most emblematic figures, tending to assimilate the lifestyle experimentation of this counterculture within the individualistic and depoliticized paradigm of modern aesthetics, which was imposed as hegemonic. In fact, the great misunderstanding is to confuse this world with what in fact was its decline and transformation into a culture of individualist consumption, during the years of the so-called 'Movida' in Madrid. But, on the other hand, as Labrador asserts, the transitional underground was a culture that

> in its moral order, in its world view, had a collective definition of identity; there the subject was a social being who needed relationships with others, destined to grow and better herself by living in community, with her limits and opportunities determined by the community, and committed to its improvement to achieve in this way her own improvement. (2008, 410)

It seems to me that we should never lose sight of this communitarian understanding of life held by the underground if we want to understand figures like Ocaña. He was a contradictory character whose stripteases and homoerotic shows scandalized even the anarchists of the Jornadas Libertarias de Barcelona in 1977, but also returned regularly to his hometown to organize *pasacalles*, costumed musical events held in the streets with local youngsters. In one of them, Ocaña ended up getting burned by accident when his elaborate sun costume caught fire from some firecrackers. He would not survive his injuries.

One might think that comparing someone like Juan Benet to Ocaña doesn't make much sense. But do they not both represent fundamental reappropriations of the tradition of modern aesthetics that are produced in the same historical moment? Ocaña, too, believed in 'style,' in his own way. While Benet practiced style in art, Ocaña practiced it in art and in life. But also, and this is the key to their differing modern aesthetics, Ocaña understood that the power of his style was only validated in community, in the construction of a daily relationship with others.

For the type of aesthetics, of style, that Benet represents, leaning more towards the formal and hermetic than towards the performative and common, the relationship of the artist with the communities of which he forms a part in his daily life isn't relevant. For Ocaña, it was just the opposite: living with the prostitutes of the Plaza Real in Barcelona was a central part of his life's aesthetics. But I don't think Benet would consider important aspects of his private life relevant to his *grand style*; for example, the fact that he worked as an engineer constructing reservoirs to help Francoism in its 'colonization' of farmland. Having said that, however, there were still times when Benet would let the two domains meet. The writer Javier Marías, disciple of Benet, recently shared an anecdote about this very thing: 'One time, they gave him a medal from the School of Engineers, and he made sure all his literary friends went to the ceremony, although it didn't matter to us and we couldn't care less, but it *was* important to him' (González 2014).

In few cases like this does that tandem between technocratic, engineering modernization and aesthetic modernity go so well together, perhaps because they are so well separated. But in many other cases, thanks in large part to the canonization of a depoliticized version of aesthetic modernity in which Benet was key, a fluid convergence can be seen between that aesthetic modernity and other aspects of capitalist modernization, which, considered as the only economic-political framework possible, would generate those dynamics Ferlosio condemned, in which the artist and the intellectual are reduced by the market and the state to the 'decorative emptiness of their fame and their name.' Especially since the onward march of neoliberalism intensified the search for brand names and tended to turn every culture into an object of economic speculation.

2.4. 'Normalization,' Deactivation, and Culture Bubble in the CT

2.4.1. A 'modernizing, normalizing' intellectual

Let's rewind for a moment to 1985: only three years have passed since the PSOE's historic rise to power, which the sociologist Lamo de Espinosa considered the victory of the 'immense, historic national modernizing and Europeanizing project that first inspired the Enlightenment thinkers, and later the regenerationists, the Generations of 98 and 14' (13). Javier Marías, Benet's disciple—and one of the most distinguished heirs of both his paradigm of depoliticized 'aesthetic modernity' and that tradition of cultural elites to whom Lamo alludes—returns from Oxford and is surprised to find a country already very critical of the government. 'I must admit,' he says in his article 'Visión de un falso indiano' (1985), 'that my surprise was considerable upon hearing opinions, reading articles, and studying supposed news reports about that same socialist government that had inspired both hopes and improvised support when I left.' It concerns him, he says, that people now often say things like:

'Before, we thought that in Health, in Education, in Housing everything was screwed up because it was *them*, but now it turns out it's also us. There's no doubt any more of how little the country gives back.' That argument, as simple as it is simplistic, is what, to my way of thinking, is most surprising and worrying. It ominously recalls the somber comment that often closed political conversations in Franco's time: 'There's no hope for this country.'

Even in a moment when one might expect collective enthusiasm for the new era just begun, people seem not only disillusioned with the government, but also, possibly, at a deeper level with themselves. But perhaps Marías shouldn't be so surprised by the Spaniards' lack of self-esteem. He himself would go on to write numerous articles that were critical of the socialist government and very critical of various aspects of democratic Spain. More importantly, he would admit only five years later that he couldn't help but be happy despite himself when someone occasionally told him that 'he didn't seem Spanish':

Unfortunately, every time some foreigner has said to me for some reason that I didn't seem Spanish, I have had the embarrassing sensation that they were complimenting me and that I should therefore consider it an insult to my country, or at least to my countrymen. This didn't seem like such an odd occurrence when I was younger; that is, in the past, when Spain was a despised nation that was then promptly associated with a decrepit dictatorship, with bullfighters, with a high crime rate where cases never got solved, with loud, rude people, with tricorn hats, with stone lifters,[13] clay water vessels, guitars ... But the most offensive thing is that even today, when one would think our country has changed so much, and always for the better, I still occasionally hear (not as often as I would personally want, and much more frequently than a civic perspective might want) someone tell me in the most complimentary tone, 'You don't seem Spanish.' (2011, 30)

Marías's statements here remind me of the dilemma of those who feel 'avant-garde' among their people. On one hand, they want to lead everyone to the long-awaited 'modernization.' But at the same time, their mission links them annoyingly to those 'backward' people—or at least, to an image of backwardness—from whom they want to differentiate themselves at all times.

---

13 *Levantar piedras* is a traditional sport in the Basque Country, practiced by a *harrijasotzaile* or *levantador de piedras* (stone lifter).

The topic of negative self-perception is a slippery one. Thus, even when they are happy for the small progress of their compatriots, it seems that the avant-garde can't help but be offended, as when in the same article, Marías pats himself on the back because

> something very worthy, though arbitrary, has been achieved: people in Spain today are blond and blue-eyed in ridiculously greater numbers than in the fifties or sixties, which, unlike the increase in average height, cannot be explained. But it is a great achievement, at least for the existence of a variety of images or physical types and the suppression of the monotonous individual of the past. (33)

At the same time, Marías says, 'Spanish women are the cleanest and most conscientious [women] on the continent,' and that men, 'although less attractive ... have made a tremendous effort to seem like normal beings and not delinquents, which is in itself a lot' (33).

However, it isn't all good news, it seems. If Marías still feels extraordinarily complimented despite himself when someone tells him he doesn't seem Spanish, it is because the image of the country, 'which, when all is said and done, is what counts in times like these, much more than the country itself for all intents and purposes,' often keeps reproducing, out of sheer inertia, the backwardness and folkloric vulgarity that has been expected of it 'for the last couple of centuries,' despite the fact that in the last few years there has been 'an awareness that such an image was not easily compatible with modern—or yet postmodern—aspirations' (34).

Marías has returned repeatedly, in articles and interviews, to this topic of the supposed 'backwardness' or the 'poor image' of Spain. As noted in the previous chapter, in 2006 Marías was already complaining that 'Spain is being destroyed by the trickery of construction firms, mayors, owners of public works, and independent counselors,' but he also had time to continue developing his classic theme of the supposed 'backwardness of Spain.' So, in a long interview granted to *The Paris Review*, Marías responded in these terms to a question about the criticisms he had received throughout his career 'for not being Spanish enough':

> There are people who expect Spanish literature, theater, movies, and painting to be folkloric, but the Spain I know is a fairly normal country. It was normal even during the dictatorship, in the sense that our cities aren't so different from other European cities. In Spain there are educated people who haven't been represented in any Spanish novel. There was a certain tendency to write about rural passions and rural

crimes, and women with a switchblade in their garter. (Marías and Blanca 2008, 379)

In other texts, Marías elaborates what he probably understands by that urban, educated 'normality' that, surprisingly, goes back all the way to the years of the dictatorship. In an article from years earlier about the Madrid of his childhood, entitled 'En Chamberí' (originally published in 1990), Marías defends his belonging to that 'pure-blood' *barrio* and compares it mockingly to the criticisms often made about it being 'foreignizing.' But pure-blood or not, it is interesting to note that what Marías highlights with pleasure about the Chamberí of his childhood is, for example, that 'the sidewalk was a civilized, respectful place,' in which the only vehicles to be seen were 'very clean, shiny automobiles whose owners drove them as if they were apologizing.' This was in stark contrast to 'the indescribable flood of cars driven by habitual criminals' that inundates Madrid today. Likewise, he entertains himself remembering how to his childish eyes 'Madrid, or if you prefer, Chamberí, was a city dominated by bakeries and import stores, scenes of abundance and even of good taste' (2008, 38).

Together with those symptoms of civility and abundance, there also existed some picturesque touches, like the 'mule- or burro-drawn carts' in which the junkmen carted their wares or, 'always standing with her back turned, and so facing the trolleys or taxis, some girl or young lady with gypsy-like beauty and light-colored eyes.' To that touch of archaic exoticism Marías adds another, rather less erotic one: 'in the middle of the intense refinement of that *barrio* it was not unusual to suddenly smell a strong odor of cows,' which came from the still existent 'milking parlors.' In any case, with those picturesque nineteenth-century details, Marías concludes, 'the memory of the Madrid of those days is one of an unhurried and orderly city (perhaps too orderly; it is where I have seen the highest concentration of police in the streets)' (39).

If we pay attention to Marías's other related texts, they confirm that in fact his ideal of 'normality' seems to fit better with that city of businesses, civility, good taste, and sparse traffic that was Madrid under Francoism, that with the noisy, crowded, vulgar neoliberal metropolis it became during the 'democracy.' I will not travel too far down the thorny path that would open up if we began to wonder why in that orderly Madrid of the 1950s some traveled in shiny cars and others in donkey carts, or why some lived in a world of abundance and 'good taste' while others' lives were merely 'picturesque,' or even why there were so many police in the streets. I will merely recall that after a civil war that resulted in half a million deaths, the state went on to kill some 100,000 more of the defeated parties until

1949; that 200,000 people ended up dying of hunger the decade before; and that in the years following the establishment of the dictatorship, 20% of the population would migrate from the countryside to those 'normal' cities in which so often the recently arrived migrants, without access to such central districts like Chamberí, were crowded into shacks on the outskirts of town.

But what I want to do now is show that the efficacy of Marías's discourse, while representative—voluntarily or not—of the thesis of Spain's 'normalization,' is to some degree independent of his opinions about the time period and places that best embody that normalization. For the stability and hegemony of the CT, which I see here as the legitimizing framework of a project of neoliberal transformation which mainly uses that modernizing, pro-European discourse, what is important isn't that Marías sees the Francoist city as more 'normal' than the democratic one, but that it disseminates and embodies an idea of what is 'normal' (and, in contrast, what is 'abnormal') which is compatible with that modernizing, pro-European tradition. Thus, Marías can both praise the civility of the Chamberí of his childhood and criticize the management of the first PSOE, or regret the survival of Spain's 'poor image' into the nineties. At the same time, he can keep adding material that will construct a desire for modernity and Europeanization which is understood as 'normality,' even though at times it is expressed in very surprising ways.

Marías recently compiled an enviable number of political articles in his book *Los villanos de la nación*, most of them very sharp and critical of various institutions and governments. This would seem to contradict the image of the 'disactivated' culture in the CT proposed by Guillem Martínez. But I think that the loyalty to the roots of the CT felt by intellectuals and artists like Marías is more structural than deliberate. This kind of structural coincidence can be better understood if we add to the analysis not only the 'standardizing' discourse of notable cultural figures but also their occasional activity as 'columnists.'

2.4.2. The columnist's individual authority

The literary critic Ulrich Winter (Abiada, Neuschäfer, and Bernasocchi 2001) has called attention to the growing importance of the 'columnism' of Spanish writers since the middle of the 1980s, in parallel with the commercialization of the literary industry. Winter relates this columnist figure to the classical roots of the intellectual *à la* Bourdieu, which I mentioned earlier. To be an intellectual, says Winter, 'one must have or be a confirmed authority because of competencies or achievements acquired in a relatively independent field like science, the humanities, literature, and culture in general' (294).

Examples of this type of intellectual would, for Winter, include some notable columnists from the democratic period, like Manuel Vázquez Montalbán, Rosa Montero, Francisco Umbral, Antonio Gala, Juan José Millás, or Antonio Muñoz Molina. We could also add Marías himself to this list. What worries Winter, in line with Ferlosio, is that besides these writers, there are also those who have gained access to the intellectual's position when the only thing they have achieved is 'commercial success.' This preoccupation seems, in fact, to contain an element of suspicion regarding the legitimacy of the very position of authority held by the intellectual—in general—in the mass media: 'Once she appears in the opinion pages, the writer gains a certain moral authority; she is granted relative superiority to symbolically interpret the world, simply because of the fact that she appears in mass media, that she expresses an opinion and is heard' (297).

I think it is especially important to consider what happens with intellectuals like Marías, whose achievements in the literary world no one will deny, and who, thanks to that legitimacy, have access to the media. It is important to analyze these figures by remembering above all that the artistic field—literary in this case—in which they earn legitimacy has been conceived from that hegemonic 'aesthetic modernity' in post-dictatorship Spain which tended to erase the necessarily common aesthetic dimension: that 'revealing the authentically common at the heart of the common' to which Laddaga refers, and which has occasionally been interpreted as a possibility for uniting art with life.

In an interview in 1995, Marías said 'with democracy, political activity can been pursued through political channels, thus ending the subordination of fiction to external factors' (invoking the phantom of those 'fraudulent interruptions' that Benet condemned in the 'social novel'). But this assertion denotes a very narrow conception of the possible political consequences of the aesthetic. As Labrador explains in his analysis of the poets of the transitional underground, there is no reason why loyalty to the experimental principles of aesthetic modernity should eliminate the necessarily relational, community aspect of artistic creation.

The key question is where to obtain that artistic 'authority' that will then allow the intellectual to participate in the political arena. Does that 'authority' not develop, like every human value, from the 'relationships with others' that always constitute our frame of meaning and through which, says Labrador, the transitional artist was 'destined to grow and better himself by living in community, with her limits and opportunities determined by the community, and committed to its improvement to achieve in this way her own improvement'? (2008) But the 'depoliticized' artist believes that, in fact, aesthetics is the suspension of community.

Only after having found her aesthetic enlightenment in solitude will that artist become an 'intellectual' and be able to enter into 'relationships with others'—but she will do so from an already elevated position that articulates those relationships pedagogically, like lessons, or at least 'guidance' for those not in the same elevated position. Thus, Winter notes:

> The loss of universal reference points in the increasingly impenetrable political and economic world does nothing more than increase the need for guidance in every one of the domains of daily life. That is where the successful writers and their columns come into play; their presence is also a consequence or a symptom of the changing function, or of the concept, of 'intellectual' in today's world. (296)

Intellectuals, already unable to impart 'guidance' to their peers through universal truths, will do it now by concentrating on those 'domains of daily life' from a 'premeditatedly subjective or personal perspective.' This turnaround is interesting: the intellectual who has been legitimized through a 'pure' art of 'great style'—that is, an art supposedly practiced individually and without reference to the community of meaning from which the intellectual came and to which he will necessarily return—can now not only give lessons on politics, but also 'guide' his audience on how to live their daily lives. This intellectual had eliminated his own attachments to networks of daily relationships to become legitimized as a creator distanced from 'external factors.' But now he uses his legitimacy not only to chant Zola's 'I accuse,' but also to share the prevailing postmodern disorientation, from a platform that keeps up a pedagogical pretense. That is, the intellectual answers questions that are neither technical nor specialized—and thus could be answered by anyone—but on which he still has more of a right to express an opinion than others.[14]

This way, the columnists of the Spanish democracy whom Winter discusses would become an odd mix of those artists and intellectuals who were asked, as Ferlosio said, to write 'whatever occurs to them' (from their 'premeditatedly subjective or personal perspective') and the classic figure

---

14 Bauman explains that in the intellectual's transition from modern 'legislator' to postmodern 'interpreter,' he retains part of his privileged authority, even if he no longer tries to make his discourse universal: 'While the post-modern strategy entails the abandonment of the universalistic ambitions of the intellectuals' own tradition, it does not abandon the universalistic ambitions of the intellectuals towards their own tradition; here, they retain their meta-professional authority, legislating about the procedural rules which allow them to arbitrate controversies of opinion and make statements intended to be binding' (1987, 5).

of the Philosopher as described by de Certeau, who is legitimized precisely by going beyond the technical, specialized knowledges that make up the nucleus of technoscientific modernity.

Thus, erasing her specific position in any community, speaking from the authority of one whose 'personal' achievements (aesthetic, cultural, intellectual) are supposedly due only to herself, the archetypical individual of the Spanish world of institutional, celebrity culture could produce copious critiques of the political and economic powers. But it seems to me that these critiques were in some sense stillborn.

2.4.3. Structural deactivation of intellectual critique in the CT

As noted earlier, it isn't as easy as one might think to find public intellectual demonstrations that defend explicitly the great milestones of the CT. Rather, the kind of participation that predominates is critical, at least in part. It is also more 'subjective' and 'personal' the greater prestige of the author in that cultural field. And, of course, it is always very discreet regarding the collective processes which generated that prestige, and therefore, regarding the criterion of the validity of what he expresses.

Paradigmatic of this is a column by the journalist and writer Juan Cueto (1985) published in *El País* the day after Spain entered the EEC, which was one of those 'great milestones' of the CT: 'Just one detail worries me after yesterday's signing of the Treaty: the European demand for specialization. Everything else can be taken care of, from the sweaty cultivation of unirrigated farmland and the national bad temper to the snooty smoke of our protected red-brick chimneys.' From the beginning, the columnist's 'I' is presented as the source of the discourse, with no need to explain the source of 'whatever occurs to him'—thus running the risk that it becomes a mere 'whim.' But what is interesting about this article is that in it, form and foundation coincide, because what Cueto's whimsical word defends is precisely a defense of the 'specialization in everything.' Indeed, once those 'little problems' of agriculture and industry were 'solved' (which was done, as we know, through subsidies granted for not planting and intense modernizing), Spain could join Europe and, in the face of excessive technicalities, contribute her so-called 'wisdom of the ages':

> In the tower of free-trade reason they want us specialized, and that's why they tempt us with all kinds of materialist happiness to pull us from the old historical mistake. For now, that aspiration is non-negotiable. We know that 90% of everything here is unspecialized, and even unrefined. But in exactly that arcane resistance to the discipline of the specific lies our wisdom of the ages. ... We will contribute to

Europe our famous specialization in everything, and in the Whole, to counteract so much abstraction of the specific.

Despite the apparent contradiction, the complementarity of this type of discourse with that of technoscientific modernity is made clear in that 'Just one detail worries me ...' Opening a window of critique and 'subjectivity' on the empire of the technical surely constitutes 'just one detail' when so many other technocratic experts—here supporters of free trade—agree not to question the narrative of necessary political and economic 'modernization' that legitimized the pacts for the transition to a parliamentary monarchy within a globalized capitalist framework. The rest is, essentially, 'details.'

As early as 1977, Fernando Savater, one of the most celebrated intellectuals of Spanish democracy, had already exemplified in his analysis of the transition that mix of apparent lack of enthusiasm and structural acceptance that has seemed to characterize the 'opinion makers' and columnists since the beginning of the 'democratic' era:

> Now at last we are included in the game of Europe, of the West. But every once in a while, one remembers with longing the covert clarity of that indistinct hatred for the dictatorship and, with the proliferation of new political definitions and explanations, one mutters glumly into one's beard that famous saying of the small-town mayor: 'How can things be so bad that I don't even know if I'm on our side!' I don't doubt that this 'defusing of national coexistence'—the saying, one would suppose, is from a liberal commentator of the day—is, generally speaking, the best that could happen to this country, but those of us who don't understand politics, the few of us that are left, now find ourselves, even with so much light, more in the dark than before. (Gracia García and Ródenas de Moya 2009)

I understand that the danger whenever one talks about the transition is, indeed, the same one that Savater tacitly acknowledges in this text when he asserts the unquestionability of that 'defusing of national coexistence': that of minimizing the threats of violent political conflict that were still latent at that time. But it seems unnecessary for my argument to evaluate that danger. Never mind whether there was a little or a lot of precaution or whether the level of criticism of one or the other was greater or lesser. I believe we have the right to ask what is the place of the intellectual who, like Savater, accepts the model of columnism in particular, and that of the 'depoliticized' capitalist liberal modernizing paradigm in general. It is more a structural than a personal problem; it doesn't actually matter for my argument who may have done what, or whether or not they did it. Rather, what matters is which cultural repertoires were hegemonic and which remained arrested possibilities.

In this sense, I repeat that what interests me is the figure of the intellectual who, although he says he speaks as one of 'the people,' does so from a space that can only be reached through the prestige obtained from supposedly individual activities—according to the depoliticized aesthetic individualism predominating in the cultural panorama of the post-dictatorship, and by which the 'intellectual' was granted a 'letter of authenticity.' I am interested in that intellectual who speaks as one of 'the people' without revealing the relationships of interdependency with them that have made it possible for him to be able to say what he says. This invisibility permits things like using the names of these intellectuals, rather than the culture of the 'provincial' people, to represent Spain. For instance, upon Spain's entrance into the EEC, *El País* began to publish examples of the excellent cultural products that Spain exports to the world despite its inevitable 'backwardness' in its opinion section. In these, the names of Fernando Savater and other 'exceptional individuals' were 'taken out for a walk' (to use Ferlosio's expression):

> It's true that Spain still has to make up a lot of lost time, and has a lot to learn about Europe, from which it was cut off for so many years. But if you've spent almost 20 years away from Spain, as I have, and been around the globe more than 15 times, maybe you will better understand why, other than the provincialism of some Spaniards who can be heard saying on the buses in Rome, 'Well, I don't see anything for Ciudad Real to be jealous of in this city,' I can't help but recognize that Spain has a lot to export besides oranges and wine. What is true is that Spain, in today's world, is proud of its culture. Gades is applauded, and Savater and Vázquez Montalbán is read here in Italy, and people line up to see one of Saura's films, and our orchards are insignificant. (Arias 1985)

In conclusion, it seems that at best, the cultural world that had been 'disactivated' during the CT produces interesting critiques of political and economic power from people such as Marías, Cueto, or Savater. But they pay a high price for their structural complicity in that same power, because they have effectively 'deactivated' the necessarily relational, communitary, and interdependent aspect of every cultural production (in part thanks to their identification with the figure of the 'columnist'). Perhaps they confuse the hoped-for 'de-emphasizing of national coexistence' that Savater discusses with an acritical acceptance of liberal, capitalist, individualist modernity as the only frame for reality (something none of the other 'offspring' of aesthetic modernity—avant-garde, counterculture, civic—had done).

And at worst, the culture of the CT would be reduced to a sometimes grotesque decoration, ridiculously 'transgressive' and swollen with empty prestige, that serves to reinforce the austere authority of the technocratic experts, simply for being such a striking contrast to it. I offer a classic example that allows us to explore interesting continuities with Francoism. In that historic act of joining the EEC, someone decided that it would be a very good idea to add a little art to the occasion, and commissioned Salvador Dalí to do a personal interpretation on the topic of the 'Rape of Europe.' And so, as explained in *El País*, 'all the signers of the accord and the protocols for Spain's entry into the EEC, will receive, after signing their names at the ceremony to be held tonight, a violet-colored file folder containing 25 pages, with Dalí's signature thermo-engraved in gold on the cover' (García Santa Cecilia 1985).

Doubtless this fact would have delighted Ferlosio. For his part, Dalí himself took advantage of the opportunity to declare, in a kind of megalomaniacal contribution to the never-ending motif of 'Spain is different,' 'The only one—the only one!—who understood that myth was Salvador Dalí. The bull, which is Spain, did not rape Europe; it took her with all its spirit, with all its courage, and it keeps her where she is. Europe owes her entire being to Spain.'

2.4.4. Artist and intellectual in the image domain

The technoscientific and political experts have directed and executed the program of implanting neoliberalism in the Spanish state for the last three long decades. But it is worth asking whether they could have done it without the army of public intellectuals and artists who have embodied the model of modernity and pro-Europeanism that has served as a justification for this transformation.

Marías observes in his article 'No pareces español' (1990) that television and the other mass media have become 'the most reliable reflection that citizens have of themselves, much more so than "reality".' If Spain's 'poor image' is too well kept, he adds, the fault belongs to the leaders who decide what gets shown on television. In the image era, the pedagogical mission of teaching the masses (in this case, regarding how they should represent themselves) normally claimed by the liberal elites must be shared with political and media power. But the compensation for the intellectuals is that they can now blame that media power for 'backwardness,' for promoting a poor image.

The entire population might also share part of the responsibility.

Nevertheless, Marías asserts, magnanimously offering up a kind of postmodern version of the elitist meta-story of Spanish modernity:

> this [entire population] can't be blamed too much, since fortunately it is always characterized by its anarchy, its contradictions, and its limited vision of the future. But the professionals of the future, that is, the politicians, *are* guilty of cowardice, negligence, and cynicism at the moment of directing, configuring, and manipulating the image of Spain in the present. (1990, 37)

What seems a diatribe against politicians and an excuse for 'el hombre vulgar,' as Marías likes to say, can only run the risk of falling into extreme paternalism, if not outright disdain, for the multitudes. Marías gleefully takes up the peoples' supposed 'anarchy' and 'lack of vision for the future,' but in other cases the tone of the pro-European intellectual, above all the one who isn't willing to so easily accept the fact that image is more important than reality, takes on darker tones, close to those of the illustrious and foundational precedent of *La rebelión de las masas*.

This is the case of the quasi-Hobbesian lament of Antonio Muñoz Molina in *Todo lo que era sólido* (2013), his recent book on the current Spanish crisis, a lament in which he seems to come to the conclusion not only that Spaniards seem to be or act like 'delinquents,' in Marías's words, but are thus by nature:

> In thirty-odd years of democracy and after almost 40 of dictatorship, there has been no democratic pedagogy. Democracy must be taught, because it isn't natural, because it goes against the deeply-rooted inclinations of human beings. What is natural is not equality, but the domination of the strong over the weak. ... Barbarity is more natural than civilization, the scream or the punch and not the persuasive argument, immediate gratification and not long-term effort. ... Ignorance is natural: there is no learning that does not require effort and that does not take time to bear fruit. (103)

The other side of the ideology of pro-European, modernizing normality is the scorn for 'backwardness,' for the *paleto*, the lack of 'culture' that is occasionally seen, by desperate metaphysical extension, as a natural characteristic of human beings. In this sense, perhaps the public intellectuals of 'Spanish democracy' contribute significantly to the 'standardization' of society by disseminating and embodying an aspiration for modernity and progress. But, more significantly still, they disseminate and embody the idea that only a certain few are prepared to guide the masses towards that modernity, because in general the masses are incapable of thinking and of improving their lives for themselves.

In any case, it seems to me that while the human ability for collective self-representation is being appropriated by the mass media, the importance of the pedagogical role of intellectuals and artists is growing, since they are the ones who will be in a more favorable position in the media environment. While experts and politicians undoubtedly have considerable visibility and authority in that media 'reality,' their discourse is dull, limited, and excessively specialized. This is in contrast to the humanistic depth, the aesthetic development, and the proximity to the daily worries of the 'common people' that intellectuals and artists include in their repertoire, especially those who have adapted better to the tyranny of the 'image,' who give more ground to so-called 'entertainment.'

In these media versions of the intellectual and the artist, the values of modernity, progress, and Europization are often reduced to an even greater simplification, which consists of nothing more than 'international impact.' During Francoism, the regime's constant aspiration to be legitimized by demonstrating the exportability 'abroad' of Spanish culture, art, and sports was already well known (Jorge Luis Marzo (2010) has researched this in detail with respect to art). But later, the years of democratic 'standardization' would take this ambition even further, with the leitmotif of the famous 'incorporation into Europe,' which is often announced as an incorporation into the group of 'most advanced countries.'

2.4.5. Culture as 'Brand Spain'
Now we are approaching the present, in 2009 now, and the narrative about Spain being the 'eighth world power' is still very fresh. In a book that incidentally hopes to offer a critique on the spectacularization and commercialization of culture, the previously cited *Más es más*, we find a brief assessment of the cultural value of Spain in these classic terms. Using metaphorical language that reveals a conception of culture as a matter of individual competitive exchanges, the authors assert:

> Spanish letters have very seldom enjoyed the credit they have today in other European countries. ... The same thing is happening in other cultural spheres, which doesn't change an obviously deficient trade balance. But it does partially correct the tendency, which is what happens with the exportation of values (including of consumption) that could be painters and sculptors (Eduardo Chillida, Miquel Barceló), architects (Santiago Calatrava, Rafael Moneo), actors (Antonio Banderas, Javier Bardem, or Penélope Cruz), movie directors (Pedro

Almodóvar, Alejandro Amenábar, Fernando Trueba), athletes (Miguel
Induráin, Pau Gasol, Fernando Alonso, Rafael Nadal, or Sergio García),
musicians or designers. (12)

Finally converted into a product ready for export, 'culture' will be difficult
to distinguish from consumption, and so the arts, sports, design, and
entertainment form an amalgam in which the only important thing is
the ability to impress, or at least *sell to*, other countries. The world of the
culture-product ('the Spain brand') thus inherits, like mass media, a version
adapted to the new times of the program of intellectual elites who aspired
to Europeanization, modernization, and international incorporation. The
elitist meta-narrative of modernity behind it all doesn't disappear, it is
merely transformed.

Even in its most crudely consumerist, mass-market manifestations, such
as the sporting victories attributed to 'Spain,' that desire for incorporation
and international recognition, that 'negative balance' of modernity the
country must exorcise however it can, reappears. Many of us remember, as
an iconic representation of the years of the 'economic bubble,' the image of
those great postmodern mausoleums of culture, left half-built or now falling
down, which the real estate-political-construction complex proliferated
throughout Spain during its years of speculative frenzy. It is well known that
the dizzying increase in the price of housing created a 'wealth effect' for the
87% of Spaniards who became homeowners. Something similar happened
due to the magnification of Calatrava's 'cultural success' in architecture, or
the success of others like Almodóvar in movies or Barceló in painting. Such
magnification produced an analogous kind of 'culture effect' whose true
value, beyond intensifying the 'manic' anxiety of modernity discussed by
Ángel Loureiro, is questionable.

It might even be worth reading the increasingly buoyant universe of the
tabloids as a kind of negative catharsis in which free rein is given to all
the 'backwardness,' 'folklorism,' and 'delinquency' that the elitist modern
paradigm constructs as a collective phantom to serve as the opposite of its
ideal. Probably a large part of the humor that appears in the mass media
during the years of democracy is built upon similar foundations of obsession
with the *paleto*, backwardness, and folklorism, although these are questions
that I won't be able to examine directly here.

The commercialization of culture and the spectacularization of big media
have come very far during the years of Spanish neoliberalism. I would like
to point out, however, that despite this, the model of the classic intellectual,
with his pedagogical legitimacy and his aura of aesthetic exceptionality, is
far from gone. As Labanyi (2013) said, with the coming of democracy to Spain,

literature went from being an elitist practice managed by 'well-intentioned bureaucrats' like the editor Carlos Barral to a panorama commercialized and dominated by the big publishing groups and cultural supplements in the mass media, which clearly implied a certain 'departure of literature from the ghetto of intellectuality' (147).[15] But Labanyi and Graham also indicated that, while it is true that this commercialization increases access to the 'high culture' distributed commercially by the same mass media, that doesn't mean everyone can understand and enjoy it equally. Perhaps it should be added that those who do understand and enjoy it also can't help but receive with that culture a model of valuation ('*high* culture') that tends to assume the exceptionality of the individual author, relegating the majority of people to simple passive access.

A good example of the survival of this type of cultural exceptionality attributed to authors, and to their ability to keep legitimizing the political discourse of public intellectuals, would perhaps be the emergence of new figures who have acquired important public visibility, years after the 'hard core' of the intellectualism associated with democratic 'normalization' was forged, but who continue to perform a similar function of legitimation. I am thinking, for example, of the figure of Javier Cercas. The mass media didn't 'discover' him until 2001, but he then became a key voice in opinion columnism in the same newspaper, *El País*, that, as we saw with Manuel Vicent, represented itself as heir to the tradition of 'enlightened minorities' which supposedly brought Spain into 'modernity.'

Cercas criticizes various powerful institutions and key aspects of the workings of the neoliberal system, such as the submission of the state to commercial speculation or the weakening of institutional democracy. But as with Marías and the PSOE government, these criticisms are by no means incompatible with his ascription, conscious or not, to that tradition of cultural elites who have become an essential tool—as defenders and symbolic bearers of the ideal of European modernity—for the legitimation of the same neoliberal system they criticize.

---

15 The commercialization of written culture is inscribed within the much broader context of the turn towards informational or cognitive capitalism in the final decades of the twentieth century. This has been analyzed by theorists of the Italian post-workerism tradition related to the journal *Multitudes*, like Negri and Hardt, Blondeau and Lazzarato, and Franco Berardi ('Bifo'). These authors have called attention to the fact that the great innovation of post-industrial capitalism has been the potentiation of the 'immaterial goods' sector (knowledge, relationships, emotions, communication, subjectivity, etc.). I touched on some of these developments relative to Spain in my article 'La imaginación sostenible: culturas y crisis económica en la España actual' (2012).

Since the crisis began in 2008, the visibility of this contradiction has increased, as the failures of the political, cultural, and economic spheres—built with the help of these intellectuals inheriting the modernizing project—have become more evident. But the same thing hasn't happened by any means with the connection between their critical ability and the legitimacy of the social order—an order which, despite themselves, these intellectuals cannot help but support as long as they continue to occupy the hierarchical position that has historically defined their work.

CHAPTER 3

Arrested Modernities:
The Popular Cultures that Could Have Been

3.1. Arrested Modernities I:
A Culture Rooted in Tradition Faces the Transition

3.1.1. Counter-figures of the modern intellectual

The modernizing paradigm of the liberal Spanish intellectual elites is deeply rooted in the cultural scene of 'democratic' Spain. In that scene, the figures capable of embodying modernization, or its degraded version of 'international success' in the culture and image markets, have been models and agents of legitimation often perhaps even more potent than the expert counselors, technical managers, and political executives for the actual integration into neoliberal Europe. But if we explore the genesis of this intellectual figure, which frequently seems to be the only one possible, we soon find other counter-figures and cultural alternatives, like those of the underground whom Germán Labrador studies, who were ultimately unable to dislodge this figure from his hegemonic position.

To complement the brief incursions I have made up to now into the genealogy of that pro-European or 'modernizing' public intellectual, I would now also like to propose the outlines of an intellectual counter-figure. This figure is neither as compact nor as able to create community as the 'enraptured' poet studied by Labrador, but he has the very interesting characteristic of maintaining a dialogue with a Spain that is neither as 'civic' nor as 'abundant' as the one that appears in Javier Marías's memories of the 1950s, a Spain made up of other people and places. The places are the rural areas that lost a large proportion of their inhabitants to urban emigration; and the people, the workers and peasants who were defeated in the civil war, and their descendants, who suffered economic hardship and political repression as a two-pronged punishment.

With these people and places I want to contribute in some measure to the construction of counterfactual reflections such as the one suggested by Sánchez León in his article 'Encerrados con un solo juguete,' when he asks:

What would have happened if the dictatorship had lacked the capacity for institutional penetration and/or time to destroy the social bases of traditional Spanish culture with its roots in the community? What would have happened if, as in the cultures of most other emerging democracies, Spain had had a greater short-term swing between dictatorship and democracy in the twentieth century, and the successive transitions had been obliged to recognize those cultures that were impermeable towards liberalism—call them cultures of class, ethnicity, language, and culture, etc.—that are today the required interlocutor of every alternative political agenda in the era of globalization and interculturality?

In the world of Spain in the forties and fifties, in which the divide between science and popular knowledges had not yet completely split reality in two, collective self-representation had not yet been captured so intensely by the mass media (despite the crucial importance of radio and American films), and consumerism had not yet been instituted as the basic organizational form of desire, the system of constructing reality had of necessity to be different from the later 'democratic' (postmodern, neoliberal) Spain. Out of this difference some people were nurtured who would later become intellectuals in Spain's public sphere—but in the process, they brought with them echoes of those other ways of distributing collective knowledges and abilities to produce meaning (oral and written).[1]

The case of the Leonese writer Luis Mateo Díez is paradigmatic with respect to his relationship with rural cultures, as is that of the Catalan Juan Marsé with regard to Republican working-class cultures. Both enjoy

---

1 I choose to focus on this 'counter-figures' of the modern intellectual that, in a sense, act as mediators between the privilege of those 'in the know' and the under-recognized subaltern and everyday cultures, aware that this may run the risk of reproducing the tendency to attribute cultural agency only, or at least primarily, to intellectuals and writers. It is by no means my intention that this research should substitute or compensate for the lack of studies directly focused on subaltern and everyday cultures. But due to limitations of time and resources, which of course are themselves effects of the structures of cultural and material domination I am studying here, I haven't been able to delve as deep into such a study of unlettered everyday, oral, and subaltern cultures before the period of the neoliberal crisis in Spain. I have quoted and will quote later several studies that go in that direction, such as those of Sánchez Vidal, Uría, Arguedas, Ariès, Berger, Cazorla, Díez, Izquierdo, Montalbán, Martín Gaite, Pérez Díaz, Candel, Molina, and Ong. However, I believe there is still an urgent need for more research that presents the ways in which subaltern and everyday cultures have created value and meaning in the midst of capitalist rule and cultural hierarchy in Spain.

considerable commercial success: their popular books can be found on the same new-release tables as those of Marías, Muñoz Molina, and Cercas, and their publishers, who frequently belong to major communications conglomerates, launch them with similar promotional schemes in the mass media. Furthermore, they are undoubtedly very prestigious authors in the critical and literary studies fields. They have both received numerous prizes, including some of the most renowned, and their names appear frequently in the culture sections of major newspapers.

In any case, Díez and Marsé, like other writers, intellectuals, and artists who followed a similar path, are heirs to cultures in which the system for creating reality did not stress the authority of specific individuals, enabling them to become Authors or Experts. Rather, it focused on methods of collective transmission and re-creation of traditional knowledges. In this sense, only in irregular, atypical ways do their career paths embody that ideal of pro-European modernization associated with the cosmopolitan intellectual: internationally appreciated, situated in the vanguard of a cultural development that takes charge of a 'backward' country. Precisely because Díez and Marsé have spent most of their lives outlining dialogues, demanding dignity for and remembrance of the peasant and working-class cultures that have typically been blamed by the literate elites for the country's 'backwardness,' their position is not easily included in the 'standardized' cultural and political model during the early years of Spanish 'democracy.'

It must be noted that this isn't because Marsé and Díez have a kind of 'conservative' (in the most literal sense) relationship with those cultures, and thus a frontal opposition to the complex cultural, political, and economic processes—usually called 'modernization'—that made them disappear. Rather, what happens is that in the appropriation of these traditional cultures lie projects or possibilities of other 'modernities.' These possibilities were cut short or buried under the hegemony of the hybrid of bourgeois culture and neoliberalism that has marked the Spanish post-dictatorial order and, within it, under the hegemony of the cultural scene and even of the very figure of the successful writer of which Marsé and Díez have become the embodiment.

3.1.2. Peasant cultures and regional effervescence in Spain's autonomous regions

Díez's active recuperation of the *filandón* (the name given to rural social gatherings in the northeast of the Iberian Peninsula) is very well known as the cultural environment from which his own writing springs. This kind of 'primal scene,' as the critic Ángel Loureiro (1991) calls it, has a specific time and place, which Díez describes poetically: 'hours after dusk, calm kitchens, the atmosphere of smoke and firewood, of wine heavy with dregs reheated in their cups, and winter creeping around there outside' (Aparicio, Díez, and Merino 1985, 40).[2] And in that space-time of legendary aroma, which is gradually populated to perform an act 'as natural as dinner,' the narration begins, as Díez wrote in 1977, with stories that

> linked us, that helped to draw the outlines of a sensibility, like one more attribute along with all the others that nourished our culture. And ours was a peasant culture, strict, tied to the land, as much of the land as the plowed field itself. Maybe that's why the fascination for the imaginary, the attraction of fictions, permeated our spirits, like a counterpoint to the vast reality of the land and its labors in which we were immersed. (42)

No doubt it has to do with the construction of an 'origin myth,' the foundation of a literary poetic that wants to be rooted in the traditional community practice of narration as one more activity among those that made up the daily life of peasant cultures. A possible 'writer's fate' is specifically drawn: 'What a good writer's fate it is to be there for the future like one of those anonymous voices telling stories to their neighbors' (41).[3]

It should be kept in mind that Díez shared these reflections about peasant cultures in 1978 along with two other Leonese writers, Juan Pedro Aparicio and José María Merino, under the shared pseudonym of 'Sabino Ordás,' a character they invented and used to sign a series of articles in the newspaper *Pueblo*. These articles would later be collected in the volume *Las cenizas del Fénix*. Ordás was, according to the biography his three inventors had created, an old, exiled Republican intellectual who had returned to his tiny village in the province of León after the death of the Caudillo (Franco), only to face the tumultuous Spain of the transition to democracy. In particular, he was confronted with effervescent regional autonomous cultures that were dedicated, among other things, to the recuperation of native cultural

---

2 Significantly, the Peruvian writer José María Arguedas draws a similarly constructed scene of his 'origin myth' as a writer: a kitchen populated by people who narrate and listen in community, far from family and political centers where power is managed.

3 In the prologue to *El pasado legendario*, published in 2000 (13 years after 'Sabino Ordás' wrote these words), Díez used the same expression to refer directly to his own 'writer's fate': 'Some of the neighborly rituals of orality, so unique to certain rural Nordic and mountain cultures, were a part of my childhood. That circumstance marks, in some way, my own fate as a writer, and I accept it without nostalgia, without romanticizing it, the same way I like to accept everything to do with my childhood' (20).

traditions like the Leonese *filandón*. In this sense, it is necessary to frame his literary project of 'being there for the future like one of those anonymous voices chatting with the neighbors' within Labrador's 'transitional cultures' that were resistant to the mesocracy, and particularly within the small Leonese autonomous 'counterculture' in which the invented Sabino Ordás appears.

Ordás writes at the time when the so-called 'Spain of the autonomous regions' was being politically and legally formed, not without considerable controversy. From the initial euphoria to the later disappointment over the 1981 'cerrojazo autonómico,' in which Adolfo Suárez's government reduced the amount of political self-determination it had originally promised to the autonomous regions, the 'provinces' experienced a frenzy of collective activity in which the literary and the political were often conflated into a single amalgam. All this was still far, however, from the professionalization and specialization of the fiction writer that the growth of the publishing industry would later promote around the middle of the eighties.

During the years of the transition, provincial writers often shared physical and symbolic space with local ethnographers, folk musicians, members of rural communes, neighbors from towns threatened by reservoirs, militants working for regional autonomy, and ecological activists. In fact, there is no reason to consider Díez during these years merely as a fiction writer who develops an individual creative project. (Similar examples of other such narrators would be Julio Llamazares, Manuel Rivas, and Bernardo Atxaga, to name some of the better known ones.) That is just one more facet of his production, which can be found clearly imbricated in networks of social interaction and in collective projects, which often go beyond literary creation.[4]

So, for example, Díez worked in those transitional years on anthropological approaches like 'Una introducción a la literatura popular leonesa' (1980) and others that result from his active involvement in the House of León in Madrid and its journal (*León*). He also participated in numerous activities of cultural diffusion and investigation that were compiled under different names ('Gumersindo Azcárate study group,' 'Papalaguinda Press,' 'Compendium

---

4 This type of work on the boundaries between 'creation' and 'documentation' is notably similar to what the numerous folk music groups of the Spanish transition did, performing an extensive job of compilation and ethnographic study while also developing their own style (examples include Oskorri in Euskadi, Al Tall in Valencia, Chicotén in Aragón, and Fuxan Os Ventos in Galicia, to name just a few). This last group, according to González Lucini (2006), usually ended their concerts by asking the audience to teach them some native songs of the region where they were performing.

of Fish Street collection,' and the apocryphal Sabino Ordás himself), and shared a common interest in popular culture and Leonese identity.[5] Those projects were defined in large part by a desire to create regionalist 'popular culture,' which had to share space with the criteria of 'aesthetic quality' that belong to the literate traditions of high culture, so they often managed to reach diverse sectors of the population (from young writers and intellectuals to old peasants). In fact, in this type of forum there is often a great concern for being open to citizens who don't belong to the cultural elites. Thus, they always insist that regionalism is not a means of producing exclusivity, but rather, is exactly that, a 'popular culture' that tries to differentiate itself from the culture of the elites.

Ordás's articles return again and again to the problem of cultural elitism, which frequently associates the authoritarian vices of the dictatorship with the 'cliques' that govern the literary world from Madrid or Barcelona (and even with the hegemony of formal experimentalism). Thus, in connection with a comment on the career of the critic José María Castellet, Ordás indicates that the power coming from the use of those cultural argots is comparable to the model of dictatorial political power that had permeated all social functioning:

> Over the flowchart *par excellence* (Dictator exercises his authority absolutely from the top down, through successive layers of obsequious petty dictators) was layered the map of general performance, and therefore, of the cultural world. Whether he wanted to or not, the intellectual who 'constituted a nucleus of influence' ended up becoming a dictator capable of exercising absolute power in his field, using dogmas and clichés without even imagining disparities or replicas, and thus converting the rest of his sphere of influence, through a set of subsidiary petty tyrants, into a submissive and obedient—if not terrified—group. (69)

In a society deeply impregnated with relationships of authoritarian power, culture could not keep from reproducing those schemas of authority and submission; rather, it propagated them through the argot of the intellectual field. In 1978, after three years of a still insufficient transition to democracy, things hadn't changed much.[6] Ordás proved, for example, in connection with

5 Asunción Castro Díez (2001) has identified in detail all of Díez's 'paraliterary' activities based on her study of Sabino Ordás.

6 There are, however, studies that have highlighted precisely the emergence of living civic languages, unaware of elitist jargons, in those transitional years and even long before. Jordi Gracia, in *La resistencia silenciosa*, investigates the tenuous line

a polemic about a public sculpture in Chillida, that both art critics and the Spanish media took shelter 'in a jargon equivalent, for their shortcomings, to what Valle-Inclán blamed on the "divine words," jargon that makes possible some powers of restricted access and giving blessings to whomever it wants' (127).[7]

For Ordás, the mistreatment of words practiced by the elites in power for the almost 40 years of the dictatorship had produced a 'disarticulation between culture and society,' and resulted in the creation of 'a state culture, or, at times, an anti-state culture (as over-structured as its opposite, if not more so)' (44). Both Francoist and anti-Francoist culture created a language apart from 'the people'; hermetic, 'rootless' argots designed for the use of a few. In general, Ordás confirms the survival in Spanish society of 'the idea that the cultural world should not be easy to access, that a knowledge of art should be surrounded by special difficulties, that only through suffering, even if only mental, can cultural riches be obtained' (98). This idea seems to make an even stronger impression on precisely those people who have managed to become administrators of the cultural patrimony, and are dedicated to creating obstacles to prevent the common man from participating in this patrimony.

When Ordás counterposes his project of recuperating the 'anonymous voices' of the peasant *filandones* against that cultural elitism, he doesn't do it out of a kind of conservatism that desires a return to an ideal past. Rather, he wants to provide Spanish 'modernization' with true democratization, which for him must include attention to the native popular cultures. The comparison between elitist culture and the rural cultures constitutes in and of itself the embryo of a whole politico-cultural program of rapprochement between culture and society (culture and 'the people') that Ordás (and other cultural agents close to him) will defend: 'let us guard ourselves against the cultural bureaucracies, let us leave places that send letters of this or that kind of quality, of this or that style, let us pursue spontaneity, connections, the articulation between culture and society, between art and the people' (67).

---

drawn during the years of the dictatorship by various cultural manifestations that opted for clarity and sobriety in the face of the darkness and petulance of fascist style.

7 The metaphor of religious language is also used by Ricardo Piglia to refer to the elitist argots that require 'experts' to interpret them: 'Perhaps the dominant discourse in this regard is that of the economy. The market economy defines a dictionary and a syntax and acts on the words; it defines a new sacred, cryptic language that requires priests and technicians to decode it, to translate it, and to comment on it' (38).

There is in Ordás's articles an exaltation of rural egalitarianism and independence that has to do with their desire to 'root' the new Spain of post-Francoism in regional and anti-imperial cultural traditions, no matter how far back in time they might go. Thus, Ordás associates, for example, the rebellious spirit of the Leonese anarchists, like Buenaventura Durruti, with the resistance of the Asturian-Cantabrian people against the Roman Empire. Likewise, in an essay entitled 'Una carta al ministro de cultura' (1979), he advocates for the creation of a Museum of Anthropology and Ethnography that will show the wealth of diverse cultural identities Spain is home to, precisely with the intention of not losing those that have not supported projects of imperial expansion: 'A permanent temptation between *cantonalism* and *imperial unity* seems to be marking our historical avatar: from that tension the originality of our human panorama is fed, filled with different cultures, some holding their own, still alive, ancient embers' (168).

The burning question is, however, how alive can those embers remain when the phantom of museumification hovers over them? To what extent, and how, can fires still be started from those ancient embers of ancestral cultures in the Spain of the transition? When Ordás proposes the need to create an anthropological and ethnological museum in Spain to promote 'the cultural reconciliation of the Spains' (167), not only does he want acknowledgment of the regional cultural specificities that Francoism had buried, but he also wants that museum to house objects pertaining to rural ways of life, 'before this stubborn race towards who-knows-where leaves our villages in ruins and forgotten forever' (169).

It must be remembered that, in the context of that biopolitical transformation of farming carried out by Francoism to which I referred in the first chapter, between 1955 and 1975, 6 million Spaniards (20% of the population) had moved away from the provinces. Of those, 2 million migrated to Madrid, 1.8 million to Barcelona, and 1.5 million elsewhere in Europe. With these massive displacements, 60% of small farmers and 70% of laborers disappeared from the rural world. At the same time, the number of Spanish cities with more than 100,000 inhabitants jumped from 20 (in 1960) to 40 (in 1975).

At the end of the seventies, the project of creating a 'rooted' culture, a modernity that doesn't bet everything on the false cosmopolitan novelty that masks cultural elitism, confronts its greatest obstacle in the very extinction of those rural cultures on which it wants to base that rootedness. In terms of Díez's literary and intellectual project, the difficulty can be simply stated: how can someone keep being an 'anonymous voice chatting with the neighbors' in a society that tends to turn anonymous voices into Authors and the neighbors into publics or consumers?

3.2. Words in the Kitchen:
Subsistence Cultures and Productivist Cultures

3.2.1. Peasant *tertulias* as images of a culture in Luis Mateo Díez

According to the Real Academia Española's dictionary, a *filandón* is an 'evening get-together of women to spin and chat,' and this is how Mateo Díez uses it (partly because the maintenance of that dictionary has been one of his responsibilities as an academic since 2001). But the Leonese writer has always suggested in his work that these get-togethers served to construct, maintain, and reactivate the cultural patrimony of the rural, eminently peasant communities that practiced them. In his book *Relato de Babia* (1991), Díez deliberately played on that function, including a central chapter titled 'Filandón' that presents, in dialogue form (and with no substantial modifications in the three extant editions of the book), an encounter between neighbors or friends (men and women) who recall various local anecdotes, stories, legends, jokes, and ballads relating to cultural, geographical, and historical characteristics of the Leonese region of Babia.[8]

Díez's Babia is the epitome of peasant cultures, which for him are, above all, *filandón* cultures; that is, cultures that constantly negotiate their meaning and their identity through the collective narration of oral stories. Stories that people speak to explain what they are and where they are: that, for Díez, is Babia. John Berger corroborates this in his quote that Díez put at the beginning of the third edition of the *Relato de Babia*:

> The self-portrait of every town is not built with stones, but with words, spoken and remembered: with opinions, stories, eyewitness accounts, legends, comments, and rumors. And it is a continuous portrait, it is a

---

8 Regarding the question of gender's relation to narration, it is very interesting to observe that although Mateo Díez broadens his version of *filandón* to include both men and women, in his conception of 'popular' narrative, women continue to have a certain priority. Often women appear in his narrative to be the best prepared to tell the story of the 'forgotten ones' left behind by modernity and 'progress.' This characteristic is in line with the construction of narration as 'feminine space' which the Argentine Edgardo Cozarinsky uses in his essay 'El relato indefinible' (2005). According to Cozarinsky, the link between the feminine and narration goes back to the early Middle Ages, when, while men hunted and warred, women studied nature and transmitted 'legends passed from mother to daughter, where the gods of pagan antiquity found a fragile but persistent survival' (21). For a historical analysis of the relationship between women and popular culture, I think it is essential to relate both terms to the arrival of capitalist productivism, according to Silvia Federici's study in her book *Calibán y la bruja: mujeres, cuerpo y acumulación originaria* (2004).

never-ending job to paint it. Until relatively recently, the only materials a town and its inhabitants had at their disposal to define themselves were their own spoken words. The portrait that each town made of itself, apart from the physical achievements of the fruits of their labor, was the only thing that reflected the meaning of their existence. (29)

'Until relatively recently' is crucial in the consideration of peasant cultures. In the *filandón* narrated by Díez, the elaboration of Babia's collective self-portrait is constantly swinging between a before and an after: the chapter is narrated in the present, and the temporal references situate the encounter at a time close to the writing of the book (1980–81), but the question of Babia is constantly posed in terms of a comparison between the Babia of the present and the Babia of the past. So they discuss changes in agriculture and in social composition, the erosion of local dialects, the durability of popular knowledge like recipes, and even the imprint of macroeconomic changes like the arrival in the area of the coal industry.[9]

Time changes lived practices and how they gain meaning. Televisions that have already found their way into the homes of Babia have begun to form the self-portrait, or those writers who, like Mateo Díez, sat in on the *filandones* as children, and as adults write their 'literary' versions of the stories they heard there. It's beginning to be done with words and voices that come from other places and tell of other experiences, until Babia's very existence, and that of other peasant cultures, is called into question by the whirlwind of migration, the proliferation of the mass media, and the diffusion of the urban, capitalist way of life.

In that whirlwind many things were broken, among them perhaps some of the things that could have provided that democratizing, anti-elitist component that Ordás and Mateo Díez wanted to bring from the peasant cultures to the post-dictatorial present of the 1970s. Of course, the capacity

9 'Here in Babia a lot of us still bake cakes. Other things are lost, but not that' (Díez 126). 'Agriculture here went to hell in a handbasket. You go around looking for a pound of lentils, you know we were famous for our lentils in Babia, and they still talk about them in cookbooks, but now you can't find them' (134). 'What there are, in spite of everything, are different degrees of preservation in the different areas of Babia. There are towns that deliberately hang onto their old ways of speaking, for instance in Quintanilla, in Babia Alta, and in Robledo down in Babia Baja' (135). 'Well, you could say that all the towns have good infrastructure: streets, running water, good light, television, and bathroom and heating equipment' (134). 'For example, see what kind of impact the coal industry has had, especially in Laciana and Babia Alta, the huge social changes that cause changes in our way of life, and at the same time they attract a huge number of people from other regions who bring their own influences with them' (135).

of human communities for self-representation through orality is one of those broken threads, but it's important to find that thread within the complex fabric of peasant cultures, which compose and weave symbolic needs and tasks with materials in an especially compact way.

So not only stories are told in the *filandón*, but also recipes, home remedies for ailments, and, in general, any type of eminently practical knowledge (such as, in part, the fictions themselves, for their exemplarity). In the *filandón*, of course, not only do they talk, but they also drink and eat; it is no coincidence that these *tertulias* are held in kitchens. What's more, people sing and dance at these gatherings. And, as the Peruvian writer and sometime anthropologist (like Díez) José María Arguedas related, the peasant gathering was the natural place for the young men and women of the village to meet someone special and fall in love.

3.2.2. Disarticulation of a way of life: Sayago through José María Arguedas's eyes

Arguedas's book, *Las comunidades de España y del Perú* (1968), is an exceptional document for understanding the process of disarticulating the peasant cultures during the period when Francoism began opening up to capitalist 'modernization.' He documented his research and his stay in several towns in the Zamora region of Sayago from 1958 to 1962, in connection with a project funded by UNESCO to investigate the possible survival of rural Spanish communitary cultures that might have an impact on the colonization of Peru. Arguedas found himself in a changing world and, among other things, he noted a particularly striking symptom: in the towns he studied, there was a growing number of single people, and fewer and fewer marriages. Speaking with people, he discovered that the general perception was, 'It's too expensive to get married,' and so men preferred to stay single. This is particularly striking in an agrarian society that only gives the title of *vecino* (neighbor) to married men. With that title come the rights to use parcels of the community fields and pasturelands that are redistributed annually. True, the benefits to be gained by exploiting those community parcels are not great, but it hasn't always been seen this way. The elders of the place speak of an even more miserable past, when wheat—now the main source of food—was not yet cultivated, and when country folk made their own clothes, slept on the floor, and 'hardly even knew what money was.'

Certainly Arguedas found a small, very isolated society, but it was already highly destabilized by the transition towards what the geographer David Harvey has called 'the money community.' Harvey analyzes the urban experience under capitalism by foregrounding the substitution of traditional ways of organizing mutual human dependence that is based on direct social ties and relationships with others based on 'objective' relationships. This substitution effectively creates a situation where the use of money is the only measure of all social wealth. The arrival in Sayago of wheat as the main subsistence crop could be a decisive moment in that transition, in that it brought with it the more generalized use of money as an organizational system for subsistence. But the most truly destabilizing moment for this type of Castillean peasant (who for the most part had supported Francoism during the civil war), the moment that put an end to what the sociologist Víctor Pérez Díaz calls the 'traditional model' of Spanish peasant communities, happened when the regime rescinded the 'autarchy' policies that had directly favored them, through key organizations of the postwar statist economy, such as the National Wheat Service. At that moment, Francoism produced a progressive economic liberalization that would force traditional peasants to either become 'businessmen farmers' (through the mechanization of agriculture) or to migrate to the cities.

This is precisely what was happening when Arguedas arrived in Sayago, and he personally observed the pressure these changes brought on the financial situation of those who couldn't buy agricultural machinery, in the '*quiñonización*' (parceling and privatizing) of the common lands of some towns, as well as in the state's appropriation of communal forests. In general, he saw the breakup of a hybrid economy in which money and state protection through a controlled wheat market were key, but in which certain institutions were still maintained that were unfamiliar with the logic of monetary exchange—notably, the common lands, which were often called *vecindades*.

Arguedas's sensitivity to questions of daily life, and to its symbolic and affective dimensions, also makes him an excellent witness to the parallel breakup of the processes of creation and transmission of meaning that underpinned that not entirely monetarized world. He realized that if getting married, and thus becoming a *vecino* (someone who had a share in the *vecindad*) with all the rights that entailed, 'is very expensive' in Sayago, it's because, in fact, everything was becoming very expensive in a community that was being urged to complete its transition to the monetary quantification of all its social wealth. He also realized that this monetarization of life affected the ways a traditional society managed its own reproduction without needing recourse to money. At the center of those traditional institutions facilitating the reproduction of community life was what in Sayago was called the *tertulia* (gathering, get-together) or *serano*.

One particularly eloquent informant, who is identified by the initials C. A., revealed several key issues to Arguedas: the *seranos*, he says, were to help young men and women meet; after the *tertulias*, couples would 'lose themselves in the fields.' There was a tacit sexual freedom, which was what usually initiated the processes of dating and marriage. But this disappeared after the civil war. The informant lists the causes of the change: 'money, the war, priests, the severity of the authorities, which are the work of the masters; all that has come down on these young men's heads, it's intimidated them. Now all they do is work, talk to their families, or watch girls singing in sunny meadows ...—they're afraid' (143).

When Arguedas was in Bermillo, the capital of Sayago, a new dance hall opened up with a cover charge (one *duro* for the young men). Children weren't allowed in, changing a long-standing custom of allowing children at the dances, all adults spontaneously sharing the responsibility of looking after them. In the new dance hall, 'modern slow dancing' was imposed, contributing to the gradual demise of native songs and dances. Only young girls kept them alive, like games, in the 'sunny meadows' mentioned by C. A. They have become a kind of entertainment for the adults, who watch the songs and dances but don't perform them anymore. One *vecina* said of the new dance hall: 'the damn business creeps everywhere, it's a sin!' (113).

These tensions articulate the problematic transition between what the writer and researcher of peasant cultures, John Berger, called 'survival cultures' and the very different 'cultures of progress.' In the former, eking out a living, or what is sometimes called the reproduction of life, is the most important thing, and it is inconceivable that the state of permanent scarcity which impels that constant struggle for survival might someday disappear. In the latter, in contrast, the emphasis is on the future, precisely because one always hopes to gain greater abundance and better living conditions in the future.

In the case of the Sayago peasants, the introduction of wheat into their economy meant an extension of the subsistence mentality, supported in this case not only by their work, which would be used for their own consumption (and often sustained by community property structures), but also by the sale of their agricultural product in a state-protected market. But only when that system starts breaking down does the demand to think in new ways become stronger, to produce not just for subsistence, but for 'progress.' This is clearly seen in the investments required of the peasant who wants to mechanize his work to be able to become a 'businessman farmer,' according to the program that technocratic Francoism had designed for this population. Money very quickly began to be in short supply for everything, including for cultivating the land, and therefore, for surviving. Whoever couldn't adapt to that new way of life in the field, had to emigrate to the city, where in the vast majority of cases, he would come to depend directly or indirectly on salaried work.

Without a doubt, as Berger affirms, it is extremely unfair to idealize the very difficult conditions of life for the peasant cultures, no matter how traumatic the processes may have been that ended up dismantling them. But at the same time, that shouldn't prevent a critical analysis from also being made of these processes of change. What happened in rural Spain during the fifties was that the Francoist dictatorship forced an adaptation to capitalism, which in turn forced many to emigrate. As opposed to what could have been an idealization of subsistence, feminist historical and economic analyses such as those of Silvia Federici or Amaia Pérez-Orozco remind us that the problem of 'cultures of progress' based on capitalism is that they tend to put all the emphasis on production and accumulation (of products or capital), making invisible and even putting at risk the reproduction of life itself.

Therefore, Federici has critiqued Marx's concept of 'primary accumulation,' as noted in a previous chapter. It's true that the privatization of lands and common resources, which often served to guarantee European peasants their subsistence (and therefore a certain autonomy from the feudal lords), constitutes a central process in the implantation of capitalism. However, she explains, another, no less important, process is the constant appropriation and exploitation of the work necessary to maintain and reproduce life (caring for children, domestic work) by a system that doesn't recognize it as creating value, and therefore doesn't integrate it into its system of wage distribution.

Without the millions of women, customarily in charge of doing that reproductive work, who have brought into the world and taken care of the men whose manpower would drive capitalist production, this system could never have existed, no matter how much it had pulled them from the communal lands to those proletarian futures. The interesting thing about the rural cultures of survival is that within them, despite their many problems, including the maintenance of violent precapitalist versions of patriarchy and many other forms of hierarchy, reproductive work was recognized as a fundamental source of value, because in fact, as Berger explains, it was inconceivable that there could have been valuable work beyond the reproductive.

3.2.3. From reproduction to production: A writer between two worlds
The management of human subsistence by means of communal structures foreign to the productivity and monetarization of social wealth was not the only thing, therefore, that is profoundly alien to the type of individualistic and consumerist urban society that most of Spain quickly became during the fifties and sixties. So too was the mentality that puts the reproduction of life at the center, that doesn't understand the separation between work

and play, that believes that the stories, the recipes, the jokes, the dances, and tumbles in the hay shared by young men and women all form part of a single continuum of the reproduction of community life, as much as the work in the fields or the meetings to decide what to do with communal lands.

Referring to the kitchens in which the *filandones* were held, Mateo Díez (2000) said, 'what was told in them, what was heard, with that point of respect and entertainment from which the knowledge of things, pleasure, emotion, mystery, is best derived, was not separate from the fire and the food; not even words conflicted with the wood and the pots and pans' (20). That continuity between language and food, between the symbolic and the material, is found in rural cultures because both aspects are indispensable to the unquestionable priority of the reproduction of community life. As that priority is increasingly replaced by the production of quantified monetary wealth and applied to individual (as opposed to community) use, both words and material goods become segmented into distinct functions organized to make them produce that new type of wealth.

Just as the cultures of survival based on the reproduction of life become 'cultures of progress' based on the production of private property and exchange value, reality remains divided into two halves: the 'productive' half, supported by technoscience, and the half that is not yet productive but will be as 'progress' advances. The artist, and in particular the fiction writer, can oppose projects to this model that radically question productivity, and this is what many have been doing ever since modernism and the avant-garde all the way up to postmodernity. But that doesn't mean that an individual artist, confined to the aesthetic sphere, is able to construct the conditions for her symbolic work to function as an element incorporated into the reproduction of community life, when this reproduction has been subsumed into the productivity of money and the markets.

This, I think, is the main difficulty facing the project of translating the rural subsistence cultures' experience of traditional collective oral narration into the world of written authorship as the cultures of progress understand it: how can one now be not only 'an anonymous voice chatting with the neighbors,' but a voice that integrates narration into the reproduction of community life when one lives in a society that has subordinated reproduction to production and the community to the individual?

Perhaps in institutions like the Casa de León in Madrid or the CCAN in León, Mateo Díez and his colleagues in the autonomous Leonese culture could recreate in some measure situations in which words recuperated the nourishing value they had in the traditional cultures, at least for communities that still believed in the primacy of reproduction over production. Or rather, to use the language of the cultures of the transition, the value of 'the millenary culture of the people' against the domination of the cities.

Those autonomous cultures were subjected to countless contradictions, and the history of their attempts to construct a 'rooted,' civic, foundational alternative that was both ecological and pacifistic towards the neoliberal 'Europeanization' already under way is complex and still unfinished. The same is true for other democratic cultures born out of the transition (including the neighborhoods movement, youth countercultures, and working-class autonomy). One of the threads of that history, and perhaps not the least significant, is constituted by the evolution of artists and writers who, like Mateo Díez, were heir to the symbolic heritage of the peasant cultures of survival and tried to keep it alive in a culture as markedly *progressive* as the Spain of the transition with its hopeful eye on Europe.

Two central elements ended up channeling the fate of that evolution: on one hand, the specialization and 'professionalization' of the artists, which involved distancing themselves from those civic cultures in which they acted as ethnographers, journalists, activists, or cultural agitators. On the other, there was a progressive mythologization of rural cultures and their symbolic legacy, which allowed a pushing to the background of the historical material transformations—the implantation of capitalism in the context of the Francoist dictatorship—which led to their breakdown. In light of these two elements, writers like Mateo Díez ended up finding a space of recognition in the highly commercialized culture of post-dictatorship Spain, after encountering many difficulties in even getting published during Francoism and the transition.

These types of stories promote a non-elitist use of fiction, as Ordás intended. They become material that is particularly appropriate for circulation among the broad sectors of society that the new culture industries of the democracy wanted to attract as consumers of novels.[10] So it's not unusual to find, among the rolls of the 'banners of literature' of the political, cultural, and economic ecosystem forged in the Spanish state of the early eighties, writers who

---

10 Which doesn't mean that the only literature produced during Francoism was 'elitist' or 'not appropriate for consumption by broad sectors of the population.' There was a broad spectrum of ways of writing and editing that in many cases tried to reach a wider public. Examples range from pulp fiction like the famous westerns and romances of Bruguera Press to prestigious literature written in accessible language published by Destino Press (which included the greats of realism like Delibes, Matute, Cela, and Martín Gaite). However, as Labanyi and Graham and others have shown, it is not until the arrival of democracy and the appearance of the big culture-media groups of the eighties that literature becomes a true mass phenomenon in Spain.

prefer a 'rural' or 'provincial' poetics, including Mateo Díez himself during his first phase, as well as Julio Llamazares, José María Merino, Manuel Rivas, and Bernardo Atxaga, among others. Close to them on the new release tables, although with perhaps an even more central position, the publishing industry would place another 'great narrator,' also with ties to cultures that tend to be mythologized, but who had already managed to get published during the years of the experimentalists' hegemony: Juan Marsé.

3.3. Arrested Modernities II:
Postwar Cultures and Creative Consumption

3.3.1. Building 'cardboard ghosts' with Juan Marsé

At the beginning of his novel, *Un día volveré* (1982), Marsé presents a panorama offering glimpses of certain tensions and transformations that recall those that Arguedas experienced in Sayago. The difference is that these are now situated in an urban environment, and told from a narrative voice that invokes the resurrection of a legendary storytelling spirit that belongs to the past of the 'cultures of survival,' but that can return when least expected:

> And then, when the *vecindario* was already replacing its capacity for surprise and for legend with resignation and forgetfulness, and the asphalt had already buried forever the tortured map of our knife games in the streambed of packed earth, and some cars on the sidewalks were already beginning to replace the old people who sat outside to enjoy the cool night air; when indifference and tedium threatened to bury forever that grinding of trolleys and of old *aventis*, and the men in the tavern no longer told anything but uninteresting stories about their families and their boring jobs, when that little bit of hatred and rejection needed to keep on living began to falter in everyone, he finally returned home: the man who, according to old Suau, more than one person in the *barrio* would have preferred to see far away, dead, or locked up forever. (14)

Those men who 'in the tavern no longer told anything but uninteresting stories about their families and their boring jobs' no doubt remember the young men of Sayago who 'now only work, talk to their families or watch girls singing in sunny meadows,' as the informant C. A. told Arguedas. But is this similarity a coincidence? Marsé's characters have almost always been interpreted as representatives of the Republican working-class world of the groups defeated in the civil war, and no doubt they are. That 'minimum of hate and rejection needed to keep on living' to which Marsé returns in almost all his texts has been understood as the reaction to the overwhelming, annihilating defeat that affects both bodies and collective identities, threatening to completely erase them. But perhaps that emphasis on the Republican memory has tended to blur other cultural elements present in his novels that have to do with those streets that still exude 'a musty, wet-earth smell like in the days when asphalt wasn't used yet, and their daily hustle and bustle, their pulse, was different' (24).

The world of Marsé's defeated people is a world where people struggle to keep not only their Republican identity and memory, but also their 'right to an epic and an aesthetics,' as Manuel Vázquez Montalbán, another essential explorer of those worlds, said in his *Crónica sentimental de España* (first published in 1969, quoted here in a 1986 edition). Marsé's characters have been stripped not only of their freedom and their political identity, but also of that still unpaved street in which the neighbors of the working-class *barrios* sat to reproduce the immemorial habit of the *tertulia*. Notably in his long-awaited novel *Si te dicen que caí* (1976), but also in many of his other texts, Marsé gives narrative centrality to that residue of oral cultures that he calls 'las *aventis*' (a neologism based on 'adventures') told by the youngsters of the defeated postwar period, in a kind of clandestine recuperation of the *tertulia*, or at least of the narrative ability that was cultivated in these gatherings.

The culture that supplies these youths with their ways of telling, their tactics, and their cosmovision, is not only the culture of those defeated by Francoism, but also an 'agro-urban' culture formed by rural emigrants or *vecinos* who have seen their towns annexed to cities through industrialization. The institutions of the modern world (school, factory, state, etc.) entered this culture more slowly than in the metropolis, which is why they have maintained an understanding of the world based more on narration than on information. In addition, of course, we can't forget the (more or less remote) ties between that traditional world and the cultures of survival in which all things material and symbolic fed the reproduction of community life, including knowledges and tactics of orality.[11]

---

11 I am not trying to essentialize the 'peasant or rural culture,' nor to consider it a 'native' environment; rather, I am trying to theorize the cultural hybridity of a transitional Spain in which strong oral traditions coexisted with a bureaucratic, institutional world based on writing, and an important audiovisual sphere that was rapidly expanding. There are two interesting sociological books about this world of 'agro-urban' *barrios* (because of their strong element of immigration from rural areas) on the outer edges of cities: *Los otros catalanes* by Francisco Candel (1965), and *Los otros madrileños: el pozo del tío Raimundo* by Esperanza Molina (1984). Both contain testimonies about the importance of orality and narration in the cultures of these *barrios* during the last phase of Francoism and the transition.

For an investigation in more abstract terms about the relation between oral cultures

But at the same time, and in contrast to the case of Mateo Díez and other 'rural' writers, for Marsé another central aspect is working with the materials of the incipient mass culture that fed those capacities for memory and oral narration in the Spanish postwar period. So, for example, when the gang of boys to which the narrative voice of *Un día volveré* belongs first discovers the mysterious man who has returned to the *barrio*, the moment is inscribed in relation to the movie theater: 'We had a sensation of déjà vu,' says the narrative voice, 'of having lived this appearance in a dream or maybe on the screen of the Roxy or the Rovira in the Saturday afternoon matinee' (10).

The movie cinema theater, together with the native legends of the *barrio*, is a constant source of language and models for construction of meaning for the young protagonists, as well as for Marsé's novel itself, which owes a lot to American *noir* classics. There is a confluence here between the threads of the *barrio* culture and American mass culture that focuses on the character of old Suau: besides being the bearer of collective oral (Republican) memory, he has worked all his life (and still does) as a theater sign painter. At one point, when the diverging narrative versions of Suau (the clandestine version) and Polo, the *barrio* policeman (the official version), clash (the two old men meet every day in the painter's workshop to argue), it might seem like the signs come to help that 'ruinous memory' defended by Suau:

He thought that, despite Polo's scornful indifference, despite his boasts and his insults, his memory of that rainy night must also be infected by fear; and that the presence of those colorful figures now surrounding him, those poor cardboard ghosts condemned to be forever trapped on theater walls, caught in the act of shooting, or kissing, or dying here and now, must make much more real for him, in his exasperated mood, the presence of those other ghosts who populated his dirty cop's memory. (24)

But 'those poor cardboard ghosts' serve not only to torment the guilty memory that hides behind the official version: they are also utopian models,

---

and narration, see the works of Walter Ong (1982) and de Certeau. For a sociocultural analysis (based on the French model) of the transformation of urban *barrios* during the second half of the twentieth century, see 'The Transition from Neighborhood to Metropolis' in *A History of Private Life* (Ariès and Duby 1987). This chapter stresses the importance of orality in the 'old' *barrios* (the ones that did not experience major urban changes). In particular, it shows how access to details of the private lives of the *vecinos* completely changes the use of 'conventional wisdom' and the proverbs used in daily life (107).

the stuff of dreams. The narrative voice talks about 'the ominous darkness of old Suau's workshop, with his cardboard imitations of a life more intense than the one we would ever have' (33). And the desire to appropriate and recreate the fictions of mass culture is one clear and deliberate choice here for a type of discourse that can resist the overwhelming weight that is reality for some people. From among all the voices that circulate through the city, these *barrio* boys (children of those defeated in the war, poor boys, condemned to witness the humiliation of their elders and to work, themselves, in tedious or grueling jobs) do not choose the ones that celebrate the status quo. They do not choose the proclamations of the regime, nor lessons on the Imperial History of Spain, nor even the promises of social mobility offered by development policy through advertisements. They choose the Hollywood epic, the epic of comic books or of radio adventure programs, because it is the voice most disconnected from the world around them: they can get close to those figurations of a life more intense than they will ever have, while allowing them, as de Certeau would say, to affirm 'the lack of coincidence between facts and meaning.'

Essentially, it is not so much a matter of trying to bring into reality those other models to replace the official version, but to open a utopian, impossible space in which things happen differently.[12] What Marsé calls the 'thwarted illusion of the defeated ones' (287) must remain an illusion. De Certeau talks about the function fulfilled by the miracle stories of popular cultures, in terms that also seem pertinent for our case: 'Without removing whatever one might see every day, miracle stories respond "on the edge," in a twisted way, through a different discourse that one can only believe, much like an ethical reaction must believe that life is not reduced to what can be seen of it' (21).

That's why, when they discover that Jan Julivert Mon—the mysterious Republican fighter and member of the first armed resistance against the dictatorship who has returned to the *barrio*—isn't seeking revenge, the

---

12 As de Certeau explains, 'In narration, it is no longer a question of approximating a "reality" (a technical operation, etc.) as closely as possible and making the text acceptable through the "realism" that it exhibits. On the contrary, narrated history creates a fictional space. It moves away from the "real"—or rather it pretends to escape present circumstances: "once upon a time there was ..."' (79). That movement, that declarative gesture that restores fiction is parallel to the notion of 'surprise' and 'occasion.' The narrator gets sidetracked towards that other place with the intention of taking advantage of the occasion offered to him and surprising his listeners (or readers): '(Narration) is a detour by way of a past ("the other day", "in olden days") or by way of quotation (a "saying", a proverb) made in order to take advantage of an occasion and to modify an equilibrium taken by surprise' (79). The power of narration, then, lies in surprising or causing a change through the creation of a fictional space.

lesson the boys learn in *Un día volveré* is not merely a rejection of violence, or of the discourses that support it, but also a lesson of fidelity to that other reality 'that is not seen,' and which they reactivate with their '*aventis*,' inspired by the epics of mass culture.

3.3.2. Theater and song: Creative appropriations of mass culture from the postwar period to disillusion

Transformed into consumers, no matter how much Marsé's characters may still inhabit a very marginal place in the increasingly totalizing 'community of money,' they are still the grandsons of the peasants of the *filandones* and the *seranos*, and they now continue constructing their popular culture by appropriating the cultural products of consumption that are offered to them. De Certeau explains that, in fact, this type of operation is common, quotidian, and massive in a technocratic consumerist society, in that it floods our lives with products whose consumption is never completely neutral. Consumption, says de Certeau, can be understood as a secondary form of production that is not manifested through its own products, but through the ways it uses those of a dominant economic system.

In particular, Hollywood cinema was one of the more fertile objects of consumption for this secondary production during the Spanish postwar period. As Labanyi (2011) indicates, 'the pleasures offered to Spanish film audiences by Hollywood cinema ... in a time of political repression and extreme material hardship after the Civil War, was the main form of entertainment and thus played a huge compensatory role' (2). She also indicates the shortage of studies on the quotidian, active, creative reception of Hollywood cinema in the postwar period, and the importance of fiction writers like Marsé and Montalbán when it came to understanding these phenomena.

In his much-quoted *Crónica sentimental de España*, Montalbán called attention to the popular appropriations of another product of basic consumption in postwar Francoism: the so-called 'national song.' In principle, this type of popular song emerged as a pro-Spain reaction in the face of the arrival of the *cuplé*, the tango, jazz, and other 'foreign' sounds. The national song was constructed from two traditions, the *tonadilla* (a popular Spanish ditty) and traditional lyric poetry, and was anticipated by the Generation of '27. But in the forties, the Francoist autarchy took advantage of those roots to move it towards what was considered 'typically Spanish,' according to Montalbán: 'individualism, peculiar historical destiny, women, wine, music.' Interestingly, these songs also revealed two great contradictions: on the one hand, the immorality of the female characters, who articulated the possibility of a rebellious reading, and, on the other, the background sadness of a people who had just suffered through a war.

Montalbán chose some key songs as examples of both contradictions. Thus, the 'Romance de la otra' was for him particularly interesting because its protagonist is a wicked woman, the 'lover' who breaks with social conventions, who feels mistreated by them and therefore questions them: 'I am the other, the other / and I have no right to anything / because I don't wear a ring / with a date on the inside / I don't have a law that supports me, nor a door to knock on.' The song 'No te mires en el río' also expresses a type of sadness and frustration that could be reinterpreted as protest, but in this case it wasn't centered on a female character of dubious morality, but on what Vázquez Montalbán called a kind of sense of the absurd that resonated with violence and misfortunes. 'This song was a crowd-pleaser,' affirmed Montalbán:

> because, like a work of Shakespeare, it has different levels. There is a sentimental, primitive song: a boyfriend, a girlfriend, a tragic, atavistic death in the water. But the logical relationship between all these elements is irrational. There is a logic, but it is not the logic that pertains to the common theme of the song of consumption. It is a 'sub-normal,' retarded logic, for which one must develop one's eighth sense of subnormality. And those beings of the precarious epic, those Spaniards of the forties who had been lost in the river of uncontrollable events—girlfriends, boyfriends, homelands, memories, honors, sacred words, ideas, symbols, myths, joy in one's own shadow— had developed it very well. That song helped them express their right not to understand things completely and to make of that profession of the absurd an extreme declaration of lucidity. (11–12)

The rebellion, the sense of the absurd, burst forth along with expressions of a collective wounded sentimentality that appropriated elements of the culture of consumption, like those songs that provided people, says Montalbán, with 'that small ration of aesthetics and indispensable epic to keep living with their heads on straight.' Both Marsé and Montalbán understand the culture of the Spanish postwar popular classes as a fundamental element of their survival, as much as or more so than the pathetic rye bread they ate to fill their hungry stomachs.

What we have here is, again, an understanding not only of aesthetics and epics, but of the entire symbolic universe in general, like one more dimension integrated into the material universe, with both constituting a single system of reproduction of a life and a 'sentimentality' that are perceived as collective. But unlike what happened in the rural cultures of survival, in these postwar popular cultures portrayed by Marsé and Montalbán, the symbolic universe has begun to fill up with 'products' offered for individual consumption, which are slowly replacing the traditional communal properties entrusted to memory and orality to guarantee the reproduction of collective life. This does not assume that those 'products' are not constantly reappropriated on a daily basis by communities that reintegrate them into their collective systems (typically oral) of symbolic reproduction, particularly into their systems of epic and aesthetic reproduction.

In his novel *El pianista* (1985), Montalbán draws one of the richest portraits of those postwar cultures, this time in fiction. In the second part of this novel, Montalbán describes a daily gathering of neighbors on the roof of a building in the working-class *barrio* of Raval in Barcelona during the forties. Once again, it is an account of a moment of leisure when people get together to share their indispensable ration of epic and aesthetics: a spontaneous *tertulia* among the *vecinos*. During this get-together, they bring up references to boxing, the *copla*, and cinema, but also secret stories from *represaliados* (people who had been punished for their participation in the Republican side of the Civil War) and *maquis* (members of the antifascist resistance), anecdotes about the food shortage, and even urban legends of the time, like the one about the tuberculous vampires.

In the comings and goings of the *vecinos* on the roof there also appear a whole series of elements that construct a hybrid land between 'high' and 'low' culture, like the realist novels of Blasco-Ibañez and Fernández-Flores, which are secretly exchanged, comments on the *zarzuela*, the rhetoric with which Mr. Enrique suddenly surprises everyone, a newspaper salesman who 'when he was young did theater in the Ateneo Obrero de Sants' (169), or the pagan wisdom of a *vecina santera* who invokes 'God or the Great Fate.' Montalbán thus astutely paints a portrait of a class that was punished but still filled with creative abilities and a desire to live; a class which seems to echo what one of the characters, little Ofelia, says just before starting to dance: 'I'm so fed up of mourning and tears.'

Dance, music, and, again, song are, in fact, the central thread of this novel which features a Catalan pianist and composer, Albert Rosell, who returns to Spain when the civil war breaks out, instead of remaining in Paris among the avant-garde circles to which he has risen. This effectively cuts short his career and almost his life; he ends up in jail and later in poverty and anonymity, until finally finishing out his days playing banal pieces in a nightclub in the Barcelona of the transition to democracy. Or rather, in the Barcelona of *desencanto* (disenchantment, disillusion), because that feeling, which became the name for an entire era, is what gives consistency and force to the novel *El pianista*, no less than to *Un día volveré*, and to that time to which, directly or indirectly, both of them contribute.

In *El pianista*, the 1982 transition to democracy commanded by the triumphal Social Democratic party is portrayed explicitly and extensively as a betrayal. The war and the dictatorship took bread from the mouths of the defeated Republicans, and very nearly took their lives; but the transition, as the novel tells it, 'robbed [them of] their song.' The pianist Rosell had a companion, Luis Doria, during his avant-garde days Paris. Luis is a figure that embodies betrayal, because he decided to remain in Paris and subordinate politics to his personal artistic career, which continued to flourish during Francoism and reached its zenith during the democracy, surrounded by the halo of a revolutionary tradition to which others like Rosell were sacrificed.

In Marsé's case, it seems to me that the false hope placed on the arrival of a possible legendary avenger recounted in *Un día volveré* need not be read as a condemnation of the violent Spanish past and an exaltation of the new democratic times. Rather, I see it as a vindication of a critical space in the present to confront the forgetfulness of past defeats (political, social, cultural) at the hands of Francoism. In this sense, it is possible to understand why in the last paragraph the narrative voice, now an adult, affirms: 'today we no longer believe in anything, they're cooking us all in the rotting pot of forgetfulness, because forgetfulness is a strategy of living—although some of us, just in case, still keep our finger on the trigger of memory' (287).[13]

We have seen that Díez and his writer colleagues who took their inspiration from rural life also faced the destruction and forgetfulness into which the

---

13 Santos Alonso emphasizes the demystifying aspect of the novel, based on the undoubtedly central issue of the divergence between Jan Julivert's behavior and what his legend expects of him: 'that's why, and herein lies Marsé's realist lesson, [Jan Julivert] doesn't enjoy being a myth of political idealism committed to the *barrio*. What's more, he rejects it, and only aspires, in what remains of his life, to become a person, something that in the novel he achieves through all the realistic characteristics of his personality' (123). Nevertheless, I insist on the sweeping defense of the capacity to invent stories that runs through the novel (and which doesn't exclude a clear look at the dangers involved in that invention). With regard to the question of memory, clearly it is not separate from the utopian tension: having 'one's finger on the trigger of memory' assumes the same insurrection in the face of the reality imposed by the powers that be as inventing legends about other possible worlds. To reject the myth, as Alonso suggests, would also be to reject the memory. Rafael Chirbes reflects on these themes in relation to novelistic practice in *El novelista perplejo*: 'Every era produces its own injustice and needs its own investigation, its own laws,' he asserts. 'Walter Benjamin knew that legitimacy lies in the permanence of the resentment of an injustice that was committed in the past, and that the struggle for legitimacy is the struggle to appropriate the injustice of the past' (35).

peasant cultures were falling due to 'capitalist progress.' In the same way, Marsé and those who worried about Republican memory in the early eighties faced the decaffeinated reappropriation that built the triumphant social democracy from that tradition, in the era of *desencanto*. But unlike Díez and colleagues, who wove their program to recuperate those past traditions into the framework of the foundational civic cultures of the transition, Marsé and Montalbán acted more like memory 'snipers,' working those subjects on their own in times when they still were far from fashionable. In fact, this would only happen later when, as Chirbes—another of those few pioneer snipers of 'historical memory'—writes, the PSOE found itself in opposition and decided it was an opportune moment to revitalize those subjects (in a new and unexpected 'theft of the song' of the defeated Republicans) to reap electoral 'profits.'

3.3.3. Adaptation of the 'writer-worker' to his circumstances

It seems, then, that writers like Marsé, Montalbán, and Francisco Candel, among others, developed their work of reconnecting with working-class cultures and with the Republican tradition from positions that were less porous to nonliterary manifestations of civic cultures of transition. Perhaps this was in part because they belonged to an earlier generation than Díez, Aparicio, and Merino; because of their age, they were already professional writers during Francoism. Thus, they arrived at the transition from a well-defined, specialized place, from a position as more established, recognized fiction writers. This could have meant that they experienced the political and cultural effervescence of the moment differently, including the intense irruption of working-class autonomy in the seventies. One might think this a possible space of affinity for them, but there are not many indications of a connection, or even inspiration.

Marsé, Montalbán, and Candel came, in different ways, to embody a marginal figure that finally earned its place in the literary establishment of the anti-Francoist opposition of the fifties and sixties: the 'writer-worker.' This doesn't mean that their access to publication and to that same establishment was easy in general—it was not by any means—but unlike what happened with 'provincial' writers or those inspired by rural life during those final years of the dictatorship, those literary power groups of which Sabino Ordás spoke ended up making a space for them in their rarefied circle.

The biographies of these 'writer-workers' are simultaneously atypical and characteristic. They all include new arrivals to fiction writing from unsuspected places, never from a position of the subject agent who sits down to a blank page to say what he wants to say, always from collective flows of appropriation (or, as de Certeau would say, of 'secondary production') of discourses and symbols used to reproduce a community's universe of meanings.

Marsé began listening to the oral histories of Barcelona's *barrios* when he worked as a commercial distributor, later writing film critiques and letters to a lady friend from which his first novel would emerge. Montalbán soaked up the folk songs and ballads he had heard rural emigrants singing and reciting for their elders, and he combined that heritage with mass culture and 'high culture' in his first poetry. But, at the same time, he earned a living as a journalist writing food articles in sometimes odd magazines like *Hogar Moderno*. In his childhood before the dictatorship, Candel read kiosk novels like those of the anarchist collections 'La Novela Ideal' and 'La Novela Libre,' and Andersen, Salgari, and Verne in the local Republican Library of his neighborhood, 'Casas Baratas,' which, in turn, was completely permeated by the rural orality of Murcian and Andalusian emigrants. Later, as an adolescent he began to write to fill the long hours of his convalescence from tuberculosis.

All these 'writer-workers' gained access to publication, and later to the consecration of precarious and contingent ways. Marsé's mother worked taking care of Paulina Crusat's mother; Crusat was a writer who collaborated in the literary magazine *Ínsula*, and she would help Marsé publish his first stories. Later, Marsé submitted his first novel for the Seix Barral publishing house's prize without knowing anybody. To his great surprise, the 'popes' of the literary left, Carlos Barral and José María Castellet, were interested in the novel, and even more in Marsé himself, as a paradigm of the 'writer-worker' they longed to discover. From then on, they protected him and intervened in his never fully complete integration into the circles of the so-called *gauche divine*. Montalbán, on the other hand, was secretly communist from a very young age, and was one of the 0.07% of children of workers who were able to go to the university at the end of the fifties. He was arrested and jailed when he was 23 years old. When he was released, he worked hand to mouth as a freelance journalist until the *Crónica sentimental* assignment earned him the confidence of the magazine *Triunfo*, a strong institution of the (crypto) anti-Francoist culture. Only later would he attempt fiction writing, devoting himself to his series of crime novels featuring the detective Pepe Carvalho.

Candel's case is perhaps even stranger. Completely lacking contacts or any kind of access to literary circles, he spent years trying to publish his first novel. Later he wrote another one that specifically dealt with young writers ignored by the publishing industry, *Hay una juventud que aguarda*, and submitted it for the Editorial Destino prize. No writer had come from Candel's *barrio* before, but there was a soccer player, Eduardo Machón from

Barça, who hooked Candel up with the famous publisher Janés, of the publishing house Plaza y Janés, whom he knew because Janés was a big soccer fan. Surprisingly, Janés liked Candel's novel precisely because it was controversial in the publishing world, and so he published it. Later, Candel became relatively famous due to his exceptional status as a writer from a marginal *barrio*, notably with his novel *Donde la ciudad cambia su nombre* (1957) and his chronicles on emigration *Los otros catalanes* (1965).

There is an episode in Candel's literary career that is especially illuminating about what it meant to become a 'writer-worker' during Francoism. In the novel that gave him his first taste of popularity, *Donde la ciudad cambia su nombre*, Candel recounted many real anecdotes of events that had happened in his and other working-class *barrios* in the Barcelona suburbs. Candel included himself as a character in these stories, and was so integrated into the narrative flow of oral self-representations of those *barrios* that he wrote so straightforwardly that he even used the real names of all the characters. This made many of those people angry to see themselves exposed this way, because often their actions in the stories left them looking very bad. Candel was the target of hostility and threats that nearly resulted in attempted lynchings. This experience of 'the characters' rebellion' served him, however, as material to write another novel, *¡Dios, la que se armó!* (1964), in which he recounted what had happened, this time with greater nuance and without real names.

This anecdote can be read as a problematic episode of adjustment in the transition from a model of community that collectively satisfies its need for representation, to another in which an individual (an author) arrogates the authority to represent a community, which is hoped to play the role of 'public.' This transition, which, as we have seen, is produced in 'rural' or 'provincial' writers through their professionalization in the publishing market of the democracy, also had to be undergone by these 'writer-workers' in the process of becoming integrated into the elitist, sectarian world of Spanish letters during Francoism. In both cases, in fact, the paradigm that prevails is clearly that of the writer of 'aesthetic modernity' (sometimes known as the 'bourgeois writer') who follows an organizational model of production of (aesthetic) meaning based on the premise that said production acts as an interruption of the common, socially shared meaning, so that it can appear 'singular.'

Artist, work, and public were the three distinct instances in the process of production of aesthetics as understood by this 'modernity' that developed in parallel with industrial capitalism and its disciplined 'community of money.' Remember that this was outlined increasingly as the only possible way to organize social wealth, promoting the production of exchange value that could be appropriated by isolated individuals instead of the reproduction of the uses necessary for the survival of interdependent communities.

In the Spain of the transition, given the renewed strength of the modernizing, pro-European ideal as a driving social force, both capitalist modernity and aesthetic modernity prevailed decisively, displacing those other possible alternative modernities that might have been constructed in dialogue with the heritage of the rural cultures of survival and popular working-class cultures.

An important form of this displacement occurred through the absorption of elements of those alternative cultures. The aim was to assimilate them into the hegemonic paradigm seen in processes like those just described, by which hybrid figures such as the 'rural writer' or the 'working-class writer' were slowly incorporated into the 'modern' requirements of separation of author, work, and public, and into the primacy of individual production and consumption (of meaning and materiality) as opposed to collective reproduction.

But at the same time, and fundamentally, capitalist modernity and aesthetic modernity (in that particularly 'depoliticized' version which became hegemonic towards the end of Francoism) also held fast through processes of transformation of industrial capitalism into financial and service capitalism. It also took root through the appearance of a creative class of 'authors' and 'artists' who embodied the ideal of aesthetic modernity, like the descendants of the tradition of bourgeois culture that was formed through industrial capitalism in the eighteenth century, but was at the same time adjusted little by little to the exigencies of a culture industry in transition towards the model of neoliberal capitalism that was permeating everything.

In this sense, the transition to democracy produced an extraordinary demand for individuals who could embody the ideal of the modern, cosmopolitan intellectual while now simultaneously producing not only 'works,' as defined by a logic that belonged more to the manufacturing spirit of industrial capitalism, but also 'names' that could function as 'brands,' that is, as immaterial merchandise able to produce tendencies (to provoke desire for what others desire) in the new neoliberal market.

On the other hand, as I will explain in detail in the second part of this book, in a contradictory relationship of continuity and separation relative to the omnipresent commercializing logics of neoliberalism, recent decades have seen the emergence of other forms of production and maintenance of culture that are more reliant on interdependence and collaboration than on the value of the 'big names.' Forged from the convergence of multiple factors, among them the relative democratization of access to technologies of written and audiovisual culture, along with a certain depletion of the modern models of cultural authority I have been examining, these cultures of collaboration and interdependence have proliferated, mainly in the wake of the neoliberal crisis that began around 2008, partly because their value as possible alternatives to that neoliberal model in crisis has been perceived.

In the following chapters, I will try to draw a map of the emergence in the Spanish state of what we could call 'cultures of anyone.' I will draw on the analysis of political processes that have been decisive for their expansion. These include, first, the struggles against the so-called 'Law Sinde-Wert,' which seeks to regulate forms of cultural sharing on the Internet, and then, the 15M movement, or the *Indignados*, as well as the subsequent cycle of mobilizations and social and cultural transformations which this movement drove.

PART II

Cultural Democratizations

CHAPTER 4

Internet Cultures
as Collaborative Creation of Value

'un mundo solo se para
con otro mundo'

4.1. Genealogies and Contradictions of Digital Cultures

4.1.1. How is the authority of a manifesto in defense of the Internet constructed?

Questions such as the following have often been posed, completely reasonably, it seems to me: Who excavates the minerals necessary to build the machines that make the 'New Technologies of Information and Communication' (NTIC) possible? Who gives up their health and dreams to work impossible hours for ridiculous pay to assemble the pieces of those computers and cellphones? And who spends their life cleaning rooms, washing clothes, feeding, and caring for the 'creative workers' (and their children) who use the NTICs?

With all due respect for the differences, which are many, these questions resonate with others that perhaps allude to similar situations, in a sense that must be determined: who finds the time to write and correct the thousands of entries in Wikipedia? Who spends their nights subtitling the films and series that circulate in P2P networks? Who spends their free time responding to strangers' questions in Internet forums? And who takes on—without being asked—the mission of producing, labeling, ordering, distributing, and making attractive all the uncountable, anonymous, accessible content on the Internet so others can use it?

Let's take, for example, a 9.5-byte file, a pdf document called 'Manifiesto en defensa de los derechos fundamentales en Internet.' No matter how almost irrelevantly small it might be, just like any other fragment of digital information, it wouldn't exist without a series of material processes dedicated to it through the limited abilities and finite energy of a few human beings. Many people today have easy access to writing or reading a text file like this one. But the apparent immediacy and ease with which they do it tends to obscure some of its conditions of production—in particular, everything related to building the hardware and the minimum quality of life requirements that will enable us to read it and write about it. But it's also true that another type of condition, which in some sense can also be considered one of production (particularly related to the file's circulation and reception), far from being concealed, becomes especially necessary and obvious, especially in cases of information that generates a lot of interest, like this file.

So, it would in fact be unfair to think of the 'Manifiesto en defensa de los derechos fundamentales en Internet' simply as a specific digital file that is already published as soon as it's written. That would mean artificially separating it from the enormous collective effort that went into it. Hundreds of thousands of operations of revision, commentary, and diffusion accompanied it, and these really must be considered an essential part of its production as a fragment of information whose existence developed like a living process in what Franco Berardi calls 'the infosphere.'[1]

It was published for the first time on December 2, 2009. Three days later, the Manifiesto had a million Google hits, more than 100,000 people had joined the Facebook group that supported it, and it had become the number one trending Twitter hashtag in Spain (#manifiesto). In addition, it was translated into English, Catalan, Galician, Aragonese, and Asturian, and was the object of 210 articles in print media, 500 in digital media, 174 television spots, and 207 radio spots in its first week of existence alone. In that same week, a wiki version of the manifesto was published online, with its own domain name and a forum dedicated to debating future actions ("Manifiesto 'En defensa de los derechos fundamentales en internet'" 2014).

But why did this Manifiesto spark so much interest? Why did so many people participate in its production? Why did so many people devote themselves to do something that could be called 'work' on it, knowing that most of them would never see any money for it? Did they perhaps expect recognition as its authors? Or did they simply want to support what some 'public intellectuals' had declared in that manifesto?

---

1 'The infosphere is the interface between the media system and the mind that receives these signals—the mental ecosphere, that immaterial region where semiotic fluxes interact with the reception antennae of the minds scattered across the planet. The Mind is the universe of receivers. These receivers are, of course, not limited to receiving signals; they also process and create them, thereby setting in motion new processes of transmission and provoking the continuous evolution of the mediascape' (Berardi, 2007, 81).

Of course, it must be remembered in the first place that the Manifiesto was published the day after the introduction of the bill that would become the Law on Sustainable Economy. This included a clause about regulating the Internet and protecting intellectual property, and would become known as the 'Ley Sinde' (the Sinde Law, from the second last name of the Minister of Culture who promoted it, Ángeles González Sinde).[2] The Sinde Law proposed, among other things, creating a commission of experts unconnected to the judicial branch, to which power would be granted to shut down websites that did not respect intellectual property rights. This provision was widely interpreted as an attack on the Internet and gave rise to an unprecedented mobilization in its defense. The Manifiesto constituted a significant chapter in this effort. And, as was only to be expected, it also expressed a range of diverse and contradictory traditions and cosmovisions that coexist in the vast world of digital culture.

So, on one hand, the Manifiesto effectively reproduced, up to a point, the traditional move of 'public intellectuals,' that of denouncing a political situation from the position of legitimacy gained from having distinguished themselves in cultural spheres supposedly unrelated to the political arena. It did this in particular by using the form of a 'manifesto' and by using the language of the liberal political tradition, from which the very figure of the public intellectual historically emanates. Even the title itself appealed to those 'fundamental rights' pulled straight from constitutional language. Then the document as a whole operated through the legal discourse of the state to which it was addressed, holding up classic values of the liberal political tradition, such as, notably, the separation of judicial and executive power, freedom of expression, and the presumption of innocence.

But this was not the only cultural or political tradition that fed the rhetoric, and above all the pragmatics, of the Manifiesto. Its authorship, for example, was ambiguous, contrary to that of a typical manifesto produced by public intellectuals, which requires lots of names, and the more famous, the better. Instead of signatures, the 'author' appeared in the text as a diffuse 'we': 'the journalists, bloggers, users, professionals, and creative people on the Internet.' Later, the newspaper *20 Minutos.es* (the only newspaper that endorsed the manifesto) explained that the text was developed collaboratively by 'some 40 journalists, bloggers, and Internet

---

2 It was also later called the Sinde-Wert Law, because the Minister of Education, Culture, and Sports of the Partido Popular government (José Ignacio Wert), who joined the government in 2011, continued to promote it, and was, in fact, the one who finally implemented it. In reference to the pressures the North American government exerted on its Spanish counterpart to pass this law, its critics have also sometimes called this law the 'Biden-Sinde Law' for Joe Biden, the US vice president.

professionals' (20minutos.es, 2009) using Google Wave, a digital tool still in beta, which allowed collective writing in real time on a single platform (a tool that, incidentally, disappeared shortly afterwards).

The next day, Minister González Sinde tried to respond to the uproar online by organizing a conversation with some of the voices that opposed the new law. In the process, the names of the 14 'professionals' who attended the meeting became known, and it turned out that they were among those who had participated in writing the manifesto. They appeared in media like *20 Minutos.es* (whose own director was one of the 14) classified respectively as 'journalists' or 'businessmen'—plus a single blogger or 'internaut'—and so each one was identified by his or her allegiance to certain journalistic media or business projects.

Thus, those who introduced the 'authors' of the manifesto contributed, to a certain extent, to locating them in a space of legitimacy associated with that concept of 'professionalism' which, in all its ambiguity, comes from the same modern genealogy I mapped out in Part 1: a genealogy that starts with an ambition to monopolize cultural value through a specifically 'modern' type of power/knowledge, founded on the pillars of Western technoscience. The cultural authority that invokes this concept of 'professionalism'—associated here with the figure of both 'journalist' and 'businessman'—simultaneously resonates with the competitive, *business* interpretation of that modern power/knowledge which neoliberalism creates. Only that one lone blogger (or 'internaut') among the 14 names of what was, with typical 'web humor,' soon called 'Sinde's List,' would open the door to more amateur and 'countercultural' traditions that would operate through other, less competitive ways of producing value and cultural authority. In light of this fact, it is significant that, unlike the others, this 'internaut' appeared on the list without a last name, and gave every impression of being a pseudonym: 'Alvy.'

But there were still more latent tensions regarding authorship. At the end of the text it was asserted that 'This manifesto, developed collaboratively by several authors, is by everyone and by no one. If you want to join, spread it online.' In contrast to attempts by journalistic media to attribute authors and perhaps even 'authorities' ('outstanding professionals,' 'Internet personalities,' etc.), those 14 guests invited by the minister to engage in a dialogue constantly rejected the idea that they were 'representatives.' 'We don't represent the Internet,' they asserted repeatedly. 'All we did was write a manifesto that a lot of people are joining.'

As Margarita Padilla noted in her book, *El kit de la lucha en Internet* (2012), during that meeting with the minister some of the 14 invitees were tweeting to the multitudes of uninvited internauts affected by the law. This effectively established a practice that, says Padilla in her astute analysis of the situation, 'diminishes opacity and secrecy, relaxes the weight of representation on the group sitting at the negotiation table, and extends the situation throughout a public-private space that exceeds the virtual-real duality' (114). For Padilla, this type of practice, which alters representation, doesn't come out of thin air; rather, it has to do with what she calls the 'political architecture' of the Internet:

> The Internet is ungovernable and is made up of intelligent and autonomous nodes. From the interconnection of these nodes a new public-private sphere arises in which, simply by existing—publishing a post, commenting on it, connecting to it, resending it, tweeting and retweeting it, tagging it, sharing it ...—politics is already being practiced. (123)

Putting special emphasis on the importance of technological infrastructures in potentially 'democratizing' situations—as in this case, on the existence of the social network Twitter used as a tool of instantaneous communication between those who were at the meeting with Minister Sinde, and those who were not—can cause (over)simplifications. We live in an era given to 'cyberfetishism,' as Cesar Rendueles (2013) explains, and idealized, quasi-determinist versions of technological changes abound. Those versions are also pushing us always to forget or ignore the concrete historical processes that link the Internet with the expansion of neoliberal globalization and its financiarization of the economy.

Silvia Federici (2011), among many others, has called attention to the simple fact that 'online communication/production depends on economic activities—mining, microchip, and rare earth production—that, as presently organized, are extremely destructive, socially and ecologically.' To this it should be added that, as Stefano Harney (2013) has explained, the whole new 'deregulated' economy that emerges around 1998, with the ascent of financial products such as 'derivatives' and 'hedge funds,' could not exist without the infrastructures provided by the new digital technologies, which allowed real-time global trading. Internet and digital cultures have obviously been instrumental for the shift towards what is sometimes called the 'immaterial,' 'creative,' or 'cognitive' economy, but the problem is that it is impossible to separate this economy from the destructive dynamics of neoliberal financiarization.[3] Harney (2010b) explains that the 'cultural

---

3 Copyright is often a key tool for the financiarization of 'immaterial wealth,' which in turns allows for speculation and anti-social accumulation by the biggest corporate monopolies of neoliberalism. César Rendueles (2013, 60) has explained

commodity' has actually been the model for neoliberal capitalism, because of its 'unfinished quality,' which allows constant renovations of its value. Capitalism has understood that society is always producing this 'unfinished cultural value,' and has developed the means to expropriate it. This is, as Margarita Padilla (2010) herself has pointed out, exactly what often happens in the so-called *web 2.0*, a concept for 'entrepreneurs of themselves'—says Padilla, echoing Foucault's analysis of neoliberalism, a market milieu in which collective creativity becomes the motor of capitalism—although this, she adds, doesn't prevent the appearance of multiple tactics that 'use the market against the market.'

In a world with a high risk of 'cyberfetishism,' fortunately, and as Padilla's own example shows, complex explanations focused on material historical processes related to digital cultures also abound. It may be useful to bring together several more of these explanations to effectively situate this question of the relationship between technology, capitalism, and democratization. This will avoid tedious debates about supposedly 'essential' properties—whether negative or positive—of the new technologies.

4.1.2. 'Shared agency' with technologies and a genealogy of its democratizing uses

In this regard, it seems to me that the sociologist Amparo Lasén (2009) offers a very acceptable starting point when she proposes that human beings have something we could call a 'shared agency' with technology: 'Shared agency means that technologies are not passive instruments, they make us do certain things, and we make them do others.' There would thus be, in Padilla's terms, a technological 'architecture' that in no way predetermines human behavior, but which is in constant interaction with the uses socially assigned to it. Accordingly, it is always a 'political architecture.' Lasén confirms: 'In our daily activity with technologies there are power conflicts (contrasting interests:

this situation clearly: 'Since the 1970s, the rich countries have simultaneously tried to accumulate the production processes with higher added value and increase their speculative gains. The protection of intellectual property legally connects both dynamics. Industries that generate higher profits depend on some sort of protection of intellectual property and governments are very predisposed to provide this legal coverage. At the same time, these companies routinely use that position of technological predominance for speculative purposes. Monsanto has the technology and resources to conduct biological research and, therefore, it uses the protection of this investigation as an umbrella for biopiracy. Hollywood has the ability to flood the world with its products and, therefore, tries to prevent the passage of its movies to the public domain. Microsoft and Apple (or on a smaller scale, Oracle or Adobe) have acquired a monopoly position that allows them to charge usurious prices for their products.'

intellectual property, control, commercial uses).' Rubén Martínez (2014a) has written in similar terms about 'Internet y política':

> A static, predefined set of political practices does not arise spontaneously from the web. Rather, as with all cultural production, the web can be used, sampled, or assembled with practices, processes, and uses that understand it (by theorizing it and using it) in very different ways. In turn, the web contains ways of doing things that influence the collective ways of communicating and producing, creating feedback cycles between users and technology.

Having established these general parameters to help us move away from all essentialization or idealization of technologies (digital or any other kind), what I want to do is contribute to the specific historical analysis of what happened that December morning when 14 people met with Minister Sinde, 'armed' with their Twitter accounts. In doing this, I hope to contribute more broadly to the specific historical analysis of the types of cultures and policies that have sprung up in digital environments—always in continuity with those that move beyond the digital—in the context of the struggles against the Sinde Law in Spain. This context seems to me to have been decisive for fulfilling those 'ungovernable' potentialities that, as Padilla says, are offshoots of the 'autonomy' and 'intelligence' of each of those online nodes. Thus the genealogy of *that* specific version of the Internet, of *that* digital culture which values autonomy and distributed intelligence, is important for the material and historical analysis to which I want to contribute.

I will not be able to develop that genealogy in depth here, but I do want to briefly mention a couple of scenes that function, up to a point, as 'origin myths' for those collaborative, decentralized digital cultures. These examples can shed light on the digital cultures' reappearance in relation to the struggles against the Sinde Law. One is the well-known story of the origin of the Internet itself. As Padilla explains, the fact that it is a decentralized network is no mere chance. Rather, it is the result of the persistence of many people who have fought for many years to maintain this democratic architecture. At first, it was a military strategy, a response to the desire to create a communications system that could survive a possible nuclear attack: 'in a situation of "every man for himself," it is necessary to respond fast and well, so intelligence must be distributed throughout the whole network, and not just at one or some centers' (41). Later, it was the university community, and later still, the hacker culture that sprang from it, that completed the project:

> [I]t was in the universities that this strange network without a central

authority and with intelligence and autonomy distributed throughout all its points began to be developed. It was there that these developments connected with the hacker counterculture, a techno-elite that departed from the script and not only created the Web, but also recorded in its DNA the characteristics with which we have inherited it today: openness, flexibility, and distribution. (41)

What interests me about the culture of the first Internet is precisely that hybrid nature between different traditions and ways of creating value that, I think, survive in the contradictions I have been indicating, as a result of the 'Manifiesto en defensa de los derechos fundamentales en Internet.' So, as Txarlie (2012), a member of the group Hacktivistas, indicated in a talk on social movements and the hacker tradition, in the university context that created ARPAnet—the academic ancestor of the Internet—software was shared, 'and nobody suggested putting restrictions on that "knowledge," just as they wouldn't put restrictions on a chemical element or a theorem.' In other words, as has been repeated often, we must consider the importance of the enlightened spirit and its affirmation of the universality of knowledge in configuring the 'political architecture' of the Internet.[4] On the other hand, the Web was born in an environment that was not, in other respects, at all unfamiliar with what would become the other, less amiable side of that enlightened spirit: the type of technoscientific cultural authority that tends to monopolize the production of meaning.

But the Internet also incorporated important democratizing elements from the North American countercultural tradition that would serve as a counterbalance to those tendencies to monopolize meaning. Emmanuel Rodríguez explains it very well in his book *Hipótesis democracia* (2013):

---

4 Robert Darnton's well-known arguments are not so much about the historical enlightened origin of the Internet and digital culture, as they are about the need to use technological means to recuperate the enlightened project of the 'Republic of Letters' in an even more democratic version. In an article titled 'Google & the Future of Books,' he said, 'The eighteenth century imagined the Republic of Letters as a realm with no police, no boundaries, and no inequalities other than those determined by talent. Anyone could join it by exercising the two main attributes of citizenship, writing and reading. Writers formulated ideas, and readers judged them. Thanks to the power of the printed word, the judgments spread in widening circles, and the strongest arguments won.' And from the appreciation of that model in the past, he concluded with a program for the present: 'Yes, we must digitize. But more important, we must democratize. We must open access to our cultural heritage. How? By rewriting the rules of the game, by subordinating private interests to the public good, and by taking inspiration from the early republic in order to create a Digital Republic of Learning' (2009).

Its genesis [that of the Internet and 'cyberspace'] is in those libertarian, countercultural media whose main current showed a preference for a kind of ingenuous naturalism, scattering later into all kinds of Orientalisms and 'new waves,' but it also had a side current that leaned towards playing with electronic gadgets.

The luck of this 'other counterculture' was forged in the crossover between the intense existential revolution of the moment and the passion for knowledge and technological experimentation that had been preserved in academic and scientific cultures. An alloy that acquired a special hardness in the field of new kinds of engineering that were just taking their first steps (cybernetics, computer science).

There were two great landmarks of this movement. The first was the creation of the first prototype of the web of networks. The second was the miniaturization of some technological devices that, in line with the current catchphrase among yippies, 'just do it,' would very quickly put into the hands of a lot of people the technological and productive powers that until then were only within the reach of states, large universities, and multinational companies. The resonance of this movement with what in older terms we might have called 'socialization—from below—of modes of production' is evident. (190)

Perhaps another of the great scenes that mark these 'origin myths' is that famous fight in 1980 between Richard Stallman, then a programmer at the Massachusetts Institute of Technology, and a printer that constantly broke down on him, causing him no end of annoyance. His annoyance was not so much due to its constant malfunctioning, but because those who programmed its software didn't allow users access to it, so Stallman couldn't solve the problem using his own abilities as a programmer.

This was in the early eighties, and some companies had decided to begin to restrict access to the programs they produced. Stallman and many others 'geeks' and 'hackers'—located at the crossroads between academic cultures with enlightenment roots and the anti-authoritarian countercultures of the sixties—wanted to change this. They wanted the code for all computer programs to be accessible to everyone; they were used to it being this way and they couldn't accept having to consider private something that was produced and maintained collectively.

They began to take steps to achieve this. They created legal tools, first the successive versions of the General Public License (GPL), then the Creative Commons licenses. These were two milestones around which were woven the rich, diverse threads of the world of free software, and later also that of the so-called 'free culture.' It's a complex history, with many curves, which

David Bollier calls 'Viral Spiral,' because he understands it as a propagation and acceleration of shared creative processes to which each generation adds improvements, thanks in large part to the connective capacity of the Internet.[5]

4.2. Unpaid Work and Creation of Value on the Internet

4.2.1. Job precarization and increase in Internet use

But to understand at what point on that 'viral spiral,' and at what point on other spirals (commercialization, privatization, or even criminalization) that turn in opposite directions, digital cultures had become heir to these complex processes by the time of the struggles against Spain's Sinde Law, I now want to raise a fairly pedestrian question relative to the internauts' meeting with Minister Sinde which was tweeted live: Who had time at that hour on a Thursday morning—a normal, ordinary workday—to be following Twitter, and even, as Padilla notes, 'to provide arguments, data, documents, or consensus' to those who were meeting with the minister?

Apparently, quite a few people, judging by the number of messages on the subject that day, and which can still be found today thanks to the free search tool Topsy. It is that availability, that capacity to do something that could well be considered 'work' on the Web, even if it's unpaid work, that interests me now. Because, once again, it seems that these processes cannot really be understood without taking note of their conditions of possibility; that is, without attending to the question of sustainability. This is not necessarily

---

5 In the definition of 'free culture' offered by the jurist and activist Lawrence Lessig, in his first book on the subject, an understanding of culture is proposed as something that is done collectively, and thus benefits from the greatest possible access, without implying an erasure of ownership or property: 'A free culture supports and protects creators and innovators. It does this directly by granting intellectual property rights. But it does so indirectly by limiting the reach of those rights, to guarantee that follow-on creators and innovators remain *as free as possible* from the control of the past. A free culture is not a culture without property, just as a free market is not a market in which everything is free. The opposite of a free culture is a "permission culture"—a culture in which creators get to create only with the permission of the powerful, or of creators from the past' (2004). Within this tradition, however, there are multiple interpretations, the confrontation between Stallman's and Lessig's positions being particularly notable, along with their respective models of 'copyleft' licenses, the General Public License (GPL), and Creative Commons licenses. The essential difference lies in Stallman's—and others who think like him—opinion that the author doesn't have the right to decide how her work will be shared, or to impose certain restrictions (in contrast to the Creative Commons licenses, which do allow this). Rather, he believes that the author should be obliged to respect free access given to the culture in general. For more details on this, see chapter 9 of Bollier's 'The Many Faces of the Common.'

always a question of money, nor of salary, nor even of employment, but in societies that have essentially entrusted most of the population's sustenance to those mechanisms, it does tend to come down to that, at least in part.

And that is why perhaps an enlightening way of approaching the problem can be to contrast—with no intention of giving the last word to statistics, or of trying to establish simple causal relationships—employment and job insecurity data with Internet usage data in Spain. We know that precarization of work has been a continuing and rapid process in the Spanish state since the Moncloa Accords of 1977—which prepared the great neoliberal transformation—opened the door to temporary contracts, as the sociologist Angel Luis Lara (2003) tells us. The following decades witnessed the birth of a whole raft of measures that have basically facilitated job terminations, made wages 'flexible,' and broadened the repertoire of unstable, unguaranteed contracts that generally offer insecure conditions for workers.[6]

For the rest, as Lara and other activists and researchers (like those of the collectives 'Precarias a la deriva' (2004) and 'Espai en blanc' (2006), and those participating in a monograph issue of the journal *Sociedad y Utopía* about precarity (Gálvez Biesca 2007)) have shown very well, it makes no sense to limit oneself to viewing the insecurity created by neoliberal capitalism solely in relation to the state's labor policies. Precarization is inseparable from the uncertainty created by many other factors related to habitability, like transportation, urbanism and housing, childcare, health, education, etc. In light of this, 'Precarias a la deriva' preferred to talk about precariousness as the 'set of material and symbolic conditions that determine an uncertainty about sustained access to essential resources for the full development of one's life' (28).[7]

---

6 Ángel Luis Lara details these measures, recalling, for example, the National Employment Agreement (1982) in which, he says, 'The upper echelons of the majority unions accepted the development of precarious employment modalities as a supposed means to halt unemployment.' He also mentions the following decisive moments in the growth of job precarization at the legislative level:
'—*Year 1992*: Royal Decree-Law of April 5 decreasing unemployment benefits ...
—*Year 1993*: Royal Decree-Law of December 3 introducing the apprentice contract as a means of reducing salaries for a period of three years for people up to 25 years of age; it includes a new regimen of part-time hires and causes greater flexibility in the regulatory framework, legalizing private employment agencies and the so-called Temporary Employment Agencies (ETT).
—*Year 1997*: Interconfederate Accord for employment stability, which seeks to guarantee greater stability by increasing the flexibility of the hiring system. Terminations are reduced and the Workers Statute is modified by broadening the nature of terminations with cause to help businesses adjust to the movements of the market' (2013, 220).
7 Judith Butler has clearly distinguished three dimensions to this problem, which

In any case, if there were any doubts about precarization as a generalized problem among Spain's population during the years of the so-called 'economic bubble,' these have been more than cleared up since the beginning of the 2008 crisis. The unemployment figures are perhaps the most spectacular, holding at around 25% from 2008 to 2015 and a scandalous 50% among the young during the same period. But these data constitute only the beginning of what is needed to get a good idea of the degree of pessimism and lack of expectations that have spread during these crisis years, especially among young people. Other indicators should be mentioned along with unemployment: the 700,000 Spaniards who emigrated between 2008 and 2014; the exorbitant cost of living along with frozen wages; the consequent delay in young people moving out of their parents' homes (the average age is around 29); as well as the proliferation of all types of low-wage jobs and the dismantling of social services and basic public aids, including education, which has produced an increase of up to 50% in the cost of university tuition.[8]

On the other hand, it is precisely this young sector of the population so pummeled by unemployment and instability that has been responsible for the exponential increase in the use of the Internet. Sixty-nine percent of Spanish homes had gained access to it by 2013, the year when 53.8% of

she identifies as 'precarization,' 'precarity,' and 'precariousness': 'In some economic and political theory, we hear about populations that are increasingly subject to what is called 'precarization.' This process—usually induced and reproduced by governmental and economic institutions that acclimatize populations over time to insecurity and hopelessness (see Isabell Lorey)—is built into the institutions of temporary labor, of decimated social services, and of the general attrition of social democracy in favor of entrepreneurial modalities supported by fierce ideologies of individual responsibility and the obligation to maximize one's own market value as the ultimate aim in life. In my view, this important process of precarization has to be supplemented by an understanding of precarity as a structure of affect, as Lauren Berlant has suggested, and as a heightened sense of expendability or disposability that is differentially distributed throughout society. In addition, I use a third term, precariousness, which characterizes every embodied and finite human being, and non-human beings as well. This is not simply an existential truth—each of us could be subject to deprivation, injury, debilitation or death by virtue of events or processes outside our control. It is also, importantly, a feature of what we might call the social bond, the various relations that establish our interdependency. In other words, no one person suffers a lack of shelter without a social failure to organize shelter in such a way that it is accessible to each and every person' (2011).

8 Regarding the increase in the average age at which Spanish youth leave their parents' homes, see Valera (2012). Regarding the increase in the cost of college tuition, see *Publico.es* (2012).

Spaniards between the ages of 16 and 74 used the Internet daily (according to data from the INE). Among that general population, young people shine as the most dedicated users: 81% log on every day, and 96% search the Web in general. Numerous studies show that the famous 'divide' between young 'digital natives' and adults continues to grow. One such study indicated that 53% of young people prefer to use the Internet for entertainment, as opposed to 16% of adults; 70% of young people prefer to study online, as opposed to 35% of adults; and finally, 41% of young people choose the Internet to stay informed, as opposed to 16% of older generations. Another recent study found that:

> 5.5% of young people, who, according to the INE's most recent survey in 2013, do not use the Internet or social networks on a regular basis, could run the risk of being 'left behind' in an environment in which so many aspects of life for people between 16 and 24 years old are developed partially or totally through the web.

More specifically, it refers to aspects such as 'the broadening of their sphere of relationships in their free time, their training, their sources of information, and their work.'

At the risk of coming across as trying establish rigid or unambiguous causal relations between these data, it would nonetheless be misleading not to look at the job insecurity and uncertain living conditions experienced by a large part of Spain's youth when trying to understand their Internet use.[9]

4.2.2. 'Copyleft' activism and new sharing practices in mass culture

At the same time, however, this Internet use cannot be understood without also being aware of the influence of what Martínez calls the online 'culture of freedom,' which comes from the 'enlightened' and countercultural origins described earlier. Because, in fact, no Internet use can be understood without being aware of defense mechanisms against the privatization and regulation efforts that have marked its history, as Martinez indicates:

> In the face of attempts at regulation, control, stratification, privatization of the web by state organisms or market agents, different social and collective organizations defend its original principles and liberties so it can continue to offer its full potentiality as an open system. To a great extent, other forms of policy on the web are unthinkable if we don't take into account the culture of freedom—which, we must remember,

---

9 For more information on the use of the Internet by young people, see Europa Press (2014).

is not synonymous with cost-free—that arises from the defense of its interrelated protocols and technical diagrams.

In Spain's case, the influence of this online 'culture of freedom' could be included in two spheres, one more militant and politicized, and another that grows in the massive spaces of the mediatized consumer culture. In the first case, we are speaking of what Guillermo Zapata (in Martínez 2012) has called a 'copyleft movement' that clashes head-on with the 'monopolistic copyright culture of the CT.' Zapata asserts that 'Spain is one of the countries in which copyright has been most effectively delegitimized. Since the end of the nineties, the copyleft movement has been growing spectacularly.' According to Zapata, the causes of this could be

> The interaction between the Internet and the street, the so-called *hacklabs* (laboratories experimenting with new technologies to serve political ends), the existence of a critical mass of publishing and cultural projects, along with a critical mass of lawmakers producing legislation, as well as a population willing to break the monopoly of that content production (mainly for television) by constantly sharing in a never-ending cycle. (146)

Padilla concurs by noting the importance, since the end of the nineties, of the Social Centers of the autonomous squatter tradition (like the mythic Lavapiés 'Laboratory' where the digital platform *Sindominio* was created) on the 'militant' side, and of the hacklabs and hackmeetings where those cultures of independent activism converge with the technophile cultures of the geeks. But in addition, Padilla indicates the importance of the proliferation of what she calls other 'politicizations in cyberspace,' which account for the vast preponderance of such activities, like the dynamism of swarming, which spring up in environments like 'fan' cultures or among videogame and film download 'addicts,' when they see their practices being threatened. The anons are a famous case in point. They came from the world of 'fan' cultures and reinvented themselves as Anonymous to fight (in swarms), first against somewhat secondary 'supervillains,' like the Church of Scientology, but later also against the most powerful neoliberal elites.

It is especially interesting to observe how it is the mass, consumerist culture itself that has developed these collaboration logics which, up to a point, undermine their individualistic, instrumentalizing foundations. Henry Jenkins (2006) calls attention to the unexpected effects of the proliferation of interaction among NTICs, which one would expect to lead to more personalized consumption. In other words, each individual could choose from among a much greater supply and thus come up with a completely unique path through the world of mass entertainment, information, and communication available through the multiple screens and formats at his or her disposal. However, what has happened instead is that the individual facing this intermedia culture has mostly met up with other individuals who also inhabit that universe of screens, and begun to interact with them.

Michel de Certeau (2010) had already warned against prejudices occasionally based on readings of the great critics of mass culture like Adorno and Horkheimer, which tend to view the consumer as an isolated, passive individual. For de Certeau (who wrote at the start of the explosion of the 'digital age'), consumption is a secondary form of production that doesn't actually produce products of its own; rather, it is manifested through the *ways of using* the products imposed by a dominant economic system. In those ways of using, thousands of tactics are condensed to form an entire informal substrate of collective meaning production, which he called 'practices of daily life.' With the appearance of the intermedia world, all that richness of life finds new channels and, in fact, increases its ability to appropriate the products launched by consumer society.

Jenkins gives a few examples from the entertainment culture, such as the 'spoiler' communities online. One of most notable examples is that of trying to discover what really happened during the taping of the North American television reality show/contest *Survivor*, before it was aired. This effort mobilized all kinds of investigative resources, from satellite cameras to workers and local inhabitants actually trying to infiltrate the filming zones, and included analysis of images aired during previous editions to try to guess routes, and so on. The interesting thing is that this type of collective effort, says Jenkins, is not always dedicated to such banal causes. The same logics of collective investigation were activated, for example, when a series of American bloggers joined forces to send impartial reporters to Iraq, with the aim of getting to the bottom of the scandal over the tortures in Abu Ghraib prison.

Consumption in the intermedia era is no longer conceived as an individual activity, but a group one. This gives rise to enormous communities, with much broader and more complex spheres of human relations than ever before. Although they develop around commercialized consumption and entertainment culture, these communities are often able to come up with their own objectives that can clash head-on with those that states and media conglomerates try to set. Pierre Lévy (1999) viewed these communities in terms of 'collective intelligence,' and described them as groups in which everybody knows something they are willing to share, but nobody knows everything the community (as a whole) knows. Lara (2013), in another revealing article about these matters, uses the concept of 'prosumers' to synthesize the most important characteristics of this type of 'active public':

> In Fordism, the consumer delegated to production the definition of his or her necessities in exchange for the possibility of accessing standardized products at a limited cost. But the dissemination of new technologies of formal production (flexible automation) and of communication (telematic networks) has prefigured new organizational forms for the relationship between producer and consumer based on the principle of interaction. However, the transformation has included a still more pronounced change, which has been defined by a transition *from the interaction to the integration* of both spheres, production and consumption, even generating a form of hybridization that has given rise to the phenomenon of the *prosumer*. (16)

Mapping the increasingly varied practices of prosumers and online collaborative cultural practices in general that have prospered in recent decades is an extremely complex task. Regarding the question of their sustainability, it seems to me that it is useful to maintain a certain separation between those that emerge in the culture of mass consumption and those that are more consciously inscribed in the tradition of the fight against privatizations and restrictions which the hacker cultures articulate with free software and free culture. Regarding the first type of practice, Lara proposes this useful classification:

> Some of the practices which lead many young people join the participative cultural universe are: *affiliations* (membership, formal and informal, in online communities around various forms of media, like Friendster, Facebook, Myspace, meta-gaming, chat rooms, etc.); *expressions* (producing new creative forms, like digital sampling, writing, audiovisual creation, mash-ups, etc.); *collaborative problem solving* (working together in teams, formal and informal, to solve tasks and develop new knowledge, as in Wikipedia, alternate reality games, 'spoiling,' etc.); and *circulations* (giving form to the media flow through podcasting or blogging, for example). (13)

In the same article, Lara emphasizes the special vulnerability of these practices to exploitation by companies of the so-called Web 2.0. These are companies that have adapted the competitive, privatizing spirit of neoliberalism to the prosumer ecology, creating business models based on exchange and access to information stored 'in the cloud' (data system clouds). This system became hegemonic around 2006, with the explosion of some very familiar businesses that adopted this model: Google, Facebook, Twitter, Flickr, etc. I will return to this danger of commercial, privatizing exploitation of the value collaboratively produced online. For now, I merely want to repeat that in very close proximity to this 'participative cultural universe' of which Lara speaks—sometimes to the point of being indistinguishable from it—could be located an equally participative but more 'militant' one, which is more directly related to the 'culture of online freedom' that tries to defend itself from those forms of privatization of value in Web 2.0.

The paradigm *par excellence* of that free digital culture continues to be free software, and in particular the operating system Linux, closely followed in its capacity for massive social impact by Wikipedia. Both cases have in common the focus on communities of 'produsers,' which Mayo Fuster Morell calls Creative Communities Online (CCOs) (2011). These communities take on the production and self-management of their platforms' cultural content with the expressed desire of defending them from privatizing appropriations. In the wake of these hugely successful collaborative models, a whole constellation of practices can be found related to what has been called the 'Free Culture Movement.' Fuster and Subirats (2012) propose the following categories to catalogue the agents, projects, and processes that comprise it: lawyers specializing in intellectual property, hackers, free software programmers, journalism that uses 'creative commons' licenses, free publishers, pedagogical projects, online creation communities (OCCs), cyberactivism campaigns, 'file sharing' (platforms to share archives), institutional policies, startups, promotion of the 'commons' paradigm, and associations to work with people who don't have access to TICs (15–16).

4.2.3. 'Fansubs,' altruism, and developing unrecognized abilities
I would now like to cite a Spanish example of a type of activity that occurs in the culture of mass consumption, and which doesn't have the 'militant' profile of the free culture. My point is to call attention to forms of online collaborative production of cultural value that can illustrate some of the complex relations between precarization and young people's online collaborative creation of cultural value.

More than a decade ago now, when the phenomenon of new fiction television series was bursting onto the Spanish scene, accompanied by the no less important phenomenon of downloading files through P2P (peer-to-peer) networks (something to which Zapata alludes), a remarkable event took place. One of the reasons why so many people downloaded series episodes was that either the series weren't aired on Spanish television networks or they were aired much later than in America. That was why, when it came to very popular series like *Lost* or *House*, one could typically find an episode already available for download on Spain's most popular P2P networks the day after it aired in the US. But in addition, and this is what's odd, those files were even already subtitled in Spanish, thanks to the generous work of series fans who collectively created the so-called 'fansubs,' in the slang of the Internet.

In 2008, the author of the blog Yonomeaburro ('I don't get bored') interviewed several people who offered this work anonymously. 'We got up at 3 or 4 in the morning,' said somebody known online as Smalleye, 'the time when the episode was usually already online. We downloaded it, and everyone did a part that we had decided on earlier. Then we helped each other figure out problems, and when we had them straightened out, one person joined all the pieces and uploaded them to the web.' This has been going on since 2004, when Smalleye collaborated on subtitling *Lost* for *Lostzilla*, the most important Spanish fan page for the series. Later, Smalleye decided to create a tool that would facilitate this job, and launched the site *Wikisubtitles*. 'If I hadn't invented it, somebody else would have, since it was necessary to improve the workflow of online subtitling,' said the 26-year-old computer scientist. He also said that not only did he not earn any money, he lost it on this website, but he's motivated because 'the spirit of Wikisubtitles is like the spirit of Wikipedia, we all help for nothing, and as long as it's like this, you feel like keeping going. The site exists because of people's goodwill, something that's not very common nowadays.'

Both he and the two other people that were interviewed for Yonomeaburro have college degrees and jobs—although not necessarily ones they want; in other words, they have other things to do besides subtitling, and they say that to be able to do all that 'they lose hours of sleep.' In a more recent article that appeared in *El País*, 'Subtítulos por amor al arte' (Marcos 2012), the same subject was presented, giving testimonies of people with very similar profiles, who also referenced altruistic feelings to explain their motivation.

But along with these feelings, it's important to emphasize that often in these cases references are made to the satisfaction of a job well done. Marga of the Asia-Team website (Yonomeaburro 2008a) reported that what kept her going was 'seeing that a good subtitle, or a not too bad subtitle, is well received,' and that she started because she thought 'that people had a right to see the series downloaded from P2P systems with good subtitles. I don't think that because something's free it has to be low quality.' It would seem, then, that there's a fuzzy line between the narrative of altruism ('I do it without expecting anything in return') and the narrative of a job well done ('I do it because I like to do things well'). 'Some of the subtitles I downloaded weren't very good, and I thought I could help make them better and "give back" for everything I'd received,' says another computer scientist who collaborates with Subtítulos.es.

Replacing bad subtitles with well-done ones, but also practicing languages, solving programming problems, meeting people from around the world, and even acquiring a knowledge of history or a better understanding of the characters of the series are some of the activities these people see as related to their work as subtitlers, and in which various fundamental abilities are undoubtedly put into play (linguistic, social, epistemic, aesthetic, etc.). The importance of cultivating these abilities as an element (sometimes unconscious) of their motivation complicates the reading of this type of online phenomenon in purely 'altruistic' terms. It is not only the individual desire to do something unusual for others that's in play here, but also a series of technological mechanisms and informally instituted practices that favor the cultivation of individual abilities in service to the creation of collective value.

This is a key question that concerns not only the fansub phenomenon, but the entire Internet. It is the same decentralized political architecture Padilla spoke of that favors the possibility of collectively producing value by exercising abilities that, in the realm of a job market destabilized by neoliberalism, often are not considered pay-worthy skills.

Bollier (2008) has called this 'the great value shift.' According to him, around 2003, when fast connections became widespread and the Internet reached 600 million users, the beginning of a radical change took place in how value was produced and distributed online. A type of wealth appeared that is no longer necessarily private, nor does it translate into money: 'On the Internet, wealth is not just financial wealth, nor is it necessarily privately held. Wealth generated through open platforms is often socially created value that is shared, evolving, and nonmonetized. It hovers in the air, so to speak, accessible to everyone' (126).

There are problems with this idea that the wealth produced online remains 'in the air,' which I will return to later. However, I will say now that the danger here is twofold. On one hand, it's easy to forget that the collective wealth of the Internet is only possible thanks to all those other people who make possible the existence of the hardware and the conditions of life necessary for some people to be able to spend time online. On the other hand, there's the danger of underestimating the enormous capacity of the monetary, capitalist economy to reappropriate that public wealth 'accessible to anyone' online, and make it private. But even with all these problems, it seems to me that there is something fundamentally important in what Bollier proposes. Most certainly, to an extent that should not be too easily dismissed, the Internet has facilitated the creation of the type of wealth that, to say the least, exceeds the (individual, privatizing, competitive) logic of what David Harvey calls 'the community of money,' because it has made accessible mechanisms of value creation that are alternative to the system of valorizing social wealth constituted by money in the capitalist system.

Truly, it seems that cases like those of the people who get up at four in the morning to translate subtitles without getting paid for it are good examples of that capacity to create value. The hypothesis I propose, no matter how impossible it may be to verify completely, is that the lack of recognition of many people's basic human capacities, especially young people's, during the precarization of the job market associated with neoliberalism, has been a fundamental incentive for that collective creation of nonmonetarized value. In the face of the ever-greater difficulty of translating their abilities into money, these people throw themselves into the search for other ways to produce, use, and recognize value that do not necessarily go through the market economy, and they find the Internet to be the most appropriate space for it.

Perhaps, after all this, we are in a better position to understand why so many people found time to be following Twitter on that workaday Thursday morning when Minister Sinde met with 14 'notable internauts.' Perhaps now we are also in a better position to understand why many perceived the minister's actions as a frontal attack on a space where, no matter how precariously, amateurishly, and sometimes unsustainably, their abilities had finally managed to contribute to something valuable.

By following the thread of the defense of that space of shared value creation, perhaps it will be possible to explore a little further what that creation of shared value consisted of, and how it kept getting stronger in keeping with the necessity to defend it, besides sometimes allowing the wise advice of John Locke to be read in Spanish. I am not referring to the philosopher—whose work will also be relevant here—but to the character from *Lost*.

4.3. The Pleasure of Doing, and Telling What One Does: Self-Representation of Internet Cultures

4.3.1. Choosing a culture of collaborative practices

In a survey comprising part of an excellent study carried out by Martínez, Fuster, and others (2013) about collaborative audiovisual projects developed online—called 'audiovisual commons'—many of the participants declared that they didn't expect any economic repayment for their participation in these projects, and that their main motivation was 'the pleasure of doing it' (86%). The second most frequently mentioned motivation was 'recognition'

(76%), and the third, the 'experience' (72%), perhaps ambiguous elements as far as their possible 'utilitarian' underpinnings. This utilitarian aspect can be plainly seen in the minority who declared that 'entry into the job market' (29%) was the goal they pursued with their unpaid online activity. The most typical response to such results would probably be to class the first type of motivation as 'altruism' and the rest as 'utilitarianism.' It seems to me, however, that doing so runs the risk of making invisible the other type of value creation that Bollier speaks of: a collective value, not necessarily privatizable, not necessarily monetarizable.

The philosopher George Caffentzis (2013) explains that, given the growing pressure on the economics field to stop ignoring activities that generate wealth not translatable into money, one of the great answers offered has been the 'rational choice theory.' This theory compares all human conduct to a monetary commercial transaction, in which the protagonist is an individual—a 'rational agent'—who calculates the costs of his actions to obtain as much satisfaction as he can:

> A 'rational agent' would treat all the alternatives 'as if' they were commodities with a price attached, calculated by how much time and money it would take (for instance) to bring up a child, or spend an evening with one's lover, where the value of one's time is measured by the amount of money one could earn in the formal labor market in same time period. (261)

Contrary to what one might tend to think—and as César Rendueles explained very well in *Sociofobia*—belief in altruism does not deny this theory, at least not completely. The theory continues to operate from one of its fundamental assumptions: that human existence can be explained based on the instrumental actions of isolated individuals. If we start from the consideration of human existence as something that basically consists of the decisions of individuals who choose between maximizing their actions or being generous and doing something for others, we are trapped in an individualistic worldview that neglects two facts that seem quite evident. First, human life is always interdependent (being an individual is only a 'moment' in being human); and second, above all else we need to look to our own survival, implementing mechanisms of reproduction for the social conditions necessary for this survival.[10]

---

10 This is how Judith Butler explains it in *Frames of War*: 'There is no life without the conditions of life that variably sustain life, and those conditions are pervasively social, establishing not the discrete ontology of the person, but rather the interdependency of persons, involving reproducible and sustaining social

The feminist tradition has been one of the richest spaces in recent decades for the recuperation of these two basic facts displacing the individualist perspective and, consequently, the theory of rational choice. As noted in the first chapter, researchers of feminist economics like Antonella Picchio (2009) have analyzed the blindness of the economics field, which is heir to 'neoclassicism' with respect to these issues—and these issues escape its narrow concept of humanity. Caffentzis indicates that it was the Marxist feminist tradition in the seventies that was truly able to theorize in all its complexity the problem of the existence of forms of social wealth, value creation, and nonwage-earning work outside the circles of the formal capitalist economy—the problem the rational choice theory tried to solve by turning all of human existence into a kind of capitalist market. And the Marxist feminist tradition could carry this off because it recuperated the question of classical economics, especially Marx's but also Adam Smith's and others, about 'social reproduction.' That is, it looked at how society not only creates new wealth, but also maintains itself, subsists, 're-produces' itself (in Marxist terms, the specific question was how to reproduce a labor force capable of producing value).

More recently, thinkers like Judith Butler (2010; 2011) or, in Spain, Marina Garcés (2013), Amaia Pérez Orozco (2014), and Silvia L. Gil (2011), have offered a worldview that would reread the question of classical economics in these terms: if society needs above all to be reproduced, it's because human life is interdependent and needs constant care to survive. Before 'production,' before 'rational' decisions of individuals who want to maximize their interests or be generous with others, there is always—tacitly or explicitly—the establishment of conditions that will make possible the continuation of one's own life. This is what Picchio calls 'living, like a daily process of reproduction of bodies, identities, and relationships.'

It is especially important to emphasize that these 'identities and relationships' are a fundamental part of what needs to be reproduced, as much as the bodies. Human life is never mere biological subsistence, it is always determined culturally, and understood and characterized linguistically. It doesn't exist as an absolute fact, life is always socially thought, valued, felt. That's why an offshoot of Picchio's arguments is that in the process of the social reproduction of life there are always in play implicit or explicit conceptions of what is a life worthy of being reproduced. Or, as she says, what 'quality of life' must specifically consist of, 'quality of life' generically defined as 'a state of well-being of individuals, men and women,

relations to the environment and to non-human forms of life, broadly considered' (2010, 19) characterized by a set of abilities to do, to be, and to operate individually and collectively in a social space' (29).

Let's return now to that answer the majority of the survey respondents in the study on 'audiovisual commons' gave about their motivations: 'the pleasure of doing it.' Of course, the way the idea is expressed already invites a reading in terms of rational choice theory, or at least from one of the variants of an individualistic worldview: the individual seeks not only money; she also seeks pleasure or recognition, and that causes her to participate in collaborative projects online. However, why can't we understand that 'pleasure of doing it' as one of those tacit answers to the question of a worthy, decent life that is constantly raised in the 'daily process of reproducing bodies, identities and relationships' that constitutes living? In that case, we might think that saying 'I do it for the pleasure of doing it' was equivalent to saying something like, 'Instead of giving my abilities and energies to a job market that subjects them to the market's ways of creating value, I choose to give them to another space of identities and relationships, the online collaborative cultures where projects are supported without having to go through money, private property, or competition among individuals.' The pleasure of doing *that*. Because doing is never only doing, but also reproducing certain 'ways of doing,' 'systems of value creation,' 'models of a life with dignity,' or maybe simply '*cultures*,' at the same time as rejecting others.

4.3.2. Beyond utilitarianism vs. altruism: Identifying practices

If we view the cooperative, unpaid work done online in this light, we escape the (false) dilemma between altruism and utilitarianism. Because then it is no longer (only) about a job that an individual chooses to do, but about activities that contribute to creating necessary infrastructures for a type of collective reproduction of relations and identities based on collaboration, and not on competition among individuals. It is undoubtedly risky to contend that online collaborative work constitutes such a thing: a mechanism or system for reproducing relationships and identities (and even bodies, since culture is inseparable from them). Especially since that would make it comparable to the immense, omnipresent machinery of social reproduction that is the capitalist system. But why can't we accept that it is comparable, even on a much smaller yet still significant scale?

Emmanuel Rodríguez claims that cyberspace has given the world three fundamental cultural dimensions (which he considers potentially democratizing): a system for mass self-organization, a sphere of 'postmedia' communication (independent of the influence of big media and capable of squaring off with them), and a much broader and faster environment of rich daily sociability 'among peers' than others that have historically fed social movements, like the factory or the city. Much has been said about the first two (for example in the well-known works of the sociologist Manuel Castells) and I will keep them in mind here also, but it seems to me that the third is perhaps the most important. Rodríguez certainly thinks so:

> The Internet and [social] networks are today an existential territory founded on exchange among peers; a much broader social medium has been created that operates at a much faster speed than previous socialization spaces, like the factory for the labor movement, or the city for earlier democratic movements. In this sense, it has recuperated for the present the prior functions of those spaces, simultaneously public and private, where contact becomes routine and daily, where affection accompanies messages, and where the circulation of ideas, projects, and alternatives becomes possible again. And this, even when their scent is neither that of industrial oil nor of the sweat of bodies. (207)

In the face of this affirmation of the *existential* importance of networks, perhaps the most recurrent objection comes, very eloquently, from Rendueles: 'Often the production of free content online is parasitic, in the sense that it depends on the existence of other sources of support and free time. As the joke goes, the best way to make money with free software is to work as a waiter' (107).

Perhaps the problem with this type of objection is that it still takes too narrow a view of the meaning of 'sustenance' for human life. As Picchio says, there is no support for life if there is not also at the same time support for the culture that elucidates what constitutes a life worth living. Cultural life and biological life are inseparable parts of human life. So if the Internet is capable of contributing to the reproduction of a culture based on sharing without the need for money, no matter how often the bodies that maintain that culture also need to participate in the system of capitalist reproduction, then that online culture of sharing is in itself a remarkable 'source of support,' or at least of 'cultural support' (and the cultural is, according to Rodríguez, *existential*), as an alternative to the hegemonic support system for capitalist life (which, of course, is increasingly revealed as unsustainable in so many ways).

From there it becomes a question of degree since, naturally, the same could be said of many other social spaces that contribute in some measure to 'supporting' cooperative cultures that slow down the neoliberal commercialization of life to some degree. In that sense, Rendueles criticizes the excessive attention paid to the Internet while many offline cooperative work projects, like those of the Mondragón Corporation (for one well-known example), are ignored.

But to compare different cooperative cultures, again, it isn't enough to say that some provide their members with money to pay the bills and others only provide good intentions. The power of spaces like the Mondragón cooperative is that their workers receive money without having to go through all the unfair logics of the capitalist social reproduction system. But the power of the cultures of online sharing is to call attention to the possibility of and the need for alternative spaces to reproduction systems based on competition, scarcity, and the privatization of wealth. It seems to me that neither of these two powers should be underestimated, and the specific nature of both should be studied.

So when Rendueles says that the problem with the cultures of online sharing is that they don't guarantee any commitment, that they are not sufficiently 'normative,' it seems to me that something important is lost in the argument. 'If I systematically sabotage the conversations in a forum [on the web], the worst than can happen to me is that they kick me out' (107). But, first, what if it is, for example, a forum like *Spaniards.es*, where very precise, up-to-date information is shared about matters that affect the emigration of Spaniards to other countries? And suppose, as the last person to post in that forum at the very same time I am writing, you have two children, you are a heavy machine operator, you are on the verge of emigrating to Norway, and you need very specific information that will affect the viability of your family's emigration, and you need it as soon as possible? Perhaps we were a little hasty in underestimating the sometimes less than evident connections between the cultures of online sharing and the survival of those who use them.

Mainly because, second, we undervalue the cultural importance of social relationships and identities for survival. A life without human relationships and the construction of meaning is not a human life. Rendueles reminds us that in addition to 'instrumental behavior,' which is the only type considered by rational choice theory, there is 'normative behavior,' 'which is based on shared rules' (97). But it seems to me that the things that guarantee that human life has meaning are not just 'norms,' beyond individual instrumental decisions. They are, on an even more basic level, all those practices through which human life takes on some identity—and therefore some meaning—through exchanges in the bosom of groups (empirical or abstract). Or what Pablo Sánchez León and Jesús Izquierdo (2003), borrowing from the work of the sociologist Alessandro Pizzorno, call 'identifying practices':

[N]umerous social activities function as identifying practices for the members of different groups constituting the social fabric: the casuistry of these activities is enormous, ranging from reciprocal exchanges of material and symbolic goods to communicative interactions using particular languages or meanings. Each one of these presupposes a community that grants them value. Integrity in the subjects' time depends on these practices, because they assure group cohesion, and with it the 'circles of recognition' in which moral criteria embody what individuals use to construct their identity. (80)

These identifying practices are the flow of construction of collective meaning that sometimes becomes cemented into explicit or implicit social norms, but that always comes back to 'values or groups' with which the subjects that use them express identification. For this reason, an evident condition of possibility for these practices is the visibility of those 'values' or 'groups,' since that visibility is sometimes essential for their ability to *matter* to the subjects.

In the case of cultures of online sharing, the struggles against the Sinde Law constituted a defining moment in the creation of that visibility. This happened as a kind of self-discovery as a group by those who were giving more and more time and energy to online sharing practices that 'had no name,' so to speak, for those who practiced them (or at least, they didn't have as powerful a shared identity as they would later achieve). From those struggles arose, above all, a characterization of what was rejected (the law itself and the restrictive conception of the Internet and the culture that inspired it), but also a rich, proud (though also often contradictory) perception of what was being defended.

4.3.3. 'The dinner of fear': Dignifying Internet users

For the construction of that positive self-perception, the debates around the 'Manifiesto en defensa de los derechos fundamentales en Internet' were very important. But perhaps even more so were those unleashed by a post by activist, researcher, and editor Amador Fernández-Savater, called 'La cena del miedo' (The Dinner of Fear) published January 11, 2011 (2011c) on the blog of his publishing house, Acuarela Libros. The text included essential fragments for the self-representation of the rising online culture in the Spanish state, among them:

> [T]he idea that stereotypes try to impose on us is the following: if I hang out with my girlfriend at the movies on a Sunday afternoon watching any film at all, I'm putting a value on culture because I paid. And if I spend two weeks translating and subtitling my favorite TV series to share it on the web, I'm nothing more than a despicable

parasitic consumer who is sinking the culture. Incredible, right? Well, the Internet is made up of a million of those altruistic gestures. And thousands of people (for example, cultural workers pressured by precarization) routinely download material from the web because they want to do something with all of it: to know and to nurture themselves to [be able to] create. It is precisely this active, creative tension that moves many to seek and to exchange. Think about it!

Operations like this, of 'dignifying' the identity associated with web users (operations in which it was tacitly debated just what was the 'decent life' that needed to be reproduced) must have contributed to the fact that progressively more and more people felt that something essential about who they were had to do with the Web (and that therefore it was no longer so clear that when somebody was thrown out of an Internet forum, absolutely nothing happened to him). Fernández-Savater himself said in an interview in the newspaper *Público* that he personally tried to explain to Minister Sinde that 'the Web is not only a useful tool for many of us, but a space for life and even an important part of our brain.' Indeed, one only needs to see the explosion of favorable reactions to Fernández-Savater's text to understand how the online culture of sharing was certainly becoming a dense nucleus of 'identifying practices' where many people risked not insignificant pieces of the meaning of their life.

The enormous interest and support the text generated was not due only to its defense of the Internet, it was perhaps even more its ability to create a critical image of those who were attacking the Web. Starting with its poetic title, the text asserted that it was the Web's critics who were scared: 'fear of the Internet,' 'fear of people,' 'fear of the future,' it was saying. But the important thing, I think, was the pragmatics of the text itself, its format of a 'revelation of the elites' secret.' While the 'Manifiesto' continued to adopt some forms that owed much to the tradition of the cultural elites, and which fit poorly with the decentralized Internet culture, 'La cena del miedo' looked, as Padilla indicated, like a text from 'just anyone' who had infiltrated enemy lines and shared with other 'anyones' the information obtained from the powers that be.

The story is well known, and Fernández-Savater told it all in the text itself: he had received a surprise invitation to a dinner meeting arranged by Minister Sinde to talk about the Internet. When he got there, he discovered he was the only attendee in favor of free culture, surrounded by a cast of 'culture professionals' and defenders of 'intellectual property.' These included some very well-known names in the public sphere: Álex de la Iglesia, Antonio Muñoz Molina, Elvira Lindo, Alberto García Álix, Ouka Leele,

Luis Gordillo, Juan Diego Botto, and Manuel Gutiérrez Aragón. Perhaps the most impressive thing about Fernández-Savater's text was the way it exposed with critical clarity not only the opinions but also the attitudes of these well-known people who had prestige in the cultural world. Even more so because in doing it, he broke the secrecy that usually surrounds this type of gathering of 'important' people.

It was shocking to learn that somebody at the meeting (Fernández-Savater did not attribute words to specific people) had praised the United States' repressive Internet policies by saying, 'That's it, at least you need to make people afraid.' It was shocking that another of these figures complained bitterly that 'People use my photos for their Facebook profiles!' And it was shocking that, in general, Internet users were referred to as 'those irresponsible consumers who want everything for free' and 'those selfish, willful people who don't know the value of a job or the effort that goes into it.' Fernández-Savater sprinkled his report with these quotes to illustrate his assertions about the ignorance and fear that characterized the position of his dinner companions. 'It seems a very serious fact,' he concluded, 'that those who must legislate on the Internet should not know it or appreciate it for what it really is, that they should fear it. They don't understand it technically, legally, culturally, or subjectively. In any way.' The power of this assertion was multiplied by the fact that it was based on an observation of a 'they' from much closer than is normally possible for most people.

Time and time again, in the 461 comments on the original post, in the 135 that appeared on the shared news site Menéame, and in many other places online, people who read the text referred to the matter of excessive secrecy: 'These meetings really are the kind they don't invite the press to.' 'Thanks, Amador, for telling us what happens in those high circles and what they try to hide.' '[It's] a pleasure that you share conversations, that you infiltrate the secrets, and that you let us see what's cooking.' 'It seems that the Minister of Culture is so inept that she doesn't even realize she invited somebody from the Copyleft world to a discreet meeting.' 'I doubt they'll ever invite you back, knowing that afterwards you'll "air" what happened there,' etc.

The abundance of comments, on the other hand, shows that, again, we're not dealing with a simple text written by a single author, but rather with a collective process of thought and action initiated, to be sure, by a written contribution. Fernández-Savater was very careful, besides, to present his report not as the text of a cultural authority but, again, as a text by 'anyone.' He uses colloquial language, presenting himself as a 'small publisher' who has nothing to do with those famous ones, and showing his own vulnerability ('I wasn't what you'd call a conversational shining star'). He even includes references to mass culture, like the film *Downfall*, which helped him create an image of the minister and her fellow dinner guests locked up in bunker, 'raving about inapplicable plans to win the war.'

But in addition, people would soon make his text their own, responding to the thread with other articles and infinite debates, extracting fragments and phrases. (One of the favorites was, 'what we have here is an elite that is losing the monopoly of the word and of the formation of reality,' which alludes to the CT hypothesis.) Web users even came up with initiatives like the creation of offline meetings (called 'Dinners against Fear') to discuss the subject in several cities.

The text became a fundamental weapon in the struggle to defend the Internet, and huge numbers of 'technopolitical' actions proliferated around it. Technopolitics is, according to the research group DatAnalysis15M (2013), 'the tactical, strategic use of technological devices (including social networks) for organization, communication, and collective action.' This research group has studied in great detail some of those technopolitical tactics and strategies that drove the cycle, from the first struggles against the Sinde Law to the irruption of the 15M movement (cyberactivism campaigns, collective learning on how to use digital tools, connections between the Web and protests in the street, etc.). Somewhat more difficult to decode, but no less important, are the often unconscious processes of subjectification— understood as the cultural configuration of identity and ways of life—that accompanied those other processes. Moments like the 'dinner of fear' seem especially important in terms of the configuration of a 'we,' no matter how contradictory, diffuse, and still embryonic, that will serve as one of those arrays of meaning that allow the development of 'identifying practices' around Web cultures.

Synthesizing greatly, and at the risk of simplifying, we could say that the 'Manifiesto' suggested a plural 'we' made up of Internet users demanding their 'fundamental rights,' using the legalistic language of the very institutions they questioned. 'La cena del miedo,' then, proposes that this same 'we' is also made up of the 'thousands of altruistic gestures on the web'; in other words, the 'we' of a culture of sharing that confronts a 'they' of cultural and political elites characterized by fear and ignorance.

As these identification arrays become stronger, they will keep forming more solid alternatives to the hegemonic forms of producing and reproducing cultural value associated with capitalism, the power of the experts, and individualistic consumerism. But that doesn't mean there aren't important overlaps between those different ways of articulating what a life worth reproducing is. The emergence of the cultures of online sharing, or at least of the defense of Internet freedom, like recognizable spheres self-represented by those who identify with them, is in no way the 'pure' emergence of something completely new in the cultural panorama of a neoliberal Spain in crisis. Nor will their evolution move these cultures towards a clearer (self-)definition, but it will maintain their contradictory plurality, and may even exacerbate it, in mixing them with other 'we's,' as more and more subjects try to flee from a 'them' no less hybrid than themselves, who identify with the 'Establishment' that has brought the country to this hard economic crisis.

4.4. Two Overlapping yet Clashing Value Systems

4.4.1. 'Don't vote for them': Between liberal politics and collaborative cultures

The next, perhaps more significant, moment in the fight against the Sinde Law, the so-called cybercampaign 'No les votes,' is a good example of the hybrid and contradictory nature that continued to develop in those moments of the increasingly mass culture of the Web.

Let's recall the history: the 'dinner of fear' took place on January 10, 2011. At the end of that same month, the PSOE managed to reintroduce the Sinde Law in the Senate, thanks to the Partido Popular's support. The PP had previously opposed it, causing its rejection in the Congress. The tension among the Web's defenders increased, in part because the previous month *El País* had published revelations obtained by WikiLeaks that showed direct pressure exerted by the American government on its Spanish counterpart regarding downloading from the Internet.

So the moment when the PP changed their mind and decided to support the Sinde Law resonated with secret reports that had been leaked about their 'unofficial' position towards this law. For instance, there was one in which the American ambassador himself, Alan D. Solomont, declared, after meeting with Mariano Rajoy: 'On Intellectual Property Rights, we understood Rajoy's message to be that although the PP understands the necessity for Spain to do more, he is going to extract every political benefit from the debate that he can' (*El País* and WikiLeaks 2010a). In similar terms, another, earlier, American embassy dispatch, written soon after the PSOE's arrival in office, stated, 'Given the number of stars in the entertainment industry with a clear preference for the socialist government, it is possible that this government is especially sensitive to doing something in this sector' (*El País* and WikiLeaks 2010b).

The agitation against the Sinde Law, and against the whole world of secret meetings and dark strategies that seemed to surround it, would be channeled in February 2011 into the creation of the 'No les votes' campaign. This initially appeared to be an invitation to refuse to vote in the municipal elections, to be held in May, for the parties (all the majority ones) that had supported the Sinde Law, which had finally also been approved in the Congress.

But something else extremely important was happening. On March 30, following the trend revealed by the debates about the campaign, the project's initiators decided to change the manifesto ('NoLesVotes.com' 2011) that appeared on its main page, and to remove all references to the Sinde Law, now putting all emphasis on the problems of endemic corruption plaguing the Spanish political system. What was, in principle, a 'sectorial' fight related to a specific legal matter (regulating Internet use) thus became a huge challenge to what the manifesto defined as 'the corruption at the very foundation of the system.'

In the new text, this corruption was attributed to a series of institutional and social problems: the perpetual alternation of 'political organizations grasping at power for decades,' the lack of mechanisms for 'active participation of the citizenry,' a voting law that had been 'jury-rigged to favor the major parties by excessively handicapping minority representation,' and, perhaps even more incisively, a 'party-tocracy' that internally imposed a hierarchical discipline within each political organization and which externally made decisions according to 'pressure groups that only represent the interests of economically powerful or media minorities.' It was, therefore, a turn towards that type of 'crisis of the system' narrative I talked about at the beginning of the first chapter, which was characterized by bringing up the need for drastic changes. Changes that, once again, would not mean merely a change of actors participating in that social and political game that is 'the system,' but a profound transformation of its own 'rules of the game.'

However, since it couldn't be any other way, the action-oriented part of this new 'No les votes' manifesto was left with the difficult task of translating that anger with 'the corruption at the very foundations of the system' into concrete suggestions for action. This consequently included having to enter the thorny terrain of explaining what, exactly, that 'corrupt system' consisted of, and what parts of it could and could not be saved to be able to transform its corruption. In fact, the manifesto suggested a specific measure that for many may well have sounded like a clear acceptance of one of the prime rules of the very system that was being condemned. They encouraged the exercising of what was, according to the manifesto, 'our primary democratic right: the vote.'

Of course, reducing the proactive dimension of 'No les votes' as a political platform to this phrase would be a terrible simplification. Even at the level of explicit language, besides requesting a vote of conscience, it also inspired an involvement in 'the network of fed-up citizens who think that improving the situation is in our hands.' But perhaps even more importantly, it is necessary to consider not only language but also the sphere of practices, because again, we are not simply dealing with a manifesto here, but with a text that opened the door to the creation not only of broad debates in this case, but of a whole movement. At the moment the second version of the manifesto appeared, this movement had already generated more than 700,000 unique users on its main page—shared some 7,800 times on Twitter and more than 36,000 times on Facebook—and above all, had inspired an active, diverse wiki (a website made by users) with 143 pages, 196 stored files, and 374 registered users. This movement, moreover, would shortly be mixed with others springing from diverse platforms, among them, significantly, 'Democracia Real Ya!' It would come together in the demonstrations that gave birth to the 15M movement, considered by many to be the most important political event to happen in the Spanish state since the transition to democracy.

As I noted earlier, the technopolitical dimensions of these connection processes and the viral growth of protests online that would later take to the streets in May 2011 have already been investigated carefully and exhaustively by others. But what I want to do here is delve into the different traditions and mechanisms of creation and support of material and cultural value that were latent in them, and that often clashed with each other, producing contradictions, or at least constant tensions. So when 'No les votes' proposes simultaneously that, on one hand, the voting law, the parties, and the existing mechanisms of political participation are all insufficient, and on the other, that the most important political measure is still the vote, this would seem to be a manifestation of one of these tensions. In fact, it was perhaps the most crucial tension, which would remain present during the whole course of the 15M and its later mutations. This is the tension that arises between the liberal political tradition and its way of understanding value—individual, private, convertible into money or at least into some type of instrumental 'profit'—and the large outskirts of that 'modern' Western hegemonic tradition, made up of cultures in which value is understood as something that is always produced and enjoyed from relationships of interdependence, of which the individual, the private, and the quantification of wealth can only be derived, secondary moments.[11]

11 David Graeber has compiled quite a number of anthropological studies that show ways of life very different from the liberal organization of value around private property, the individual, and monetarization. For instance, he speaks of the existence of societies that use a kind of 'primitive money'; he calls them 'human economies' (as opposed to 'market economies'). This 'primitive money' served to organize and maintain relations between people, not to sell or buy people or objects—it wasn't about accumulating wealth, but about making arrangements

This tension began to make itself strongly felt as soon as the taboo surrounding the notion of 'democracy' in the Spanish state ceased to be accepted. In that sense, the 'No les votes' campaign and later 'Democracia Real Ya!' constitute fundamental references for introducing a massive questioning of institutions that tacitly tended to identify with democracy itself, so that judging them was almost considered an assassination attempt against that very system.

4.4.2. 'National sovereignty' vs. 'passion for the common': Two concepts of democracy

Rodríguez clearly explains how problematic such an identification becomes when these institutions are analyzed from a historical perspective. Thus, as he indicates in his book *Hipótesis Democracia*, the belief that the only possible democracy is one, like the Spanish state, based on the principle of representation by 'popular sovereignty' (instead of self-government), and on political parties and parliament as mechanisms for exercising that representation, implies deliberately ignoring the actual history of political institutions.

It is necessary to understand, he continues, that the type of representation politicians exercise in the system of liberal democracies like Spain is not the only one to have existed, nor is it the best fit to the etymological definition of democracy (government by the population, government by the people). In this sense it must be seen that the representation exercised by elected political officials in Spain (and in liberal democracies in general) is not by any means a representation of its voters like that exercised by a mere spokesman, or a 'chief executive,' but something much more complicated and with less than democratic roots:

> The chief executive responds to his 'superiors,' he must be revocable and subject to the decisions of the assemblies that have granted him his 'mandate.' On the other hand, the representative is much more than 'the representative of his voters.' First, and above all, he is representative of something much more abstract and difficult to comprehend, something that in the French Revolution took the name 'national sovereignty.' Sovereignty is, throughout the whole liberal tradition all the way up to the present, a transcendent authority inherited from the monarch's powers. That's why sovereignty, even when it resides in the citizens, is understood as unique, indivisible, inalienable, the result as much of

between people (marriages, treaties, solving crimes and disputes, gaining followers, etc.) (2011, 130).

the formation of a 'general will' as an expression of a 'general interest.' In short, it is the incarnation and legitimation of the state's powers over society, to which it only responds through 'sovereignty.' This explains why 'representatives' are legally invested with such a show of pomp, ceremony, and dignity that seems excessive to their condition as mere chief executives. (Rodríguez 216)

When, as in 'No les votes,' it is continually declared that the vote is 'our primary democratic right,' a tradition is assumed—or at least it is not being questioned directly—in which voting means choosing this type of *sovereign* representative. Nevertheless, when the same manifesto alludes to 'party-tocracy' and the need for greater mechanisms of 'civic participation,' it is moving more in the direction of other democratic traditions distinct from liberalism, for example, Athenian democracy. The latter, notes Rodríguez, is more in agreement with two principles that can be considered essential for the existence of something that could be called 'democracy' from a critical, well-informed perspective on the history of political institutions: on one hand, the existence of the conditions of equality necessary for anyone's participation in explicit power, and on the other, the existence of a truly common public sphere (and not just one of 'representatives') in which that participation can be exercised.

That truly common sphere, he asserts, is more than a mere aggregate of individuals, as liberal tradition would have it. Rather, it is a 'social body able to maintain its passion for the common.' The idea of 'popular sovereignty' (in itself an inheritance from monarchical absolutism) used by liberal democracies is founded on a supposed pact between individuals who would decide to transfer their 'sovereignty' to their representatives. But democracies like the Athenian (or those of the experiments of working-class democracy carried out in the Paris Commune, the Soviets, or the collectivities of the Spanish Revolution of '36), don't view society as an aggregate of individuals that possess a 'sovereignty' *per se* that they could transfer by mutual agreement. Rather, they are a 'social body' of interdependent individuals who, in the proper and necessary management of that interdependence, already exercise direct self-government. They have no need, says Rodríguez, 'to invoke laws that transcend the social body' (217).

In that sense, it seems to me, what is behind these different models of democracy is, once again, the difference between the liberal cosmovision that views society as an aggregate of individuals who have decided to be associated (who have decided to accept a 'social contract'), and the (premodern, communitary, etc.) worldviews that conceive of society as a weave of interdependent relationships without which individuals would not exist, beyond their personal decisions, and which therefore it is necessary to reproduce for human survival. The interesting thing is that, even though individualistic language often speaks of liberalism, the tradition of collaborative online cultures has developed certain practices that, in a sense, are more attuned to a nonliberal worldview: they place more value on the reproduction of interdependent relationships that generate collective goods than on the production of private goods for supposedly independent individuals (or, rather, individuals who hide their relations of interdependence behind a veil of monetary quantification of their valuables).

In this regard, the tensions that surround the recognition of democracy as a political system in the online environment always involve other background tensions that concern the different ways of understanding, anthropologically, the relationships between individual, work (value creation), and property. It is here that we need to remember that other John Locke, the one who did not appear in *Lost*. As is well known, it was this philosopher who originated the famous theory about private property understood as the result of individual work with the resources of the earth. For Locke, property is individual because it is the fruit of individual work that transforms the earth, producing a value that can later be quantified in the market to enable its exchange.

However, what more and more people online experience daily is that work (or the creation of value) is never, in fact, purely individual. Furthermore, valuables tend to stop being valuable when they are privatized and quantified in the market. In other words, the experience of collective, open online work can easily lead to the realization that, as David Harvey says in *Rebel Cities*, the capitalist system, in converting everything into goods exchangeable for money, privatizes the greatest good humanity has at its disposal: its own, always necessarily collective work.

Much has been written on the 'hacker ethic,' on the new forms of sociability enabled by the Internet and NTICs, as well as on the general transformation of the human experience in the 'information era.' But perhaps, with respect to the question of human subsistence and the reproduction of (material and cultural) necessities for it, the most interesting thing about online cultures is that they have recovered the value of something so *un*-novel and so simple as collective work—in fact, a form of collective work in which it is not necessary to collectivize everything, or even to agree on everything, but rather to distribute tasks according to different abilities and come to a 'rough consensus.' Txarlie, the Hacktivistas member quoted earlier, claimed that this type of distributed work is a legacy of the online cultures to the social movements that started springing up in Spain, beginning with the 15M movement. Specifically, he recalled that it was the mythic

'Internet Engineering Task Force,' created in the eighties to standardize online communication protocols, that began using the expression 'rough consensus' to refer to its methodology, in which it wasn't necessary for all the developers to agree on something explicitly for it to be considered acceptable.

The maxim of 'not solving a problem twice,' transparency in everything that's done, decentralization, and, in general, the capacity to do things together without having to be together on everything, are characteristics of the work of free software developers, 'hackers,' and those who customarily ascribe to the 'free culture.' In the historical circumstances of recent decades, and particularly in the recent years of the Spanish economic crisis, these characteristics have been an inspiration and a direct source for a revaluation of collective work, understood in its broadest sense. In other words: understood not just as production of goods, but rather as reproduction of the necessary value for collective subsistence, at least for 'cultural subsistence.'

This revaluation is essential for the practices developed by the cyberactivist campaigns I have been analyzing (the 'Manifiesto,' the 'Cena del miedo,' 'No les votes'), as it will be for the 15M movement. But if this is so, as I have tried to show, it's not just because these political campaigns and movements have used the work distributed online to make things they needed, but because that distributed work was already being experienced in many other social spaces as a way to create value capable of constituting an alternative, no matter how insufficient it might often be, to the hegemonic way of creating value based on liberalist assumptions and capitalist mechanisms of reproduction.

4.4.3. Possibilities for cultural autonomy: Internet vs. school

To what extent, then, can online collective cultural work constitute an alternative to the mechanisms of creation and support of cultural value that reign in a neoliberal society like Spain? In an excellent study, 'Jóvenes y corrientes culturales emergentes [*trends*],' the anthropologist Francisco Cruces (García Canclini et al. 2012) emphasizes that although fundamental class restrictions obviously still exist, which determine which young people will be able to 'be creative' and to 'start a trend,' his fieldwork revealed that 'cultural reproduction (in Pierre Bourdieu's (1990) sense of the ability of dominant groups to perpetuate their distinction through generations) does not seem to take place automatically. There is no direct correlation between economic position and the ability to promote oneself in the new social space.' This could be, says Cruces, because we find ourselves 'in the process of a profound change in the reproduction of symbolic capitals.' And this change would be brought about especially by the appearance of two aspects that seem to escape the established cultural power's logic of reproduction:

> On one hand, a new type of specifically technological capital, which indicates differences in access to and familiarity with using TICs. On the other, the structure of opportunity certain communicative aptitudes offer, like extroversion, easy sociability, and the game of negotiating that characterize current well-known subjects of the Web 2.0. (This would undoubtedly be the case of a successful blogger who introduced herself as 'jack of all trades, master of none,' and was meteorically promoted to host/anchor of the television network Antena 3.) (165)

Perhaps the very framing of Cruces's study within the concept of 'emergent cultural trends'—whose aptness, by the way, he himself questions—causes him to interpret the new value these technological and social abilities produce in terms of 'access and familiarity' or 'notoriety.' But there are two things we must not forget. On one hand, those abilities don't necessarily pre-exist their use online; often they are developed because Internet use encourages them and enables their development. On the other, the value created with those online abilities is not always channeled towards the competitive logics that underpin the hegemonic system of value creation. Given that, often those young people who become proficient online users of technology and highly sociable subjects do not need to be 'promoted' to anything; that is, they don't need the recognition of institutions like a television network to be able to value themselves and to be valued by their peers. In short, they don't need society's 'teachers' to give them a certificate of value, because they share sufficiently rich learning networks to provide them with the cultural abilities they need and want.

Ultimately, if the ways of creating value shared online are often not enough to replace the institutions that manage goods as necessary as food, housing, or healthcare, they *can* be enough to unseat others like museums, big cultural industries, or even schools. Regarding this last possibility, young Mei (her online nickname) is a case in point. She was 19 years old in 2008, when discourse analysts Daniel Cassany and Denise Hernández (2012) interviewed her for their research on the online reading and writing practices of young people. Mei interested them because she was the prototypical young person who was active and creative on the networks:

> She was webmaster of a forum called *Neolite*, where 12 young people wrote, read, and commented on 'stories' and poetry. There she had written fantastic narratives of more than 25 chapters, which her

companions evaluated positively. She also maintained a personal
photolog and a private diary on paper, in addition to chatting online
with friends and surfing her favorite sites. Every day she spent a lot of
time reading and writing online. (127)

But if Mei was chosen as an especially interesting person for Cassany and
Hernandez's study, it was because, in addition to (or in spite of?) developing
such a rich online life, she had failed several subjects in her second year of
a humanities *bachillerato*. She had to repeat a course twice and still never
managed to complete the *bachillerato*. Consequently, she wasn't accepted at
the university, which she considered important.

Cassany and Hernández studied her case thoroughly to reveal the number
of online abilities Mei had developed. They highlight in particular her
writing and reading in three languages (Castilian, Catalan, and English),
which she translates, transcribes, and uses indiscriminately within a single
subject, moving between and among them, and among different registers
depending on her audience. She is also proficient in the use of rhetorical
tools as a result of her facility with narration, theater, comics, and the
ubiquitous SMS language of texting, and in the use of computer programs
that help her in her writing and her role as webmaster. If none of these
abilities seems to have helped her pass subjects like Catalan and Castilian
language classes, Philosophy, Latin, or History of Art, it is, argue Cassany
and Hernández, because she applies them online within a context they call
'vernacular,' under conditions that don't exist in the educational sphere.
Vernacular conditions basically consist of the immersion in 'groups or
informal gangs of friends who act as "communities of practice," where they
teach each other cooperatively and share each other's linguistic resources
online and off' (135).

Faced with the activities of these 'communities of practice,' or cooperative
learning, the school often demonstrates a lack of understanding, if not
disdain. The researchers quote one of Mei's teachers: 'I've seen the photologs
... I don't know how to define it. ... [T]hey say a lot of nonsense, I suppose
they'll outgrow it ... Me, I haven't been able to make anything of it' (137).
Cassany and Hernández point to the advisability of changing this attitude,
and of opening the school system to these types of online practices, seeking
'contact points.' They argue that 'If school is supposed to teach our future
citizens how to live better, it should also teach to them how to do better what
they like to do in their free time and their private life' (138).

But wouldn't it also be interesting to invert the argument? Since it is
clear that in the collaborative online communities of practice, young people
develop abilities and create value in a way the school can't emulate, wouldn't

it be more interesting for the school system to learn to do the things that are done online, instead of relegating them to the sphere of 'free time' and 'private life'? Wouldn't it be better for the school, as a place where citizens are prepared for the world of work and public life, to allow itself to be exposed to the kind of collaborative work and rich sociability found in online cultures, instead of trying to 'integrate' students and teach them to do what they already know how to do very well?

Ever since the advent of the narratives of 'standardization' and pro-European modernization that have served as a frame of hegemonic meaning for the Spanish CT, citizens have been treated a little like those 'struggling students' who, just like Mei, never manage to pass the subject of 'modernity.' But now we can theorize that online cultures also have their own important potential: the potential to transform that 'great school' that is society. A society in which, as Rancière says in *Le Maître ignorant*, 'The government is nothing more than the authority of the best ones in class' (12).

4.4.4. Construction of 'democratic subjectivity' online

However, it is clear that adapting the online (digital) collaborative forms of creation and diffusion of value to analog contexts is no easy task. On this subject, Margarita Padilla (2013), defender, participant, and expert of those cultures, is emphatic: 'Social change cannot come only from the Internet. It has to be done with bodies. We must go out and demonstrate in the streets, we must find food for those who don't have it, stop evictions, protect the undocumented ...'

But at the same time, perhaps the best way of doing all those things is to have confidence in the abilities that online experience tends to foster in anyone, and which was essential when the movements in the plazas started:

> What the Internet gives us is another way to experience the world. A joyful experience of abundance, cooperation, creativity, authorship ... I think that experience influenced many people to go to the plazas and not to see others simply as someone who walks all over you or bothers you, but as a potential associate.

The spread of this experience to a massive public is turning out to be a powerful antidote to that 'passion for inequality' produced by the still-hegemonic cultural elitism in Spanish society. The world of free software and hackers has contributed at least two fundamental things that are transforming the subjectivity of many people: the tendency to see the other as a potential collaborator, more than as a potential competitor who will set himself above or below me; and pride in one's ability to create and distribute cultural wealth (code, information, etc.) not so much from a group identity, but in collective processes open to anyone.

There is something crucial in the online world, and it is that, unlike modern bourgeois culture and the fields of aesthetics and the sciences that harbor it, the Internet is a space under construction, in which competition for prestige (the production of symbolic capital) is still to a great extent subject to the struggle for the reproduction of the common space itself (neutral network, 'free' information). But, in addition, in the neutral, decentralized network that hackers have built and that now defends many people who use it as a common space, 'intelligence is everywhere,' as Padilla says. In other words, it is a system that works not so much, or at least not primarily, because of the desire that my altruistic contributions be recognized, because of the desire that my intelligence be appreciated, but because of the desire that there be a common space where intelligences can freely develop their abilities in collaboration.

It's interesting to keep in mind, then, the exceptional potential for creation of subjectivity of ways of life oriented towards commonality rather than towards competition, which this version of the Web represents. It is, we could say, a whole 'passion for commonality' that proliferates around the experience of the decentralized network and, notably, around its defense. The struggles against the Sinde-Wert Law were a decisive moment for the construction of a subjectivity that was perceived as different, foreign to the rancidly hierarchical, competitive world of political parties, mass media, and even of the cultural, sports, intellectual, and artistic 'star system.' A rupture has occurred: not so much an attempt to defeat those elites, but to play a different game.

However, in emerging into the field of creating computer code and potentially transmitting all that immaterial culture, the cultures of sharing that extend from the Internet to the new movements locate their struggle for a common space, for good or for bad, in the heart of the capitalist economy, affecting the spheres of work, politics, and aesthetics. The interesting side of this is that they can't be easily locked up in the 'ghetto' of 'free time' or the 'art world,' as happened to the popular cultures of the twentieth century. The most complicated side of the matter is that, precisely because they affect the heart of the institutions of economic capital production, the capitalist systems for extraction of collectively produced wealth constantly find ways to benefit themselves, as they have always done, from these forms of collective value creation.

The lack of a strong identity and dense social ties, such as, for example, those possessed by the peasant cultures of survival, rooted at the local level, makes it difficult for the 'free culture' to limit, support, and defend the wealth it produces collectively, in the face of the large mechanisms of privatization that parasitize the mutant space of the Web. When it comes to communities open to anyone, it becomes difficult to avoid the intrusion of 'free riders' like the big digital companies that make money thanks to the collaborative work of users to whom they give nothing in return. On the other hand, the pragmatic 'hacker' or 'geek' mentality, focused on the solution of specific problems, can lead to a certain degree of blindness regarding those same indirect processes of privatizing collective wealth, which often are not resolved simply by granting an open license or by the opening of a specific protocol. These types of 'free culture' resources can end up like small boats adrift on the sea of neoliberal privatization.[12]

In this regard, I think an interesting way to approach the 15M movement, which is the topic of the next chapter, is to understand it as a kind of attempt to respond to certain questions that arise from the contradictions inherent in the experience of online cultures, and particularly in the attempt to translate that experience to the analog world. Questions that, perhaps, could be formulated more or less in the following way: What if we constructed a small city where we could make everything we needed and it seemed worthwhile to us to do it using only distributed collaborative practices like those of the Web? What if we constructed a city removed from neoliberalism in the very heart of the neoliberal city itself?

12 The study about 'audiovisual commons' I mentioned previously points out that some businesses are commonly seen to commodify the volunteer work that sustains those 'commons,' thus privatizing the wealth that others produce without contributing anything. This is because, the authors assert, the value is not just in the results, in the shared resources produced, but also in 'the information generated during the interaction process needed to produce them' (142). And this interaction and information is sometimes used for private, profit-making purposes. In this way, 'Wikiwashing' practices are undertaken—a term coined by analogy with the 'greenwashing' of the oil companies. This happens especially in the case of big profit-based companies like Yahoo and Google, which associate their image with 'the values of collaboration and sharing' by disguising their profit mechanisms.

In this respect, see Lara (2013) regarding the unpaid collective work that benefits, for example, Twitter; see also Padilla (2010) on the inevitable ambiguity of Web 2.0 that makes it a niche for open value production, but also for privatizing business practices.

CHAPTER 5

Combining the Abilities of all the Anyones: The 15M Movement and its Mutations

5.1. Anyone's Word and the Expert's Word: An Alliance

5.1.1. Affected voices and technical voices: 15M, PAH, and Mareas

May 2011. A trembling voice; words heard over street noise—or perhaps cut off by a bad Internet connection in a YouTube video: 'It's just that you're doing things I've always dreamed about being able to do ...' A pause, the voice breaks, and applause explodes. 'Excuse me, but I'm just ...'—more applause, and little by little the older woman speaking to the assembly, bending over the microphone, hands trembling, manages to go on: 'What I meant to tell you all is that I think you are so much more creative than our generation, and so I'd like to ask you something, something I think we all need, and it's that we not forget that ...' She falters for a moment, and then continues. 'There's a part of the population that's not here. There's part of the population missing here. It's the population that's even lower than low, the people who don't have something to eat every day, who live in slums, the *barrios*—' Applause bursts out again, interrupting her, and a hand settles on the woman's back to support her. '—where the average life expectancy is lower than in other *barrios*, where illiteracy is much higher, where people die, they're sick and they suffer in horrible situations.' Another supporting hand appears on her back, as if sharing the weight of the words she's still trying to say. 'And we have that in almost every town in the region, and in Murcia itself, and somehow they have to have this life, it has to fall on them. I don't know how to do it, but you do, I believe you do ...' Applause bursts out thunderously now, while the woman leaves the microphone and walks towards the people—who all stand up—and she loses herself among the crowd.

Shortly before or shortly after this, in May 2011, self-convened meetings in other plazas in cities and towns throughout Spain will see myriads of similar moments, at which so many other trembling voices will speak, often beginning with an apology. 'I'm sorry, it's hard for me to speak in public.' This phrase, emphasizing the speaker's own vulnerability, becomes a habitual introduction for moments of exceptional sincerity and collective emotion.[1]

But at the same time, another style of words, completely different in their format, tone, and presentation would also shortly spring forth from those assemblies and *acampadas*. Let's take, for example, some lines from point #14 in the document titled 'Propuestas abiertas de la comisión de economía del 15-M (Sol)' (2011):

Establishment of a moratorium on the payment of the Spanish state's foreign public debt until a full audit (including economic, social, and environmental aspects) can be made, with the participation of social agents and independent experts, to determine its legitimacy or illegitimacy. Should a debt be declared illegitimate, its payment shall be denied, and civil or criminal penalties for both debtors and creditors shall be required.

This proposal appeared as part of a document drafted collectively by the Economics Working Group of the *Acampadasol*. It included 16 specific political measures for resolving the crisis and changing the model that had caused it. These proposals were compiled and approved by the subgroups on Political Economy, Finances, Housing, Employment, Dissemination, Action, and Global Relations.

As Pedro Martí (*15M.cc – conversación con Pedro Martí* 2012), one of its members, explains, the power of the Economics Working Group came from having pooled together many 'creative minds' in an open discussion space where anyone was welcome. Martí asserts, in this regard, that one of the most important characteristics of the 15M movement in general, to which this Working Group belongs, has been knowing how to combine the production of 'collective thought' ('without that psychological process it would have been hard for us to move from such a competitive society to understanding and listening so much to others') with the recognition that

specialization is essential in a horizontal system; when there is no hierarchical system that unites us all, it's efficiency [that unites us], and it's much more efficient for those who know how to do something

---

1 As Amador Fernández-Savater says, 'In the assemblies, the most *personal* contributions were applauded (in silence, with hands only), for example, those who stammered and struggled to find the right words. Arms crossed in rejection were raised immediately against any speeches that sounded more automatic, more rote, less affected by the situation' (2014).

to dedicate themselves to that, regardless of the fact that all spaces are open to everyone so that anyone can participate in them.

This combination of fragile voices, that is, of 'anyone' with technical, specialized proposals and languages, no matter how strange it might be, doesn't seem to have disappeared from the social arena since the 15M occupations of plazas ended. On the contrary, we can see it constantly reappearing throughout the cycle of mobilizations and social transformations that have taken place in the wake of this movement. It perhaps reached its most intense moments around the campaigns of the People Affected by Mortgages Platform (or PAH, the acronym for its Spanish name, Plataforma de Afectados por la Hipoteca) and the so-called Mareas Ciudadanas (with particular emphasis on the Mareas in defense of public health and public education). I offer two brief examples.

March 2012. The documentary 'La Plataforma' is released, telling the PAH's history. In it we see Matías González, a citizen affected by the real estate bubble who was evicted from his house—another of those 'fragile' voices—recounting how he made contact with the association:

I went to Obrador Street one Friday afternoon, to see what that thing was all about, and I saw what was happening: just like me, well, there was tons of people, thousands. So I told 'em about my case and they supported me ... and they gave me the strength to be where I am, and now I even support the people who support me. I mean, if we don't support each other here, there's no way to get nothin' done. And I give thanks for the Platform, 'cause, well, it gave me the strength to be where I am, 'cause this'll drive you crazy ... This'll just drive you crazy.

Months later, Matías González had his mortgage debt reduced. His voice, along with many others, had influenced the production of legal documents like the resolution of the Court of Human Rights in Strasbourg that prevented the eviction of people living in a block of apartments in the town of Salt that had been occupied by PAH's 'Social Work' campaign. Based on that resolution, PAH itself (2013) produced a legal document to be presented to any Spanish court processing an eviction, which began with these words:

XXX, *Solicitor of the Courts and of XXX, as I have duly verified in foreclosure proceeding nº XXX//// eviction for rent, before the Court and according to law I hereby SUBMIT:*

That in accordance with articles 10.2, 47, and 96.1 of the Spanish Constitution, with international regulations on the right to decent housing and the prohibition of forced evacuations without prior relocation, and in light of the recent ruling on the matter by the European Court of Human Rights in Strasbourg, I solicit postponement of eviction from my house, on the basis of the following allegations ...

In 2014, another legal decision marks what is perhaps one of the most important victories of the political cycle the 15M helped to initiate: preventing the privatization of six public hospitals in Madrid, as evidenced by the following decree from the Superior Court of Justice in Madrid:

> The Court (Section 3) RESOLVES: ACCESS to the preventive measure requested by the claimant and consequently suspension is granted of the Resolution of April 30, 2013 from the Vice Ministry of Health Assistance of the Ministry of Health of the Community of Madrid, which publicized the call for bids on the contract of services known as 'Licensed Management of the public service of specialized health care of the university hospitals "Princess Sofía," "Princess Leonor," and "Princess Cristina" of the Southeastern Henares and el Tajo.'

This judicial decision led to one of the extremely rare resignations from a public position to be seen in Spanish politics since the crisis began—that of Javier Fernández-Lasquetty, the ex-Minister of Health in the Community of Madrid. It would not have been possible without the whole process of strikes, protests, and legal actions taken by what came to be called the Marea Blanca, a huge public mobilization that reacted rapidly and forcefully to the attempted privatization orchestrated by Lasquetty.

But again, one of the main characteristics of the Marea Blanca was precisely its open, nonhierarchical, and, given its connection with something as historically stratified and corporatist as the health sector, surprisingly un-corporate organization. In addition, the Marea Blanca, like the assemblies of the 15M movement and PAH, was conceived as a space with room for voices with different types of authority, ranging from that gained through the personal experience of being affected by common problems, to that obtained through having specialized, technical kinds of knowledge. In fact, in the Marea Blanca it has been common to hear voices recognized as professionals, but also as patients. As one woman said on the radio program 'Dentro de La Marea Blanca' (2012):

> We are very alarmed, but not by fear of losing our jobs; nor are we fighting to earn more money. We simply see a threat to the rights we've gained during these thirty-odd years of having public health, and against all the patients, and that includes us professionals, the doctors and nurses.

Also recurring in the Marea Blanca's mobilizations are references to the diversity of abilities necessary to maintain the public health system. There have been posters that say, 'The kitchen is as important as medicine, let's defend both,' strikes by hospital janitorial staff supported by the entire medical sector, and, in general, a constant appreciation for those with the caregiving, logistics, and social skills so necessary to the practice of medicine and who have set aside the strongly hierarchical distribution of value imposed by the tradition of expertise that surrounds the medical field. This redistribution of values has had an almost playful echo in the sudden transformation of healthcare personnel, patients, and hospital neighbors into 'activists' who have been able to pull together huge strikes overnight, to spread their message to all of society, and, several times, to paralyze downtown Madrid. An article in a local newspaper said, 'You can see doctors-cum-"community managers" compiling information and distributing it through social networks. You can see nurses giving press conferences and speaking in front of television cameras, aides designing posters and placards, technicians, physical therapists, all of them moving in the same direction' ('Desde Fuera …' 2014).

The blog maintained by Hospital de la Princesa personnel ('Salvemos la princesa' 2014), who managed to avoid its shutdown after weeks of mobilization (in another remarkable victory for the Marea Blanca), evidenced the unity of the various hospital workers. They considered it not only a coordination of efforts to reach a goal, but also as something that is, in fact, quite distinctive: a victory over a world that proposes competition as the general form for relationships:

All the groups that have participated in this movement—doctors, nurses, aides, technicians, unions, watchmen, cleaning personnel, kitchen workers, maintenance staff, etc., etc., almost 3,000 people— have learned to reconcile their interests into one: our hospital.

Don't you believe for a minute that that's easy to do in a world dominated by ambition and 'I want to be more than you.' Every one of you guys knows that.[2]

Ultimately, if this characteristic combination of expert and everyday knowledge bases and abilities came together in these movements (15M, PAH, Mareas, and others), I think it's not just because everyone had something they felt the need to protest against. They also had the will to find ways of collaborating that offered alternatives to a competitiveness and hierarchy

---

2 Some of the most illuminating texts about the Marea Blanca that I know can be found in the blog *Al final de la asamblea*, to which I will refer later.

that was perceived—even if often only tacitly—as part of the problem being protested.

5.1.2. A 'protest style' and a 'climate'

The accelerated pace of today's multiple narrations by the big mass media companies—and often also by digital networks, which usually follow the former in this regard more than in others—makes it difficult to draw analogies like the one I suggest. The constant need to report as news what happens in the social sphere, to which the majority of the media succumb, also permeates civic self-perception. However, that has not prevented the recognition, from multiple perspectives, of the continuities between movements like 15M, the PAH, and the Mareas. These are no longer seen only as timely responses to the government's management of the economic crisis, but as moments in the same political and social cycle that involves a fundamental rupture in the tacit agreements that supported the foundations of Spanish coexistence. (This was particularly true of agreements about the democratic operation of the political party system, previously considered acceptable, if imperfect, and about the acceptability of the economic system itself.)

This brings us back to the idea of the 'crisis of the system' I spoke of at the beginning of the book: it's not only a crisis of 'the economy,' it's not only an economic situation caused by the poor management of particular individuals. It's something deeper that has to do with the way the Spanish state has been organized since it was 'democratically' established after Franco's dictatorship.

Beyond the fact that this perception has been proposed as an interpretive thesis by some of the investigators working on the notion of the CT, and beyond the fact that many sectors of social movements habitually maintain it, it seems to me that it's a narrative that is pretty well accepted by the general population. There's a feeling that something fundamental is broken, or at least being questioned. Along with that, there are unavoidable perceptions that now something different has been opened. These perceptions often include, consciously or subconsciously, that of protests in general—and the 15M movement in particular—as triggers of that opening.

Thus, Fernández-Savater's proposal to view the 15M movement not only as a specific social movement limited to the experience in the plazas, but also as the opening moment of a different climate that is altering the limits of what is possible in Spanish society, seems to be in harmony with a certain 'common sense' shared by large sectors of the population. As early as January 2012, Fernández-Savater stated in the article '¿Cómo se organiza un clima?':

The official reality is the map of what's authorized as possible: what it's possible to see, to think, to feel, and to do. *We have opened that map.* Now other things can be seen, thought, felt, and done. The party system is no longer taboo. We conspire to interfere in the elections, although we may not agree among ourselves on how to do it, because it's the *vox populi* that they are a fraud. The relationship between democracy and capitalism is no longer so clear. The previously invisible reality of the evictions is now out in plain sight. It's possible to think and make policy without being affiliated with a party, or even a member of a social movement. We use the Internet every day to collectively construct another point of view about the present. We've learned that the unknown other is not only an enemy or an irrelevant object, but that he or she can be a friend. We've discovered that we can do things we had never suspected. The map of the possible is different, the climate is different.

Perhaps one of the versions of this idea that has caught on in a big way, as the years pass, is that of a new 'protest style.' Even though these continuities may not be spoken of explicitly in media forums and among the general public, it is very difficult to deny that such massive mobilizations as those of the Mareas, PAH, or the Marches for Dignity in March 2014, share with the 15M movement the choice not to use the more usual (although hardly unique) organizational forms of social movements, unions, and other leftist organizations: those in which some type of strong identity—activist, worker, sectorial, 'subordinate,' gender, etc.—tends to play the role of protagonist, and to generate spaces for a 'vanguard' composed of those who represent that segment of the population to all the rest of the population.

This 'inclusivity,' as it is often called, of recent movements has been generated through a whole series of procedures, expressions, and we could even say 'tics' (none of which are exempt, at times, from a certain fetishization) that have become emblems of that 'new style of protest,' and which are often put into practice and recognized almost automatically. I am thinking mostly of assemblies, with their turn-taking, facilitators, codes of gestures to express agreement or disagreement, etc. But we cannot forget the posters of various sizes and styles that fill demonstrations, contrasting significantly with the uniformity of those distributed by political parties and unions. Then there is the broad repertoire of slogans and characteristically nonsectarian and nonsectorial chants ('Yes, we can,' 'They don't represent us,' etc.) that accompany a use of public spaces that is hospitable and respectful of others (even—in general—of those who in principle would not expect that hospitality, like the riot police).

Often the dizzying pace of 'the present' and the urgency imposed by increasing structural violence (unemployment, precarization, etc.) make it very difficult to look back, and a few years seem to be enough to blur past events. It seems to me, though—and this is difficult to prove, because it's based on my own daily monitoring of the mass media, my participation in digital networks, and on personal conversations held during these years— that at least a certain feeling has been engraved into the recent collective memory that the 15M movement opened another type of political space that has been constructed more 'by anyone' than by a certain social group or ideology, with its corresponding 'vanguard.'

'We are everyone,' was one of the more oft-repeated slogans of the movement. And the truth is that more than 80% of the population declared their support for it, in addition to the approximately 7 million people who participated directly, united by very general mottos like 'Real Democracy Now!' or 'We're not goods in the hands of politicians and bankers,' but without necessarily identifying with any particular social group or ideology.

Likewise, one did not and does not have to be a member of anything, nor adopt any strong social or ideological identity—nor submit to any vanguard—to agree with the PAH or the Mareas, or to participate directly in their mobilizations. That is something that, I dare say, few people would doubt today. And in any case, the phenomenon has been thoroughly studied and theorized by social scientists, philosophers, and other scholars of such movements, especially those that have put the 15M movement in relation to its other 'sister' movements that arose around 2011 in the global wake of Tahrir Square and the Arab Spring. All of these movements have been characterized by their 'absence of leaders,' their 'horizontality,' and as already mentioned, their 'inclusivity.'[3]

On the other hand, the tacit or explicit notion of an inclusive, horizontal 'style of protest' keeps recurring when mass media and researchers represent these social processes. At the same time, and this is the nuance that I particularly want to introduce, along with that perception of its 'open, nonmilitant style,' an awareness—often silenced by the media—has also crystallized among the people who have lived it up close and personal that there are fundamental aspects of these processes that exceed 'the protest' as such; that is, the complaint or the demand for solutions from institutional powers.

3 Some examples include Graeber (2013), Hardt and Negri (2012), Jimenez and Estalella (2014), Lawrence (2014), Morell (2012), Moreno-Caballud and Sitrin (2013), Romanos (2014a, 2014b), Sitrin and Azzellini (2014), Toret, Monterde et al. (2013), and Gould-Wartofsky (2015).

I will propose shortly that these other aspects have to do with those two dimensions to which I have alluded: the appearance of the voice of 'anyone,' which expresses their shared vulnerability, and the construction of political alternatives by resorting to specialized, technical ways of knowing. I will emphasize primarily the feedback of these two dimensions and their equal importance within these processes, since—and this is my main thesis here—the value placed on the 'unauthorized' or vulnerable word, and the ability to combine this word with specialized, technical discourses is the main cultural tool of these social processes that, besides protesting, manage to simultaneously promote and support nonneoliberal ways of life. In other words, they are foreign to the principles of competition and corporatization of life (i.e., treating life as if it were a business) discussed in chapter 1. But before beginning to elaborate on this topic, I want to give a clearer idea of the space-time coordinates of the processes I am talking about.

5.1.3. Mapping ways of life in the face of dispersion

Despite the greater visibility of movements like the PAH and the Mareas, the political, social, and cultural transformations that have taken place in that new 'climate' are undoubtedly open to very heterogeneous possibilities surrounding the 15M movement. They also appear in different spaces: some more *macro* and others more *micro*, some openly political and formally organized, other more routine and almost invisible. Furthermore, as I noted above, it is especially difficult to perceive those transformations and give them value in a society that is not only forced by mass media to accelerate and scatter its self-representation in supposed 'news stories,' but which, in general, is articulated based on the neoliberal principles of widespread competition and the corporatization of life, which produce what the psychoanalyst Franco Ingrassia (2011) understood as an intense, pervasive tendency towards 'dispersion.' Ingrassia defines this tendency as 'that which makes the social ties we establish ever more unstable, weak, and heterogeneous.' Dispersion, therefore, is an 'effect on the social aspect of market transactions there where the state weakens its regulating, structuring function of intersubjective relationships,' given that 'the market today is constantly assembling and disassembling bonds based on its incessant search for the maximization of profits. Disturbance becomes the norm and stability the exception.'

These conditions of dispersion caused by the neoliberal market hegemony strongly affect society's self-perception. In this sense, it is easier to count the processes opened by the 15M movement, like the swell of always apparently novel protests, than to try to trace the continuities between processes that sometimes are indeed protests, but often, in fact, are much

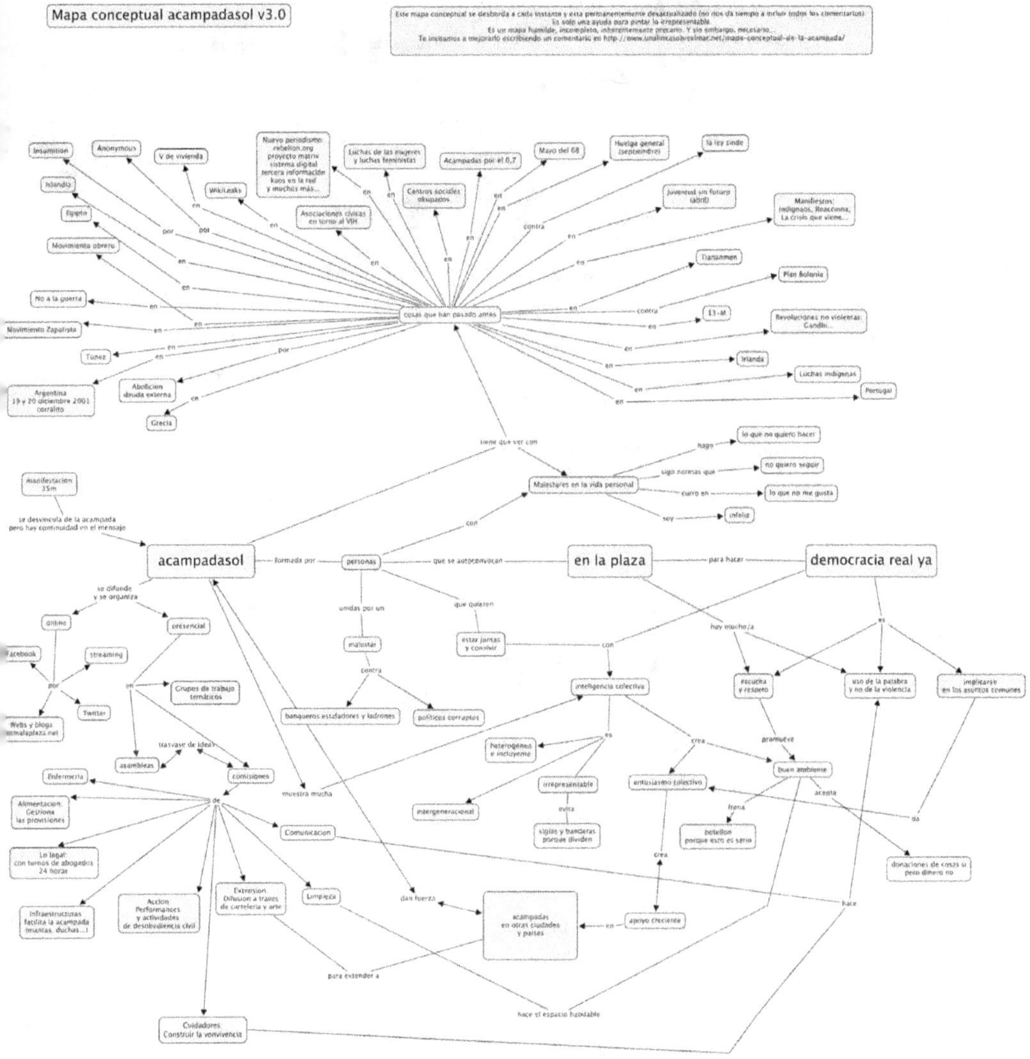

FIGURE 1. 'Conceptual Map of Acampadasol,' in its 3.0 version

more transformative in their propositional, affective, or subjective aspects—precisely those most capable of creating the social tie that neoliberalism tends to destroy.

In response to these difficulties of self-perception, agents of the movements have produced, among other things, instruments of rapid visualization like the 'maps' shown in Figures 1 and 2. Figure 1 is the 'Conceptual Map of Acampadasol,' in its 3.0 version. It was produced by Acampadasol's Thought

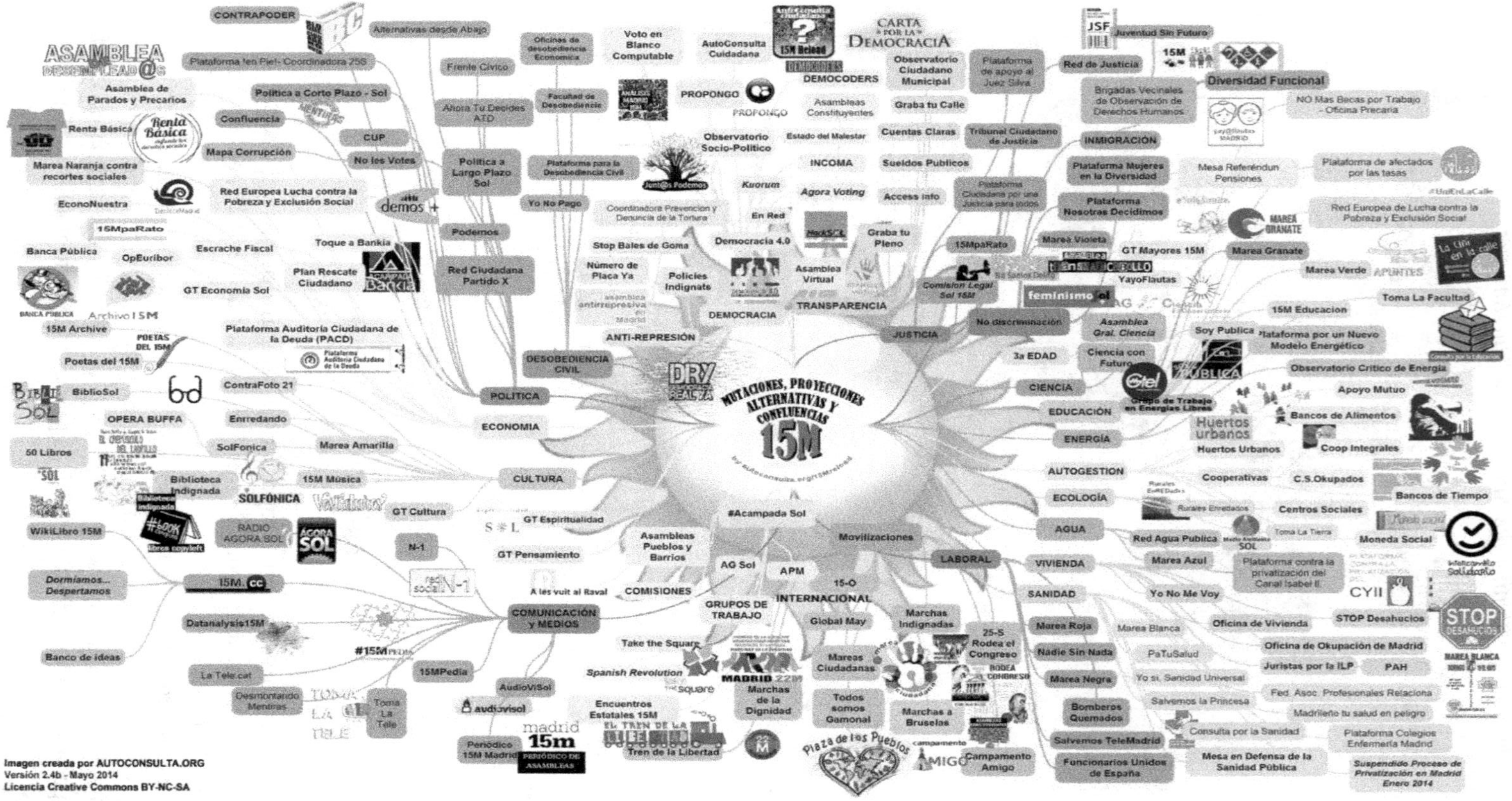

FIGURE 2. '15M Mutations, Projections, Alternatives and Convergences'

Commission in May 2011, and extended based on suggestions made by people 'on the ground' in the plaza itself and also online, through the blog of the radio program 'Una línea sobre el mar,' where it was originally published. Figure 2 is called '15M Mutations, Projections, Alternatives, and Convergences,' and was prepared by the Civic Self-Consultations Working Group at the beginning of 2014, as a tool to help in the process of 'updating' the 15M that was proposed by this group.

The first map was produced closer to the time when the plazas were occupied, and not for nothing does it appear to be a map of Acampadasol. But at the same time, it shows the camp's 'present day' in the light of a recent past of 'things that have happened before.' These range from very specific protests in the Spanish state—like the 'Acampadas por el 0.7%' that took place during the nineties, or the general strike of September 2010— to great historical political movements like the 'women's struggles and feminist struggles,' the labor movement, and indigenous struggles, moving through experiences related to emergent online cultures, like WikiLeaks or Anonymous, and to revolts of the new global wave, like those of Egypt, Iceland, or Greece.

The second map, on the other hand, focuses more on the post-15M period, when a climate of politicization or the 'new style of protest' develops. The explicit intention, as the Autoconsulta Ciudadana ('AutoConsulta Ciudadana' 2014) website says, is

> to evaluate the experience of these three years of the 15M, to synthesize its proposals and thesis, to show and make a map of what is alive and working, to visualize our social support graphically, the social movements' successes in their forms of struggle (demonstrations, marches, 'Silent Shout,' Mareas, Civic Consultations, halting the privatization of healthcare, PAH, demonstrations in Gamonal, etc.).

This idea of showing the social movements' 'successes,' often also called 'victories,' has circulated widely among the '15M climate' networks. This is in line with their continued success at getting political, legislative, and judicial institutions to respond with concrete measures—though, it's true, these may be few and far between—to the pressure and specific proposals of the movements. From this motivation, which is central in the Civic Self-Consultation map, it's easy to tend to give more value to the specialized, technical aspect of political projects in the wake of the 15M movement—because it is the people with such skills who communicate directly with the institutions—than to their capacity to create spaces for everyday, experiential, or affective abilities and ways of knowing; in other words, spaces for 'anyone.' In this sense, it's almost inevitable to grant a central value to mobilizations that obtain judicial victories because they have support from lawyers who play an essential role, as seen in both the PAH and the Marea Blanca.

Likewise, the thematic organization in 'commissions' or 'working groups' that was carried out even in the 15M camps, and which serves as a guide to this map for categorizing the 'post-15M,' always runs the risk of emphasizing the more instrumental aspects of these social processes, and of erasing their more expressive, affective, or relational aspects. In other words, those involved in the 'construction of subjectivity,' and who, despite being—it seems to me—essential for all areas, would be relegated quietly to the headings of 'culture,' 'spirituality,' or perhaps simply 'thought.'

The map developed by Civic Self-Consultations is, in any case, an excellent tool to show the plethora of initiatives taking place in the wake of the 15M movement that have specific intentions, and often with the specialized, technical capacity to obtain small and large institutional victories. That plethora of initiatives is what is so difficult to reconstruct in the middle of the dispersion produced by mass media, and in general by the precarization of life under neoliberalism. The map shows, for example, the existence of initiatives that combine technical abilities related to the economy, law, or audiovisual media. Some examples include the Platform for the Civic Audit of the Debt—which emerges, in fact, from the aforementioned Economía Sol proposal number 14; the 15MpaRato project, which is lodging a civic complaint against Rodrigo Rato, the head of Bankia, the financial organization that received the most public money to avoid bankruptcy; the Record Your Meeting Platform, the Precarious Office, the Platform against the Privatization of the Isabel II Canal, the Offices of Economic Disobedience, and many more.

Just the *possibility* of mapping conceptually, beyond an organization around 'subjects' (politics, economy, justice, education, health, etc.) that came into the 15M world already preconceived, is what enables the *conceptual* Acampadasol Map. For reasons of chronology, it can't include the post-15M, but it does allow an approach to its dimension of subjectivity construction. Thus, playing with the possible routes suggested by this other map, we can describe the 15M movement by creating phrases like the following from the proposed nodes: 'people who want to be together and coexist by using collective intelligence, which creates collective enthusiasm' or 'in the plaza people listen to you and respect you, which promotes a good atmosphere.'

Regarding the organizational structures of Acampadasol, we can read in the map:

> Acampadasol is disseminated and organized face-to-face in thematic working groups and commissions on nursing, food (arranging

provisions), legal (with 24 hour shifts of lawyers), infrastructures (providing the camps with blankets, showers, etc.), action (civil disobedience performances and activities), extension (dissemination through poster-making and art), cleaning, and communication.

Together with those commissions is also the more general idea that there are 'caretakers who facilitate coexistence and facilitate the use of words and not violence' (perhaps the most specific translation of this function in the field was the creation of the so-called 'Respect Commission,' which I'll return to later).

What I find interesting about these conceptualizations developed by the Acampadasol Thought Group is precisely their capacity to show the importance of ways of life and meaning production, like collective intelligence, respect, mutual care, enthusiasm, coexistence, and listening, that are cross-sectional and essential for the explicit thematic and organizational orientations of both the 15M movement and those later 'mutations, projections, alternatives, and confluences' shown by the other map.

I want to return now to the nuance I want to contribute to these debates on the 15M movement and the social processes it has opened. I believe that, once again, as happened with the online cultures, the issue of this 'subjective' or 'cultural' aspect that moves beyond the protest and 'institutional victories' dimensions cannot be understood without relating it to the mechanisms that support it; that is, the mechanisms that allow all the work of production, circulation, and transformation of meanings that are the material substance—and there is no other—of this cultural dimension.

As I noted at the end of the previous chapter, what the 15M *acampadas* intended was precisely to create a space where not only culture—that is, the collective production of meaning—but also life as a whole, could be maintained. This would be accomplished through collaborative practices as far as possible from the neoliberal 'way of the world' that foregrounds competitiveness and the corporatization of life. This meant getting to work: if things couldn't be done with money—which was not accepted within Acampadasol—if certain words could not be imposed upon others by pre-established criteria of hierarchical authority—if we really 'are everyone'—it would be necessary to produce materially and to maintain *other mechanisms for valuing existing abilities and needs.*

Thus, it seems to me, in the same way that it was essential for the camps to construct material infrastructures for the collective management of food, rest, or physical care, it was also fundamental to ensure a space to collaboratively manage everyone's 'cultural needs.' This translated into the creation of spaces of respect, valuing, and listening for vulnerable voices, which spoke from their personal experiences about common problems, and not from the positions of authority habitually used in the competitive neoliberal dynamic.

Beyond the protests, then, was a whole other dimension, one of constructing ways of life that replaced competition with collaboration, that were respectful of vulnerability and able to value different kinds of knowledge and everyday or experiential abilities. That does not mean by any stretch of the imagination that specialized, technical abilities were cast aside. On the contrary, what happened was that the latter were combined with the former, within a logic of collective cooperation that was promoted intensely through its embodiment within a specific limited space—the plaza—where, unlike in digital cultures and many of the post-15M spaces, all the basic aspects of the coexistence of daily life have a place. The plaza was a space to find 'solutions' formulated in the technical languages that institutions wanted to hear; it was a space to experiment with alternative ways of life, through words and affection, sociability and bodies.

In short, the 15M plazas could be described as spaces where all kinds of knowledge and abilities were welcome, as long as they were used to help support a way of life based on the collaboration of anyone, and not on competition.

5.2. Sustaining the Plaza and Beyond: Towards a New Cultural Power

5.2.1. Building abilities, resources, languages

In order to think about this better, we return for a moment to the scene of the trembling voice that appears, apologizing, before the assembly. The example I gave comes from the Acampada Murcia, but really, it could have happened in any other camp—and here in this section my observations are based on research done mainly on Acampadasol. But in any case, what interests me are those hands that settle on the woman's back as her speech progresses with difficulty, a difficulty usually heard in voices 'unauthorized' by modern neoliberal paradigms of cultural authority to speak in public. In this case, the speech that progresses with such difficulty talks about the need to include those who live a more difficult life. In some way, those hands are supporting the body that speaks, making its words possible. But they are not the only ones.

If we imagine a wider view of that same scene, and we begin to observe everything around the speaker, we will see that there are many more elements necessary for those words to be said. When seen from further away, the assembly sometimes has the appearance of a 'spontaneous' meeting. But during the 15M occupations an entire logistics and a series of very complex protocols were developed that enabled the organization of assemblies that were consciously structured so that not only could anyone participate, but their participation would not get lost at the anecdotal or individual level, but rather, would help to create what was constantly called 'collective thought' or 'collective intelligence.'

So as we continue to look around, we will notice that beside the microphone there is, of course, sound equipment, and several people responsible for making it work. Who brought the equipment, and the necessary electric generator? Remember, we're in the middle of a public thoroughfare. The testimonies on the matter all say the same thing: 'Things appeared, people brought them, nobody had to pay for anything. Everyone contributed what they had and what they knew how to do.'

However, it isn't enough to set up a microphone so that a voice can not only be heard, but also be 'actively listened to' (another common expression in the camps). For this to happen, many other things have to happen too. First, the subgroup on Assembly Logistics has prepared the way. It has created corridors with adhesive tape on the ground so that people can enter and leave comfortably without bothering others (remember that there were often more than 1,000 people gathered at the assemblies). It has distributed pieces of cardboard for anyone who wants to avoid sitting directly on the hot ground baked by the Spanish summer sun. And it has found chairs 'for people with limited mobility or energy.'[4]

With the assembly already under way, the Assembly Logistics subgroup still doesn't rest: its members can be seen circulating among the people with water diffusers for whoever wants to cool off (a playful element, and one that helps to 'create a good atmosphere'). They also distribute parasols. Alongside them, the members of the Turn-Taking subgroup circulate with posters plastered to their bodies to identify themselves. Not only do they note the names of people who want to speak, they also ask on what subject, and negotiate the relevance of the intended contribution. But it isn't up to them to decide. They transmit the information to the Turn-Taking Coordination team, which, since it has greater contact with the Facilitators group, can make a more informed decision.

The Facilitators, in turn, don't have to communicate that decision directly to the assembly. That task belongs to the Moderators, who are dedicated entirely to interacting with the public, because the Facilitators are giving

---

4 As recommended by that fascinating document, the 'Quick Guide for Energizing Public Assemblies,' published in May 2011 on Acampadasol's blog, 'Toma la Plaza' (DifRed 2014).

them all the necessary clues (when to move on to the next point of the daily schedule, how to paraphrase a contribution, what is the best decision at any given moment to reach a consensus, etc.). Flanking the moderator, who always faces the assembly, are the iconic simultaneous interpreters of sign language—a language everybody at the assembly participates in to some degree when they show their agreement or disagreement with their now no less iconic hand movements to express applause or rejection, among other things.

In some assemblies there were even enough people working on the Facilitation group that some could personally approach any person who showed their displeasure with the process, trying to get their opinions to include them later. Needless to say, anyone could belong to the Facilitation group, as long as they showed up for group meetings. Of course, one had to know when and where those meetings were being held, but this wasn't hard. The information points had lists of everything that happened in the plaza, updated constantly and in plain sight. In just a few hours, a new arrival could know practically the same things about the operation of that small city as somebody who had been there for a month.

Because, let's not forget, people were living in the 15M *acampadas*, at least in those of the biggest cities. The assembly was only a brief moment out of the daily life in the plaza, although, in some sense, the whole *acampada* had been constructed so that they could keep holding assemblies where 'we look for solutions' or, as Acampadasol's first tweet said, 'we reach agreements.' Because, while the Tahrir Square demonstrators promised not to disband until Mubarak resigned, Sol swore—not without some ambiguity—in that first message: 'We have just set up camp in the Puerta del Sol. We will not go away until we reach an agreement.'

In order to maintain that long, arduous search for an 'agreement'—to obtain that meeting between anyone's voices and the expert voices that wanted to decide how to live a life with dignity—many things needed to be done in turn. When the assembly was over, the cleaning team had to make sure to leave the space as it was before, while at the same time the Infrastructure Commission made sure that the plaza was still walkable, directing traffic through contributions from 'micro-urbanism.' There was one zone for camping and sleeping, and a different one for daytime activities. People ate there—and pretty well, too; there were even vegetarian options. The locals were constantly bringing homemade food to Acampadasol, although cooking was also done there in the camp.

The body was very much in evidence, because so much work had to be done. It was necessary 'to take care of oneself': 'We take care of each other' was a constant refrain. The members of commissions who used computers ceaselessly and spent whole nights without sleep, like Communications or International Outreach, received visits from the Spirituality Group offering them Reiki massages. The Feeding Commission offered sandwiches to the Carpentry Commission. Seniors and children each had their own spaces. There was, mostly during the early weeks, a somewhat contradictory atmosphere of emergency: a peaceful, careful kind of 'trench' atmosphere. A poster in Sol said 'Rest and get organized: your exhaustion benefits them.' Another one, with certain older resonances, said: 'Madrid will be the tomb of neoliberalism.'

Sound technicians, electricians, carpenters, cooks, translators, hackers, journalists, social workers, economists, lawyers, architects … in Acampadasol, all easily found ways to use their abilities to collaborate with others. An exceptional mixture of knowledge bases, aptitudes, and ways of doing things arose. The professional, the expert, the technical were mixed with the affective, the experiential, the everyday in a way that couldn't happen in neoliberal society.

Fernández-Savater quoted in his 'Notes from Acampadasol'—an exceptional document for understanding these dynamics—the following comment: 'A friend who is very involved in the organization, who dedicates her life to the camp, says, "Shit, we can't get a job in our own fields, but we'll know how to do a little of everything."' In Sol, a city was built in four days. In spite of the urgency, they created a daily life rich with activities: while an older gentleman lovingly prepared a huge paella, a few meters away the Legal Commission drafted a proposal to change the Electoral Law. Climbers scaled the scaffolds that surrounded the plaza to hang banners; others planted gardens in the flower beds. In the library, at the beginning, there wasn't enough room for all the donated books, but later they were catalogued scrupulously, and as with the Archive that contains every document produced in the plaza, all those books can still be freely consulted today.[5]

One of the many documentaries and semi-amateur videos recorded in those days about the march, titled *No nos vamos* (We Are Not Leaving) (*No nos vamos - Comisión de Respeto* 2011), attempted to chronicle the activities of each of the Acampadasol working groups. In one of its sections, dedicated to the emblematic Respect Commission, the language used by a young man explaining the daily life of that commission is noteworthy. 'What are we doing?' he says in a didactic tone to the camera that follows him as he walks

5 As I write this, both Archivo Sol and Biblio Sol are housed, after having taken various trips, in the CSA 3peces3, as explained in a recent informational note ('La Biblioteca Sol y el Archivo del 15-M perviven en Lavapiés' 2014).

through the crowded plaza. 'Well, right now we're organizing the Respect Commission, we're gathering resources. So what does this mean? Well, first, personnel resources: people to be able to cover the area covered by Respect Commission #2.' When he reaches a small stand where his companions are, he explains, 'Another job of the people here in reception is to control human and technical resources. What does this mean? Well, for example, keeping track of whether the walkie-talkie needs batteries, to fix those kinds of things. They also manage any displaced personnel. Third function: internal communication with Respect #1.'

It is striking to hear language full of expressions belonging to a business management vocabulary coming from the mouth of this experienced member of the Respect Commission to describe perhaps one of the most representative groups of that collaborative, inclusive culture that characterized Sol. This same person, switching to a much more colloquial register, also says about Respect, 'We are not an authority, what we do is mediate and raise awareness, we're not going to tell people what they should or should not do.'

A young woman, explaining to some newly arrived volunteers how to collaborate, is much more colloquial: 'If you get nervous in a bad situation, you split, so things don't get out of hand, okay?' And 'if someone comes around being a jackass, and someone always does, just stay calm, chill out, and most of all, don't get nervous, never lose your cool ...'

Sol was said in many ways. During a meeting of the Respect Commission with the Thought Group, they drafted a text (2014) in which the former represented itself in these terms:

> The Respect Commission, originally fed by prior knowledge bases (Crisis Intervention, Social Work, Sociology, Psychology, Linguistic Pragmatics, Philosophy of Language ...) is enriched with knowledge derived from action and praxis. Instead of a competition between voices, the Commission relies on empathy and mediation for its dialogue. Instead of conflicting interests, motivations are heard and prejudices are battled to collaborate on a beneficial result for everyone.

These types of crossovers between professional, specialized, intellectual, and even business languages and traditions with other everyday, experiential ones—all of them in service to collaboration—are the ones that interest me. In order to live collaboratively in the *acampada* it was understood that all those languages, knowledge bases, and abilities were necessary and worthy of respect. Despite the logical desire and hope that 'something else would result' from the plaza, that 'specific proposals' would be agreed upon (these were recurring expressions), it was also understood that in the camp something important was already happening, because of the way coexistence was lived and organized day by day. It was understood, I think, that the goal was not to distill the knowledge of ordinary everyday 'anyones,' to obtain a specialized, technical knowledge, but to blend one with the other in spaces where collaboration was prioritized over competition.

This is one of the reasons for the mysterious phenomenon of the faithful endurance of very many people in assemblies of endless duration, lasting hours and hours without reaching many concrete decisions. Again Fernández-Savater (2011b) gathers testimony that offers a key: 'Another friend: "What works in the assemblies is not the assembly format, but an energy that comes from somewhere else: the need and the desire to be together and to keep going together. Only this way can we put up with it, that's what needs more care."

In another vignette, Fernández-Savater talks, now in the first person, about the same phenomenon:

> In the group I'm with in the evening there is not a single thought in common. Monologue after monologue. And even so ... Someone trembles with emotion when taking the megaphone, people going shopping in calle Preciados are caught up, glued to the group, overwhelmed, so much is said from the heart ... So definitely, something is happening.

Among the string of opinions offered by various intellectuals in the mass media about the 15M movement, to which I will turn shortly, there was no lack of those that emphasized, in a critical tone, the aspect of the 'viscerality' or the 'emotiveness' of the movement. This was the case, for example, of the reading of Zygmunt Bauman himself, from a perception that was inevitably distanced from the 15M's daily life, and armed with his theory of the 'liquid society.'

However, I repeat that those aspects of emotional expressivity related to the creation and material support of an ordinary life not governed by competition cannot be separated from that context. From that context of 'a nonneoliberal city within the neoliberal city,' the emotivity released by the 15M movement takes on another meaning.

5.2.2. Empowering the new 'experts in what happens to them'

Of course, the biggest problem was that this ordinary life based on collaboration, and distanced from (at least rendered indirectly related to) money and the relations of neoliberal competition and corporatization, couldn't be maintained indefinitely in the camps. Everybody knew that the camps' days were numbered, they weren't made to last. Just like the assemblies, the camps had what was often called a 'symbolic value.' It was a matter of demonstrating that it is possible to live another way, even if only for a while and only within that enclosed space.

But during that demonstration, procedures were constructed, sensitivities and ways of knowing that, unlike the material infrastructure of the camps—all those precarious constructions of cardboard and wood that often ended up in the trash—they *could* continue to be used, wherever other places and other energies could be found to reactivate them. Specifically, as I have shown, that peculiar combination of the knowledge of the citizens affected and the knowledge of the experts is probably one of the most strongly exported of the cultural dynamics cultivated by the 15M movement. And perhaps, therefore, it is also one of the nuclei of that new 'style of protest' or 'climate of expansion of the possible' that was opened by the movement, and which Fernández-Savater has called 'the birth of a new social power.' It seems to me that it's also about 'a new cultural power,' since it promotes that 'culture of anyone' revalorized by the 15M movement. This is thanks in part to the new collaborative abilities acquired online discussed in the previous chapter, which enabled the construction of all kinds of nonhierarchical knowledge and abilities capable of creating 'collective intelligence.'

If we observe what happens in social processes with roots in the 15M movement, like the PAH (which, although it was created before 2011, owes much of its massive success to the plazas' spirit of solidarity), or the Marea Blanca in defense of public healthcare, we can confirm that there is an important transmission of that new 'cultural power.' It is notable, for example, how in the case of the PAH, the assembly where all voices are important continues to be a central organizational tool. In fact, the exceptional 'empowerment' the PAH inspires must be attributed, among other things, to its determined rejection of a 'service' model through which the problem of mortgages would be confronted with the aid of a series of legal experts, mediators, or activists offered to an undifferentiated contingent of so-called 'victims' whose abilities and ways of knowing would not be relevant.

The key to the PAH's success—as noted by those who began it and maintain it day to day—is that everyone who was affected participates in all the processes of the struggle for all the cases, everyone contributing his or her own kinds of knowledge and abilities, and themselves becoming advisers for other affected people. This is how Montserrat Hernando, housing adviser for the Federation of Neighborhood Associations of Barcelona, and customary collaborator of the PAH, explains it in the documentary *La Plataforma*:

> Every Friday in the assembly you see people who come, at first very fearful, very afraid, they don't open their mouths, they won't stop crying if they do, and they even feel guilty, they feel like a failure.

And these people, you see that as time goes on and they attend more assemblies, and more than anything from that collective advising that the assembly does, they start latching onto that strength, and even that leadership, like in Matías's case. So then they can become the strength for other affected people, and they can move and publicly denounce what's happening, with no worry at all, no fear, and with so much honor, and really with everything they have ... And that, I believe, is the great formula of the assembly. When I came for the first time it hit me, and it really works.

Antonio Lafuente (2009), a multidisciplinary researcher whose roots are in the field of history of science, coined the very useful concept of 'expanded authority,' which can help understand these processes better. By this he means 'a heterogeneous, delocalized cluster of experiences that produce knowledge, meticulously confirmed, outside the limits and borders of the academy, outside the laboratory.' And he enumerates some of those experiences:

[T]ogether with the market and the state, there is a third sector, based essentially, although not exclusively, on the economics of the gift. It is constituted by NGOs, antinuclear, pacifist, and ecological movements, the local movement, or the collectives of affected or concerned citizens; i.e., patients whose identity has been designed based on science and who rebel against what seems more punishment than diagnosis, struggling to construct their own identity. The most advanced, most recognized experience, which constitutes the flagship of the third sector, is the hacker movement and everything there is around the operating system GNU-Linux ... All of them are, as I say, 'experts in experience,' experts in what happens to them.

It seems to me that this figure of 'expert in experience or expert in what happens to her' is a wonderful way to conceptualize the breakdown of the arbitrary barrier between the expert as understood by the modern technoscientific tradition and 'anyone,' the person culturally unauthorized by that paradigm. The 'expert in what happens to him' would be nothing more than 'anyone' who has freed himself from the prohibition against recognizing himself as a thinking being capable of producing meaning and knowledge, and who has therefore begun to value and expand his abilities. Thus, for example, the citizens affected by mortgages who approach the PAH become 'experts in what happens to them' when they are mutually empowered to understand better and to fight against their problem, shedding the role of victim but also the position of 'those in the dark.'

I understand that when Lafuente speaks of 'communities of affected people,' he is referring in particular to groups of people who suffer from environmental diseases seldom studied by medical science, and who are united to elaborate their own theories collectively. But at the same time, Lafuente also indicates the enormous importance of all the types of knowledge that have not historically been considered scientific, and have even been persecuted ('described as superstitious, charlatans, prejudiced, ignorant, plebeian, etc.') but that comprise a whole unrecognized, 'amateur' tradition that has been fundamental for the construction of modernity as we know it. If we think of the PAH as a 'community of affected people,' we realize just how the technical, specialized knowledge bases of lawyers and social workers are allied with social, relational, experiential, and emotional ways of knowing that make up the element of solidarity and mutual aid. And without these things, the assembly, and therefore the PAH itself, would never work as it does now.

It seems that the 15M movement itself—and not only the political but also the cultural climate that was opened with it—could be thought of as a great process of collective learning of certain kinds of knowledge restricted until then to experts—as when they say (and it's true) that with the 15M 'we've learned a lot about economics.' But at the same time, it allows an intense revaluation of those kinds of ordinary, everyday, unauthorized knowledge and abilities 'of anyone' needed by those affected by the crisis of neoliberalism to defend themselves from its consequences. Those affected by the neoliberal crisis unite, then, regardless of their class and condition, to become 'experts in what happens to them'; but they understand that to be expert, in this case, doesn't require only specialized knowledge, but also those others situated, everyday ways of knowing that are usually called 'experience.'

The case of the Marea Blanca, finally, particularly corroborates this tendency. In it, the hyperspecialized, prestigious world of medical science coincides with the strong belief that such specialization and prestige are nothing if not used in service to the health—and therefore the dignity—of anyone. Time and time again, it has been repeated, even by some who are otherwise 'ideologically' very conservative (and abound in the medical profession), that public health also needs to be universal, as a matter of dignity. But what is even more interesting and unusual is that when massive protests have been staged to defend that universality, the very spaces of the protest have been infected with the positive valuation of 'anyone' implicit in the recognition.

And thus, as indicated earlier, we have seen medical specialists, along with nurses, other health personnel, users, and neighbors of the hospitals sharing those protest spaces, and doing so with the blend of expert and everyday kinds of knowledge that is typical of the 15M movement. The Marea Blanca, like the PAH, has broken with the 'service' model typical of NGOs and even many activist groups. This has led to the understanding not only that medical 'experts' are also potentially 'patients,' as the previously quoted doctor indicated, but also that the defense of public health has no meaning if we do not incorporate an open space for everything that 'anyone'—whose dignity must be safeguarded—can contribute. This way, the 'patient' stops being a victim, or the passive recipient of a service, and becomes, in fact, an 'anyone' who has to be taken into account. In the same way, those affected by mortgages can also be 'anyone,' although now it may be more directly one or another specific person, and that 'anyone' is always going to contribute something in the assembly.

The right to health or housing stops being only a need, and becomes a source of active abilities that are multiplied when they are woven in collaborative ways. Thus, it is possible to understand that 'yes, we can' which we heard chanted in the streets not only as an affirmation of the possibility of defeating the institutions and policies that oppose those universal rights but also precisely as an assertion of empowerment and the multiplication of abilities implicit in recognizing the very legitimacy of 'anyone' to establish what constitutes that dignity.

5.2.3. Social differences and practices of equality

It is important to make clear that the openness to 'anyone' I have been identifying as characteristic of the '15M climate' is not at all incompatible with a special sensitivity to knowledge, ways of life, and sectors of the population usually excluded and marginalized from the production of and access to recognized social value. Some rather hasty characterizations of 15M as a 'middle-class' movement have perhaps underestimated the ability of the various processes related to the '15M climate' (not just camping in plazas) to compose bodies, lives, and experiences marked by very different 'levels of exposure to the crisis,' to use Labrador's expression in his article 'Las vidas subprime' (2012), which addressed this plurality in 15M. That is, I think the ability to combine the material and symbolic capacities of people suffering different forms of cultural and material domination that have accumulated up to the neoliberal crisis has been underestimated.

Indeed, Labrador notes that the circulation of what he calls 'stories of *subprime* lives' is one of the main features of 15M 'as a social movement and discursive world.' These are stories of 'lives that cease to be viable,' stories of poverty that had been marginalized in the official culture of Spanish democracy, and that emerge articulating new politicizations, with particular strength in the early moments of the assemblies in the plazas. I say that they articulate new politicizations because they call attention to the kind of life that 'embodies and experiences *in situations of serious biopolitical risk* the conditions caused by the last economic cycle' (570), not because they intend to individualize that life or segregate it in a space of the 'other,' but because, on the contrary, they want to build an inclusive 'us' with those life experiences:

> At the meetings people spoke in the first person, but also brought the experiences of others. They told the stories of their own *subprime* lives, but also those of others, just as in neighborhood assemblies *subprime* life stories of others were told, some of them about people who were going to be evicted. The permanent remembrance of those who were not in the plaza tried to include other *subprime* lives (those of immigrants, elderly, disabled ...), so that *all* were in the plaza. (573)

Thus, as in the example of the woman talking to the assembly about 'those who are not here' with which I opened this chapter, there was a constant effort to build a discursive and material 'space of anyone' that was not at all politically neutral or immune to the existence of different social conditions. On the contrary, it would only become possible when it was accessible to those in situations of greater danger of social exclusion because of the crisis.

At the same time, there was also a constant effort not to lock people into rigid social categories, that is, not to decide for them what their capabilities and aspirations were, but to allow them to self-represent. Perhaps it is, again, the PAH which has led this type of dual approach further and more effectively. It is an approach that includes sensitivity to the suffering and particular vulnerability of some, while at the same time creating a situation of equality that empowers everyone to change things (although there are other remarkable examples, like Yo Sí Sanidad Universal or the Brigadas Vecinales de Observación de Derechos Humanos). In the PAH assemblies, from the beginning, university graduates, precarious workers, migrants, skilled professionals, people with little schooling, the unemployed, and even some individuals with access to the mass media (among many other conditions and situations of relative dispossession or relative stability) have sat together. The differences in these different people's access to cultural and material capital are not, in any sense, hidden or erased. What happens is that the PAH launches forms of collaboration in which those differences are no longer in the forefront, because what counts is what each person can contribute to change the 'housing emergency' situation that affects everyone. In this sense, it is particularly striking, for example, to see the fluidity of cooperation between people who personally suffer a problem with their home and others who feel concerned and sympathize, but are not themselves at risk of losing their own home.

Such differences are what have traditionally resulted in hierarchical situations in the history of the political left. A political and intellectual vanguard decides that some part of the population does not have the material and cultural ability to represent themselves, being subjected to forms of domination and social exclusion that prevent it. As Pablo La Parra explained in his illuminating article 'Revueltas lógicas' (2014), 15M involved the implementation of something that, following Rancière, we might call 'equality practices,' which seek to disrupt these hierarchical dynamics:

> The fact that the 15M assemblies were based on what was agreed to be called 'inclusiveness'—i.e., on discussion among peers without establishing a prior identity requirement or aspiring to monopolize participants' commitment—not only helps explain the extraordinary capacity for social aggregation and the legitimacy of the movement, but also constitutes the practice that confirms its egalitarian ideal. (11)

La Parra also echoed Rancière's criticism of Althusser, to warn against the risk of putting oneself in a privileged position from which the attempt to 'discuss among equals' is quickly characterized as an (unconscious) 'middle-class' trend to erase the differences between oneself and the subaltern classes (an accusation launched against the 15M movement, among others, by the anthropologist Manuel Delgado). Indeed, Rancière has devoted much of his extensive work to dismantling such an intellectual position that seeks to constantly denounce delusions of emancipation, 'unmasking' them as hidden ways to play the system of domination in which each social class acts inevitably as determined by its place of privilege or subordination. In a critique of the sociologist Pierre Bourdieu, Rancière (1984) synthesized as a circular argument the alleged discovery of such an intellectual position: first, that the system of domination is reproduced because people do not perceive the way it functions; and second, that the way the system of domination works is by making its functioning imperceptible (Ross 1997). Imperceptible to 'the people,' yes, but not to the intellectual who, like Bourdieu, claims the ability to avoid that deception.

I will return to clashes between the egalitarian practices of the 15M with forms of authority indebted to this intellectual tradition that claims to see 'what people do not see,' but first I want to propose very briefly three arguments that may be useful to illuminate the issue of social class differences in the '15M climate.' The first is a corollary of the above: following Rancière, it is interesting to emphasize the impossibility of finding a privileged position from which to think about the 'equality practices' that are deployed in the 15M climate, for those of us who study these practices

are as immersed in systems of domination as those who implement them
(and sometimes we are, in fact, the same people). That does not prevent us,
I think, from helping to build an account of these experiments; nor does it
prevent this account from including references to the different situations of
social exclusion or privilege with which said 'equality practices' must deal.
In this sense, I greatly appreciate the contribution of Charlotte Nordmann
(2010) in her book *Bourdieu/Rancière*. She proposed, from a casual and creative
relationship with the texts of these intellectuals, that it would be much
more useful for emancipatory practices of equality to admit, in contrast to
Rancière's position, that they do not come 'out of nothing,' but rather from
concrete, and sometimes contradictory, social positions that need to be
studied. Furthermore, contradicting Bourdieu, they are capable of breaking
the cycle of domination, creating new, more egalitarian social compositions
that redistribute social order.

So, entering the second argument, 15M is a political and cultural process
that is quite difficult to understand without talking about social situations
like the neoliberal precarization exerted on segments of the population that
have, it is true, different levels of access to cultural and material resources.
At the same time—and I am not trying to fetishize the event or the climate
of the 15M movement—it is also important to think how both opened a
new space of 'anyone.' Or, to put it in another way, to accompany them in
their egalitarian experiments without trying to reduce them to a game of
predictable exchanges between fixed and pre-existing identities or social
'classes.' To do this, it may be useful, as La Parra does in quoting Espinoza
Pino (2013), to recover E. P. Thompson's (2013) notion of class: it is not a
matter of 'a static, homogeneous category,' but 'a dynamic historical and
social process, the result of the exchange of experiences, social trajectories,
historical memory, and various socio-political objectives' (La Parra 11).

In this sense, as La Parra reminds us, the very 'transverse, interclass,
and intergenerational' reality (Gálvez Biesca 2007) of the precarization
phenomenon already clearly requires, in and of itself, a complex approach
to 'social class' phenomena, such as that proposed by Thompson. I referred
in the previous chapter to precarization during neoliberalism, especially
among young people, as one of the processes that have motivated the search
for other spaces in which to cultivate skills and forms of collaboration,
generating subjectivities that were later tested in the 15M movement's
'practices of equality.' But it would be very important too (and unfortunately
I will not be able to do it in this book due to lack of resources) to track
in more detail many other precarizations and their consequent creative
responses. Some of these include migrants who have moved from allegedly
'buying' the dream of an 'ownership society' to joining the front ranks

of the PAH, or those public workers who have distanced themselves from a supposedly 'privileged' corporatism to meet on an equal footing with the rest of society in the Mareas, or of those retired people relegated to an alleged depoliticization or to forms of 'old' politics, which have become creative and solidary 'yayoflautas.'[6]

In any case, I think the 15M climate has been able to combine these and many other processes of precarization, through different levels of risk and exclusion. It has done so by building the legitimacy of 'anyone's' experience. Being 'affected' has been considered something worthy of greater value and greater respect, allowing the building of equality practices to which, I think, we should apply the same 'presumption of intelligence' that they apply to anyone.

There are still, of course, 'authorities' who will not recognize that legitimacy, even if they defend very similar things to the 15M movement, such as the universality of the rights to housing, healthcare, education, etc. So it's one thing to think that 'anyone' has those rights, and another to think that 'anyone' has the right to participate actively in the elucidation, conquest, and specific construction of those rights, with no need for anybody else to authorize him or her with their expert knowledge. From this there arises a latent—and sometimes a manifest—'conflict of authorities,' which seems to me to be another fundamental element for understanding the cultural climate generated by the 15M movement.

5.3. Conflict of Authorities: Intellectuals, Mass Media, and the 15M Climate

5.3.1. The 'intellectual leader' in his circle of impotence

On October 27, 2013, about 4.7 million people listened to the journalist and writer Arturo Pérez-Reverte say the following things on the television program *Salvados* (2013):

Can nothing be done? Is there nothing we can do? Well, sometimes the answer is no. At least, the answer I give myself is no ... It won't change anything, nothing will change anything. If there were a revolution today, people would go out first to see if their car had been burned

---

6 'Yayofalutas' is a derivation of 'perroflautas', a pejorative expression used by some people to disqualify 15M participants. 'Perroflautas' alludes to the stereotypical figure of a young punk or hippie that asks for money in the street, surrounded by dogs and playing the flute. It was reclaimed by the movement, and later creatively transformed into 'yayoflautas' to refer to the elder participants in the movement ('yayo' is a familiar word for 'grandfather').

> ... Do you know why people want the crisis to be over? To go back to
> doing exactly what they did before: to buy a car again, a mortgage, to
> go to Cancún for vacation again ...

He listed with a certain nostalgia some causes of this supposed widespread
selfishness: 'Before, when things went bad, in other times, there were
ideologies that supported those things, there were ideas, there were even
intellectuals who made use of those ideas and disseminated them to
the people ... Now those leaders no longer exist, society is defenseless,
orphaned.' He concluded:

> People don't want an education, they don't demand an education
> for their children ... The whole problem with Spain is a problem
> with education, because we are who we are; politicians are only one
> manifestation, the symptom of a disease of who we are: the acritical
> stance, the lack of culture, fratricide, vileness, envy—that is who
> we are, we are Spaniards. The politician is nothing more than the
> officialization of our essence ... it's a culture problem.

From among the innumerable reflections and critiques on the Spanish
economic crisis and its possible alternatives expressed by intellectuals,
opinion makers, participants in talk-shows (*tertulianos*), and other heirs
of the elitist, exclusivist conception of culture, those expressed here by
Pérez-Reverte have the virtue of clearly identifying the central stereotypes of
this tradition: 'people' are uncouth and selfish, only the intellectual leaders
can change things, and without them society is 'orphaned.'

In this sense, it seems to me that Pérez-Reverte's position perfectly
exemplifies a particular viewpoint on the phenomena I have been studying—
phenomena of empowerment of 'cultures of anyone' and of their blending
specialized kinds of knowledge. Instead of despising or attacking them, he
ignores them, because, I would dare to say, they don't fit within his framework
of 'what's possible.' Pérez-Reverte's conception of politics is simultaneously
and very clearly one of pessimistic essentialism and individualism that
doesn't seem to consider the possibility that collaborative, supportive forms
of politics, capable of respectfully articulating human interdependence and
of empowering anyone's abilities, could exist as anything more than isolated
and even 'heroic' acts:

> What prevents someone from saying, 'Let it rain napalm!' is precisely
> the fact that there is always one just man in Sodom, there is always
> that little seed, that teacher, that solitary hero there waging his small,
> individual battle, and he'll manage to get another kid to do it, too.

From this viewpoint, then, it's no wonder that in the same appearance on the program *Salvados*, Pérez-Reverte also projects a pessimistic vision of the 15M movement:

I—the 15M when I saw it emerge, I said: 'Look, there are still heroes. Heroes can still reach an agreement' ... After just a few days of observing it, I began to see how it changed, how the boy disappeared, how the demagogue occupied his place, how rhetorical speech replaced rational speech, how the most populist and ignorant replaced the smartest and the most astute, and how little by little it disintegrated into the miserable human condition.

No doubt this inevitable triumph of 'the miserable human condition' resonates with the feeling that 'there's no hope for this country' of which Javier Marías spoke, and with the view that 'barbarism is our natural state' asserted by Muñoz Molina. But it's worth asking: Why is this type of reading of the 15M movement, and of political and human nature in general, still so attractive and gaining so many adherents? After all, it completely contradicts the relatively mass 'common sense' I mentioned before—that is, it ignores the 'climate' of possibility that has opened up in recent years.[7]

Obviously, centuries of hegemony of the modern power/knowledge complex will not vanish overnight, nor probably in decades of proliferating online collaborative cultures, or of horizontal, anti-elitist social movements. But besides all that, perhaps the greatest power of the modern belief in the cultural inequality of human beings—in the existence of a minority of heroes and intellectuals and an egotistical, stupid majority—is still that it offers a type of moral justification for the political inaction that is especially useful in a crisis.

---

7 If we contextualize Pérez-Reverte's words in the program during which he utters them, we realize that, in fact, they exert the seductiveness of a familiar, paralyzing pessimism that, paradoxically, has been partially weakened during these years of crisis. In fact, the host of the program himself, Jordi Évole, conducts the entire interview as an attempt to move Pérez-Reverte beyond his pessimism. This wouldn't, however, necessarily mean taking him beyond his elitism and individualism (and in that sense, *Salvados* often tends to feed its own optimism with the logic of 'isolated heroic gestures'). But the show does express a certain boredom with that type of defeatist explanation, which is probably one of the main factors for this television program's huge success.

In this regard, minutes earlier, another 'testimony' invited by Évole, that of philosopher Txetxu Ausín, had mentioned the Marea Blanca as an example of civic mobilization. He emphasized its ability to fight and win in the legal arena, thus suggesting, no matter how fuzzily and fleetingly, the argument for the characteristic ability of these movements to mix everyday kinds of knowledge with specialized ones.

Of course, the existence in any society of selfish, passive, or simply stupid attitudes like those noted by Pérez-Reverte is undeniable, and it is to those attitudes that commentators turn time and time again to justify their disdain for human nature and the pointlessness of all political effort. But, as Rancière might say, that type of defeatist criticism forms part of the 'circle of impotence' associated with the 'pedagogization of society': it is postulated that to 'have culture,' one must submit to the guardianship of the avant-gardes that control it. In doing so, the rest of the population is thus being turned into supposedly ignorant, dependent beings who—and this is worse—will internalize this judgment and begin to believe they really are incapable of learning on their own, and therefore of changing things. This is how the image of a society divided between the few 'in the know' and the majority 'in the dark' is consolidated, and it has a corrosive effect on everyone, sowing both elitist scorn and inferiority complexes everywhere. In the end, a structural distrust of the other develops, which leads to the same 'selfishness' that Pérez-Reverte criticizes. This only leaves the door open to change through 'education,' as Pérez-Reverte himself does. But this is often an education that, as demanded by the myth of pedagogy, must be authorized by 'those in the know,' thus perpetuating the existence of that group and, therefore, of cultural inequality.[8]

In contrast to this 'circle of impotence,' I have shown how the 15M movement and later social processes like the Mareas or the PAH are, among other things, precisely political efforts that reject the need for 'teachers' or intellectual leaders as guides to bring everyone else towards 'education,' 'culture,' or social change. On the contrary, in these movements it is assumed that things are done better with everyone involved, when everyone contributes their abilities and ways of knowing. Its dynamic consists of multiplying these capacities and ways of knowing by creating collaborative networks in which anyone can participate. That doesn't mean, once again, that these abilities

---

8 In an interview, César Rendueles said the following about the internalization of cultural elitism and the disdain for the masses in Spanish culture: 'Nineteenth-century elites did not hide their panic and disgust at the possibility that the working classes might gain access to political institutions. They thought the masses would disgrace Western civilization to the point of destroying it. At the start of the twentieth century, during the colonial era, that hate became a racist fear that the populations subjugated by imperialism would become uncontrollable and would end up invading the metropolis. This discourse has been internalized and endures even today. We see ourselves the same way the rich previously viewed the dangerous classes. We have incorporated that elitism into our ideological genotype. This is why egalitarian projects have practically disappeared from the political sphere. We radically distrust our own capacity to debate together; we view democracy as a competition among private preferences' (Arjona 2013).

and knowledge bases can't be valued for their differences: the movements understand perfectly that specialized, technical knowledge is necessary for some things, and for others, everyday or experiential kinds of knowledge are needed. Likewise, they understand that not everything has the same value within each of these ways of knowing, and so filtering and refining mechanisms are implemented with the goal of creating 'collective intelligence.' But mainly what the practices of these movements propose is precisely that politics and culture are things in which everybody must participate actively. After all, everybody lives in society and everybody needs to give meaning to their existence, and it is not fair that others decide how it should be done.

In this sense, perhaps even more so than the technical or expert authorities, it has been the intellectual and political authorities that have been deeply questioned—even if only implicitly—by this cycle of movements and its emergent 'cultural power.' The responses to those challenges have not been long in coming. But as far as I can find, they have tended to appear in critiques that, like those of Pérez-Reverte, in fact do not address this central question of a cultural transformation involving the appearance of collaborative networks which reject the guardianship of any avant-garde. Rather, they are limited to wielding multiple, many-hued, and often contradictory reasons for denying that the movements—particularly the 15M—have any value.

5.3.2. Deaf ears, insults, advice, and reaffirmations of authority

The op-ed article '5 articles not written about the 15M,' published by the writer and columnist Javier Cercas in *El País* on June 24, 2011, is especially useful as a quick review of those critiques, because it suggests a classification of some of them. Cercas begins the text by saying that he has been wanting to write about the 15M movement for weeks, but for several reasons he never got round to it. Already in that first statement we can find hidden a central characteristic of the way many intellectuals have related to the 15M: they have wanted to write *about* the movement. That is, they have wanted to take it as one more in the infinity of current 'subjects' or 'issues' they write about every day in the mass media from the position of authority granted to them by the tradition that guarantees the figure of the intellectual, charged with all the problems I have been analyzing.

They have frequently wanted to read the nonauthoritarian, noncompetitive culture of the 15M from the logics of an authoritarian intellectual tradition and a competitive political economy. So, perhaps inevitably, they have tended to emphasize or even invent rather partial, lesser aspects of the movement that allowed them to read it without calling into question the culture from within which they read it.

Thus, for example, the first of the five articles on 15M that Cercas says he hasn't written—and also the one 'he is happiest not to have written'—would have been 'an article written on the spot,' or rather, he says, 'an act', since in it he would have announced that he was leaving his newspaper column, the novel he was writing, and his 'father–son duties' to go to the plaza de Cataluña in Barcelona 'to throw in my lot with the *acampados*.'

Of course, Cercas uses a humorous tone here, but the type of joke he decides to use is significant. He compares joining the 15M camps during the early days of the movement—something, remember, that several million people of all the ages did all across Spain—with a kind of voluntary enlistment in a war. This understanding of the movement as a (violent) rupture of the everyday, prevents him from seeing that other fundamental dimension of collaborative support for daily life the plazas had from very early on—day-care centers, senior centers, food service, and all the other devices for a mutual care sensitive to vulnerability, were already present from the beginning, and they fit very poorly with Cercas's warlike metaphor.

In that sense, curiously, Cercas's own position would perhaps not be so far removed from those other types of article he might have wanted to parody: those of the old 'revolutionaries' from '68 that react critically to the *Indignados*, 'first calling us,' says Cercas—again in a humorous register—'pansies, and the movement, queer: a serious revolution burns the Parliament or takes the Bastille or the Winter Palace with blood and fire, for fuck's sake.' Later, however, they would also label 'the 15M as demagogic, populist, fanatic, antipolitical, and antisystem, and the campers as hordes or violent mobs.' I say his position would perhaps not be so far removed from these revolutionaries turned—he says—'extreme right-wingers as a consequence of being so modern,' because they both focus their attention on the protest aspects of the movement, ignoring its capacity for collaborative support of democratic cultures and everyday life in the *acampadas*. Neither Cercas nor just about anybody else in the mass media has said anything about this last aspect, as far as I know.[9]

In an earlier article, I discussed the existence of some curious contradictions, similar to those Cercas presents, in contributions from intellectuals, particularly in the conversation published by *El País* between the publisher Mario Muchnick and the painter Eduardo Arroyo (Cavero 2011), titled 'Sol visto desde mayo del '68.' In it appeared the recurring idea alluded to by Cercas: the 15M as a 'revolution of lies,' a simulacrum of revolution, an insufficient gesture. 'These guys want to fix the system. We

---

9 Notable exceptions would be José Luis Sampedro and Manuel Castells, among others.

wanted to blow it up,' said Arroyo. In an article in *La Vanguardia*, Catalan writer Quim Monzó (2011), for his part, asserted on the one hand that it was shameful to call the 15M a 'revolution' because is not a true change in political and economic structures, but just a 'camp-out.' At the same time, venting his spleen with 'I won't be the one who defends the politicians in power; they give me the heaves,' he pushed the vote as the only way of fighting against bipartisanship.[10]

Felix de Azúa (2014; Sainz Borgo 2014) also stood on shaky, ambiguous ground when he said, 'The inability to understand violence, the absolute forgetfulness that war implies, functional illiteracy, all lead to schoolyard revolts.' Feeling the need to clarify, he added, 'I'm not insinuating that the 15M must move into terrorism … I am saying that if a movement wants to fight this war successfully it needs leaders, study, planning, and a program.' In the end, for Azúa, as for Pérez-Reverte, it all it comes down to a problem of education: 'They have not been educated in how to study, in discipline, in effort, in sacrifice.' Although, in fact, with or without education, 'the human way of life' consists of 'huge catastrophes generated by our own stupidity.'

It seems to me that perhaps this type of criticism, along with Cercas's article, would also fit into another category of participation, which has perhaps actually been the most frequent kind among intellectuals regarding the 15M: that which consists of telling the movement what it should do. Thus, completely ignoring the possibility of working to construct the 15M movement from within so that their ideas would add to its collective intelligence—the same possibility that so many millions of other people had assumed—intellectuals like Cercas simply prefer to recommend from outside that, for example, they put 'more emphasis on Europe,' because Europe, he says, is 'our only reasonable utopia.' Which, by the way, confirms Cercas's allegiance to that intellectual tradition that, voluntarily or not, has helped so much to justify the construction of neoliberalism through its Europeanism.

---

10 Kiko Amat and Manolo Martínez answered him in an open letter. They asserted that Monzó preferred to focus on superficial aspects of the movement rather than try to understand it and take it seriously. They recommended he read several of the first documents of political proposals produced in the plazas. Furthermore, they waxed ironic about his criticisms of the 15M for not being 'sufficiently revolutionary': 'In a last pirouette, Monzó also suggests that the reason for his lack of interest in the *Indignats* movement is that it is insufficiently revolutionary, and that what they are doing is not revolution, but 'camping out'; perhaps insinuating that, if they were armed and wore ski masks, he would cast aside his laptop and hit the streets with fists at the ready to combat those 'powerful politicians' that he so firmly swears he detests, like a crazy *sans culotte*' (2011, 43).

In the intellectual world, everyone has their own recommendation for the *Indignados*, regardless of their ideological allegiance. Thus, Ignacio Ramonet (2011), in a conference in Heidelberg, wished that there were more concern with the power of the *mass* media in the movement, because he had seen very little of it reflected in its slogans. Meanwhile, Francisco R. Adrados responded to a survey of 'intellectuals' in *La Razón* (2012) saying, 'information, still scarce, indicates decay,' and recommends that the 15M movement 'should not live for a date, for an obligation, that is self-imposed.' In a manifesto titled 'Una ilusión compartida' (Público.es 2011) names such as García Montero, Almudena Grandes, and Joaquín Sabina, for their part, spoke of 'taking advantage of the civic energy of the 15M' to mobilize the left. Another of the *La Razón* survey respondents, however, the university professor Ángel Alonso Cortés, said, 'its strength is low because its persuasive ability is weak, and to have a future it would need ideological discipline.'

There are many more examples, and if there is anything surprising about them, at least if you know the least little bit about the 15M, it is how colossally capable they all are of ignoring the possibility of using channels opened up by the movement to incorporate any proposal. These intellectuals toss out their own proposals as if they were unavoidably—through some kind of magical, existential quality that would make them different from millions of their fellow citizens—prevented from taking their ideas to the street just like anyone else.

Finally, there is one more type of contribution to talk about, which, even if these contributors don't put a positive value on the 15M, or even explore in depth those cultural dimensions of it that clash directly with the tradition of modern intellectual authority, at least 'sniff' around them, that is, they notice some of their aspects. Perhaps the article 'Empobrecimiento' by writer Enrique Vila-Matas (2011) could be included here. In it, he drew a connection between the 15M movement and the use of digital social networks, in particular Twitter. His idea was that the brief format (140 characters) of the messages or tweets sent by the *Indignados* was one more indicator of the widespread impoverishment of the language in current times. This assertion, as I have noted elsewhere, comes across as quite odd coming from a writer who is heir to the avant-garde, defender of 'portable literature,' a style of writing that practices self-restriction and plays with self-imposed formats.

Sánchez Dragó (2011) would do something similar. He seemed to understand the 15M movement's dimension of opening up politics to anyone, but he did so only to criticize it and defend just the opposite: a type of politics that would function as a professional job done by a series of salaried technicians. In other words, a 'technocracy':

Like everyone, I pay some men to manage public affairs, not so that they can allow or force me to butt in on something that bores me. If a businessman hires an accountant, it's so he doesn't have to bother with the boring accounting, not so he can go poking around in it. Wouldn't that be something! Out of the frying pan, into the fire ... Let the politicians manage politics honestly and effectively, and not bother those of us who have other jobs, vocations, and interests.

In a similar vein, albeit using less expressive terms, the responses of many of those 'professional' politicians, such as those Sánchez Dragó likes, have flown past. Mostly they have reminded the citizenry that politics is done at the ballot box, and that's it. In some cases, they even urged the 15M movement to form a political party or, better still, join theirs. I will not take up time or space reporting these types of response, which are much more monotonous than those of the intellectuals. What I would like to do is examine the intersections of both types of response with representations of the 15M movement and its 'climate,' from some of the prevailing logics of the big mass media outlets. These media representations—and in general all those coming from the cultural establishment—have provoked direct and indirect responses from the movements that allow a better understanding of the conflict between diverse forms of authority that is put into play in these dialogues.

5.3.3. When 'anyone' responds to the cultural authority
Much has been said about the increasing distance between the politicians and the citizenry of Spain. Somewhat less has been said about the latter's possible emancipation from the establishment of reality performed by the mass media, and perhaps still less about the increasing distance between intellectuals and average citizens. Nevertheless, they are strongly related phenomena, and thus became obvious at many times during the 15M movement.

Let's recall, for example, the airing of the Spanish National Radio program 'En días como hoy' on Tuesday, May 17, 2011. Two days after the demonstration on May 15, and in the face of the incipient encampment at Puerta del Sol, the *'tertulianos'* (a hybrid species between the figures of the intellectual and the journalist, these are participants on television and radio political programs, mostly journalists, sometime politicians, or 'experts') present on this morning public radio show, Miguel Larrea and Javier García Vila, spoke frankly about the subject, expressing opinions like the following: 'It's an embryo of something, but confusing'; 'There's a mix of antisystem forces and all kinds of other forces there'; 'The slogan is taken from Stéphane Hessel's book, *Indignez-vous!*, a worthless book, it's nothing': '"Real democracy": as Churchill said, democracy is the worst of all possible systems except all the others, and that's the reality, there *is* no other alternative to democracy'; 'Everything about assemblies is so passé since the French Revolution, it doesn't make much sense'; 'I think it's great they've been kicked out, because they were turning Madrid's Puerta del Sol into a camp where all kinds of strange people were showing up ...'

To all of this, which was contributed by Larrea, García Vila indicated his agreement, adding that in Sol they were expressing 'a feeling of orphanhood relative to the political class,' but that it was a mass of 'confusing assemblies that led nowhere,' and furthermore, 'they are used by violent antisystem groups to do their little things.' From there, both *tertulianos* began a spiral of mutual reaffirmation that led them to build the following series of stereotypes: 'Can the world be changed? It's very hard, we're seeing a world dominated by money, by consumerism ...' 'Esperanza Aguirre said what they have to do is go and vote, but that's exactly what they *won't* do, the kind of young people we have today.' 'It's necessary to be organized, to have spokesmen, it's necessary to establish structures, which is exactly what they're criticizing.' 'One of the leaders is a lawyer who's running for office, I say it with the greatest affection, but there is nothing more bourgeois,' and to top it off: 'Young people today have it so much better than 40 years ago.'

Up until then, everything was rolling along like something we could call 'any given day in the CT,' any given day in the world of the *tertulianos*, daily defenders of the limits of the possible from their position of semi-intellectual, semi-mediatized authority. But something was changing. A few minutes later, the program was opened to callers, and the telephone call of one listener—Cristina from Burgos—would soon go viral: 'I'm speaking on public radio, right? The one that represents us all, the one we pay for with our taxes?' This was how Cristina's contribution began, but she then went on to say the following clearly and confidently:

> I'm 46 years old, I was at the demonstration in Madrid this Sunday, and I have something to say: there *were* a lot of young people, but there were people of all ages and conditions. Antisystem? Yes, obviously: politicians and bankers and those who really support these measures that are cutting all the rights it cost our parents and grandparents blood, sweat, and tears to earn; our politicians, who we voted for, who are evidently managed by the same hands of capital that are also managing the mass media, are the ones who are making our young people, our sons and daughters, antisystem. Because they are leaving them out of the system.

After continuing to develop these ideas, Cristina alluded directly to the *tertulianos*: 'One of you said, "the kind of young people we have" ... This kind of young person is the one who's going to give us a big surprise.' She concluded with these words:

> You've thrown them out of Puerta del Sol, but we're all there, supporting them. And we don't need political parties or economic parties, we don't need any of that. We're more than capable of getting things done: our parents and grandparents raised us with the dignity to always move forward, following our dreams. There we all are. No, there are no *antisystems*, there are not four lamebrains, no. We are all of us defending a better world. That's all I wanted to say.

Moments like these exemplify very literally the 'rebellions of the publics' about which the texts of Amador Fernández-Savater and Ángel Luis Lara (among others) talk. This type of situation almost always tends to be explained in terms of responses to the 'media's manipulation of information,' but I think it's important to also put them into the wider context of the proliferation of participative cultures to which I referred, along with Henry Jenkins, in the previous chapter. In this sense, not only would there be straight answers to the distortions or twisted views of reality from the big media outlets, but also, in a very important way, these would occur within a pervasive climate of circulation of 'post-media' voices in the digital sphere, capable of recounting their own versions as well.

Cristina's call can be seen in the YouTube video 'Cristina, la oyente que exigió a RNE respeto para los manifestantes del 15m' (2011). It belongs to a tacit subgenre of what we could call 'straight answers to media powers on their own turf,' and when this happens, always with an aura of exceptionality and challenge, they are widely disseminated through social networks. They are moments when the word of 'anyone' (of someone who doesn't try to give value to what he or she says from a supposedly exceptional knowledge base, but from an everyday, experiential position) directly confronts the authorized discourse of the media, *tertulianos*, or intellectuals, and which the post-media sphere later celebrates and spreads. They couldn't exist as such, or at least, they couldn't achieve massive dissemination, without that post-media sphere that is in charge of selecting them, extracting them from the media ocean—which sometimes even censors them—and distributing them virally.

A pair of good, more recent examples of this genre took place as a result of another of the important victories of these social movements: that of the inhabitants of Gamonal, a *barrio* in Burgos, who in January 2014 managed to stop an urban planning project suspected of political corruption in their region. Thus, the video 'Un vecino corrige a un periodista de Radio Nacional que estaba mintiendo' (2014) (with almost 1.5 million hits on YouTube) shows an even more direct irruption of 'anyone's' voice into the media discourse. In fact, it is literally an *interruption*, and thus different from Cristina's call, which was part of the segment of the program called 'Listeners' Conversation.' In this case, what we have is a radio reporter in the street, covering the protests live, and saying, 'Groups of citizens have become violent, they're burning containers and they've broken the windows of some businesses.' But as he speaks, we hear some voices trying to talk back to him, until finally one of them interrupts him outright—we understand that somebody has probably snatched the microphone from him—and protests: 'Don't lie: not a single business, they're banks. Banks, which we understand are guilty, too. But not a single business.'

Another video related to the Gamonal protests ('Manipulación y acoso en TVE. El portavoz de Gamonal calla la boca a Mariló Montero' 2014) also gained considerable dissemination on the networks. This one showed a verbal confrontation between Manuel Alonso, a spokesperson for the inhabitants of Gamonal, and a group of *tertulianos* from TVE. In the face of presenter Mariló Montero's insistence on asking about the throwing of liquids and eggs by the Gamonal demonstrators, Alonso answered: 'And of all the problems the people face, this is what's important? Whether an egg or a bottle of beer is thrown, that's what's important? Or is what's important the problems that the people, the *vecinos*, the citizens in general have?' Montero responded with the myth of journalistic objectivity: 'My opinion isn't what matters here, I have to stay focused too, on the information about what we're seeing.'

Given that answer maybe ten years earlier—if I might be permitted this small flight of fancy—before social networks had turned the public sphere into a much more plural and accessible space for many citizens, perhaps then the neighbors' spokesperson would have been left speechless. But on this occasion, what Manuel Alonso's reaction shows is that the myth of journalistic objectivity has lost much of its force in the last decade. Also, although not many people use the term 'agenda-setting,' that doesn't mean they don't know very well that the veracity of information depends as much on an accurate representation of the facts as on which facts are chosen for representation, and with what degree of priority some are chosen over others.

'Look, I'm going to give you top priority information, eh?' says Manuel Alonso, pulling out a document that certified, he explains, that the business developers who had time and time again denied any involvement in the Gamonal project, resigned from the business that was to supply all the cement for the works, and would therefore profit from the project, just a few days after the protests started.

The TVE reporter responds rather disconcertedly and decides to turn things over to another reporter, but not without first dropping a veiled question regarding the authority of that paper—in her words, not a 'document'—which Alonso has already clearly identified as an official document from the Certificate of Incorporation: 'María, do me a favor,' she says. 'We're going to take a closer look at that paper, while I go to the plenary, I want to look *that* paper over closely, the *seal* of that paper, the *heading* on that paper, *who's* sealed that paper, *what* kind of documentation it is ...' She pronounces this list emphasizing its monotone rhythm, as if explaining that there are many requirements 'that paper' is going to have to fulfill to earn some credibility as a 'document' in her eyes.

This exchange seems particularly revealing because it shows how the myth of objective reporting is ultimately supported by the expert, technocratic power at the core of cultural authority in the modern West. What Manuel Alonso does here, and what the conjunction between the climate of widespread illegitimacy causing the economic crisis and the informative plurality opened up by digital cultures has done, is break the cycle of belief in mass media discussed in the first chapter. Manuel Alonso and his Gamonal *vecinos* have stopped believing that reality is what becomes visible through the media, they have stopped believing something is reality just because it's what *everybody* believes. The myth of media objectivity is laid bare: the inhabitants can produce their own versions of reality, which they well know are much less biased, and they do it by contributing documents if necessary.

Faced with this gesture, the media discourse has no other choice but to step back, turning to a supposedly higher authority than their own, an authority that would have the power to '*certify*' with their seal what is truly real, from among the different versions. That authority, even if it is not named straight out, can be none other than that which emanates from the modern power/knowledge complex in its many and varied sources of legitimacy, from the technoscientific to the intellectual, by way of its bureaucratic and institutional derivatives. It is the same tradition to which Manuel Alonso also turns when showing his legal document—but he doesn't wield it from public television's position of power, nor by hiding behind that supposed informative objectivity. He acts from the power of a local movement which also values another type of authority: the authority of anyone to participate in the necessarily collective debate over what constitutes a life with dignity—the debate about 'what is really important' that Manuel Alonso proposes to the reporter, and which she is unwilling to join unless she has an official seal.

So, in essence, the demands of those 'voices of anyone' from the new movements arising in the wake of the 15M, when they break out in the media or other public forums, are no more and no less than demands to be allowed to talk about what's really important, even if they are not voices gifted with hegemonic cultural authority (technoscientific, intellectual, media, etc.). In that sense, it seems to me that what they do is somewhat more complex than 'denying' or 'correcting' wrong information, although that may often be the immediate intention. It also has to do, at least tacitly, with the public arenas—which are neither 'neutral' nor 'objective'—where what will pass for reality is established, and where, therefore, expectations are also constructed about what a life with dignity should be. The movements protest that these arenas should not be monopolized by voices that wield expert authorities (such as those of the *tertulianos*, journalists, intellectuals, politicians, and others belonging to the group of 'those in the know'). Such a monopoly would imply that they were the only ones to elucidate something that nobody should delegate to others: the meaning and dignity of their lives.

This 'conflict of authorities' is often expressed as a confrontation, a clash, like those indignant responses in the media, interruptions, and exchanges of proofs and counterproofs. Recent years have seen more public challenges to authority in the Spanish state. We have seen students who, when receiving their National Award for Excellence in Academic Performance, ignore Minister Wert, the person responsible for cuts to education. We have seen former spokesperson for the PAH, Ada Colau (now mayor of Barcelona), stand up in the Congress of Deputies and call 'supposed financial experts' criminals for praising the Spanish legislation on evictions 'while there are people who are taking their own lives over this problem' (an event that gave rise to another viral video); we have seen Spaniards who have emigrated to Paris and belong to the Marea Granate (the *marea* for exiles of the economic crisis) publicly confronting the PSOE candidate to the European elections to remind her that her party is responsible for the 'austerity' her campaign is now aimed against. We have seen a woman approach Philip of Bourbon in the middle of the street to demand a referendum on the permanence of the monarchy. And we have also seen innumerable recordings circulating online that show actions and events that contradict official and media versions, such as, notably, the active role of the secret police in provoking violent confrontations in the street. This includes a video where one of these secret police, disguised as an 'antisystem,' was beaten by the riot police themselves while he yelled at them, 'I'm one of you, for fuck's sake!'

But there have also been other types of manifestation, more indirect and elusive, of that conflict between the authority of the established cultural powers and that of 'anyone' who collaborates to prevent the monopoly of those powers over the meaning and dignity of human life. I want to take the time now to talk about them, because in fact, it seems that they are the most characteristic of the political cycle I am investigating, generally not much given to straightforward antagonism. Rather, they are rich in strategies of 'withdrawal from the established order,' as the philosopher Santiago López-Petit would say—at times even through refusal to be set against whomever should have fulfilled the role of 'enemy' (as had happened with the police). In considering these alterations of established identities (and their habitual conflicts), which have been so characteristic of the 15M, I want finally to return, once again, to the question of the sustainability of the cultural power generated around the movement, especially complicated once the plazas are deserted.

5.4. 'The Boxer and the Fly': Nomadism and Sustainability after the Plazas

5.4.1. Deserting 'police logic'

May 27, 2011, eve of the grand finale of the 'Champions League,' in which F. C. Barcelona will face Manchester United. The television newscast of TVE's first network connects with London, where the match is to take place, to show the Barcelona fans spending time in the 'entertainment zone' organized for that purpose in Hyde Park. Behind the correspondent, people are reserved and silent. But suddenly a voice bursts in: 'Now, now!' Immediately a large group with posters stands up and choruses noisily, 'They call it democracy, but it's not!' The correspondent, who can barely be heard now, keeps calling them 'fans of Barça,' denying the obvious. And the report continues without the camera focusing on them.

Where fans should have been, the *Indignados* had appeared. This is one of the typical maneuvers of displacement of identities that characterize the 15M movement. These maneuvers at times even lead to situations where the *Indignados* should appear, but nobody is there at all; that is, the very space assigned to the movement has been 'vacated.' So, in effect, as the 15M movement is assimilated like a new actor in the reality which the mass media and cultural authorities describe and guarantee, stereotypes, expectations, and forms of representation begin to arise that catch on within those 'official' narratives, which the 15M has often tried to avoid. Let us consider, to give an idea of the popularity of the movement, that by the time of the local elections on May 22, 2011, only a week after the *acampadas* began, the mainstream television networks had already included among their live broadcasts of the meetings of the various campaigning political parties, another obligatory one at Puerta del Sol. This was how, from very early on, a codified and increasingly routine space was reserved to represent 'the *Indignados*' protest,' according to the language typically used by the media.

I have already commented that limiting the understanding of the movement to nothing more than a protest is perhaps one of the most habitual and effective means of erasing its potential to create collaborative ways of life and democratic cultures in the long term. Given this, it's no wonder the collective intelligence of the movement often resisted engaging in direct conflict and resistance or 'shock'—the types of logic that were expected of it, based on that limited understanding.

Perhaps the best example of that type of collective intelligence is what was seen when, after the police took down the information booth on August 2, 2011, which was the last piece of physical evidence of Acampadasol left, a series of mass 'walks through the plaza' arose spontaneously, and led to the police's decision to close the plaza to the public completely. Then, instead of continuing to try to reoccupy the plaza or dispersing, the people went to other plazas, and began to hold assemblies and meetings again there. These meetings attracted growing numbers and reached great intensity, giving rise to a kind of rebirth of Sol outside of Sol. Meanwhile, the Puerta del Sol itself remained completely empty and surrounded by police, day and night.

This situation unleashed the humorous wit of the networks, which quickly invented a fictitious protest called '#Acampadapolicía.' On August 2, a Twitter account was created with that name, and sent this first message, parodying those of Acampadasol: '#Acampadapolicía needs: tear gas, rubber balls, extendable nightsticks, and walkie-talkie batteries, this is going to last a while @acampadasol.' And many more followed: 'We're buying the tomalaporra.net domain and the Facebook spanishinvolution'; 'We've set up camp in Sol and we won't stop until they order us to'; 'Tomorrow 11:00 peaceful anti-disobedience workshop with Mossos [Catalan police], 12:00 practice evictions with senior citizens, 20:00 how to stop an *Indignado* tsunami'; 'The spokesmen for PRY (Policía Real Ya) are here already, taking all the credit. Let's assemble to see if we run them out on a rail'; 'Last assembly of bosses for tonight: they call it democracy and it is'; 'If you don't let us sleep we won't stop beating,' etc.

This type of wit capable of revealing repressive or antagonistic situations through creative, satirical re-creations has been fundamental to the 15M climate. There are already specific studies about it, such as those of the sociologist Eduardo Romanos (2014a). He frames the use of humor in the 15M movement within a more general turn towards aesthetic and identity production in social movements, and differentiates the uses of instrumental versus expressive humor. I particularly want to note that humor often has a lot to do with the movement's ability to elude what Rancière calls the 'police,' in his oft-quoted distinction between 'police' and 'politics'—which, of course, is crucial for my overall analysis of these 'cultures of anyone':

> *Police logic* thinks and structures human collectivities as a totality composed of parts, with functions and places corresponding to those functions, with ways of being and competencies that likewise correspond to those functions, with a government as government of a population, which divides that population into social groups, interest groups, and that offers itself as an arbitrator between groups, distributing places and functions, etc. *Police logic* today takes the form of a solid alliance between the state oligarchy and the economic oligarchy. Politics begins precisely when the system departs from that functional mode: hence my assertion that the people, the *demos*, are not the population, but nor are they the poor. The *demos* are the *gens de rien*, those who don't count, that is, not necessarily the excluded, the miserable, but *anyone*. My idea is that politics begins when political subjects are born that no longer define any social particularity. On the contrary, they define *the power of anyone*. (interview with Fernández-Savater, 2007)

One of the ways to exercise that 'power of anyone' in the 15M movement has been, literally, to avoid being in the place where not only the 'police logic,' but the police themselves, that is, the forces of public order, expected the movement to be.

Another notable example of this kind of feint to fool the police order can be found in connection with the European Central Bank summit in Barcelona in early May 2012. The authorities decided to call out a completely unexpected full deployment, putting 8,000 policemen on the streets, and even temporarily suspending the Schengen Treaty to be able to close the country's borders. However, the expected protest in the streets, which the authorities and some mass media had practically considered a given, never happened. The police presence was clearly seen to be a waste. This caused another flood of creative jokes on Twitter, this time under the hashtag #manifacción: 'The first attendance counts range between 0 and 100,000 invisible, violent demonstrators in the #manifacción'; '200,000 violent demonstrators according to police. 0 according to the organization. The serious press estimates an average of 100,000'; 'The Mossos develop sophisticated mime and body language techniques representing combat with a powerful enemy'; 'Mossos vans speed across the city filled with dummies with dreadlocks'; 'The president of the BCE declares: "I've never seen so much violence. In fact, I don't see it now, either"'; '#manifacción leaves zoo open: the ostriches head towards Fitch, the snakes to Moody's and the kangaroos pound the Mossos'; 'Trias includes "invisibility" among the crimes in city ordinances'; 'Puig doubles his bet: "In the next few hours, groups of hungry pumas and burning snakes on llamas will invade"'; 'Puig accuses AcampadaBCN of resisting authority for avoiding the summit and orders the arrest of its leaders.'

5.4.2. The technopolitical speed of networks

The speed of mass communication enabled by digital networks has been crucial to the flow of these kinds of frequently humorous 'rebuffs'—and the identity displacements that accompany them—and has contributed to a certain, not only physical, but also, we could say, 'existential' nomadism that characterizes the 15M movement. Spontaneous marches, proliferation of names, changes of plans, crowds pulled together in just hours, disguises, simulations, playful appropriations of 'enemy' speeches, and, in general, all kinds of surprising, unpredictable tactics for occupying both physical and symbolic spaces have all been regular occurrences in a movement with a very active, flexible presence which is, above all, combined and coordinated between the streets and digital networks.

Of course, this 'nomadism' was multiplied in the 'post-plaza' stage. It gave rise not only to such 'disappearances' or 'camouflages' of the movement in the face of power, but also to their encounters with other social protests and processes. These were not specifically identified as '15M,' but they tended to come together in, or at least to cross, the somewhat unforeseeable drifts the movement had inspired. Thus, as was intelligently narrated in the blog *Al final de la asamblea*—which constitutes one of the best sources for understanding these 'post-15M' dynamics—in the summer of 2012, shortly after the Barcelona 'manificción,' there arose a series of very interesting convergences of protests by various groups of civil servants with '15M-style' mobilizations. It came to the point where the police and members of Acampadasol found themselves on the same side for once, when the police organized protests against public spending cuts that also affected them. The interesting thing was that, as a post in the above-mentioned blog noted ('El desconcierto (Cuerpos y Fuerzas del Estado de Indignación)' 2014), the framework of inclusive practices 'of anyone' that the 15M movement had created—or at least strengthened—including their 'street nomadism' and their rapid-fire use of [social] networks, was adopted even by their supposed 'natural enemies,' the police, when they wanted to protest. The post posed the question:

> I wonder where the anger of the indignant police might have taken them? Where would the people-of-order of another time in another country have ended up in other circumstances?

Several options seem to be very easy choices: on the street but behind Le Pen in France, in Jobbik in Hungary, with Berlusconi in Italy, with Clean Hands and Spain 2000 in Spain today, in the hands of the PSOE in Spain five minutes ago, as the saying goes, or behind big union flags and union leaders, or behind the UP&D-style third ways, genetic recyclers of the system. Or, who knows, rabidly burning cars and [breaking] shop windows like in Paris or London.

It's possible that any of these things could still happen, but not today. It's possible that the municipal police officers I'll talk to couldn't care less about the litanies of 'they don't represent us' and 'these are our weapons.' However, de facto, they've begun their mobilization by threatening an *acampada* in the Congress, using networks to organize anonymously (as well as using certain platforms), and they've started to copy the first *perroflautada* that they have seen, roaming the streets without permission, running around and around the locked-down Congress, visiting the offices of the majority parties.

An 'indignant policeman' had already appeared in Acampadasol, but for the police as a professional sector to adopt the 15M forms of protest was certainly something quite unexpected, and even disturbing for many.

Some months earlier, in February, during a protest organized under the name '#Yonopago' (I'm not paying), which invited participants to jump the turnstiles in the metro as a protest against price hikes in public transportation, *Al final de la asamblea* described another situation in which the movement didn't do what everyone expected. This inspired the following optimistic analysis from the blogging collective:

The state expects something to happen. The media expects something to happen, there were mobile units with antennas in Sol. Everyone is sure something is going to happen. They set the scene for us, opening a space in the middle. The tension is mixed with excitement. It's as if E.T. had once landed in Sol, and now at the least provocation, they all come running: federal agents, marines, NASA, and TV. There's something so hilarious about this, like a poor lover being stood up. It's like the state is shadow boxing with something it can't see. It's like a 375-pound boxer (with his head smashed in) trying to swat a fly. They waste a lot—I mean a LOT—of energy. Many young, fresh-faced men, many bosses, new suits ironed, helicopters, SAMUR [emergency medical services], thousands of brand-new vans, etc. Cameras, reporters, photos, flashbulbs. The enemy seems happy and ready ... and The Other (us) doesn't show up. Disappointment. Back home they go, with all their toys in tow.

How does that Jap thing go? Using the enemy's weight and strength against him? (15mas1 2014)

A large part of the movement's 'becoming Japs,' their ability to become a fly which the powers that be sometimes want to hunt down with cannons, is due specifically to those 'swarm dynamics' fostered, as Margarita Padilla suggested, by digital networks. The research group DatAnalysis15M has completed an exhaustive investigation that utilized a wide range of methodologies (including a huge amount of quantitative analysis). They collected numerous interactions between the streets and digital networks that came from what they call the '15M Network System' and its 'multilevel synchronization of collective behavior.' They summarized the first of their conclusions in the study *Tecnopolítica: la potencia de las multitudes conectadas* (2013):

> The centrality of the connection between online social networks and human networks for the emergence of new forms of communication, organization, and collective action mediated by the political use of technology, critical mass phenomena, and mass self-communication has been shown in the gestation, explosion, and development of the 15M. We characterize this tactical and strategic use as technopolitical, and it varies between mass appropriation and derivation of the original use of digital platforms, and the collective invention of new uses and new tools. This has meant a drastic reduction in the cost of collective action and a greater ability to construct the meaning of what happens in real time, and simultaneously to create a very strong impact with viral campaigns or events put together through digital networks.

In essence, if the new 'cultural power' coming from the 15M movement is capable of creating 'cultures of anyone' able to challenge the monopoly over cultural authority that experts, media, and intellectuals attempt to exercise, it's partly because it is capable of gaining access to a technopolitical infrastructure that allows it to 'construct the meaning of what happens in real time.' In other words, it can construct alternatives to the spin that cultural officialdom keeps putting on 'what happens.'

But that need to do it 'in real time' noted by the DatAnalysis15M collective indicates the types of event—ephemeral, nomadic, quick, one-time, exceptional—in which that 'lightness' of technopolitical structures turns out to be especially effective. In competing with the accelerated time of 'the present' marked by the media, to anticipate and surprise the police or institutional bureaucracy, that network speed becomes priceless.

However, as I continue to note, I don't think these are the only, nor probably even the most transformative, dimensions of the 'cultures of anyone' capable of defying the cultural authority establishment. In these cultures, once again, it also has to do with maintaining a cultural space in which the daily construction of meaning that is intimately linked to human dignity is democratized. This involves maintaining a space that would be difficult to make function from an ephemeral plane. It has to do, essentially, with being able to construct a culture that faces up to the dispersion created by neoliberalism, making visible and strengthening collaborative, egalitarian forms of human interdependence that, it seems to me, cannot base their strength on transience.[11]

I am not suggesting here a dichotomy between the slowness of the physical and the speed of the digital. Rather, the dichotomy I propose is between the desire to create sustainable collaborative networks that, through their permanence, end up becoming alternatives to the neoliberal organization of life (for which the digital sphere is one of the fundamental tools), and the desire to regularly sabotage that neoliberal organization by promoting the upsurge of 'illegitimate' abilities, knowledge bases, and

11 Increasingly, it is capitalism itself whose reproduction is based on speed, transience, and even destruction. As early as 1989, David Harvey indicated in *The Urban Experience* that capitalism not only needed, as Marx had said, 'to abolish space.' In its post-industrial drift, it also functioned by way of a constant 'creative self-destruction' through which it needed constantly to construct new spaces to be able to 'dissolve them in air' (to take up Berman's classic expression) as soon as possible. 'We look at the material solidity of a building, a canal, a highway,' Harvey said vividly, 'and behind it we see always the insecurity that lurks within a circulation process of capital, which always asks: How much more time in this relative space?' (192).

More recently, the economist and business professor Stefano Harney (2010a; 2010b) integrated the study of novelties presented by the world of financial capitalism within this line of analysis, taking it to an unheard-of point: the affirmation of the complete split of capitalism from the suppositions and ideology of progress. The kind of 'creative destruction' on which financial markets embark in speculating with sophisticated products like derivatives, says Harney, can no longer be thought of from that familiar perspective through which, by means that might at times be somewhat pernicious or incomprehensible to the layman, it was thought that capitalist 'modernity' would always result in a control over nature that would, one way or another, bring progress in the future. Around 1998, with the deregulation of financial economics, asserts Harney, something happens that will disrupt that familiar view: while before it had been thought that economic value should always increase, in parallel with that 'progress of humanity' that everyone hoped for, now it begins to be thought that increasing value isn't so important, but that we know how to manage ourselves through its swings. Risk becomes something desirable, productive. In fact, it becomes the main investment of capitalism, whose speculative economy is, as is well known, 30 times bigger than the 'real' one.

discourses, in that order. It is precisely the speed of word and image, the speed of the more immediate aspects of meaning construction (multiplied by digital infrastructures) that tends to cause so much energy to be put into instigating ephemeral interruptions, displacements, sabotage efforts, or insults to the neoliberal order, because everyone knows that they will achieve an immediate goal. But the danger of this specialization in ephemera is that it abandons the everyday to its fate. In other words, the everyday is left to the neoliberal organization of life, which permeates everything by default in our time.

The difference between the logic of the camps and the 'nomadism' of the movement—shown, for example, in the post-15M 'aimless indignant strolls'—is not, I repeat, the difference between the physical and the digital. The two aspects coexisted in both moments. The difference is based, rather, on the fact that in the first case a permanent forum for the democratic construction of meaning was articulated, like a kind of Trojan horse within the neoliberal city; in the second, it played cat and mouse with the 'police,' in both Rancière's and the literal sense. Both models, which have never been completely separated but simply combined to different degrees, have their strengths and their problems.

5.4.3. Advertising and commercial appropriations of collective value
In the 15M *acampadas*, as is well known, everyone was invited to participate, but not through the media, technocratic, or intellectual platforms that tend to produce a monopoly on knowledge. Rather, the invitation came from within the unique 'space of anyone' the movement was attempting to maintain, and which created its own conditions of participation. There were, in this regard, repeated debates in Sol about whether or not the media should be allowed to record the assemblies. And there were times when it was expressly prohibited, rejecting an ingenuous conception of 'freedom of expression.' They proposed the restriction as a way to defend themselves from what they identified as a danger of 'manipulation,' but which, it seems to me, had much to do with the illegitimate hoarding of cultural authority exercised by the mass media.

The plazas were inclusive, but only in terms that allowed inclusion for everybody. This was also true for intellectuals, whether they were famous or not, leftist or not, who, as Luis Martín-Cabrera (2011) said in an article on the subject, 'in the plazas they have to wait their turn just like everybody else, and they have neither last names nor pedigrees.'

When there is no camp, however, when that permanent space of anyone doesn't exist, although other opportunities for resisting authoritarian cultural powers appear, it also becomes much more difficult to make those powers respect, even a little bit, the protocols necessary for the egalitarian multiplication of abilities that creates collective intelligence. When the playing field is marked out by the media, with their *tertulianos*, their intellectuals, their constant desire for novelty, and their transformation of reality into a market, things are different.

Let me offer some examples: shortly after the 15M movement, various advertisements appeared appropriating the aesthetics and the ways, or rather, the 'tics' of the movement. One television commercial was especially striking: it staged a hypothetical, completely decontextualized 'assembly' in which people of various ages contributed ideas on the appropriate price for text messages sent through cellphones, finally agreeing that they should all be free. The voice-off concluded, 'The people have spoken and this is what it has asked for: new cellphone rates decided by everyone.' The company was Movistar, which belongs to Telefónica, the Spanish communications giant. It is well known for its commercial practices of doubtful legitimacy, as repeatedly condemned by FACUA, the consumers' association. FACUA's members have voted it the worst company of the year for several consecutive years. They likewise voted the assembly spot the Worst Commercial of the Year in 2011.

It was, stated FACUA (2014), 'pure mockery of the 15M movement trying to take advantage of their image and the decisions of their assemblies.' On the other hand, the anonymous 'communications guerrilla' that flourishes on digital networks didn't take long to upload a new and improved YouTube version of the ad, in which the characters attending the assembly talked about Movistar-Telefónica itself, and reached very different conclusions: 'Profits (€10,167 million in 2010), layoffs (6,000 or 20% of workers) and quality (the slowest and most expensive service in Europe).'

Something similar happened with a pair of television commercials for Campofrío, a brand of cold cuts, aired in 2012 and 2013 respectively. Both ads played with a vague notion of the virtues of the supposed 'Spanish character,' staged as a way 'to raise morale' supposedly depressed by the crisis. Thus, without making any reference to the causes of that crisis, they praised sports, infrastructures, a sense of humor, and Spanish sociability in an undifferentiated amalgam that ended up, in both cases, reverting to a collective desire to buy Campofrío's cold cuts, because they embodied— never better said—that revalorized 'Spanishness.' What I want to stress here is that among the list of characteristics that should be attributed to the Spanish spirit—which, providentially, were listed in the first ad as a kind of résumé—was 'solidarity' (exemplified with images of PAH protests) and the ability 'to fight even when you feel you can't go on' (as expressed by 'el Langui,' an actor and singer in the hip-hop group La Excepción, who suffers from cerebral palsy and who appeared in a t-shirt displaying a symbol against budget cuts).

Beyond the problems the commercial context itself could cause for the message—let's not forget that they *are* advertisements—and without wanting to diminish any support the PAH's struggles and those against cuts in education and healthcare may have received thanks to these ads, it is important to indicate the risks involved in integrating these struggles acritically into narratives that juxtapose them to social realities that are so dependent on neoliberal logic, such as the promotion of elite sports and the creation of overly ambitious transportation infrastructures. Campofrío's own commercial says, 'you can't turn around without tripping into an airport,' but indeed, building airports that see little or no use has been one of the emblems of the speculative real estate bubble's excesses.

In the next chapter, I will explore a little further the logics of the neoliberal system's appropriation of the value collaboratively created in 'cultures of anyone.' I will discuss the symbolic capital created by the movements and how these obvious 'thefts' perpetrated by the big multinationals that use it for their publicity, are only one quite literal—and for that reason especially useful—example. But they form part of a very complex conglomerate of indirect, hybrid, often barely visible, and ambiguous dynamics through which, in fact, any socially recognized value tends to be financiarized one way or another, and put to work in the competitive, corporate logic of neoliberalism.

Fortunately, we also have numerous, complex analyses of these dynamics, and in dialogue with these, I will also outline some concrete attempts to manage the collaboratively created value and try to protect it from neoliberal appropriation. In particular, I will talk about institutions that work with 'culture,' and try—in a way that is partly analogous to the *acampadas* of the 15M—to include both physical and digital spaces where it is possible to defend specific protocols that prevent the privatization of cultural value, and guarantee the capacity for self-management of that value by the collaborative communities that produce it.

No, there is no 'pure' outside to neoliberalism. But there are, as the historian Immanuel Wallerstein (2002) proposed, processes of 'selective decommodification,' that is, the creation of 'structures that operate in the market [and] whose objective is to offer a service and its survival, and not the profit.' 'This,' indicated Wallerstein, 'can be done, as we know from the history of universities and hospitals: not getting everything, but getting the most possible' (39).

In this regard, what I wanted to indicate here are some difficulties raised by the 'nomadism' of the 15M climate facing that 'selective decommodification.'

This is an action that seems to require, as Wallerstein says, the creation of more permanent 'structures,' like the plazas of the 15M movement, with its attempt to maintain a noncompetitive, noncorporatized everyday life, and like some of the institutions I will talk about in the next chapter, which try to do the same with the cultural or symbolic aspects of life.

5.4.4. Political talk shows and academies: The dangers of playing away from home

An especially controversial drift of the relations between the 'cultures of anyone' and the neoliberal establishment, in relation to the 'nomadism' of the former, would be certain attempts to intensify what I view as interruptions or sabotage of big media's logic on their own turf. I think about what happens, for example, with the crucial and delicate matter of the participation of people like Ada Colau, ex-spokesperson of the PAH (and now mayor of Barcelona with the platform Barcelona en Comú), or Pablo Iglesias, secretary general of Podemos on the political talk shows that have proliferated on the major television channels.

It is a complex subject about which I only want to briefly note an idea, which perhaps doesn't appear very often in the debates on the matter. I am referring to the fact that in the interesting opinions exchanged on digital networks sympathetic to the 15M climate about the advisability (or not) of these contributions in a perceived 'enemy' territory, the tactical importance played in those televised debates by recourse to specialized knowledge, or even, simply, to the authority of the expert position is not always kept in mind. As I noted above, the figure of the televised or radio broadcast *tertuliano* owes much to the 'aura' offered by that position. Thus, it seems especially difficult to reappropriate it from a position within the 'cultures of anyone,' or at least to enter into a relationship of equals with it, as has been done with so many other figures of power/knowledge (economist, doctor, lawyer, philosopher, etc.) during this cycle of cultural democratizations that was opened up with the 15M. It is especially difficult, I say, above all when it is being attempted on the 'home field' of the *tertuliano*, which is big media.

It seems that this is so in part because of a lingering misunderstanding: the usual criticism of these political talk show participants is that they act as if 'they know,' but, in fact, they don't know. This is not far from the truth since, indeed, they are asked to offer opinions on any current event, and it's impossible for them to 'really know' everything. Taking this as a point of departure, it would make sense to resort to a strategy in which a *tertuliano* is introduced who breaks that logic, and who really does know what he or she is talking about.

But again the question is, what does it mean 'to know'? If a *tertuliano* is put onstage who displays a knowledge set authorized by establishment institutions, it seems to me that perhaps that other essential type of knowing—that of 'the experts in what happens to them,' the knowledge of the affected ones, the knowledge of those vulnerable voices that know what it is to tremble—is being set aside somewhat. This is the case with Pablo Iglesias, who often introduces himself by emphasizing his specialized 'professor' knowledge, throwing his brilliant academic dossier in the face of another guest on the program (in one of the most viewed videos of Pablo Iglesias on YouTube).

There is, however, hardly any space for 'anyone's' type of knowledge in the big media *tertulias* (political talk shows). When the voice of an affected individual is allowed to make an appearance, it is to turn it into a victim, to be moved by or show solidarity with it, but not to learn with it or from it. Even the interventions of Ada Colau, who was always faithful to her role of PAH spokesperson—not 'representative'—in the media are marked by the use of expert discourse, in particular legal discourse (although not always nor totally). This is understandable simply because in those forums the choice presented is doubly disgraceful: if she speaks as an affected individual, she risks being framed as an impotent victim; if she speaks from her specialized knowledge base, she risks being assimilated as just another 'expert' more, using her cultural authority against that of her peer tertulianos. And perhaps sometimes this second type of identification is chosen as the lesser, or perhaps the less visible, of two evils.

Finally, along with these complex relations between the 'cultures of anyone' and the mass media, I would like to point out that there are other equally problematic relations that are even more directly related to the logic of hierarchical cultural prestige. Again, when the playing field is not fixed by the 'cultures of anyone' themselves, but by institutions strongly marked by the monopolistic, authoritarian logics of the modern power/ knowledge complex in its neoliberal declension, like most of the academic and cultural institutions of the globalized world, the symbolic value created by those cultures is easily reterritorialized in competitive dynamics that alienate it from the communities that produce it. The immense machinery of institutional cultural programming and academic publication—both strongly marked by the neoliberal logics of competition and corporatization—find in the material created collaboratively by the cultures of anyone 'subjects' for their events, books, and articles, just as the media intellectuals used them for their opinion columns.

These are the risks being run by the very volume you hold in your hands now, along with the growing investigative and analytical production emerging in more or less direct, close contact with the 'cultures of anyone,' but which also uses the infrastructure provided by institutions immersed in the neoliberal, 'expert' paradigm. In the face of those risks, as with those run when the 'cultures of anyone' make any incursion into institutions alien to their open, decommodified, collaborative logics, it seems to me that one of the most powerful strategies is usually to implement 'roundtrip routes' that lead the revaluation allowed by that establishment, in turn, back towards those very 'cultures of anyone.' I am referring to instances when the infrastructures, resources, and capacities provided by the neoliberal institutions are used, directly or indirectly, in efforts that try to create alternatives to neoliberal logic.

To do this, those dynamics for creating structures capable of a certain permanence, and therefore, of a certain 'selective decommodification,' are particularly necessary. These may sometimes reclaim energies being used in other, more 'nomadic' structures of online movements and cultures, and which are therefore perhaps also more vulnerable to the neoliberal dispersion paradigm. I will dedicate the last chapter of this book to a study of some of the former, from the conviction that making them visible through a historical and philosophical analysis is another way of constructing the collective value that can guarantee its permanence.

CHAPTER 6

Towards More Democratic Cultural Institutions?

6.1. The Self-Managed Culture in its Life Spaces

6.1.1. Traficantes de Sueños: Sharing conditions of possibility for culture

A few books on a folding table: a small stand for activist literature in El Rastro in Madrid.

The year is 1996, and the germ of what is today the 'political production and communication project' known as Traficantes de Sueños, a folding table, practically fits inside a suitcase. Almost 20 years later, this project comprises, among other things, a bookstore, a publisher, a distributor, a design workshop, an activist research group, a permanent program of self-education seminars, and a social space that houses all these and many other activities. In 1996, there probably weren't many people who thought this transformation would happen by 'giving away' books. But somehow that's just what happened.

So, essentially, since 1999, when that folding table became a publishing house, Traficantes de Sueños (TdS) has been making digital versions of all their published books freely available to anyone. Besides allowing copying through the use of Creative Commons licenses, TdS has always produced a pdf file of every one of their carefully edited texts, and has put them on its website for downloading. Contrary to what some skeptics claimed, *a priori*, would happen, people have not taken massive advantage of these 'free products' and 'ruined' TdS's project or made it unsustainable. Quite the contrary. The determined support for the decommodification of the book as an object, along with other important factors I will discuss, has made TdS's project especially attractive for many people, who, in turn, have found ways to support it. Through their work, TdS has become one of the clearest examples in all of Spain that the basic principles of the free culture can be applied successfully not only to digital resources like software, but also to other types of cultural processes, such as the publication of books.

The researcher and activist Jaron Rowan has published an interesting and exhaustive study about this multifaceted cultural project (2001). He indicates a number of significant factors that contribute to TdS's exponential growth. Beyond just offering free access to their books, they also possess the more general capacity to create infrastructures that others can use to carry out other processes of cultural production. In other words, they have the ability to create and share not only 'results,' which published books are, in some sense, but also the very conditions of possibility for establishing open, self-managed cultural processes.

Let's think about what happens in any given week at Traficantes de Sueños, or rather, at Embajadores 35, which is their address in Lavapiés, the Madrid *barrio* that is home to this project.[1] As I write these words, a vinyl scratching and mixing workshop is being held by DJ Caution. It's one of the activities on the program of Guacamayofest 2014, which defines itself as a 'playful platform for giving exposure to the more avant-garde artistic expressions of the heterogeneous Latin American sound space.' But in the space of a very few days before and after, this same physical space has hosted and will yet host a talk on cyberactivism in Africa, feminist theorist/activist Silvia Federici's presentation of the translation of the book *Revolución en punto cero* (published by Traficantes), a tribute concert to the Puerto Rican poet Julia de Burgos, a conference on transgenic foods, and the start of the self-education course 'The Legend of Time: Subcultures, Music, Social Change and Ruptures in Contemporary "Spain."' This latter will begin with a session on 'flamenco and power,' among other events that are free and open to the public.

In addition to offering this wealth of programming, the space is open to the general public during the day. People can browse in the bookstore or La Ceiba, the fair trade cooperative store that shares space with TdS and with the open-source software cooperative XSTO.info. Embajadores 35 is also regularly open to the *barrio* through activities for children, language classes, and workshops, and is shared with any local groups that may want to use it for their activities. This activity generates what Rowan calls a 'noticeably multiethnic and multipurpose dynamic space, quite the opposite of certain more traditional cultural spaces that have a more homogeneous demography' (2011).

From this daily activity, from this exuberant confluence of rhythms, bodies, desires, and projects springs the extraordinary production of all kinds of knowledge generated by TdS, hand in hand with the communities

---

1 Traficantes de Sueños has moved in 2015 to a new space, bigger and even more centric, in Duque de Alba 13.

and networks that move through the project. Among these kinds of knowledge are those gathered in and proposed by the press's books, which often have direct connections to specific needs and interests rooted in that everyday life. Perhaps the clearest case of this would be the books explicitly presented as 'users' manuals.' A prominent example is the *Manual de desobediencia a la Ley Sinde*, published in collaboration with Hacktivistas and the newspaper *Diagonal* in 2011, amid an atmosphere of effervescent opposition to this law. Another with similar objectives is *Copyleft: manual de uso*, which came out in 2006.

But up to a point, many of TdS's books demonstrate that same vocation to serve some specific collective need as straightforwardly as possible. *La crisis que viene*, for example, is a remarkable example written by the activist research group Observatorio Metropolitano, which is also a part of Traficantes, and published just before the irruption of 15M. It became an essential reference for the wave of politicization produced by that movement. Two years after its appearance, this analysis of the neoliberal dogmas leading to the economic crisis had reached 50,000 downloads and 2,000 print copies sold. Another important recent example among many others is the compilation of experiences and ways of knowing resulting from the encounter between the Forum for Independent Life and the Precarious Agency in *Cojos y precarias: haciendo vidas que importan* (2011). And finally, it's worth mentioning the collective volume *La universidad en conflicto* (2010), compiled by Universidad Nómada and Edu-Factory to investigate and offer analytical materials on the corporatization of institutions of higher education under globalized capitalism.

As the neoliberal crisis has deepened, TdS has become an ever more necessary and requested knowledge factory because of its capacity to harbor a kind of reflection connected directly to attempts to escape the dominion of competition and corporatization. It has its own model of sustainability, as a project that supports the 'social economy.' As explained on its website, TdS is a 'nonprofit association where the workers give the orders,' and which 'survives thanks to the community that chooses to support it because they believe it's a valuable resource for everyone.' With the aim of offering channels for that community support, in addition to offering books for sale in its physical and virtual stores, TdS has set up subscription services to its bookstore and its press, and the ongoing possibility of making donations online.[2]

2 In relation to the 'social economy' label attached by TdS, there are various definitions and modalities of support. In the text '¿Quiénes somos?' TdS offers the following: 'numerous people can come together to begin productive projects that

A fact that may seem anecdotal, but I consider relevant to this support, is that the premises of Embajadores 35 are set back a little from the street, in a passageway located within a block of apartments. If you didn't know it existed, it would be hard to just stumble upon it. Deliberately burying themselves in the small corridor leading to their door could serve as a metaphor for the active, voluntary gesture that TdS requires from its community of users to survive, beyond mere consumerism. Even though book sales are used partly to support the organization, it would be difficult for someone to buy a book in TdS without knowing that by doing so, he or she was contributing to a space that tries to create a culture whose value is not decided commercially.

Of course, the created value of TdS can also be co-opted indirectly by being used by consumerist, commodifying logics, like any other socially produced value. But that does not invalidate the existence of a whole series of specific protocols that make TdS a social economy and free culture project that tries to complicate that co-optation: open licenses, workers self-managing assemblies, interruption of profit logics, constantly offering their resources to serve the communities that participate in the project, and in general—again in their words (online)—the goal of 'generating goods and services through fair productive structures, where the most important things are workforce and gender equality, and respect for the planet.'

It is no surprise, then, that during the neoliberal crisis Traficantes has experienced an increase in participation and remarkable support for its activities. In some sense it functions as a cultural catalyst, a repository of living knowledge, a meeting place, and an enhancer of the intellectual and affective abilities of anyone. In short, it is fulfilling many of the functions that other institutions closer to neoliberal logics—and more dependent on them for support, such as universities, museums, cultural centers, and

generate jobs, goods, and services based on ethical principles. This is the basis of social economy that already has, in the whole state and the whole world, thousands of cooperatives, associations, and businesses that produce according to a different economic model. Its goal is not to accumulate profits, but to generate goods and services through fair productive structures, where labor equality, gender equality, and respect for the planet take precedence.'

In TdS's case, these basic principles of social economy are combined with those of free culture. Regarding the convergence of these two models, Ricardo Amasté wrote, '[T]hey try to see how in addition to social good, organizations are capable of promoting the proliferation of the common good(s), that is, of enabling the conditions to ensure the possibility of transference, reproducibility, reuse, and remixing of the resources that manage and produce the greatest possible number of people and collectives (from natural resources or related to healthcare, education, culture, or economy to management models, software, and digital archives or situated ways of knowing)' (2013).

foundations—find themselves less and less able to carry out because of their growing commercialization, which involves an inevitable dependence on private economic interests.

It also seems particularly relevant to highlight that along with that more urgent type of knowledge tied to specific political or even tactical processes, Traficantes generates very interesting processes of self-education and research. These give rise to more speculative, experimental activities that may lead to rereadings of long-term historical processes that often require more tranquil temporalities. For example, Silvia Federici's text *Calibán y la bruja: mujeres, cuerpo y acumulación originaria* has generated enormous interest, attaining very high sales and downloads for a history book and political essay published by an alternative press. Federici, whose theory on the origin of capitalism and its effects on the reproduction of life is central for my own research, has given talks at TdS on several occasions, and she always fills the place to capacity. She typically attracts people interested in the convergence of feminism and the critique of capitalism. But interestingly, she also attracts those willing to participate in the type of long-term analysis that is usually more difficult to carry off in activist spaces, which are often more focused on the present.

That function of learning, research, and analysis maintained over long periods—which usually occur in universities—perhaps finds its most propitious place within the constellation of TdS in the self-education courses called 'Nociones Comunes' ('Common Notions'). In these courses, collective inquiries are opened about problems that the 'alternative' spaces critical of neoliberalism tend to deal with from the position of street protests, activism, or public condemnation. Common Notions courses provide infrastructures so that in addition to those answers, collective self-education also takes place, allowing a deeper exploration of subjects typically closely tied to the present. Examples include the neoliberal crisis, struggles for online freedom, or feminisms, but also others like migrations, countercultures, processes of urban gentrification, and the burning question of the moment, the possible democratization from within of representative political institutions.

So TdS is a kind of incubator of knowledge and resources—of different scales, dimensions, and speeds—that can address the needs and abilities that arise as much in the everyday life of a multiethnic urban *barrio* in the center of Madrid as they do in the ebb and flow of global opposition movements to neoliberalism. These range from eminently practical, tactical, or instrumental kinds of knowledge tied to immediate survival, to creative, aesthetic, theoretical, or investigative long-range processes, and go through a multitude of combinations between both extremes.

6.1.2. Self-Managed Social Centers as decommodified life spaces

On the other hand, TdS's ability to build and extend networks and constellations has increased considerably as its project has continued to join with other similar ones, mostly through the creation of the Fundación de los Comunes in 2011. For quite a while, Traficantes's distributing arm worked with bookstores and presses in other cities, circulating its books through a network that has now been strengthened. So now, for example, Nociones Comunes's courses are repeated in different versions and with different facilitators in cities like Terrassa, Zaragoza, Pamplona, and Málaga, which host the main 'nodes' of the network formalized by the Fundación de los Comunes. And perhaps the strength and uniqueness of this network lies precisely in putting front and center the connection of activities normally recognized as 'cultural,' such as investigation, self-education, publishing, and 'technopolitics,' with the 'channels of living social production'—in the words of Marisa Pérez Colina, coordinator of the Fundación de los Comunes—that are generated in cooperative spaces open to the flow of daily life, like Embajadores 35 itself. Pérez Colina recently said that the collectives of the Fundación de los Comunes essentially carry out their practices of activist research, self-education, and publishing within the framework of self-managed social centers (or CSA, from the Spanish initials of Centros Soaciales Auto-gestionados) or centers of civic participation. These are 'spaces of aggregation or encounters' with a particular vocation for durability over time. She added that therefore, one of the first objectives of the Foundation is 'to serve as material and life support' for these Social Centers. (Entrevista Marisa Pérez Colina, Fundación de Los Comunes (FdlC), MUSAC 2014).

In his research on TdS, Rowan also uses this concept of 'channels of social production,' which he thinks is fundamental for understanding what distinguishes the project from other 'cultural enterprises.' Following analyses originating in the Italian post-autonomist movement and in the French magazine *Multitudes*, Rowan explains that channels of social production would be 'places where new kinds of knowledge, words, ways of relating, and new imaginaries converge,' on which the 'cultural industries' feed in order to 'capture certain flows and extract rents from them' (2011). A classic example of this type of process on a small scale would be the appropriation of urban graffiti for the aesthetics of fashion design. On a more macro scale, we have the revaluation of urban land that these productive accounts produce, and of which the real estate speculation and tourism lobbies are the main beneficiaries. With a project like Traficantes de Sueños, this privatization of collectively generated wealth doesn't occur, at least not so easily. The social wealth of the 'urban productive channels' that nourish TdS is constantly returned in the form of books with open licenses and a whole series of freely available cultural goods and infrastructures that will enrich those channels further.[3]

The support given by the Fundación de los Comunes to connecting their projects of publication, investigation, and self-teaching with the CSAs in which they take place is essential, because it's a way to indicate and pragmatically protect the concrete existence of those 'productive channels.' This makes their collective creation of wealth more visible, thus also making it easier to defend it from privatization of one type or another. It seems to me that this gesture to protect and fortify specific spheres of self-managed collective cultural production is what enables greater success in starting decommodification processes, since, as Wallerstein proposed, it makes it possible to work on particular 'structures' to open small spaces of resistance to the neoliberal logic.

Wallerstein was talking about hospitals and universities, but what is interesting about the model proposed by the Fundación de los Comunes is that it understands the self-managed social centers as 'spaces of social production' (and, we could add, simply 'spaces of life'), endowed with a multifunctionality that, to my way of thinking, directly attacks the logic of dispersion and division of experience which is at the heart of neoliberalism. One of the most important expressions of this logic of dispersion consists of separating symbolic production, 'culture,' from its material support: universities on one hand, hospitals on the other; minds on one hand, bodies on the other.

'The market is constantly assembling and disassembling ties according to its incessant quest to maximize profits,' asserted Franco Ingrassia with regard to the phenomenon of dispersion (2011). In this way, the relations of constitutive interdependence that enable the material and symbolic subsistence of humans tend to be made invisible and subjected to profound inequalities. But if, along with open licenses and spaces for planned 'cultural' activities, the life of a nucleus of organizers is independently supported so they don't have to depend on an outside salary, and useful infrastructures

---

3 TdS itself has published several studies about the processes of appropriation of common wealth produced by so-called 'cognitive capitalism.' In fact, it is one of the most useful Spanish-language presses for studying the Italian post-autonomy tradition and the environment of the magazine *Multitudes* on which Rowan bases his analysis. See, for example, the collective volume *Capitalismo cognitivo, propiedad intelectual y creación colectiva* (Blondeau, Lazzarato et al. 2004). Of course, an essential reference in this theoretical tradition regarding the 'channels of social production' and its capitalist appropriation is Michael Hardt and Toni Negri's trilogy, *Empire* (2001), *Multitude* (2005), and *Commonwealth* (2009).

for the lives of those who participate in the project are provided, as occurs in TdS, the possibility of counteracting that logic of dispersion is very significant. And if, besides, all this is done within a context in which there is a daily tumult of other projects of decommodified life—like food or software cooperatives, spaces of community-supported sociability, etc.— the possibilities seem to multiply for the people who make and enjoy that culture to be able to establish its value for themselves, without the interference of external criteria based on maximizing profits, which bring dispersion with them.

The ways of knowing, the narratives, the research, and the learning that take place in places like Traficantes de Sueños do not depend entirely on neoliberal commercial logics for their production and maintenance. Thus, they challenge the neoliberal world's separation and erasure of specific, interdependent lives from which 'culture' arises. Similarly, the CSAs provide bases where the value of the everyday, material collaboration that always enables any production of meaning is reserved and even 'accumulated.' And in using them, we could say that one can't help but *see materially* those collective processes that would often remain hidden behind commercial means of capturing collective value, such as the privatizing, speculative uses of the author figure, his 'work,' 'aesthetic quality,' fashions, 'hypes,' etc.

6.1.3. The tradition of CSAs and 'cultures of anyone'
The question of the reciprocal intensification of collective value is fundamental. This is particularly so in regard to the value produced between projects of cultural, alimentary, housing, social, and any other type of decommodification in the bosom of the CSAs. Likewise, it's important more generally as well, in any instance where they manage to protect and defend the social wealth of certain productive channels (as might happen, for instance, in the multiplication of CSAs or similar projects in a given *barrio*, town, or territory). Fortunately, research on this subject is increasing, as community and cooperative projects spread across Spain, creating fabrics of exceptional participative richness. And as this is increasingly demonstrated, in the crisis of state institutions, the function of these fabrics becomes doubly important. And so it has recently been proven, to cite a familiar example, in the mass defense of the CSA Can Vies in the Barcelona *barrio* of Sants, which ultimately stopped the city council's planned mass eviction and demolition. This inspired important protests and widespread displays of regional solidarity; it even went as far as to begin a brick-by-brick reconstruction of the demolished part of the building.[4]

---

4 For more information about this social fabric formed by the CSAs, see, for

But delving into the importance of the community fabric generated around the CSAs is not my only purpose. My focus now is the question of the relationship between ways of collectively self-managing the cultural value produced by communities defending themselves from the neoliberal 'capture' of that value, and the experience of potentiating the abilities of anyone outlined in the previous chapter. So it seems to me that despite the obvious similarities, it is worth asking whether those CSA cultures defended by the Fundación de los Comunes are also 'cultures of anyone,' in the sense that they break with the theoretical divisions between 'those in the know' and 'those in the dark'? Are they ways of bridging between specialized and everyday ways of knowing? Are they able to empower anyone by creating situations that foster the recognition of various values, and not just those endorsed by the technoscientific tradition and the modern power/knowledge complex?

These are pertinent questions, since the capacity for self-management and maintenance of cultural processes through collaborative, relatively decommodified methods doesn't guarantee only the kind of cultural democratization that I have observed in the 15M movement and the 'post-15M.' The decommodified self-management of the cultural needs and abilities of a community could still harbor hierarchical logics or logics of exclusion: perhaps not everyone is welcome in that decommodified community, perhaps they reproduce separations between different hierarchical identifications of 'those in the know' and 'those in the dark.'

However, I think there are at least three reasons for dismissing these doubts and answering in the affirmative, at least on a generic level, to the questions raised above. In the first place, the key question of the opening up of infrastructures and cultural processes—and not just 'results'—necessarily points at least in the general direction of that 'empowerment' produced when there is confidence in the abilities of anyone, when culture is understood more as something that is developed collectively, in open 'workshops'

example, the collective volume *Okupa Madrid (1980–2010)* (Seminario de Historia Política y Social de las Okupaciones en Madrid-Metrópolis 2014). Several newspaper articles have echoed the growing legitimacy of the CSAs, not only in relation to the incident in Can Vies, but also, more generally, in the wake of the politicization caused by the crisis (see, for example, Cabrera (2014), Lenore (2014), León (2010), and Peiró (2014)). In Barcelona's case, the mapping work and research being done by the Observatorio Metropolitano de Barcelona is exceptional, and can be found on its website, bcncomuns.net. With respect to the collective project Barcelona en Comú, the fabric of this city's community and self-managed projects is garnering increasing recognition for it is being presented as one of the pillars of this municipal project.

that need a material logistics, than as something that is produced in a kind of vacuum 'behind the scenes' and enjoyed in solitude, individually. Furthermore, since these cultures are deeply rooted in the everyday life generated in the CSAs, in principle it is to be expected that those culture 'workshops'—of publishing, research, self-education, etc.—that inhabit it soak up those knowledge bases and qualities so often unacknowledged by the hegemonic cultural tradition, but so fundamental for maintaining the everyday nature of the CSAs: practices of mutual caregiving, intuitive, 'amateur' social skills, traditional or extradisciplinary ways of knowledge, etc. Finally, the assembly configuration and the increasing tendency to mount projects in open networks that facilitate the construction of new 'nodes' are marks of egalitarianism that facilitate the opening of these 'social center cultures' beyond closed communities, regardless of how strong their ties are to local spaces.

None of these aspects completely guarantees that hierarchical or exclusivist reterritorializations can't occur. There could be reappearances of 'avant-garde' phenomena or sectarianisms that, in any event, are not at all alien to the history of social movements, nor, in particular, to the sphere of autonomy and anticapitalist self-management, or even to that of the Neighbor Associations Movement, which is also important to the genealogy and composition of the CSAs. The development of a sufficiently detailed and complete history of these spheres of 'living social production' is completely beyond my abilities and purposes here. Likewise, it is not my intention to establish value judgments as a supposedly neutral observer.[5] What I do want to do, however, is propose some inquiries into specific protocols of decommodified cultural self-management. This will allow me to identify the complexity, limits, and challenges raised by some institutions that practice, in one way or another, this very self-management, in relation to the type of democratization that the 'cultures of anyone' are assuming during this neoliberal crisis. The objective, therefore, is to track the possible emergence of a democratic 'cultural ecology'[6] starting from those who might construct

---

5 I must add that here I only mention a minimal sample of the many CSAs and CSOAs that exist in the Spanish state. I am particularly interested in those linked to the Fundación de los Comunes because these allow me to better analyze the problems related to self-management and cultural democratization in which I am most interested. In no way do I want to minimize the complexity of the huge number of social and cultural experiences related to self-management, I simply do not have the space here to address them all.

6 I borrow this term from Reinaldo Laddaga, who in turn borrowed it from the sociologist Charles Tilly to apply it to the field of aesthetics. Quoting Tilly, Laddaga talks about recurrent transactions among units that 'produce interdependences

its most stable nodes, those who, in some way, are suggested as 'institutions,' or who simply, as Pérez Colina said, 'have a vocation to remain.'

In this regard, it is very important to observe other self-management and cultural democratization experiments that come from a very different environment that is also able to offer durability to their projects. I am talking about public institutions, and these, in turn, present their own possibilities and limits. So I will now talk about an odd, atypical institution that in many ways is the standard-bearer for these self-managing, democratizing drifts of public space in the sphere usually recognized as 'cultural' in Madrid: Medialab Prado.

6.2. Under the Ambiguous Umbrella of the Public Sector

6.2.1. Medialab-Prado: Institutional protocols for the participation of anyone

Medialab Prado is a 'program of the Arts, Sports and Tourism Area of the Madrid City Council,' self-defined more specifically as 'a citizen laboratory for production, investigation, and diffusion of cultural projects that explore forms of experimentation and collaborative learning that have arisen from digital networks' (Medialab-Prado). Medialab introduces itself, therefore, as a type of experimental public cultural institution that departs from classical models like the library, the museum, or the auditorium. Nor does it prioritize the publication or distribution of written culture, unlike the tradition of associative bookstores or 'social center libraries' from which Traficantes de Sueños and the other nodes of the Fundación de los Comunes arise. Instead, it takes as a reference those 'forms of experimentation and collaborative learning that have arisen in the digital networks' to institute something like an attempt to 'translate' certain aspects of digital culture to the physical realm.

In this sense, Medialab's support for procedural aspects, for the opening of infrastructures and processes of cultural production, for the search for formats alien to the modern culture based on the division between authors and public, is still more explicit—which doesn't mean that it is necessarily verified with greater intensity—than that of the model of activist research collectives, self-training, and publication proposed by the Fundación de

among places, change shared understandings in the process, and return to vast cultural resources available in each particular place through their connections with other places,' through a spontaneous organization that implies 'the training and activation of individuals who initiate advances or demands on a local scale, but who in some way articulate them with large-scale identities and collective struggles' (Laddaga (2006); Tilly (2002, 49)).

los Comunes. These collectives come from the world of social movements and, of course, they have encountered the explosion of technopolitics and networks along the way. But (at least with regards to its self-representation) Medialab perhaps drinks more directly than do other collectives from these latter founts, which carry inscribed within their own DNA the centrality of procedurality and open collaboration.

The model of meaning production in social movements, on the other hand, has traditionally depended more on ideas like 'alternative information,' which continue to stipulate the need for a 'public.' It has also revolved around militant and activist figures as centers from which that meaning could emanate, although all this may have changed considerably with the intensification of the logics of 'anyone' around the 15M movement.

Perhaps Medialab's most paradigmatic activity is what has been called the 'collaborative project development workshop' or, simply, the 'prototype workshop.' This activity occupies the central position that in other cultural spaces would be occupied by book publishing, research seminars, informational conferences, art exhibitions, or musical and stage performances. It is a model inspired by the collaborative practices of open-source software and experimental technology, and has been formalized as a protocol with very precise organizational guidelines. First, Medialab sends out a call for projects, always with a very broad conceptual frame. For example, the premise of the most recent one is 'Madrid, Urban Laboratory: Practical Infrastructures and Tools for Theorizing Shared Life.' Each call is backed by three advisors chosen by Medialab, who in turn choose about ten projects to participate in the workshop.

Once these projects are chosen, 50 collaborators are convened to participate in the development of the 'tools, platforms, and actions' the projects propose as concrete objectives. Thus, in the example mentioned, these 50 collaborators, who are admitted on a first-come-first-served basis, will work to 'prototype' anything from 'a low-cost, noninvasive electroencephalograph (EEG) to use as a BCI (brain-computer interface)' to 'a proposal to help the public administration understand and standardize civic initiatives that use public space as a commons' (for example, urban orchards in vacant lots), including 'a mobile application that helps locate accessible and adapted places' for people with diverse functional needs, or a historical tour, all the way up to the present, of the Barrio de las Letras 'straight from the hands of its inhabitants and users through testimonies and photographs.'

The workshops take place in intensive sessions, in this case in two phases of six and three days respectively, and are sometimes accompanied by other reflection or exhibition modules. For instance, in this case an international conference will be held between the two phases. There is also a whole series of telematics and material infrastructures available to the projects, which can make use of Medialab's digital tools and physical space during the months that separate the two phases of intensive work.

In this way, a framework is established to provide continuity for the processes. At the same time, it also inherits the typically pragmatic vocation of open-source software programmers or those who experiment with technology, who are accustomed to working on concrete objectives for which the ideas must be proven. It should be kept in mind, on the other hand, that although collaborative workshops are perhaps the main paradigm for Medialab's activity, they are not by any means the only one. Perhaps not so unlike what happens in the CSAs—and anthropologists Corsín and Estalella have indicated the permeability and proximity of Medialab to the world of community self-management—an everyday routine is established that is rich in encounters and heterogeneous situations, going beyond the logic of the regularly scheduled events or intensive work sessions. In this regard, Medialab has been able to construct a network of participants or daily users of its infrastructures that enjoys a quite unusual autonomy in public cultural institutions, which typically rely very heavily on timely proposals from their management teams.

Furthermore, all this is not at all accidental or 'improvised': in Medialab there is a constant process of reflection about this very atypical institution that has been created and is constantly seeking to improve itself. The working group 'Thinking and Doing Medialab' indicated, in this respect, that perhaps one of their greatest challenges was precisely the creation of greater continuity for the cultural processes that Medialab facilitates or drives, as well as broadening the communities participating in these processes. Towards this end, permanent 'Workstations' were recently established, allowing Medialab's most eminently productive and procedural functions to be operational at any moment, without depending so much on the routine scheduling of intensive prototype workshops.

So Medialab's very condition as an 'experimental' institution reinforces, in a certain sense, that aspect of open cultural infrastructure creation—which is also inseparable from community culture projects like Traficantes de Sueños—with the creation of protocols, such as these 'Workstations,' designed solely to intensify it. But Medialab has also produced other protocols more directly dedicated to dealing with the no less central question of the possibility of anyone's participation or, more precisely, of the possible empowerment of anyone's abilities. (In this regard, they may have an advantage over the community culture institutions, which may not always be so well supplied with sophisticated tools.) Medialab's basic official objectives already include 'offering different forms of participation that allow the collaboration of people with different backgrounds (artistic, scientific, technical), levels of specialization (expert and beginners), and degrees of involvement.' But I think the most significant thing about it is the importance that Medialab gives to the figure of its 'Mediators,' now associated with the 'Workstations.' Their function is specifically 'to respond to the needs of different types of publics and users: from general information and consultation to training, material resources, and spaces for listening and meetings,' as well as 'to explain the nature of the space and to put people in contact with people, people with projects, projects with projects.'

In dedicating this particular effort to, say, 'getting someone through the door'—i.e., in giving priority to welcoming and listening to the various needs and desires of potential participants—Medialab is explicitly offering support not only for collaboration, but also for inclusivity and plurality. In recognizing the importance of 'beginners' or 'amateurs,' Medialab is trying, it seems to me, to tear down those barriers between those supposedly 'in the know' and those who are 'in the dark'—barriers bequeathed to us by the tradition of artistic, technical, and scientific disciplines with which, at the same time, Medialab is officially affiliated.

This all has to do with something that in principle does not exist so concretely in the tradition of CSAs or other community cultural institutions: the desire for universality associated with the public arena, the vocation of being just that: 'a public service.' However, in Medialab's case it also has to do with a particular interpretation of the public arena, which Marcos García, the institution's director, clarifies very well:

> The difference between a public project that is for everyone (the general public, a homogeneous entity) and a public project that is for anyone is one of individuality, of personalization. It means paying attention to the particular needs of each person who comes; that is, helping each one of them develop their unique abilities.[7]

6.2.2. Risks of neoliberal capture of public cultural value

Having said this, I also want to highlight a certain contradiction. On the one hand, Medialab's very experimentality as an institution and its calling to public service allow it to develop protocols both of intensification of procedurality, such as inclusivity and plurality. On the other, and paradoxically, its very condition as a public institution, dependent in this case on a local administration heavily involved in the application of neoliberal policies, always constitutes a threat to these same tendencies.

---

7 Personal communication from Marcos García.

At the risk of oversimplifying, I think this is so mainly for two reasons. In the first place, the tradition of public cultural institutions continues to be strongly associated with the power/knowledge monopoly. Those working within Medialab itself often make the self-critical observation—and they work intensely to come up with a solution to it—that many people perceive the institution as a space of 'specialists,' people with highly technical and not very accessible knowledge bases. I can't take the time to dwell on this now, but I will say that it does not seem to be an unsolvable problem by any means. In fact, everything seems to point towards Medialab already being in a position to change that perception and the realities of exclusion to which it can lead. For example, there are programs designed specifically for *barrio* residents, or for children; they could also prioritize activities for traditional, amateur, and everyday abilities and ways of knowing that do not require any technical specialization.

What *does* seem to me to be a manifestation of an ingrained structural problem is that, despite all of the above, Medialab's very condition as a public institution dependent on an administration that strongly pushes neoliberal logics also involves the inevitable activation of forces for capturing and accumulating cultural value that necessarily counteract that same continuity. The most extreme expression of these forces—and certainly we live in a time that favors the expression of neoliberal extremism in its worst forms—took place in the form of a recent threat against Medialab's very existence. A rumor made the rounds that the city council was on the verge of handing over the building that Medialab now occupies, the recently restored former Belgian Sawmill, to Telefónica's 'Open Future' project. If this threat had become a reality, a single blow from above would have put paid to practically everything Medialab stands for, in favor of a private multinational corporation. And such a decision would have had nothing to do—in fact, quite the opposite—with the people, from both institutional positions and from outside, who have managed, given life to, used, and directly and daily encouraged that institution of participative culture for about 14 years.

But this is, as I say, perhaps only an extreme example of a tension that inevitably runs through all public institutions dependent on a state that has embraced neoliberalism as a primary means of support for social life, and therefore for basic aspects of human existence like cultural production, education, healthcare, and housework. In the case of institutions like Medialab, which have a strongly democratic operation in many senses, this tension is perhaps doubly overwhelming. It means that the protocols created to help people generate their own cultural value (e.g., workstations, prototype workshops, mediators, etc.) clash head-on with an institutional framework that constantly exerts pressure to redirect that value back towards forms of neoliberal privatization.

An important way in which this neoliberal pressure is articulated every day is through the recurrent demand for the isolation of units of meaning—such as an event, a tendency, a name, or a concept—or, more classically, the insistence on the identification of 'authors' and 'works,' to turn them into merchandise susceptible to producing financiarized value—i.e., 'brands.' This always occurs at the cost of interrupting or complicating the continuity of processes of self-managed production of cultural goods that can be used directly every day by those who participate in this production.

This demand can sometimes be made directly by the public administration, for example when they continue to use quantitative criteria to value the operation of cultural institutions, at the same time as they cut their budgets. In this sense, not only Medialab but all public institutions have suffered from the infamous 'austerity measures,' also called 'cuts,' that have characterized the neoliberal management of the crisis. And yet still their activity is constantly supervised, often from productivist criteria that, instead of valuing the capacity to empower and promote cultural self-management among those who participate, simply tend to demand more events, more visibility, more attendance by the 'public,' etc.

On the other hand, and no less importantly, neoliberal pressure is also exerted indirectly through a widespread climate of precarization. This causes the work, energy, and time the communities that use Medialab can contribute (for example those 'collaborators' who participate in the 'prototype workshops') to be severely limited by their dependence on more and more demanding ways to earn an income, which are also necessary for their survival.

In this sense, it's true that, as Domenico Di Siena indicated, even the notion of 'prototype,' which has proven to be so fertile in the context of Medialab, can run the risk of minimizing the importance of, or even fueling a certain tendency towards, self-exploitation. This is why it assumes the provisional state of what continue to be thought of as 'projects,' more than as tangible realities in the present. In the end, an excessive focus on that provisional state associated with the prototype process could lead to the type of devaluation that takes place in educational institutions in the prevailing neoliberalist conditions: they tend to become a kind of incubator of a value that will only be able to be put into effect outside their walls. That is, that value only *has* value in 'the market,' when the newly prepared students leave to look for work or, in the case of the prototypes, when they are finally ready 'to be made real' by companies that commercialize them.

6.2.3. Participation without the power of decision in the economic model (the case of PECAM)

I want to put special emphasis on these tensions because I believe that they are strongly representative of the pressures that not only the public cultural institutions but also, to a certain extent, the community and self-managed ones are feeling during the neoliberal crisis. So what becomes obvious in the problems that institutions like Medialab face is that, in fact, the assumption by the public administration of the privatizing, financiarizing, productivist, and jeopardizing criteria of neoliberalism is being turned into support for public institutions that are increasingly similar, in many senses, to community self-managed ones.

As some cultural policy critics, such as the previously quoted Rowan (2013), Rubén Martinez (2014b), and Adolfo Estalella (2012), are shrewdly noting, this is nothing new. Perhaps the best-known example is what was called the 'Big Society' model by British Prime Minister David Cameron, says Rowan, 'to pressure the social base to compensate and assume the tasks not performed by the state due to budget and competency cuts.' Opening the doors of public institutions decimated by cuts to 'civic participation' therefore causes a kind of potentiation of self-management that in many cases runs the risk of instigating self-exploitation. At the same time, it prevents the citizenry from making decisions about questions pertaining to the sustainability of those public institutions that now claim to be 'participative.'

In the language of Spanish public administration, it is, in effect, more and more common to appeal to citizen participation, at the same time as line-item cuts in the financing of basic public services, including cultural ones, are already among the most significant in Europe. In the sphere of cultural institutions, to give a concrete example, this situation was clearly shown recently at the beginning of the city council's process to develop a new Strategic Plan for Culture in Madrid (PECAM in Spanish). In 2012, the council offered a comprehensive document titled *Hacia el PECAM*, which offered a series of reflections and proposals on medium-term cultural policies that highlighted, as the aforementioned critics observed, concepts that articulate the model of participative, democratic institutions, whether self-managed, like the CSA La Tabacalera, to which an entire section was dedicated, or public, like Medialab-Prado itself.

In fact, in the act of introducing the deliberation process that would lead to PECAM, and which the city council proposed as a 'participative process,' the Delegate of the Area of Arts, its highest authority, affirmed that 'the enormous effort of investment in cultural infrastructures and activities made by the previous government' would 'be unsustainable' (he didn't say why). At the same time, however, he indicated that culture was entering a new paradigm, exemplified by three concepts typical of the Medialab-Prado discourse, without ever mentioning this institution: 'digitalization, the commons, and mediation.'

From these two discursive elements, the Delegate seemed to reach the following conclusion: 'culture is made and it is lived, it is not legislated. And, of course, it is not increased or cut by decree.' Which, of course— and as Rowan incisively indicated—is quite surprising as an affirmation pronounced at the beginning of a process designed for precisely that: to legislate culture. That is, to establish a series of public cultural policies, and at a time when the administration was indeed constantly issuing decrees that cut funding for institutional cultural promotion and production activities.

Stemming from these misunderstandings or conceptual contradictions present from the very start, the supposedly participative process that was expected to lead to PECAM basically consisted of the authorization of an email address on the council's webpage to which messages could be sent. Of course, no direct answers would be issued, and the messages could not be seen by other users. The process also included a series of 'regional' meetings and another of public 'round tables' with 'expert' participants. From what I have been able to glean from the documentation on this process, it doesn't seem like these scheduled events have been sufficient to dissipate those conceptual contradictions that the process has dragged with it from the start.

There have been interesting moments, however, when these contradictions have been starkly revealed. One occurred during the round table titled 'Dialogue between Public Administration, Foundations, Associations, and Companies' (Medialab-Prado 2014b) which, as its title indicated, gathered together people with very diverse allegiances and notions of 'culture': from a representative of the Telefónica Foundation to a participant in several Self-Managed Social Centers, among them La Tabacalera, and including a Director General of the Ministry of Education, Culture and Sport, among other people.

This same heterogeneous table configuration was already revealing of a discussion framework that in itself is anything but neutral, as was noted and questioned directly by Carlos Vidania, the previously mentioned participant in several CSAs. He claimed that placing self-managing cultural projects together with corporate enterprises on the same plane, as if they were the same, was a sure way to repeat the types of error that have led to the economic, cultural, and city model crisis that defines the present situation. For him, the prevailing models responsible for the crisis are those of the great culture industry, the culture-spectacle, and city-brand. All of these are incompatible with true civic participation because they focus on the 'attraction of capital, of initiatives of greater added value.' In opposition to these models, the self-management experiences of 'weak empowerment' neither want nor need to compete, because they propose a different model of economy, culture, and city. 'It's not the same [process] to organize the Antiracist Alcorcón "Little World Cup" as it is the Olympic Games in Madrid,' asserted Vidania graphically, 'but more than that, it's possible that they're completely incompatible.'

Vidania also contributed another substantial criticism of the very process of creating PECAM, and in general of the dialogue models that propose public institutions with an associative fabric. He showed that as long as no instruments are created for citizen participation in effective decision-making on cultural policies, true participation will not exist. And he clearly explained that public institutions should promote relational paths that enable a true decision-making capacity for constructing and distributing resources, and for establishing priorities for the use of those resources. Contrarily, in the city-brand model a good number of the resources end up supporting those who, paradoxically, already have more of them: company foundations and big culture industries. Self-managed projects, however, are granted nothing more than a 'folkloric' role.

Vidania's discourse had a certain performative function in that it made the immediate applicability of his arguments obvious. It received a rapid response from Carlota Álvarez Basso, the city council's director of PECAM development, in an intervention that completely ignored both of Vidania's critiques (the incompatibility of culture models and the false 'participation' that was offered). This, of course, demonstrated just what type of 'dialogue' the administration was encouraging in that round table. Instead of responding to his specific challenges, Álvarez Basso answered Vidania by brandishing a new defense of the 'hacia el PECAM' process in terms of just how much participation it promotes. She added that representatives of 80 associations had been invited to 'regional tables,' and then, bringing things down to a personal level, finished with, 'I don't remember why you couldn't come or we weren't able to contact to you.'

Álvarez Basso also reiterated her willingness to revise PECAM afterwards based on the dialogues that were being generated in the process. In other words, her willingness, effectively, to deny direct participation in the decision-making to the associative fabric that produces self-managed culture in Madrid, and ultimately to reserve this prerogative for herself and the rest of the technicians of the city council's Arts Area designated for this purpose, exactly what Vidania had condemned.

At this point, the Telefónica Foundation's representative spoke up. It is important to remember that this Foundation belongs to the same company that was about to contribute to the expulsion of Medialab-Prado from its current location, and which also, by the way, appropriated the imaginary of one of the 15M assemblies in one of its publicity spots, even as it dismissed 6,000 workers. Its representative contributed to the debate to say, in reference to what she called models of 'subsidized culture,' that 'lamentably, throughout history there have been deaths.' She added that this fact 'is part of evolution,' and that 'subsidized culture' was one of those deaths.

In this sense also, there was something of the performative in Vidania's gesture of denouncing the incompatibility between business and self-management: in effect, the business models of culture, such as the Telefónica Foundation, seemed not to be able to exist by themselves without the need to send all the other models—what they very inaccurately called 'subsidized'—to the tomb.

6.2.4. Culture as 'resource': citizens evicted from the 'public house'

Rubén Martínez, who researches cultural policies, was also present at the round table, and he took the opportunity to nuance the idea expressed by the Telefónica Foundation representative. He chose to contribute to the distinction between the conceptions of 'culture as right' and 'culture as resource' proposed by the researcher George Yúdice. This distinction is useful for moving beyond the critique of turning culture into merchandise, because it shows how another way of endangering the right to culture is by turning it into a 'resource,' that is, into a pretext for something else.

From this conception, which has been predominant in recent decades, public institutions have been more worried about the 'impact' of culture than about culture itself, and the state has taken part to turn culture into a sector used by others: the service sector, the real estate sector, tourism, etc. Martínez therefore asserted that 'culture as resource should become a thing of the past,' although 'it is at the heart of PECAM, as seen in its use of the concept of "creative industries." This is nothing more than a state operation to favor the corporatization of freelancers, and later allow them, through self-exploitation, to take responsibility for carrying out functions that the state used to fulfill.'

Again Álvarez Basso's answer revealed the public institution's position: she said that culture as right, but also as resource, and as a service self-managed by communities are all legitimate, and that they have to share 'the space.' She added that 'there are very healthy cultural industries,' and that the associative network is also 'requesting entrance,' but that they aren't mutually exclusive.

For her part, Begoña Torres, the Director General of the Ministry of

Education, Culture, and Sports who negotiated the transfer of the building that houses the CSA La Tabacalera to the groups that manage it, expressed her disagreement with Rubén Martínez, affirming that 'the economic use of culture' has been a great discovery for Spain, because it has allowed the country to move from having one museum to having hundreds.

Thus two outright refusals to confront the disastrous consequences of neoliberal policies on culture were outlined. One insisted on the perfect compatibility of the business model of cultural industries with the associative self-managed model. The other went perhaps further still, directly defending placing culture in service to financial interests, praising the proliferation of museums by the Spanish state that has been considered one of the great emblems of the excesses of the 'bubble' (sometimes called the 'Guggenheim effect').[8]

To these two refusals to accept the disastrous consequences of the neoliberal model, I would like to add still another, fundamental to the repertoire of arguments used by public administrations to avoid directly approaching and simultaneously to justify and slyly promote the precarization of culture imposed by neoliberalism. It is the already classic exhortation for 'entrepreneurship' to cultural agents, which is nothing more, it seems to me, than another manifestation of the omnipresent pressure of corporatization that the neoliberal way of life entails.

Martínez and Rowan both participated at another dialogue table, this time with a representative of the Catalan administration, within the framework of the 2013 Indigestio Forum. These two researchers, who have extensively criticized the type of public policies that favor 'creative industries,' insisted that in the context of the crisis it was increasingly clear that those policies should not be repeated. They were met with colorfully recycled versions of the same arguments:

> There doesn't seem to be anything bad about a music group playing music and making money for playing music and being able to economically exploit their creativity ... If stimulating a company means helping a music group to form, and be able to write checks and pay bills, and know how to calculate, before writing a check, if there is enough money in the account, then yes, we are promoting companies—but the goal is not to make companies.

8 See Esteban's *El efecto Guggenheim* (2007). Regarding transformations of cultural policies in the framework of Spanish neoliberalism, the books written by Rubén Martínez in collaboration with Jaron Rowan and signed as YProductions (YProductions 2009a; 2009b) are very enlightening. Also very useful is the article 'Las políticas culturales en el estado español (1985–2005)' (Marzo and Badía 2006).

Rowan synthesized these policies clearly: 'I go with my grandmother and she tells me, "Give a nickel to the musicians playing in the metro, they have the right to earn a living." Sure, but that can't be a proposal from a political institution. Where's the political project in that?'

Co-opting 'participation' and 'self-management' to integrate them into the neoliberal system. Stubbornly defending the use of culture as resource to obtain economic profits or political capital. Urging everyone who wants to 'make culture' to start a business even at the cost of falling into precarization and self-exploitation. These kinds of administrative attitudes can be understood metaphorically as a kind of 'active eviction' of cultural agents protected by the umbrella of the public arena, to throw them to the mercy of the market. And this seems a useful metaphor to me, because it allows us to relate this situation to others that deal with the most obvious problems created by the neoliberal crisis, as well as relating it to the movements that have arisen as a result.

The PAH and the Mareas Verde and Blanca, which I have already discussed, can in this sense be understood as ways of reclaiming the space that the public sphere must safeguard for the common good and the satisfaction of peoples' basic needs, in the face of the intrusions of private interests. Housing, hospitals, and schools are the physical manifestation of that 'space,' which also entails many other resources, but these tend to converge around those nerve centers located in specific buildings. This is what seems to have been assumed by the citizenry. They have organized their mobilizations around the defense of, and in some cases, through experiments in the self-management of, those physical spaces to reclaim the function of protection of basic rights that must be exerted in the public sphere. But in the case of the right to culture, what would constitute the 'public house' *par excellence* that needs to be defended? Perhaps those museums and art centers that are supposedly so favorable for 'the economy,' and that have become symbols of the bubble? Or the libraries, the archives, the auditoriums so dependent on the elitist traditions that have dominated modern culture?

I want to use these questions now to give one more turn of the screw to the analysis of the emergence of a possible ecosystem of 'cultures of anyone' in self-managed or public frameworks. I turn to an interesting debate about why there has not been a Marea de la Cultura, or at least none with as much force as those for health and education. I propose that both the weight of modern elitist tradition and the usual view of culture as a 'less essential' need have produced its greater vulnerability to forms of neoliberal privatization, and have contributed to making the type of mobilization centralized in public spaces that we have seen in the Mareas very difficult.

In some sense, perhaps those cultural 'public' spaces have never been completely public, because of their strong affiliation with the hegemony of the modern power/knowledge complex. At the same time, it doesn't help that their process of 'selling' to the highest bidder in the neoliberal market was already much more advanced than in the case of hospitals and schools, since these turn out to be much less effective for promoting spectacular urban revaluation phenomena. All this has, of course, a series of fundamental consequences in terms of the type of cultural production that could be sustained in the absence of those 'public houses' of culture. I will also attempt to pose questions about some of these consequences, which might bring out neoliberalism's effects not only on ways of supporting culture, but also on the ways of expressing and constructing meaning.

6.3. Between Institution and Experimentation: Why Hasn't There Been a Marea de la Cultura?

6.3.1. 'Everything is culture' but there is a 'cultural sector'

In the face of the bankruptcy of public cultural institutions, their invasion by private interests, their inability to create programming due to 'lack of funds,' and their invitation to all cultural agents, beginning with themselves, 'to become a business or die,' has often left many people who want to dedicate their time and energy to cultural production, simply put, out on the street.

And it was on the street that the 'We Are All Culture' act was performed on March 9, 2014. This was part of something that was, in fact, called Marea de la Cultura or Marea Roja, but it has not yet achieved the intensity of other Mareas. In Madrid's Paseo del Prado, nine platforms were built for this act, dedicated respectively to music, performing arts, visual arts, education, patrimony, literature, dance, cinema, and civic movements. In spite of 'taking culture to the street,' it seemed then that the logic of the group of professional associations that convened the event (who called themselves Platform for the Defense of Culture), perpetuated the type of sectorial divisions practiced by those same institutions whose privatization process was being condemned.

In relation to this compartmentalized and professionalized concept of culture, Carmen Lozano-Bright (2014) wrote a timely and critical article on the eve of the act in which she indicated:

They're calling tomorrow 'the first great mobilization of the world of culture.' As if everything we're living (particularly for the last three years) were not the greatest cultural demonstration and learning in decades: recuperation of unused spaces, urban community orchards, mutual support networks, creation and articulation of *common* points of contact in the face of the Nothing left by the real estate bubble.[9]

What is here in the background, without a doubt, is the recurrent misunderstanding of, or at least the persistent tension between, the applicable 'anthropological' definition of culture, which considers as such all construction of human meaning, and the shortened version proposed by bourgeois liberal modernity, supported by the exclusivist conception of the production of meaning that I have been reviewing in this book. But the added complication, of course, is that this last conception, 'sectorial,' 'professional,' 'specialized,' is the one that has predominated in the institutions of the neoliberalist bubble, and therefore the one that has occupied its spectacular infrastructures, until these began to be drained of resources. Hence, when this type of sectorial understanding of culture 'hits the streets,' or reclaims part of the Mareas, there is no lack of critical voices like Lozano-Bright's.

In fact, a polemical debate has been generated about this situation, which Víctor Lenore (2013) summarized in the title of another article: 'Culture and 15M: A Stormy Relationship.' In it he gathered the opinions of several cultural agents on the subject. In their opinions, mixed in with other comments, we can undoubtedly find critical reactions to the indelible marks that both the elitist tradition and neoliberalism have left on 'the cultural sector.'

And so, for example, the musician Nacho Vegas said, intelligently relating both problems: 'Many "creators" mistrust any collective movement as a matter of principle, considering them meek, as if following the hyperindividualistic dictates imposed by neoliberalism was not letting themselves be acritically carried away by the current.' At the same time, as happened with Lozano-Bright, the support for the 'transversality' of culture was reappearing as a form of resistance against those abusive vices of the 'authorial,' 'professional' sector. In this sense, the writer Belén Gopegui stated:

Culture, it seems to me, shouldn't be a section in a newspaper, but rather, should be imbricated in every one of the other sections. For the same reason, I don't believe it should be a section in a movement, but an expression of it and thus be everywhere and nowhere.

9 Lozano-Bright seems to be thinking about practices that are closer to what is routinely thought of as activism, frequently linked to physical spaces. However, it would be interesting to also map the proliferation of cultural projects from or about the 15M in the sphere of written culture (something to which I contributed with the article 'Cuando cualquiera escribe: procesos democratizadores de la cultura escrita en la crisis de la Cultura de la Transición española' (2014)).

Of course, the danger of taking to extremes that logic of the transversality of culture—a danger that, by the way, none of the aforementioned people incurs—lies in diminishing the need to materially support certain intensive cultural practices that would not otherwise exist. In other words, although of course everybody is in fact a cultural producer (everybody thinks and speaks, everybody gives meaning to what happens to them), some people dedicate their lives to intensely cultivating one or another aspect of meaning production. And they need to be able to 'live on that'; that is, sustaining those intensive cultural practices *is* their livelihood, and having also to do other things to be able to support themselves to have a life with dignity would interfere with that.

Jordi Oliveras (2013), organizer of the Indigestio Forum and host of interesting debates on these questions in the magazine *Nativa*, synthesized in the following terms this conception of culture as something common and everyday, but that also allows 'specializations': 'We would have to understand creators as specialists who work the cultural magma in an implicit process of social delegation, and the managers and structures of management—public or private—as instruments in the service of these processes, and not the reverse.'

Guillermo Zapata (Lenore 2013), activist, audiovisual scriptwriter, and promoter of multiple cultural and political initiatives, also pointed out something essential in relation to those 'management structures' that are due to the 'cultural magma.' He reminds us that in addition to public and private, they can also be community, but for that we need communities willing to defend them:

> I believe that one of the keys to the Mareas is that they understand that the defense of the public sphere is no longer only a matter for professionals, but one that requires community participation. The questions raised are: What is community for Spanish culture? Can there be community if we have spent years treating people either like clients or like thieves?

In the paragraphs above, I have tried to offer an outline of how the world of Self-Managed Social Centers and some public cultural institutions especially permeable to community involvement, like Medialab-Prado, are perhaps most similar to those communities able to defend the intense processes of cultural production that Zapata demands. In no way are these exhaustive examples. Fortunately, there exists a plurality of cultural community self-management experiences capable of empowering all types of knowledge and abilities, and often these experiences do not depend directly on what can be properly understood as CSAs. Nor do they depend on public institutions, or at least not entirely. Often they are cultural processes that experiment with hybrid forms of self-managed support, public and private, in the physical and digital spheres, linking unpaid collective work with the use of public infrastructures or even subsidies, but also with certain uses of the commercial sphere foreign to the logics of privatization and competition.

6.3.2. 'Epistemic experimental communities':
Without pampering there is no experimentation

It is true, in any case—and I think it's important to make the distinction—that in among all that magma that Lozano-Bright talks about, it is worth identifying some projects or spaces that are dedicated with greater intensity to questions of learning, to working with language, with research analysis, and, in general, with experimentation in the production of meaning.

Thus, in a trilogy of articles essential to theorizing these questions, Tomás Sánchez Criado (2013a; 2013b; 2014) indicated that, in effect, the neoliberal crisis has simultaneously brought a crisis of the 'institutions of knowledge' that produce a widespread desire 'to theoretically and practically articulate "who we are," "what is happening to us," to discuss "what has come down on us," and "what we can do with it."' As he says about those '"institutions of knowledge," [given that] it has been demonstrated that "they didn't know" that this could happen, that "they couldn't" do anything to avoid it, that "they didn't predict" what would happen, or that "they didn't want" to tell us that they profited' from all the new forms of encounters that have appeared, some of them dedicated to somehow confronting the need to replace those fraudulent kinds of knowledge:

> Splinter groups or great masses that mount their own environments for creating knowledge, that strive to create climates of debate and discussion, with a great hospitality for the unknown. An entire true 'ecology of collective practices' that it would require our best talent as naturalists to try to account for, to make the most of. (2013b)

Sánchez Criado builds a small catalogue and also proposes the concept of 'epistemic experimental communities' to theorize these collective practices. Of course wisdom and knowledge, the 'epistemic,' are always involved in any human activity, and in many of the political processes initiated around the neoliberal crisis this has been obvious, as I discussed in the last chapter. Sánchez Criado clearly recognizes this issue, but he also points out some lines to map, with no intention of establishing rigid categories, those spaces or projects that have focused on that epistemic dimension of a more experimental form. In other words, those spaces, we could say, with a greater willingness to question the meaning of the reality that emerges from the neoliberal crisis, still at risk of not being fast enough about attaining specific changes in the institutionality that manages that crisis.

So Sánchez Criado speaks, for example, of experiences modeled around collective learning, such as those of the 'University on the Streets,' or the 'People's Summer University' held in the self-managed urban space of Campo de Cebada. Such experiences, he says, could become related to the old traditions of popular *barrio* schools and the movements of educational renovation. He also mentions the breeding ground of the CSAs, some projects like the Observatorios Metropolitanos of Madrid and Barcelona, and the Common Notions, for which we could use the label of 'activist research.' Furthermore, he alludes to 'hybrid institutional spaces,' among which he includes both Medialab-Prado and the CSA Ateneu Candela, integrated from Terrassa into the Fundación de los Comunes. Finally, he mentions Intermediae, ColaBoraBora, and Zemos98, plus the 'innumerable collectives of participatory architecture that have sprouted like mushrooms in recent years' (2013b). An interesting addition to this list would be that of the interdisciplinary field of studies in science, technology, and society (STS), which has called attention to the ethical and political dimensions of science and technology, producing interesting encounters with activist practices, such as Sánchez Criado's own developments around the 'material politics of care' (critical interventions in services and technologies related to the notion of 'disability').

Instead of the community/self-management/public institution axis that I have been using, Sánchez Criado here follows in particular the epistemic, experimental function of some current cultural projects. This is a function it seems essential to emphasize in order to understand the paths of the collaborative cultures emerging from the thread of the neoliberal crisis, and perhaps also to understand why they have not given rise to a mass Marea de la Cultura, like those for education and healthcare. So, besides the problem of the co-optation of public spaces by neoliberal competitive logics, it seems to me that we must also keep in mind the inevitable tension that always takes place between experimental forms and established processes.

Spaces that put the epistemic crisis in the forefront and confront it with an experimental spirit, without proposing preconceived solutions, also need to constantly reinvent themselves in some way. This is in no way incompatible with creating institutions, if we understand that their organizing and structuring tendencies can be flexible, but they do mark certain priorities in that sense.

In the third article of his trilogy, Sánchez Criado (2014) defends his use of the concept of experimentation analogously to the notion of the 'experts in what happens to them' proposed earlier by Antonio Lafuente:

I spoke, however, of experimentation not only because I like to play with words or simply to incorporate a *cool* word from the art world, but because of the proximity or vicinity of these means of knowledge production with the real practice of scientific laboratories (and not their mythical vision). Because in these spaces it becomes necessary for us to constantly explore the boundaries of our conventional ways of thinking and acting; taking charge of the changing, vibrant materiality that constitutes us, in complex worlds such as the contemporary ones, where we de/compose ourselves through our relations with microbes and very diverse somatic affections, communication infrastructures, climatic catastrophes, housing systems, intellectual property formats, etc. that enable the sociomaterial articulation of our agency. In other words, the things that allow or interfere with our particular possibilities of performance to take charge of what affects us. And I was delighting in the fact that the result of its union is a novel situation that has allowed the old guinea pigs of technocratic reason to explore and experiment with other life and existential alternatives, looking for ways to develop something like 'self-managed guinea pigs,' making 'the revolution of bodies, from bodies, for bodies, in bodies ...,' in other words, from its radical diversity.

In this same article, Sánchez Criado also recognized that the experimental practices of those 'self-managed guinea pigs' that emerge from the neoliberal crisis have been besieged by the aforementioned 'technocratic reason,' which has tried to integrate them into the world of 'innovation' and 'learning,' to fit them to the logics of neoliberal competitiveness. This is why he emphasized that it's fundamental to attend to the vulnerability of these experimental practices, developing what he expressively called '*pampering*': 'that care and daily attention that requires experimentation with passion.' And for this he proposed 'new formats of institutionality,' or '*mimatorios* [pampering places] where these experimental practices would be sheltered':

[S]elf-managed spaces to be constructed where our experimental tasks could be carried out, where we would be able to control our support, keeping alive our knowledge bases of experimentation and their particular relation with materials, practices, ideas, tools, etc. But also spaces where these practices are pampered so that they result in a good deed, where they are proven and formats are experimented with to equip them with minimum conditions of subsistence and compensation.

This need is none other than the one I have followed in previous reflections about the shelter and everyday support the 'cultures of anyone' can find, always with the expected difficulties, in self-managed or public spaces. But Sánchez Criado also emphasizes one of the essential characteristics of those intensive cultural practices, of that 'specialization' that takes place within the daily magma of the collective production of meaning: experimentation. I think this emphasis on experimentation as one of the important factors of the 'cultures of anyone' can add another layer to the debate on the possible *marea de la cultura*. It shows us that perhaps it is not only neoliberal harassment and its 'enclosure' of the public sphere that have complicated the existence of 'public culture houses' capable of inspiring *mareas* in their defense. Rather, it is the especially experimental—and therefore vulnerable—condition of the production of meaning itself during the neoliberal crisis—at this moment so strong with shared 'not-knowing'—that complicates, or at least suggests special demands for, the institutional dynamics capable of creating such 'houses' from participative and community networks.

6.3.3. Collecting answers or posing questions: Between institution and experimentation

Let's think again, for example, about the Fundación de los Comunes. Would this not be one of those 'pampering places' that must take care of the experimental practices of the 'self-managed guinea pigs' during the crisis of the neoliberal institutions of knowledge? It seems to me that the Fundación de los Comunes constitutes a privileged example because it captures a common tendency to demand the right to the public arena from a position within the self-managed spaces, analogously to what Rubén Martínez and Carlos Vidania suggested as a result of PECAM. The Fundación de los Comunes was created, as explained in its blog (Fundación de los Comunes 2013a), to

construct a territory of experimentation shared between, on the one hand, cultural or political institutions with a de-institutionalizing vocation, in the sense of not capturing others and of overcoming its limits (separation gaps with respect to truly alive social production) and, on the other hand, some spaces of independent cooperation with a desire to equip their practices with greater stability, consistency and impact; that is, overcoming, in turn, the precarization to which neoliberal globalization tries to condemn us.

In this sense, the Foundation tries to systematize or formalize these movements' collective desire for intervention in public institutions to escape that 'sentence of precarization.' And significantly, in doing so, it also appears as a legal institution with statutes, and above all, with a clear and to some degree instrumental discourse about its goals.

This is what I particularly want to highlight now, because it seems to me that when the vector of experimentation is introduced into the equation of 'cultures of anyone,' it becomes particularly obvious that there are more instrumental ways of producing meaning in these cultures, which share space with that experimentation. And such sharing can't help but be a source of diversity in the models, and even of the tensions among them.

The Fundación de los Comunes proposes itself as a *think tank*. This means that it must offer not only questions, but answers. Its coordinator, Marisa Pérez-Colina (Entrevista Marisa Pérez Colina, Fundación de los Comunes (FdlC), MUSAC 14 de mayo de 2014), has commented on numerous occasions that this means 'elevating the discourse to the level of the conflict in the street,' or, as explained in an article from the Foundation (2013b), listening and observing 'the movements,' because

> the answer to the question 'how do we win?' will not come *a priori* from intellectual discussions nor from theoretical analyses. Only the movements have the answer, and it is inscribed on their bodies, in their practices, in their ways of doing. Today we have a myriad of interesting practices to learn from, new experiments, and it is necessary to listen to them and observe them, always from a position inside these practices. To the question 'What can we do?' we can respond with another question: 'What is already being done—from the struggles?'

The think tank model means these questions must be considered valid to be able to formulate answers. Thus, more than asking what are 'the struggles' or what do they mean—or even what does it mean 'to win,' or perhaps even more importantly, in what kind of language do those struggles and movements speak and what would be the most appropriate way to translate their 'bodies, their practices, their ways of being' into 'discourse'—a certain legibility is presumed, a certain access that will allow us to offer answers. Or at least, the experimentation, the not knowing, and the uncertainty entailed in that necessary 'translation' is not the focal point.

Ultimately, what I want to point out here, hand in hand with the concept of vulnerable experimentation proposed by Sánchez Criado, is that the 'movements,' if we include those 'experimental epistemic communities,' are not only going to provide answers, but also more questions. And thus the 'translation' the Fundación de los Comunes proposes will not always be an easy exercise. This, it seems to me, does not at all mean that institutions able to defend those cultures are not necessary; rather, just the opposite. But yes, perhaps these institutions will always have to reserve an important space for the not-knowing and experimentation, for things that can't be immediately translated into the language of politics or institutional culture, which is not always easy.

Perhaps this difficulty of linking cultural experimentation with establishing practices capable of providing long-term support is more appreciated in the area of projects that have a vocation more oriented towards aesthetic questions, towards reflection on the forms of plastic, linguistic, audiovisual representations, etc.

In this sense, it seems significant to me that often when 'the 15M culture' is spoken of—and I myself have done it in previous texts—the projects that have been summarized have mostly been projects that can be more or less associated with traditional artistic or cultural forms, like cinema (15M.cc, Cine sin Autor), music (Fundación Robo), literature (Asalto), or even 'the library,' in the case of #Bookcamping. And then their relationship to the 'spaces of life' or 'institutions' have been theorized more or less indirectly, given that none of these cultural initiatives, unlike projects like TdS, are tied directly to permanent institutional structures such as CSAs, although some have occasionally been supported by them, and also by some public 'cultural centers.'

Perhaps, I suggest now, beyond the traditional tendency to separate 'culture' and, even more, 'art' from the 'social channels of production' that nourish them, it is necessary to recognize that an inevitable tendency also exists in the most experimental aspects of meaning production, those usually associated with aesthetic or philosophical exploration, to work with a high degree of uncertainty. And this does not always fit well with the need for consensus and positive affirmations that occur in the construction of institutions.

In this regard, I am not trying to establish any kind of artificial 'suture'; nor is it my intent to reduce to a single unit the multiple differences between these aesthetic projects, those more 'epistemic' ones, and the diverse experiences that ground them. What I want to do in what follows is to add a final reflection around the plural tensions and drifts that occur not only between the self-organized and the public spheres—both always subjected to the pressures of 'extraction' and neoliberal 'enclosure'—but also between the experimental and establishing dynamics that run through both fields.

For this, I now want to explore briefly and as an open ending to my journey, some examples of experimental cultural processes that arose around the types of questions with difficult answers that don't always allow progress towards the creation of institutional proposals. Even so, they are crucial with respect to the possibility of not reproducing the languages and forms of legitimation that neoliberalism co-opts with greater facility. Thus, they are also crucial for democratizing the 'cultures of anyone' at the level of the most immediate materials—linguistic, formal, conceptual—with which these cultures are granted existence and self-representation.

6.4. 'Making Us Be':
The Question of Forms of (Self-)Representation

6.4.1. 'Occupying language' to exist: The Euraca Seminar

How did we get to this point? Let's return now to those young people introduced by *El País* as 'Nimileuristas,' about whom I talked at the beginning of this book. If we pay close attention, if we look a little more closely or, simply, another way, we'll see that the photos in the news article show fairly 'normal'-looking figures (makeup, hair, clothes) against a supposedly 'neutral' background: white.

This was the way the Euraca Seminar (EURACA 2012)—which initially appeared to be a seminar on contemporary poetry and poetics—looked at the 'Nimileuristas' in its initial interventions, in October 2012. The opening group of this collective investigation wanted to exemplify with these images on a neutral background an operation of meaning that is fundamental to understanding what is in play in what I have been calling 'cultures of anyone.' It's a specific way of exerting the 'establishment of reality' Michel de Certeau speaks of. He reflected on the preconception of accepting as real only what can be shown to be visible, but in this modality, as Euraca asserts, what passes as real is not only visible, but 'transparent.' That is, it is passed off as something perfectly legible, whose meaning should be abundantly clear, ready-made, ready for consumption.

The poets María Salgado and Patricia Esteban, founders of the Euraca Seminar, proposed as one of the premises of their 'research on language and languages in the final days of the Euro' the need to question this type of operation. Taking inspiration from a text by the historic Oulipo poet Jacques Roubaud (1998), they have connected this 'transparent' language to the existence of something like a 'muesli language' of global capitalism, well mixed so that it can flow everywhere. The epitome of this language would come to be that type of completely instrumentalized, rapid, 'standardized' 'airport English' that is occupying more and more terrain in the construction of the collective experience under neoliberalism.

Euraca is opposed to this 'transparent' language, and to operations of 'soft representation' in general, like those of the newspaper *El País* and its 'Nimileurista generation.' Instead, what Euraca proposes is to recover the materiality of languages, their capacity to be located in bodies and geographical spaces that give them a concrete existence and a multiplicity of meanings which is exactly the opposite of that supposed 'transparency.'

As an example of forms of resistance to the 'muesli language' that are supported by the materiality of languages, Euraca took as its point of departure the work of some Argentine poets from the nineties who built a poetics based on the appropriation of colloquial, lower-class, teen slang, or 'street' languages. Their point was not to attempt to represent those who spoke them, but to produce an unfamiliarity in which the rhetorical operations typical of literary language were still present. It was therefore not about 'imitating' the language of others, but rather using the materiality of located languages, strongly marked, to destabilize the standardized and supposedly 'transparent' language that is invading everything.

Salgado and Esteban summarized the value of this type of operation with the help of a phrase from the critics Selci and Kesselman (2008), who analyzed one of the key Argentine poetry collections, *La zanjita* by Juan Desiderio: 'The characters of *La zanjita* barely have names, they're only vaguely described, and the story that frames them is barely intelligible. Nevertheless, they speak in such a unique way, so oddly but authentically, that the reader immediately believes in their existence.'

It is precisely that 'belief of existence,' that verisimilitude based on their material uniqueness, of which speech and language are sometimes undeniable proofs, that *El País* denied to the generation of young Spanish people suffering from the neoliberal crisis. It turned them into a kind of photogenic stereotype floating in a dehistoricized, decontextualized emptiness (the blank white background). In order to question that attempted neutrality, Euraca embarked on an intense trip in which questions were posed about the normalizing effects of the mesocratic ideal and consumerist society on language and the production of meaning in the Spanish state. These questions will be familiar to readers, as they are similar to some of those raised in the first part of this book, and also in dialogue with the historians Germán Labrador and Pablo Sánchez León.

At the same time, on its journey Euraca approached multiple Creole, hybrid, and resistant border areas in other latitudes, from the Caribbean to the *banlieus* of the great European metropolises, on the way moving through racially mixed Tijuana and other afro and native Latin American conclaves. In among all that plurality, they also emphasized two places that were, perhaps, more of arrival, or at least nearer that poetic and political 'Euraca' position they were attempting to interrogate. The first was the poetry of Luz Pichel in the Castrapo dialect, a mixture of Castilian and Gallego associated with the popular classes; the second was Luis Melgarejo's poetry in 'Andalusian.' Both problematize 'muesli languages' as much as national frameworks and their venerated representative 'high' literatures.

Another way to explain what Euraca proposes and investigates, and which is also close to central themes of these reflections on 'cultures of anyone,' would be to say that in all its work with 'marked,' located, semi-opaque languages, there is a discovery of the language of 'ordinary people,' of those people who don't belong, in each case, in each context, to the tacit group of 'those in the know.'

The elites that try to monopolize meaning production would have moved, in Euraca's analysis, from preferring 'official or high languages'—*wooden languages*, as Roubaud says, basically referring to rigidly normative languages—to also using the fluidity of the 'muesli' approach. But their purpose is always as a strategy to exert a policing control on the overflowing materiality of ordinary language, of the language of 'those in the dark.' Before, the uncouth barbarian was unable to rise to the sophistication of 'cultured' languages, and remained unable to understand its exclusive codes. Now he is the one who remains too attached to his 'lects,' his own particular speech varieties, to the local specificity of his territory, his accent or his body, too slow to be incorporated into the speed of the global commerce of meaning. The barbarian is now the one who soils and infects that international, immaculate language of airports and nonplaces with his irremediable belonging to material, located, imperfect, ordinary ways of producing meaning.[10]

But when neoliberalism enters as deep a crisis as that happening in the Spanish state, its muesli language does, too. And then all those 'barbaric,

10 Ricardo Piglia's reflections on the place of literature in the face of these tensions seems particularly relevant here: 'There is a schism between public language, the language of politicians in the first place, and the other uses of language that get scattered and twinkle, like faraway voices, on the social surface. An average style tends to be imposed—a style that functions as a register of legitimacy and comprehension—that is used by everyone who speaks in public. Literature is directly confronted with those official uses of the word, and of course its place and its function in society are increasingly invisible and limited. Any critical word suffers the consequences of this tension; it is forced to reproduce that crystallized language, with the argument that that will make it accessible. Hence the idea of whatever works being comprehensible. That is, anything is comprehensible as long as it repeats what everyone can understand, and what everyone can understand is what reproduces the language that defines reality as it is' (Piglia and Rozitchner 2001, 40).

ordinary' languages proliferate, filling the common space with improper noises, dissonances, and meanings. When the authorities that try to control language by making it transparent confront such an intense crisis of cultural legitimacy as what is spreading through Spanish institutionality, we are often left with the strangeness of the everyday.

'The ordinary always has something of the extraordinary,' said Salgado when she introduced Euraca. You go out in the street of any *barrio* in Madrid and you'll find a street vendor saying, 'fantastic red garlic, I sell for one euro what others'll give you for four.' You go on the Internet and you get a plurilingual flood of text, mostly English, but it's an English 'bastardized' by 1,000 accents, slangs, and ignorance, as the poet Kenneth Goldsmith says. You listen to the voice of your great-grandmother on cassette recordings and you discover that without realizing it, you have been using the word 'shirt' in the same, now archaic sense that was completely ordinary for her: as a metonym for 'dressy clothes.'

In the face of the supposed transparency of the dominant languages, ordinary language appears today, perhaps more than ever, as that 'ship of fools' on which we all are hopelessly stuck, and of which Wittgenstein, Merleau-Ponty, and de Certeau spoke:

> We are subject to, although not identified with, ordinary language. As on the ship of fools, we have embarked without any chance of an aerial view or any means of totalizing. It is the 'prose of the world' that Merleau-Ponty dealt with. This includes all discourse, even if human experiences aren't reduced to what can be said about them. In order to constitute themselves, scientific methods are allowed to *forget* this fact, and philosophers *think to master it*, and thus to be authorized to talk about it. (de Certeau 11)

Perhaps it is the Euraca Seminar's ability to focus on this overflowing dimension acquired by ordinary language when the permitted forgetfulness of the Expert and the attempted mastery of the Philosopher no longer work, that has turned it into an 'experimental epistemic community' capable of generating an intense desire and learning all around it. Certainly, the seminar quickly transcended the possible identity or 'sectorial' limits that its special link with poetry could have imposed upon it. As explained by one of its participants, Rafael SMP, Euraca 'posed a problem that affected many of us who aren't poets. It has to do with a battle of words, a crisis of language. It has to do with how we name ourselves, with what we say about ourselves.'

Indeed, it seems to me that of the communities of living experimentation to arise from Spain's neoliberal crisis, Euraca more directly and deliberately proposes the need to equip the emerging 'cultures of anyone' with languages that allow the self-management of their meaning production. And perhaps for that reason, it has attracted and strengthened, as can be confirmed in its activities archive and its frenetic mailing list, an impressive plurality of abilities, themes, and points of view that range from poetry and poetics itself, to activism, passing on the way through discourse analysis, work with urban spaces, cultural historiography, chronicles, music, film, architecture, and an impressively long list of et ceteras.

Instead of assuming that existing languages or forms of meaning production are good, and therefore always being 'borrowed' to a certain extent by emergent cultures from other traditions and communities—such as, notably, those of social movements, free culture, countercultures, or the long tradition of the 'political left'—Euraca has raised the question of how these present-day emergent cultures can represent themselves in trying to respond to the unique situation brought about by neoliberalism's cultural and institutional crisis. Perhaps the value of its eminently experimental vocation resides in this question. In order to think the unique situation of the cultural crisis of neoliberalism, Euraca has used the confrontation between the 'muesli' language and the 'marked' languages. Euraca has put forward the need to look for these 'marked' languages that could also become, in some always problematic way, 'common languages' that are not transparent.

6.4.2. How do we tell of ourselves and sing of ourselves? Bookcamping, Asalto, and Fundación Robo

This move of laying out self-representation more as a problem or a question to be investigated experimentally than as a technical problem to be solved with 'think tank' methods has been repeated in various ways in the political and cultural processes that 15M unleashed. Soon after the beginning of the *acampadas*, for example, the writer Silvia Nanclares sent a tweet asking, 'And you, what book would you take to your *acampada*?' As a result of this question, a kind of collective genealogy began to develop in the social networks that would help 15M participants explain to themselves along the way what was happening.

The mass media tried to explain the irruption of the most important political movement in Spain since the transition to democracy by arbitrarily referring to Stéphane Hessel's essay *Indignez-vous!*, published in Spain as *¡Indignados!* (the source of the label *Indignados*). Nanclares, in contrast, fostered a collective process of self-investigation in which participants would propose many other books as tools to explain and contextualize the 15M. From that moment began a parallel evolution of the movement itself and of the digital library #Bookcamping ('#Bookcamping' 20), in which various 'bookcases' are opened that group references (and in some cases the text files themselves) thematically, under suggestive titles like 'History: Mothers of the Lamb', 'Action Manuals: Micropolitics, Local Analysis, Free Culture,' 'Liberated Technologies,' and 'Political Economy of the Crisis,' among others.

With the identity of the 15M movement still present but now already more blurred, #Bookcamping acquired a new autonomy and a focus more oriented towards the present and the future than the past. Continuing to make lists of books, continuing to extend that reference space, is already now just one way to recognize what has happened to that diffuse community. But it is also more and more a way to encourage the continued sharing of things, to keep that community growing and enriching its common space. What was initially a gesture of genealogical contextualization that hoped to face the labels imposed on the 15M movement from outside by the mass media has now generated a certain capacity for the collective creation of knowledge that goes beyond the desire to know 'who we are' to enter the territory of 'what we could be.' One of the most active lists on #Bookcamping carries the name 'Telling Us' and is introduced through a series of questions that synthesize what is in play in cultural projects like these:

> Can we escape from the megamutant neoliberal story that absorbs everything? Do we have words and places to produce another story that contains what we want to tell? Can fiction open spaces and imaginaries that in turn affect or contribute or open political spaces? How are we going to do it? With what myths? With what stories? Where do we speak from? What paths do our ideas and words follow? What ways of producing meaning and formats do we have?

In the case of another of the better known cultural projects to emerge with direct ties to the 15M *acampadas*, the musical platform Fundación Robo could also be said to have emerged from a question: 'What can today's protest song be?' Or perhaps, 'What can today's politicized song be?' (Herreros 2011). Fundación Robo ('Fundación Robo' 2013) is a project that works in a very clear way with the construction of the imaginary for emergent cultures—we might almost say of 'hymns': songs that have the capacity to make people who are unsatisfied by the neoliberal crisis and eager for more democracy feel represented by them. And one of the ways it does this is by creating lyrics in which an everyday, nonexpert politics of anyone is constructed.

To do this they have made use of important sources of popular music culture, like protest folk songs. Some well-known ones are the versions using Chicho Sánchez Ferlosio's themes, which in their time went from being anonymous popular songs to anti-Francoist hymns. But in Fundación Robo a range of musical styles have also appeared: hip hop, techno, multimodal pop, punk, cumbia, and even country. And, furthermore, they have often produced music in more interesting ways, using unusual combinations, creating situations in which the identities of those traditions, their performers, their poetry, and their tics are displaced, overlapping and opening up to experimentation. Take, for example, the country version of legendary punk group Eskorbuto's song, 'It's a Crime'; or the song 'Fire' by the techno-pop group Diplo, using lines from Camarón de la Isla; or the collective Spanish version of the Woody Guthrie classic 'This Land Is Your Land,' adapted for current circumstances.

Fundación Robo's experimentation with popular musical traditions also has a dimension of institutional creation. According to Daniel Granados, one of its founders, the platform is claimed not only as a way 'to generate language,' but also as 'an alternative business model to that of capitalism and the record industry.' Along these lines, when DJ and techno producer Oscar Mulero introduced the song 'Poder en la sombra' (Power in the Shade), Fundación Robo proposed to move beyond the classic notion of 'committed' music like songs with explicitly political lyrics:

> The load, or rather, the political potentiality of the new music resides in what the music 'does' and not so much in what it 'says.' A self-managed techno party that recuperates dead spaces in the city and injects them with life and communication, even if it's only temporary, is in itself an event that can have a political charge. ... Creating independent distribution networks that offer an outlet for the material of small producers who contribute to the construction of a common musical heritage with an intensive use of samples, remixes and copies is the same thing. ('Poder en la sombra' 2012)

But it is perhaps another type of politicization of music that has had more resonance in Fundación Robo, especially those songs performed by the singer-songwriter Nacho Vegas, like 'Runrún' and 'How to Do Crack.' His songs are supported by a creative mixture of the personal and the collective in the lyrics, about which the musician Robert Herreros said, 'I can't think of a more honest way to explain personal problems than to write about collective conflicts.'

So Vegas's 'How to Do Crack,' which in the post-15M has come to have the feel of a 'hymn,' is an ambiguous song in which personal malaise is confused with public malaise, and is told in everyday language. Not for nothing does the song begin with the expression 'every morning ...,' and the story is about a day in the life of an anonymous someone, of just anybody at all who shops at the supermarket, who goes to a bar, who watches television and sees how his country, or perhaps he himself, or perhaps, simply, everyone *'does crack.'*

'Asalto, the literary arm of Fundación Robo' ('Asalto' 2013) emerges with a similar intention: to politicize literature, just as music is politicized. Up to now, there have been five 'assaults' (*asaltos*) published. Each one consists of the publication of a series of short texts on a website, without signatures, but with the names of the authors at the end of the page, such that it is not known who wrote what. The first assault proposed playing with 'the semantic field of the everyday, those words that designate objects, set phrases, or structures of life with which we coexist and that can be found in the title of the text.' The second was proposed as 'an adjustment, a revision or almost complete disassembling of certain linguistic expressions,' a work with 'semantic structures that are used thoughtlessly, or worse, with deliberate forethought, that confuse and can cause damage.' Because, as the introduction stated, 'Every day we have to read misleading phrases. Whoever claims to know the language uses them. Or are the semantic structures using them?' In any case, continued the introduction, 'It shouldn't be as if nothing happened when somebody takes advantage of the social position given to them to say trite, hackneyed things, and not say what's necessary.'

It is not difficult to hear in those words the echo of the fatigue with expert speeches and their empty rhetoric, the displeasure in the face of that constant fallacy according to which the expert paradigm passes off as knowledge what is in fact 'social position' or, as de Certeau says, it legitimizes as science what is in fact 'no more than the ordinary language of tactical games between economic powers and symbolic authorities' (8).

Asalto thus proposed a certain ethnography of the everyday that becomes necessary when false legitimacies are unveiled that try to control the flow of plural meanings constructed by anyone. It is an ethnography that, in the words of de Certeau, arises when one is conscious of 'being a foreigner in your own home, a "savage" in the middle of ordinary culture, lost in the complexity of common sense and of what is given as understood' (11).

6.4.3. *Al final de la asamblea* and the 'language of the 99%'
These words by de Certeau could well also be a description of the position from which are written the entries of the blog *Al final de la asamblea*, which began to publish anonymous texts related to the 15M and other similar international movements in September 2011. The uniqueness of this blog's texts lies precisely in not resorting to any source of authority supposedly external to ordinary language to face the complexity of reality. Rather, it

relies simply on narration, anecdote, and chronicle as close to 'ground level' as possible.

It has to do with naming what's there, so much in plain sight that sometimes it isn't seen. This was an observation made in the post '23-F or the Commonness of the Extraordinary,' ('#23F o la vulgaridad de lo extraordinario' 2013) as a result of the surprisingly well-attended and diverse demonstration of Tides/Mareas that took place on the thirty-first anniversary of the attempted 1981 coup: 'Unless it's to avoid telling us the obvious, the lived, what is seen, something escapes us. Let's see if we'll get used to the commonness of the extraordinary.'

So in effect, the underlying thesis of *Al final de la asamblea* seems to be, similar to what Euraca proposes, that a great change is taking place at the subjective level in the Spanish state, but that it lacks 'authorized' languages to narrate it and represent it. Perhaps this is precisely because this change contains within it a certain opposition to the very loss of prestige of the ordinary and the everyday that is at the base of modern culture, and particularly at the base of the Culture of the Spanish Transition. Another post (15mas1 2012) asserted:

> While we watched Parliament like a cat at a mouse hole and said nothing's going on here; while we declared that the day of the revolution, when everything changes, hasn't come yet; while many keep watching the sky anxiously to see if somebody arrives who can take charge of the situation and the suffering, a savior, a just and democratic liberator, a party, or something. While many get depressed between the anxiety caused by the emergency and the absence of solutions on the horizon.
>
> Meanwhile, looking away, looking at the less spectacular, perhaps, the ground keeps splitting. While we wait for the revolution and the solutions that will change everything, perhaps, around us everything is changing.

The 'nongroup' that anonymously publishes in *Al final de la asamblea* has appropriated the mission of watching in that other way, of narrating less spectacularly, and has produced striking contributions in the chronicle form. For example, there have been posts that showed the ins and outs of the White Tide/Marea Blanca in Madrid, the unexpected convergences of the 15M movement with the security forces (which I have already discussed), and many other moments of an ordinariness that, surprisingly, is much more difficult to find in writing than one might perhaps believe. And the thing is, all those events are being narrated, of course, but by a type of mechanism that is not, perhaps, democratic enough to constitute something that could be 'a language of the 99%'—and is therefore incapable of seeing the change of subjectivity at the level of the everyday. Asked by Amador Fernández-Savater about this formula, Pepe of *Al final de la asamblea* responded by talking about those mechanisms that introduce inequality in the production of meaning:

> I don't know what a language of the 99% would be, but I do know what it's not. The activist communique, journalistic stereotypes, the self-referential codes of the different intellectual or political strata, etc. A language of the 99% is not a language where the 99% already is, but where it *could* be. Not a lowest common denominator, but a (nonleveling) aggregate of voices. (Fernández-Savater 2014a)

In this sense, as happened in Euraca, it is not simply a matter of copying, of imitating or 'translating' a kind of 'popular wisdom' that is already there, hidden in principle, but at heart as accessible—once it is unveiled—as that 'transparent' language that tries to dominate reality.

The position of the 99%, the position of those excluded from true participation in neoliberal policies and their mechanisms of meaning production, is not given in advance, but rather must be built. Neoliberalism is, first of all, a machine for producing inequality through competition. And one of the vehicles for that inequality is the use of stereotypical languages, 'muesli,' which in spite of their apparent inclusivity, create spaces of indifference, arenas where the rules of the game of meaning production are already in advance, and the only thing that remains is to compete for value. Contrary to that, a language of the 99% tries to construct common spaces based on differences that are not arranged competitively.

In that sense, the chronicle work of *Al final de la asamblea* is not at all 'natural,' 'immediate,' or 'objective,' no matter how it tries to always use everyday, colloquial, or ordinary forms of discourse. The everyday is besieged by the stereotypes that divide reality into competing identities that inscribe inequality with fire in words and in bodies. Constructing a language capable of undoing those inequalities is no easy task, nor does it have to do with a kind of 'realism' that should be limited to representing what is already there. Drawing once again on the echoes of the political, epistemic, and aesthetic theory of Jacques Rancière, we can recall that equality is never given in advance. Rather, it is a hypothesis that must be affirmed to be able to verify it. 'We can be equal in this world of inequality,' 'we can speak the language of the 99% in this world of neolanguages that justify hierarchies and make us compete against each other': they are not affirmations that describe a pre-existing reality, but support for the construction of something that is not yet given.

Álvaro of *Al final de la asamblea* is very aware that although there are no strong expressions in his blog of what reality should be, there *are* fundamental choices about how to tell it:

> The blog is characterized by not having speeches, for being as bland as reality, but also for being happy. The tone comes from its strengths and positivities. It's an important choice: to come up with a description of what we can do and not what we can't do; in life, the opposite can be chosen and it is very easy: choosing impotence. There is no discourse, and therefore, there is no criticism of reality. So where do you get off saying what's missing from reality? In fact, when there is criticism in an entry, the interlocutor is usually not reality, but the other voices that tell it what it should be, the voices that make us anxious by repeating, 'the government should fall already, everybody should hit the streets already,' should, should.

*

Again, I am not trying to cover anything exhaustively when I talk about these specific cultural projects, which are just a few examples in a sea of experiments with ways of producing meaning during the crisis of the expert and intellectual tradition that has given neoliberalism its legitimacy. I only want to call attention to the way the emergent 'cultures of anyone' are being given not only strategies of composition and empowerment of human capacities in general, not only of 'spaces of life' in which those capacities can attend to community needs in a sustained, everyday way, but also of languages and ways of (self-)representation capable of naming and giving value to those ways of life based more on collaboration than on competition.

As I write this, the Spanish state is going through an exceptional institutional crisis, which is also accompanied by an effervescent creativity. This creative impulse has come not only to state cultural institutions, but also to politics, with the irruption of Podemos and the formation of civic platforms that are preparing for the next municipal, regional, and general elections. In the field of elections, of representatives, of government mechanisms implemented by the party system that up to now has served a neoliberal model, the clashes between experimentation and institution are destined to be, obviously, much more wild and complex even than those that take place in the spaces assigned for 'the cultural,' as much from self-management as from the public.

But, perhaps, if this book can be good for anything, it will be for remembering that those institutional spheres of the political are also 'cultural,' that is, that in them too is resolved the constant implicit and explicit debate about what can be a life with dignity. An essential part of that debate, it seems to me, has to do with the forms, the languages, and the traditions of meaning that can construct that dignity today.

'If we don't tell ourselves, they tell us.' If those forms, languages, and traditions of meaning with which people try to construct a truly democratic politics are not able to save us from that 'megamutant neoliberal story that absorbs everything,' as #Bookcamping proposed, many of the undemocratic logics that have led to the crisis will probably repeat themselves.

'A world can only be stopped by another world,' wrote the poet María Salgado (2014). A couple of years before, with respect to her reading of the book *El Sur* by Silvia Nanclares (2009), she had also said these words, which will serve me well as the final statement of this investigation, and perhaps the first of others:

> Then I thought that perhaps I would like somebody to write all this all this all this that's happening or that has happened, to narrate it, heck, not as a substitute chronicle, but so that those of us who are living it can perceive it. It seems simple, but it is incredibly difficult. To make us exist, I mean.' (2012)

Cultures of Anyone:
A Proposal for Encounters

N ow I imagine this whole book written otherwise. *Now*: now that the two anonymous reviewers have already given their approval to the manuscript, and it will be published by an academic publisher. Now that having secured this publication places me with options to get 'tenure,' i.e., a permanent position at the university where I work. It is, incidentally—and clarifying it for those unfamiliar with this system of academic employment—'tenure' or the door, no other option.

I imagine now, in any case, a book with a less traditional authorial voice. A book that would show more clearly—although there are some indications already—who writes it, from where he writes it, what experiences and what material and symbolic resources sustain it, what responsibilities and what vital dilemmas and contradictions traverse it. An authorial voice that did not hide its doubts, its shortcomings, its inconsistencies. And perhaps even more important than all that, a voice that does not pretend to be explaining reality from a position of traditional intellectual authority (individual, 'scientific,' sanctioned by official, supposedly 'neutral' educational and cultural institutions, but implicitly productivist and patriarchal), but rather proposing tools for the democratic development of a common story.

Some of the latter is there already, I'd like to think, at least in regard to the opportunity to give enough space for multiple 'affected' and 'placed' voices in the debates that I reconstruct. But beyond what I imagine or don't imagine, I think I still have time in this epilogue to make explicit the proposal for encounters and conversations that I would like this book to be, even with all its imperfections.

A proposal that could be formulated as questions: In what ways can categories like 'cultures of anyone' or 'cultures of experts' help deepen the democratization processes described in the book? Does it make sense to develop a story that tries to connect such disparate historical processes as Francoist developmentalism and the '15M climate' in the neoliberal crisis? *Cultures of Anyone* proposes possible elements for a common story that has democratic effects, rescuing pieces here and there, voices, memories, experiences, bodies, and languages for encounters—and not necessarily harmonious ones. It is a book full of holes, edges, and unfinished pieces; it attempts to be a tool for composing with many others. It chooses, despite the consequent risks, to put together many pieces that perhaps are not commonly put together. Its intellectual and political challenge is to draw a broad historical and conceptual contextualization of the cultural democratization processes taking place in the Spanish state during the neoliberal crisis, hoping that this contextualization can empower—to use that key word again—these processes, and other similar ones that may occur in the future.

All this does not mean that the author of *Cultures of Anyone* cares little about 'reality,' and that he is dedicated to inventing whatever he wants. It means that, as with any human artifact, this book stems from and is presented to a community of meaning, implicit or explicit, that will actually give value to or remove value from it. This book talks about and *with* people, and to their vulnerable bodies, their living conditions, their passions, their imagination, their ideas, and their aspirations for equality; it owes responsibility.

So I now reread this book as an invitation to meet people who have been and still are. 'Cultures of anyone' means those cultures who have chosen to build a collective sense of their lives so that nobody remains excluded from participation in this construction. How did they do it? How can we do it now?

To address these questions—to propose them as meeting spaces—I have had to take many detours, encounter many experiences. Now I imagine this book written as a novel, using literature as the 'philosophy of the poor' that, says Ricardo Piglia, helps us understand the 'pure forms of experience.' It would begin with a TV set, in 2008, blaring in an empty room with the news, the Newscaster's Voice, dictating the agenda of reality: every man for himself, difficult times are ahead but we will overcome with our efforts, everything is under control because we have behind us Those Who Know, the Master's Voice, the Expert's Voice. Centuries of modernity and advanced technology cannot be wrong. Keep buying, which is good for the economy, and rejoice if you have a job, because having a job today *is a luxury*.

The response to this kind of abrupt Orwellian beginning can only be to take some genealogical distance and to clarify things. The voice of the One Who Knows is not unidirectional, but distributed in echo chambers throughout society: neoliberalism has made us competitors, 'subject-brands,' 'entrepreneurs of ourselves.' There is, therefore, both a centralized power—a privileged authority in the production of meaning—and a dispersed power everywhere: the one we exercise when we all partake of the commercial model of existence, which aims to convert human life into an instrument for 'making profits.'

It is the culmination of a long project: the establishment of a 'productive' model of life that (since the eighteenth century) tries to monetarily quantify any social value, to the point of forgetting that the sustenance of life comes first, and is the condition for the existence of money (as explained by Amaia Orozco from a feminist economics perspective). Thus, money becomes paradoxically independent from the reproduction of life, and turns out to be the vehicle for a form of competitive social relationship between individuals who ignore their interdependence. In this way of organizing social relationships, many are doomed to be losers, of course: their lives become expendable because their skills and their value don't translate monetarily.

This book proposes a meeting with some of those people: both those who fall on the side of expendable lives and those who warrant authority and exemplify success in the money game. It is very difficult to do justice to all the archaeological layers of power, exclusion, and subalternity that converge; it is, indeed, ridiculous to expect one author do it in one book. For that reason I rely on many accounts, and propose two in particular as a framework, allowing me to focus the debate on the emergence of a 'power/knowledge syndrome' in modernity (Bauman), and a process of dispossession and devaluation of resources and reproductive capacities at the start of capitalism (Federici).

But back to people: there are the farmers of the Spanish state in the 1950s, at the time when Franco's technocratic disarticulation of rural subsistence cultures is complete, incorporating—precariously—all that population through major economic restructuring plans. The technocrat draws the line where the dam will be built: everything that falls on one side will perish under water. This includes, of course, hunger, endless days of manual labor, patriarchal violence, ecclesiastical control, and other scourges of the countryside. But it also includes traditional knowledge, and the many material and symbolic capabilities that guaranteed subsistence peasant cultures but would not be considered 'productive'—particularly knowledge and skills associated with the reproduction of life, care, and emotional and domestic work, the tasks usually assigned to women in a patriarchy.

In the villages of the Sayago region, notes writer José María Arguedas, there are no more *tertulias* or *seranos*: young people do nothing but go from work to home and from home to work, so much so that even engagements and marriages are scarce. The forms of sociability that do not conform to the new productivism are left out. 'The blessed business is getting everywhere, it's the very devil!,' a woman tells Arguedas. And those words travel from her mouth to these pages, in a conversation spanning decades that builds a possible historical experience.

These voices, their specificity, is, in my reading, what makes the book, yet inevitably what is most missed sometimes. I can't get enough of them. Of all the pieces that this book needs to compose itself, undoubtedly these, the voices placed in concrete historical processes, are the most precious. I wish there were thousands of Arguedases writing them down, and that I had thousands of hours to rewrite them. Not only the voices of peasants, of course, but also those of Francoist technocrats, which appear under-represented, and even those of their heirs, the experts and intellectual elites of democracy, who continue to legitimize the same guidelines for capitalist 'modernization,' through the incorporation of party politics and a Europeanism that leads to the neoliberal exacerbation.

If this book were a novel or an (openly) literary chronicle, it would get even further inside the private rooms of restaurants where the transition was arranged, inside the cocktail soirées that celebrated the marriage of state culture and democracy, and even—why not?—inside the brains of those who made hegemonic a depoliticized interpretation of modern aesthetics. It would share secret meetings with 'men who smoke' and high-flying gatherings with 'men who drink.' But, of course, it would also dive into the sewers of the ideal of the Spanish 'middle class,' which both Francoism and parliamentary democracy assumed as the sociological support to justify their policies as forms of 'normalization.' It would look for the traces of that lag historians point out between mesocratic images that have been used to represent the majority of society and the economic and cultural practices of those majorities. It would also investigate the persistence of collective inferiority complexes that have been so important to the guilty invisibilization of all forms of life that did not conform to that capitalist productivism which has been called 'modernity.'

But it would not do it simply out of an anecdotal nor even a micropolitical desire. It would just try to go further in giving space to the forms of self-representation that problematize sociological stereotypes and democratize the production of meaning. Nobody is normal when seen up close (and especially when you really listen). Up close, the multiplicity of experience appears, and it is never easily translatable into rigid social categories, especially when a transformative collective experience emerges, one that does not merely reproduce the prevailing forms of life, but reshapes them. I agree with Charlotte Nordmann's reading: neither Bourdieu nor Rancière is entirely right, but both have good reasons. The cycle of domination never repeats itself exactly, it is always transformed, but not every moment of this transformation is the same. In some cases, there is a 'redistribution of the sensible,' which always arises from concrete social contradictions. With its limitations, *Cultures of Anyone* intends, as Nordmann says, to 'circumscribe the historical conditions of emancipation' (189), i.e., to give an account of how certain transformative collective experiences have emerged, circa 2011, from a series of social contradictions—notably, from the contradiction between the extreme precariousness that neoliberalism was creating and the existence of rich possibilities for empowerment of and collaboration by large sectors of the precarized population.

'The network experience is a bit like LSD in the '60s: a different, unreal but real experience that stays in your memory because you have actually experienced what you have experienced: the ability to converse with strangers, to cross borders, to self-transform, to easily create, etc.' (Padilla 2013). In the plazas of the 15M, that experience is explored with an overwhelming passion. With much uncertainty, too, because it's not clear where you're going, as the filmmaker Cecilia Barriga (2014), who filmed this experience lovingly, said:

> [There was a] very strong impression of being cast adrift, so many different people in the same boat. The feeling that we could drown, that it could fall at any time, not because of the police but because of ourselves. Every day in Sol was a conquest, everything depended on us. (Fernández Savater and Barriga)

The experience of the squares emerges, as Julia Ramírez Blanco (2014) said in her indispensable book *Utopías artísticas de revuelta*, not just as 'political empowerment,' but also as 'expressive empowerment,' which activates the ability to experiment with building a different society (24). Not only an explicit demand, not only a series of requests to the institutions, but rather 'a systemic approach that speaks of the possibility of a radical self-organization, of an existence without formal hierarchies, of forms of volunteer work and non-monetary economy, and community life where care is collective' (236). A lifestyle that directly confronts not only the neoliberal logic, but also the monopoly of the production of meaning by the mass media, intellectuals, and the 'experts.' And of course, the revenge of the Voice of He Who Knows was swift.

But if this 'cultural revolution,' or 'process of emancipation,' fails to materialize in strong and sustainable institutions at first, I think it's not so much because of the counter-attack of an establishment whose cultural and intellectual legitimacy is rather worn. The danger, indeed, is perhaps not so much the 'police' but 'ourselves.' Or rather the police *in* ourselves. After the plazas, the order of those who know and those who don't know tends to constantly resurface, and of course the precariousness of a life forced to compete to survive remains, exerting a brutal structural violence against those who lack sufficient material and symbolic capital to be 'entrepreneurs of themselves.' Even in areas most sensitive to the 'cultural' dimensions of social movements (to the experimental construction of meaning and subjectivity), it is extremely difficult to challenge neoliberalism by building networks capable of sustainable economic solidarity while enabling spaces for 'expressive empowerment.' The self-managed community spaces and the attempts to reclaim the public for these collaborative economies and democratic cultures face the constant extraction of social wealth by the financial economy in the context of the neoliberal city. They must also negotiate the constant tension between the movements' experimental, 'expressive,' creator-of-forms-of-existence instinct and the overwhelming persistence of the neoliberal management of lives.

This raises something I have not had time to analyze directly in this book, but that inevitably overhangs it from start to finish: the longing for other kinds of institutions, not self-managed but representative, which could curb neoliberal precarization from within the system of political parties. The cycle of the 'assault on the institutions' has begun. There is little that I can contribute explicitly about this here, but at the same time, it is undeniable that if *Cultures of Anyone* can be a meeting place at the juncture of the democratization processes in the neoliberal crisis, it undoubtedly will be by offering a point of view that scarcely allows an understanding of that 'assault on the institutions' as an integrative culmination of the 'cultures of anyone.' In as much as there can be many intersections and mutual intensifications, I think this book can help to perceive them as different things, and to not give value to one by taking it away from another.

There is, however, a recurrent argument used to justify the need for taking the step from the '15M climate' to that 'assault on the institutions.' It is said (see, e.g., Alba Rico 2014) that most people cannot 'participate' in the political process because they do not have the time, resources, interest, or skills. The creation of electoral platforms would then establish a necessary political representation for those who cannot participate. But there is some misunderstanding, it seems to me, in this conception of political 'participation,' because it excludes the dimension of the construction of meaning, in which everyone is always involved: like it or not, everyone speaks, everyone thinks and gives meaning to what happens to them. Politics necessarily involves 'participation' in the construction of meaning, which in this book I have called 'the collective elucidation of a life with dignity.' During the neoliberal crisis in Spain there have been some attempts at democratizing such elucidation. Although it is certainly not obvious how to compose these democratization processes with the institutional transformations necessary to stop the neoliberal attack, I don't think the best way of conceiving their relationship is to put them in a finalist sequence in which the first would be a mere preparatory step for the second. The dimension of construction of meaning and subjectivity can never be erased; it is a form of constant political and collective participation that cannot be dismissed.

From the Argentina experience, the Colectivo Situaciones (Gago, Sztulwark, and Picotto 2014) has provided very valuable reflections on what happens when the dimension of 'subjective excess' that is part of the movements is marginalized. I think that participating in what they call 'the aspects not subject to demands' of the movements is not necessarily to become an 'activist,' but transforming the framework of sense in which one organizes its reality. And the question is, how many people did this, to whatever extent, when 15M questioned the—until then untouchable—quality of the Spanish democratic system, when it showed that the alleged passivity and egoism of 'people' could become solidarity, that one need not belong to the group of 'those who know' to have dignity? Why do we have to assume that some 'could not' or 'didn't have the abilities to' participate in that new construction of meaning?

Colectivo Situaciones raises another fundamental idea: the conception of politics that tends to ignore the value of those subjective transformations is the one that understands it as a 'conflict of interest' and 'construction of hegemony,' on a reading of Ernesto Laclau's thinking, which has influenced what they call 'progressive governmentality' in Latin America. The importance of Laclau and the experience of Latin American progressivism for members of Podemos's executive board is well known, so Situaciones raises the call for a South-South dialogue in this key moment, and also provides the suggestion to think of politics, with Deleuze, not as a conflict of interest, but as a 'line of flight' or, more specifically, as a 'subtraction from structures and hierarchies that assign values to life.' Societies are not only transformed by conflicts between opposing parties, but also because sometimes they flee the established order, paving the way for other forms of life. The *piqueteros* and the practice of *escraches* (activist demonstrations outside the target's home or workplace) in Argentina, for example, rose up not only a demand to institutions for jobs and justice, but also for an 'escape from a society of labor and justice already impossible in the terms known,' which in turn 'led—in the case of following the line of flight—to the need to invent new ways of understanding the collective praxis.'

Besides the argument about the impossibility of participation by all, there has appeared another, perhaps even more widespread, justification for a departure, or at least a change of direction from the practices of social movements such as the 15M to the 'assault on the institutions.' It is the famous idea of the 'glass ceiling': movements have reached the limit of their processing capacity, and it is necessary to conquer political institutions to go further and stop the march of the neoliberal attack. To that argument, again one could reply that it is based on a reductionist reading of what the movements do, that it underestimates their abilities to change ways of life with their 'lines of flight.'

However, it also opens another, perhaps even more disturbing, uncertainty because the truth is that almost no one denies the need for change in the political institutions in order to stop neoliberal policies (surveys show that there is, as they say in Podemos, a 'social majority' hoping for this change). But what the Latin American experience also shows is that, in reality, it is unclear whether it is possible for the state to depart from neoliberalism. What appears in Argentina's progressive governmentality, according to Situaciones, is a version of neoliberalism which, together with significant tactical advances, maintains a strong financialization of the economy, with such problematic issues as the 'pattern of accumulation and acquisition of currencies (the financial system, agribusiness, mega-mining, concentration, and foreign ownership of the economy, etc.).' Laval and Dardot have been even more emphatic on this subject: 'The populism that says it rules "on behalf of the masses" is not an alternative to neoliberal rationality, but instead merely reinforces it' (Fernández-Savater, Malo, and Ávila 2014). Raquel Gutiérrez has exemplified this in the cases of Ecuador and Bolivia:

> Mr. Correa and Mr. Morales, and the governments they lead, seem to have conceded too much in terms of reconstruction of formats and laws, an institutional and legal scaffolding absolutely consistent with the order of accumulation of capital. With a rather different order of capital accumulation that, for example, in the case of Bolivia, limits and tries to cut ties with the most powerful transnational corporations in the world that previously had a hold there; but then that capital accumulation becomes linked again to other interests, such as those of the Brazilian oligarchy. (2014)

The comparison between Latin America and Spain has all kinds of limitations, of course, and I think some of them may speak of interesting prospects for Spaniards to deal with these problems more successfully. The issue is very complex, but let me just ask here if it's not true that in some of the institutional platforms that have emerged in the Spanish state to curb neoliberalism there is a very important sensitivity towards 'politics from below.' This seems certainly true in Barcelona en Comú, which has worked hard to articulate itself with neighborhood movements—making its own the

Zapatista motto of 'caminar preguntando', to walk asking questions—but also in Ahora Madrid and other municipalist platforms. Even with respect to Podemos, despite its drift towards a seemingly more statist populism and its flirtations with a technocratic discourse, I do not think one can say that the experience of collective intelligence and empowering of the 15M cycle is no longer relevant at all.

It is not so hard to imagine, I think, a 'multilevel politics' as Situaciones says, or a network in which Podemos and the municipal electoral platforms like Barcelona en Comú and Ahora Madrid are just another node, and have to work with many other nodes of social movements and citizens, as Margarita Padilla proposes: a distribution of roles in which the takeover of the institutions would not involve an interruption of the lines of flight and the creative possibilities opened by the movements to other ways of life, but rather its intensification. A non-'state-centric' politics, as has been proposed by Raquel Gutiérrez and Amador Fernández-Savater. Because, as Débora Ávila and Marta Malo wrote:

> to break through the glass ceiling against which we often stumble, and to build the foundation for a good life, there are more ways than the electoral. Roads we travel and others that we must dare to make. Small realities, palpable, inhabited, to build an independent voice that can dialogue with institutions and demand that they 'govern by obeying,' but from a radical difference. (2014)

Finally, without further speculation about the future, *Cultures of Anyone* would also like to be, here and now, a meeting place for those who try to 'caminar preguntando' inside institutions of knowledge, which often suggest, conversely, that we 'make our way hastily without talking to anybody.' As I say, I imagine a version of this book based much more on conversations with people affected by what is told in it, but for this I must also imagine some institutional conditions that would allow it: how to not just talk about but to *do* 'cultures of anyone' from within the American Academy?

I pose this question as an invitation to collaborate. The task is immense, but there are abundant opportunities for more or less immediate action. Perhaps the first and most accessible step is that of simply improving communication between the world of Hispanic studies in the United States (and in general, but I focus on the area that I know firsthand) and different spaces and projects of the 'cultures of anyone' in the Spanish state. The relations between these two worlds can build interesting alliances as long as, I think, they involve a 'contagion' of democratic practices for academia, which can lead to institutional transformations. In the field of publishing, for example, it does not seem very risky to expect in the coming years an important extension of free culture practices to university spaces (and the publication of this book in free access is, in this sense, a small symptom about which I am obviously pleased).

But taking seriously the possibility of supporting from within academic institutions a democratization that stands up to centuries of cultural and social stratification aggravated by the wild emergence of neoliberal inequality will certainly require much more than the publication of our texts in *open access* format. Transforming research in Hispanic ('peninsular,' 'Iberian') studies into a truly democratic conversation with people who have the right to self-representation would, today, mean having to redo countless practices, theoretical assumptions, forms of distribution of epistemic and material resources. Significant difficulties persist in even developing collective research, which substantially reduces the quality of the work. The eternal tendency to self-referentiality in academic practices renders the 'objects of study' pretexts to fulfill researchers' professional demands, reducing their ability to participate in true transformations of collective knowledge. However, the explosion of collaborative practices developed by the 'experts in what happens to them' during the Spanish neoliberal crisis seems particularly conducive to altering these dynamics. The infrastructure and resources of US 'Hispanism' could help a lot and benefit greatly from contact with these processes that are already under way, often—if not always—in very precarious conditions.

There are, of course, productivist dynamics and crucial job insecurity issues hampering the development of projects of real collaboration between the university and self-organized sectors of society. In very general terms, this collaboration would require exponentially increasing recognition of 'social responsibility' across the professional activity of researchers and teachers, incorporating this recognition as a criterion of value at all levels, including job recruitment. This, of course, would clash with the individualistic, competitive dynamics that underlie the material functioning of most institutions of knowledge. Like any other institution strongly integrated into the logic of the global financialized economy, the university is structurally part of the logic of competition and the corporatization of oneself that characterizes neoliberalism.

That does not mean that concrete steps cannot be taken to adopt protocols for local action to counter these logics, and to open spaces for other ways of building collective value. Today, here and now, the studies of Iberian contemporary cultures seem, I insist, to be a particularly favorable field in which to do this.

Works Cited

15mas1. 2012. 'El deshielo.' *Al final de la asamblea*. November 26. http://alfinaldelaasamblea.wordpress.com/2012/11/26/el-dehielo/.

—. 2014. '#yonopago: el boxeador y la mosca.' *Al final de la asamblea*. Accessed July 28. http://alfinaldelaasamblea.wordpress.com/2012/02/03/yonopago-el-boxeador-y-la-mosca/.

15M.cc – conversación con Pedro Martí. 2012. https://www.youtube.com/watch?v=9-V3 7SDaPxY&feature=youtube_gdata_player.

'#23F o la vulgaridad de lo extraordinario.' 2013. *Al final de la asamblea*. Accessed July 29. http://alfinaldelaasamblea.wordpress.com/2013/02/25/23f-o-la-vulgaridad-de-lo-extraordinario/.

Abiada, José Manuel López de, Hans-Jörg Neuschäfer, and Augusta López Bernasocchi, eds. 2001. *Entre el ocio y el negocio: industria editorial y literatura en la España de los 90*. Madrid: Verbum Editorial.

Acín, Ramón. 1990. *Narrativa o consumo literario (1975–1987)*. Zaragoza: Universidad de Zaragoza.

Alba Rico, Santiago. 2014. 'El lío de Podemos y los tres elitismos.' http://www.cuartopoder.es/tribuna/2014/10/04/el-lio-de-podemos-y-los-tres-elitismos/6325.

Alonso, Santos. 2003. *La novela española en el fin de siglo: 1975–2001*. Madrid: Mare Nostrum.

Álvarez Junco, José. 1995. 'Rural and Urban Popular Cultures'. In Helen Eve Graham and Jo Labanyi. *Spanish Cultural Studies – An Introduction: The Struggle for Modernity*, 82–90. Oxford: Oxford University Press.

Amaste, Ricardo. 2013. 'Bien(es) común(es) = Bien social de código abierto.' *ColaBoraBora*. http://www.colaborabora.org/2013/01/02/bienescomunes_biensocial_codigoabierto/#more-2691.

Amat, Kiko, and Manolo Martínez. 2011. 'Esto es lo que importa, pero aquello lo que hace gracia. Una carta abierta a Quim Monzó.' *Organización. Un fanzine express sobre la marcha*.

Aparicio, Juan Pedro, Luis Mateo Díez, and José María Merino. 1985. *Las cenizas del Fénix, de Sabino Ordás*. (Breviarios de la calle del Pez ; 7). León: Diputación Provincial.

Arguedas, José María. 1968. *Las comunidades de España y del Perú*. Lima: Universidad Nacional Mayor de San Marcos, Departamento de Publicaciones.

Arias, Juan. 1985. 'No me avergüenzo de ser europeo.' *El País*, June 11. http://elpais.com/diario/1985/06/11/opinion/487288809_850215.html.

Ariès, Philippe, and Georges Duby. 1987. *A History of Private Life*. Cambridge, Mass.: Belknap Press of Harvard University Press.

Arjona, Daniel. 2013. 'César Rendueles: "Nos vemos como antes los ricos veían a las clases peligrosas".' *El Cultural*, September 23. http://www.elcultural.es/noticias/BUENOS_DIAS/5334/Cesar_Rendueles.

'Asalto.' 2013. http://www.fundacionrobo.org/asalto/.

'AutoConsulta Ciudadana.' 2014. *AutoConsulta Ciudadana*. http://autoconsulta.org/.

Ávila, Débora, and Marta Malo. 2014. 'De los caminos para gobernar(se).' *Periódico Diagonal*. https://www.diagonalperiodico.net/la-plaza/23877-caminos-para-gobernarse.html.

Azúa, Félix de. 2014. 'Soldados de juguete.' *Jot Down Cultural Magazine*. Accessed April 30. http://www.jotdown.es/2012/05/felix-de-azua-soldados-de-juguete/.

Barcellona, Piero. 2003. *Strategie dell'anima*. Città Aperta, Troina.

Barciela López, Carlos, ed. 2003. *Autarquía y mercado negro: el fracaso económico del primer franquismo, 1939–1959*. Madrid: Crítica.

Bauman, Zygmunt. 1987. *Legislators and Interpreters: On Modernity, Post-Modernity and Intellectuals*. New edition. Cambridge and Oxford: Polity Press.

Beasley-Murray, Jon. 2010. *Posthegemony Political Theory and Latin America*. Minneapolis, Minn.: University of Minnesota Press. http://site.ebrary.com/id/10448695.

Benet, Juan. 1982. *La Inspiración y el estilo*. Barcelona: Seix Barral.

Berardi, Franco. 2003. *La Fábrica de la infelicidad: nuevas formas de trabajo y movimiento global*. Translated by Patricia Amigot Leatxe. Madrid: Traficantes de sueños.

—. 2007. 'Schizo-Economy.' *SubStance* 36 (1): 76–85.

Berger, John. 1991. *Into their Labours*. New York: Pantheon.

Bértolo, Constantino. 2008. *La cena de los notables: sobre lectura y crítica*. Cáceres: Editorial Periférica.

Blondeau, Olivier, Maurizio Lazzarato et al. 2004. *Capitalismo cognitivo, propiedad intelectual y creación colectiva*. Madrid: Traficantes de Sueños.

Bollier, David. 2008. *Viral Spiral: How the Commoners Built a Digital Republic of Their Own*. New York: New Press.

'#Bookcamping.' 2011. http://bookcamping.cc/.

Botti, Alfonso. 2002. *Cielo y dinero: el nacionalcatolicismo en España (1881–1975)*. Madrid: Movimiento Cultural Cristiano.

Bourdieu, Pierre. 1990. *The Logic of Practice*. Stanford, Calif.: Stanford University Press.

—. 1995. *Las reglas del arte: génesis y estructura del campo literario*. Barcelona: Anagrama.

—. 2001. *Masculine Domination*. Stanford, Calif.: Stanford University Press.

Butler, Judith. 2010. *Frames of War: When Is Life Grievable?* Reprint edition. London and New York: Verso.

—. 2011. 'For and Against Precarity.' *Tidal. Occupy Theory* 1.

Cabrera, Elena. 2014. 'Simpatía por la "okupación."' *eldiario.es*, July 12. http://www.eldiario.es/sociedad/Simpatia-okupacion_0_279972672.html.

Caffentzis, George. 2013. *In Letters of Blood and Fire: Work, Machines, and Value in the Bad Infinity of Capitalism*. New York: PM Press.

Candel, Francisco. 1957. *Donde la ciudad cambia su nombre*. Barcelona: J. Janés.

—. 1964. *Dios, la qué se armó!* Barcelona: Marte Ediciones.

—. 1965. *Los otros catalanes*. Madrid: Ediciones Península.

Cassany, Daniel, and Denise Hernández. 2012. '¿Internet: 1; Escuela: 0?' *CPU-e, Revista de Investigación Educativa* 0 (14): 126–41.

Castellet, J. M. 1970. *Nueve novísimos poetas españoles.* Barcelona: Barral Editores.

Castells, Manuel. 2009. *Communication Power.* Oxford: Oxford University Press.

Castro Díez, Asunción. 2001. *Sabino Ordás, una poética.* León: Diputación de León.

Cavero, Eva. 2011. 'Sol visto desde Mayo del 68.' *El País,* June 5. http://elpais.com/diario/2011/06/05/domingo/1307245962_850215.html.

Cazorla Sánchez, Antonio. 2009. *Fear and Progress: Ordinary Lives in Franco's Spain, 1939–1975.* Oxford: Wiley.

Cercas, Javier. 2011. '5 artículos no escritos sobre el 15-M.' *El País,* July 24. http://elpais.com/diario/2011/07/24/eps/1311488808_850215.html.

Certeau, Michel de. 2010. *The Practice of Everyday Life.* Berkeley, Calif.: University of California Press.

Colau, Ada, and Adrià Alemany. 2013. *Vidas hipotecadas: de la burbuja inmobiliaria al derecho a la vivienda.* Barcelona: Cuadrilátero de Libros.

Comisión de economía Acampadasol. 2011. 'Propuestas abiertas de la comisión de economía (Sol).' *#Acampadasol.* June 6. http://madrid.tomalaplaza.net/2011/06/06/propuestas-abiertas-de-la-comision-de-economia-sol/.

Contratiempo, historia y memoria. 2014. 'El 15-M y las narrativas de la modernidad en España.' *Contratiempo, historia y memoria.* Accessed July 26. http://www.contratiempohistoria.org/?page_id=742.

Costa, María Teresa. 1983. *La financiación exterior del capitalismo español en el siglo XIX.* Barcelona: Edicions Universitat Barcelona.

Cozarinsky, Edgardo. 2005. *Museo del chisme.* Buenos Aires: Emecé.

'Cristina, la oyente que exigió a RNE respeto para los manifestantes del 15m.' 2011. http://www.youtube.com/watch?v=3yQxixRBCls&feature=youtube_gdata_player.

Cueto, Juan. 1985. '1291.' *El País,* June 13. http://elpais.com/diario/1985/06/13/ultima/487461606_850215.html.

Dardot, Pierre, and Christian Laval. 2014. *The New Way of the World: On Neoliberal Society.* London and New York: Verso.

Darnton, Robert. 2009. 'Google & the Future of Books.' *The New York Review of Books,* February 12. http://www.nybooks.com/articles/archives/2009/feb/12/google-the-future-of-books/.

'DatAnalysis15m.' 2013. *DatAnalysis15m.* Accessed July 29. http://datanalysis15m.wordpress.com/.

Deleuze, Gilles, and Félix Guattari. 1987. *A Thousand Plateaus: Capitalism and Schizophrenia.* Minneapolis, Minn.: University of Minnesota Press.

Delgado, Luisa Elena. 2014. *La nación singular: fantasías de la normalidad democrática española (1996–2011).* Madrid: Siglo XXI Editores.

'Dentro de la marea blanca.' 2012. *Una línea sobre el mar.* http://www.unalineasobreelmar.net/2012/12/23/dentro-de-la-marea-blanca/.

'Desde fuera …' 2014. *Plataforma H. Infanta Sofía Informa.* Accessed July 21. http://privatizacionnuevoshospitales.wordpress.com/2012/11/17/desde-fuera-2/.

Díez, Luis Mateo. 1991. *Relato de Babia.* Madrid: Espasa Calpe.

—. 2000. *El pasado legendario.* Madrid: Alfaguara.

DifRed. 2014. 'Guía rápida para la dinamización de asambleas populares.' Accessed April 17. http://madrid.tomalaplaza.net/2011/05/31/guia-rapida-para-la-dinamizacion-de-asambleas-populares/.

'Documentos TV – ¿Generación perdida?' 2011. *RTVE.es.* http://www.rtve.es/television/20111005/documentos-tv-generacion-perdida/466307.shtml.

'El desconcierto (Cuerpos y Fuerzas del Estado de Indignación).' 2014. *Al final de la asamblea*. Accessed April 30. http://alfinaldelaasamblea.wordpress.com/2012/07/17/el-desconcierto-cuerpos-y-fuerzas-del-estado-indignado/.

El País. 2005. 'La generación de los mil euros.' *El País*, October 23. http://elpais.com/diario/2005/10/23/domingo/1130038892_850215.html.

—. 2012. '#nimileuristas.' *El País*, October 19. http://politica.elpais.com/politica/nimileurista.html.

El País, and WikiLeaks. 2010a. 'Cable sobre la postura del PP en la lucha contra la piratería.' *El País*, December 3. http://elpais.com/elpais/2010/12/03/actualidad/1291367866_850215.html.

—. 2010b. 'Cable sobre las acciones legales del Gobierno contra la piratería.' *El País*, December 3. http://elpais.com/elpais/2010/12/03/actualidad/1291367859_850215.html.

Entrevista Marisa Pérez Colina, Fundación de los Comunes (FdlC), MUSAC 14 de mayo de 2014. 2014. http://vimeo.com/95377230.

Espai en Blanc. 2006. 'Espai en Blanc: [revista].' *Espai en Blanc: [revista]*. http://www.espaienblanc.net/.

Estalella, Adolfo. 2012. 'Otra cultura para otro Madrid. ¿Otra cultura para quién? Notas sobre el PECAM.' *Prototyping*. http://www.prototyping.es/cultura-digital/otra-cultura-para-otro-madrid-otra-cultura-para-quien-notas-sobre-el-pecam.

Esteban, Iñaki. 2007. *El efecto Guggenheim: del espacio basura al ornamento*. Barcelona: Editorial Anagrama.

EURACA. 2012. 'EURACA.' *EURACA*. http://seminarioeuraca.wordpress.com/.

Europa Press. 2014. 'El 96% de los jóvenes usa internet, la mayoría a diario, y el 83% utiliza redes sociales.' *20minutos.es*. Accessed July 21. http://www.20minutos.es/noticia/1350975/0/.

FACUA. 2014. 'Los consumidores eligen la "asamblea-farsa" de Movistar como El Peor Anuncio del Año.' *FACUA Consumidores en Acción*. Accessed July 28. https://www.facua.org/es/enviar_amigo.php?Id=?Id=6684&seleccion=noticias&Id=6684.

Federici, Silvia. 2010. *Calibán y la bruja: mujeres, cuerpo y acumulación primitiva*. (Historia; 9). Madrid: Traficantes de Sueños.

—. 2011. 'Feminism and the Politics of the Commons.' *The Commoner*. http://www.commoner.org.uk/?p=113.

Feijoo, Benito Jerónimo. 2014. *Teatro Crítico Universal*. Digital edition. 8 vols. Proyecto Filosofía en español. Accessed July 25. http://www.filosofia.org/bjf/bjft000.htm.

Ferlosio, Rafael Sánchez. 2000. *El alma y la vergüenza*. Ediciones Destino.

Fernández-Savater, Amador. 2008. 'Fuera de lugar.' Blog in a Digital Newspaper. *Diario Público*. http://blogs.publico.es/fueradelugar/tag/apuntes-de-acampadasol.

—. 2011a. 'Interferencias.' Blog in a Digital Newspaper. *eldiario.es*. http://www.eldiario.es/interferencias/.

—. 2011b. ''Fuera de lugar' Apuntes de acampadasol (1).' http://blogs.publico.es/fueradelugar/376/apuntes-de-acampadasol-1.

—. 2011c. 'La cena del miedo (mi reunión con la ministra Sinde).' *El País*, January 12. http://cultura.elpais.com/cultura/2011/01/12/actualidad/1294786808_850215.html.

—. 2012. '¿Cómo se organiza un clima?' http://blogs.publico.es/fueradelugar/1438/%c2%bfcomo-se-organiza-un-clima.

—. 2013. *Fuera de lugar: conversaciones entre crisis y transformación*. Madrid: Acuarela Libros.

—. 2014a. '"Saber decirnos y contarnos es parte de la batalla".' *eldiario.es*. Accessed June 12. http://www.eldiario.es/interferencias/Saber-decirnos-contarnos-parte-batalla_6_209339086.html.

—. 2014b. 'Política literal y política literaria (sobre ficciones políticas y 15-M).' *eldiario.es*. Accessed July 21. http://www.eldiario.es/interferencias/ficcion-politica-15-M_6_71452864.html.

Fernández-Savater, Amador, and Cecilia Barriga. 2014. 'Sólo necesitamos tiempo: una entrevista con Cecilia Barriga sobre cine y política.' *eldiario.es*. Accessed December 27. http://www.eldiario.es/interferencias/cine-politica-15M-Cecilia_Barriga_6_336726339.html.

Fernández-Savater, Amador, Marta Malo, and Débora Ávila. 2014. 'Laval y Dardot: "El neoliberalismo es una forma de vida, no sólo una ideología o una política económica".' *eldiario.es*. Accessed December 12. http://www.eldiario.es/interferencias/neoliberalismo-ideologia-politica-economica-forma_6_312228808.html.

Fernández-Savater, Amador, and Margarita Padilla. 2013. 'Internet puede inspirar una nueva política a la altura de la complejidad de nuestro mundo.' *Interferencias -eldiario.es*. January 10. http://www.eldiario.es/interferencias/Internet-politica-complejidad_6_88951108.html.

Ferrándiz, José J. Martí. 2002. *Poder político y educación: El control de la enseñanza (España, 1936–1975)*. Valencia: Universitat de València.

Foucault, Michel. 1990. *The History of Sexuality, Vol. 1: An Introduction*. Translated by Robert Hurley. Reissue edition. New York: Vintage.

—. 2010. *The Birth of Biopolitics: Lectures at the Collège de France, 1978–1979*. Reprint edition. New York: Picador.

Fradera, Josep Maria. 2005. *Colonias para después de un imperio*. Barcelona: Edicions Bellaterra.

Fundación de los Comunes. 2013a. '¿De qué va esto de la Fundación de los Comunes? | Periódico Diagonal.' Blog in a Digital Newspaper. *Asaltar los cielos*. May 23. https://www.diagonalperiodico.net/blogs/fundaciondeloscomunes/va-esto-la-fundacion-comunes.html.

—. 2013b. 'De nuevo al Agora99. Algunas consideraciones desde la Fundación de los Comunes.' Blog in a Digital Newspaper. *Asaltar los cielos*. October 30. https://www.diagonalperiodico.net/blogs/fundaciondeloscomunes/nuevo-al-agora99-algunas-consideraciones-desde-la-fundacion-comunes.html.

'Fundación Robo.' 2013. Accessed July 29. http://www.fundacionrobo.org/.

Fuster Morell, Mayo. 2011. 'Acción colectiva a través de redes online: Comunidades de Creación Online para la construcción de bienes públicos digitales.' *Redes.com: revista de estudios para el desarrollo social de la Comunicación* 6: 229–48.

—. 2012. 'The Free Culture and 15M Movements in Spain: Composition, Social Networks and Synergies.' *Social Movement Studies* 11 (3–4): 386–92.

Fuster Morell, Mayo, Marco Berlinguer, Ruben Martinez, and Joan Subirats. 2013. 'Modelos emergentes de sostenibilidad de procomunes audiovisuales.' *Teknokultura. Revista de Cultura Digital y Movimientos Sociales* 10 (1): 131–53.

Fuster Morell, Mayo, and Joan Subirats. 2012. 'Més enllà d'Internet com a eina "Martell" – eina de la vella política: Cap un nou Policy Making? Els casos del

Moviment de Cultura Lliure i pel Procomú Digital i el 15M a Catalunya.' Institut de Govern i Polítiques Públiques Universitat Autònoma de Barcelona.

Gago, Verónica, Diego Sztulwark, and Diego Picotto. 2014. 'El intelectual orgánico y el cartógrafo.' http://anarquiacoronada.blogspot.com/2014/09/el-intelectual-organico-y-el-cartografo.html.

Gálvez Biesca, Sergio. 2007. 'Las relaciones capital-trabajo en España: la "cultura de la precariedad" como pauta cultural.' *Sociedad y utopía: Revista de ciencias sociales* 29: 105–14.

Garcés Mascareñas, Marina. 2013. *Un mundo común*. Barcelona: Edicions Bellaterra.

García Canclini, Néstor, Francisco Cruces, Maritza Urteaga, Verónica Gerber Bicecci, and Karina Boggio. 2012. *Jóvenes, culturas urbanas y redes digitales: prácticas emergentes en las artes, las editoriales y la música*. Buenos Aires and Madrid: Ariel and Fundación Telefónica.

García, Clotilde Navarro. 1993. *La educación y el nacional-catolicismo*. Cuenca: Universidad de Castilla La Mancha.

García Posada, Miguel. 1994. 'Un renovador indIspensable.' *El País*, January 5. http://elpais.com/diario/1994/01/05/cultura/757724402_850215.html.

García Santa Cecilia, Carlos. 1985. 'Dalí dibuja el rapto de Europa.' *El País*, June 12. http://elpais.com/diario/1985/06/12/cultura/487375201_850215.html.

Gil, Silvia L. 2011. *Nuevos feminismos: sentidos comunes en la dispersión. Una historia de trayectorias y rupturas en el Estado español*. Madrid: Traficantes de Sueños.

González. 2014. 'Javier Marías: "Estamos viviendo una especie de enorgullecimiento de la ignorancia, de la bruticie."' *Jot Down Cultural Magazine*. Accessed July 27. http://www.jotdown.es/2012/06/javier-marias-en-espana-estamos-viviendo-una-especie-de-enorgullecimiento-de-la-ignorancia-de-la-bruticie/.

González Lucini, Fernando. 2006. *_Y la palabra se hizo música: la canción de autor en España*. Madrid: Fundación Autor.

Gould-Wartofsky, Michael A. 2015. *The Occupiers: The Making of the 99 Percent Movement*. Oxford: Oxford University Press.

Gracia García, Jordi. 2001. *Hijos de la Razón: Contraluces de la Libertad en Las Letras Españolas de la Democracia*. Barcelona: Edhasa.

Gracia García, Jordi, and Domingo Ródenas de Moya, eds. 2009. *El ensayo español: siglo XX*. Barcelona: Crítica.

Graeber, David. 2011. *Debt: The First 5,000 Years*. Brooklyn: Melville House.

—. 2013. *The Democracy Project: A History, a Crisis, a Movement*. First edition. New York: Spiegel & Grau.

Graham, Helen Eve, and Jo Labanyi. 1995. *Spanish Cultural Studies – An Introduction: The Struggle for Modernity*. Oxford: Oxford University Press.

Gramsci, Antonio. 1999. *Cuadernos de la cárcel*. Mexico City: Ediciones Era.

Grupo de Pensamiento de Sol, y Comisión de Respeto. 2014. 'Bonita reflexión sobre RESPETO.' *Asamblea Popular 15M Villa de Vallecas*. Accessed July 28. http://asambleavvk.wordpress.com/2011/06/15/bonita-reflexion-sobre-respeto-grupo-de-pensamiento-de-sol/.

Hardt, Michael, and Antonio Negri. 2001. *Empire*. New Edition. Cambridge, Mass.: Harvard University Press.

—. 2005. *Multitude: War and Democracy in the Age of Empire*. New York: Penguin Books.

—. 2009. *Commonwealth*. Cambridge, Mass.: Belknap Press of Harvard University Press.

—. 2012. *Declaration*. New York: Argo-Navis.

Harney, Stefano. 2010a. 'The Real Knowledge Transfer.' *Social Text*. http://socialtext-journal.org/periscope_article/the_real_knowledge_transfer/.

—. 2010b. 'The Creative Industries Debate. Unfinished business: labour, management, and the creative industries.' *Cultural Studies* 24 (3): 431–44.

—. 2013. 'Logistical Infrastructures and Algorithmic Institutions.' May 2. http://vimeo.com/65293774.

Harvey, David. 1989. *The Urban Experience*. Baltimore, Maryland: Johns Hopkins University Press.

—. 2005. *A Brief History of Neoliberalism*. Oxford and New York: Oxford University Press.

—. 2013. *Rebel Cities: From the Right to the City to the Urban Revolution*. London and New York: Verso.

Herreros, Roberto. 2011. '¿Cómo diablos se escriben canciones colectivas?' *Rebelión*. www.rebelion.org/noticia.php?id=132494.

Hooper, John. 2006. *The New Spaniards*. 2nd edition. London and New York: Penguin Books.

'Huyo de la realidad española.' 2014. *El Huffington Post*. Accessed March 20. http://www.huffingtonpost.es/2012/10/13/jovenes-espanoles-emigran_n_1963468.html.

Ingrassia, Franco. 2011. 'Por todas partes crece la sensación de ser como náufragos a la deriva.' http://blogs.publico.es/fueradelugar/280/como-naufragos-a-la-deriva.

Izquierdo Martín, Jesús. 2002. *El rostro de la comunidad: la identidad del campesino en la Castilla del antiguo régimen*. Madrid: Consejo Económico y Social de Madrid.

—. 2005. 'Morir de Humanidad. Otro Réquiem por el Campesino Español.' En presentation at X Jornadas Interescuelas-Departamentos de Historia, Rosario, Argentina.

—. 2007. 'El ciudadano demediado. Campesinos, ciudadanía y alteridad en la España contemporánea.' In *De súbitos a ciudadanos: una historia de la ciudadanía de España*, edited by Manuel Pérez Ledesma, 627–56. Madrid: Centro de Estudios Políticos y Constitucionales.

Izquierdo Martín, Jesús, and Pablo Sánchez León. 2003. 'Ciudadanía y clase social tras la comunidad.' *Cuadernos de relaciones laborales* 21 (1): 61–87.

Jenkins, Henry. 2006. *Convergence Culture: Where Old and New Media Collide*. New York: New York University Press.

Jiménez, A. C., and A. Estalella. 2014. 'Assembling Neighbors: The City as Hardware, Method, and "a Very Messy Kind of Archive."' *Common Knowledge* 20 (1): 150–71.

Jiménez, Luis Eduardo Pires, and José Luis Ramos Gorostiza. 2005. 'Ingenieros e "ingenierismo" en la economía de la España autárquica: una comparación con el caso portugués.' *Tst: Transportes, Servicios y telecomunicaciones* 8: 82–115.

Labanyi, Jo. 2011. 'Cinema and the Mediation of Everyday Life in 1940s and 1950s Spain.' *New Readings* 8 (1). http://ojs.cf.ac.uk/index.php/newreadings/article/view/23.

—. 2013. 'Narrative in culture, 1975–1996.' In *The Cambridge Companion to Modern Spanish Culture*, edited by David T. Gies, 147–62. Cambridge: Cambridge University Press.

'La Biblioteca Sol y el Archivo del 15-M perviven en Lavapiés.' 2014. Accessed July 23. http://www.cuartopoder.es/invitados/la-biblioteca-sol-y-el-archivo-del-15-m-perviven-en-lavapies/3219.

Labrador, Germán. 2006. 'Indicios vehementes: notas para un archivo cultural de la transición española.' *Revista de Occidente* 299: 83–98.

—. 2008. 'Poéticas e imaginarios de la transición española: campo, discursos, fracturas.' PhD thesis, Universidad de Salamanca.

—. 2012. 'Las Vidas subprime: la circulación de historias de vida como tecnología de imaginación política en la crisis española (2007–2012).' *Hispanic Review* 80 (4): 557–81.

—. 2014. '¿Lo llamaban democracia? La crítica estética de la política en la transición española y el imaginario de la historia en el 15-M.' *Kamchatka: revista de análisis cultural* 4: 11–61.

Laclau, Ernesto, and Chantal Mouffe. 2004. *Hegemonía y estrategia socialista: hacia una radicalización de la democracia*. Buenos Aires: Fondo de Cultura Económica.

Laddaga, Reinaldo. 2006. *Estética de la emergencia: la formación de otra cultura de las artes*. Buenos Aires: Adriana Hidalgo editora.

Lafuente García, Antonio. 2009. 'El saber, para quien lo necesita.' Blog in a Digital Newspaper. *Fuera de lugar - Publico.es*. June 6. http://blogs.publico.es/fueradelugar/73/el-saber-para-quien-lo-necesita.

Lafuente García, Antonio, Andoni Alonso, and Joaquí Rodríguez. 2013. *¡Todos sabios!: ciencia ciudadana y conocimiento expandido*. Madrid: Ediciones Cátedra, S.A.

Lamo de Espinosa, Emilio. 2001. 'La normalización de España: España, Europa y la modernidad.' *Claves de razón práctica* 111: 4–17.

Lamo de Espinosa Enríquez de Navarra, Emilio. 1962. 'El informe del banco mundial y la agricultura española.' *Revista de Estudios Agrosociales* 41: 7–60.

La Parra-Pérez, Pablo. 2014. 'Revueltas lógicas: el ciclo de movilización del 15M y la práctica de la democracia radical.' *Journal of Spanish Cultural Studies* 15 (1–2): 1–19.

La Plataforma. 2013. http://www.youtube.com/watch?v=YBFlxOBOfHo&feature=youtube_gdata_player.

Lara, Ángel Luis. 2003. 'Una aproximación al ecosistema de la nueva fuerza de trabajo. Approaching the ecosystem of the new workforce.' *Cuadernos de Relaciones Laborales* 21 (2): 215–30.

—. 2013. 'El trabajo de los prosumidores: carácter productivo y explotación de los públicos mediáticos.' En presentation at XI Congreso Español de Sociología, "Crisis y cambio: Propuestas desde la Sociología", Universidad Complutense de Madrid.

La Razón. 2012. '15-M: 15-Críticas.' *www.larazon.es*, June 13. http://www.larazon.es/detalle_hemeroteca/noticias/LA_RAZON_457708/3534-15-m-15-criticas.

Lasch, Christopher. 1996. *The Revolt of the Elites and the Betrayal of Democracy*. New York: W. W. Norton.

Lasén, Amparo. 2009. 'Las nuevas formas de acción colectiva desafían la lógica de la representación.' Digital Newspaper. *Fuera de lugar -Publico.es*. December 12. http://blogs.publico.es/fueradelugar/114/multitudes-inteligentes-y-multitudes-relampago.

Lawrence, Jeffrey. 2014. 'The Spanish Roots of the 99%.' *Tropics of Meta*. Accessed July 21. http://tropicsofmeta.wordpress.com/2013/05/30/the-spanish-roots-of-the-99/.

Lenore, Víctor. 2013. 'Cultura y 15M: una relación tormentosa.' *El Confidencial*, November 3. http://www.elconfidencial.com/48625/.

—. 2014. 'La victoria cultural de los centros sociales okupados.' *El Confidencial*.

Accessed June 23. http://www.elconfidencial.com/cultura/2014-06-23/la-victoria-cultural-de-los-centros-sociales-okupados_150024/.

León, Pablo. 2010. 'El mapa "okupa" de Madrid.' *El País*, January 6. http://elpais.com/diario/2010/01/06/madrid/1262780657_850215.html.

Lessig, Lawrence. 2004. *Free Culture: How Big Media Uses Technology and the Law to Lock Down Culture and Control Creativity*. London: Penguin.

Levy, Pierre. 1999. *Collective Intelligence: Mankind's Emerging World in Cyberspace*. Cambridge: Perseus Publishing.

López Hernández, Isidro. 2012. 'Consensonomics: la ideología económica en la CT.' In *CT o la cultura de la transición: Crítica a 35 años de cultura española*, edited by Guillem Martínez. [unpaginated] Barcelona: Desbolsillo.

López Hernández, Isidro, and Emmanuel Rodríguez López. 2010. *Fin de ciclo: financiarización, territorio y sociedad de propietarios en la onda larga del capitalismo hispano (1959–2010)*. Madrid: Traficantes de Sueños.

López, Isidro, and Emmanuel Rodríguez. 2011. 'The Spanish Model.' *New Left Review* II, 69 (June): 5–29.

Loureiro, Ángel G. 1991. *Introducción a Relato de Babia*. Madrid: Espasa Calpe.

—. 1998. 'España maníaca.' *Quimera: Revista de literatura* 167: 15–20.

Lozano Bright, Carmen. 2014. 'Todos somos cultura, pero ...' *Carmen Lozano Bright·*. March 8. http://carmenlozano.wordpress.com/2014/03/08/todos-somos-cultura-pero/.

Macasoli, Agustín, and F. Martín. 1957. *La provincia resurge: Plan de Badajoz*. Documentary, Short.

Mainer, José Carlos. 1994. *De postguerra: (1951–1990)*. Barcelona: Crítica.

'Manifiesto "En defensa de los derechos fundamentales en internet."' 2014. Wikipedia. http://es.wikipedia.org/w/index.php?title=Manifiesto_%C2%ABEn_defensa_de_los_derechos_fundamentales_en_internet%C2%BB&oldid=69812539.

Manipulación y acoso en TVE. El portavoz de Gamonal calla la boca a Mariló Montero. 2014. http://www.youtube.com/watch?v=FHTbOxWGpgw&feature=youtube_gdata_player.

Marcos, Natalia. 2012. 'Subtítulos por amor al arte.' *El País - Blog Quinta Temporada*, June 21. http://blogs.elpais.com/quinta-temporada/2012/06/subtitulos-por-amor-al-arte.html.

Marías, Javier. 1985. 'Visión de un falso indiano.' *El País*, November 2. http://elpais.com/diario/1985/11/02/opinion/499734008_850215.html.

—. 2006. 'Los villanos de la nación.' *El País*, September 3. http://elpais.com/diario/2006/09/03/eps/1157264821_850215.html.

—. 2011. *Pasiones pasadas*. Barcelona: Penguin Random House Grupo Editorial España.

Marías, Javier, and Inés Blanca. 2008. *Aquella mitad de mi tiempo: al mirar atrás*. Barcelona: Galaxia Gutenberg; Círculo de Lectores.

Marsé, Juan. 1976. *Si te dicen que caí*. Barcelona: Seix Barral.

—. 1982. *Un día volveré*. Esplugues de Llobregat (Barcelona): Plaza & Janés.

Martín Cabrera, Luis. 2011. 'Los intelectuales y el 15-M: una modesta propuesta para autoabolirnos.' *Rebelión.org*. http://www.rebelion.org/noticia.php?id=132299.

Martínez, Guillem (ed.). 2012. *CT o la cultura de la transición: Crítica a 35 años de cultura española*. Barcelona: Debolsillo.

Martínez, Jesús A, Julio Aróstegui, Carmen Molinero, and Pere Ysàs. 1999. *Historia de España. Siglo XX. 1939–1996*. Madrid: Cátedra.

Martínez, Rubén. 2013. 'La economía de la cultura no existe.' *Nativa.cat*. http://www.nativa.cat/2013/12/la-economia-de-la-cultura-no-existe/.

—. 2014a. 'Internet y política (versión 1.0).' *Ley Seca*, January 2. http://leyseca.net/articulo-internet-y-politica-version-1-0/.

—. 2014b. 'Pragmatismo en la incertidumbre.' *Ley Seca*, June 4. http://leyseca.net/pragmatismo-en-la-incertidumbre/.

Martín Gaite, Carmen. 1987. *Usos amorosos de la postguerra española*. Barcelona: Anagrama.

Marzo, Jorge Luis. 2010. *¿Puedo hablarle con libertad, excelencia?: arte y poder en España desde 1950*. Murcia: CENDEAC.

Medialab-Prado. '¿Qué es?' http://medialab-prado.es/article/que_es.

—. 2014b. 'Jornadas de reflexión "La cultura de Madrid a debate" – Medialab-Prado Madrid.' Accessed July 28. http://medialab-prado.es/article/jornadas_reflexion_pecam.

Memoria de un Consenso (Documental Canal Historia sobre la constitución española). 2004. http://www.youtube.com/watch?v=BYWyYoozExc&feature=youtube_gdata_player.

Molina, Antonio Muñoz. 2013. *Todo lo que era sólido*. Barcelona: Grupo Planeta.

Molina, Esperanza. 1984. *Los otros madrileños: el pozo del tío Raimundo*. Madrid: Avapiés.

Monzó, Quim. 2011. 'Vet aquí la Spanish Revolution.' *La Vanguardia*, May 19. http://www.lavanguardia.com/opinion/articulos/20110519/54156805721/vet-aqui-la-spanish-revolution.html.

Morán, Gregorio. 1998. *El maestro en el erial: Ortega y Gasset y la cultura del franquismo*. Barcelona: Tusquets.

—. 2014. *El cura y los mandarines. Historia no oficial del bosque de los letrados. Cultura y política en España, 1962–1996*. Madrid: Akal.

Moreno-Caballud, Luis. 2010. 'Topos, carnavales y vecinos. Derivas de lo rural en la literatura y el cine de la transición española (1973–1986).' PhD thesis, Princeton University.

—. 2012. 'La imaginación sostenible: culturas y crisis económica en la España actual.' *Hispanic Review* 80 (4): 535–55.

—. 2013. 'Desbordamientos culturales en torno al 15-M.' *Teknokultura. Revista de Cultura Digital y Movimientos Sociales* 10 (1): 101–30.

—. 2014. 'Cuando cualquiera escribe. Procesos democratizadores de la cultura escrita en la crisis de la Cultura de la Transición española.' *Journal of Spanish Cultural Studies* 15 (1): 13–36.

Moreno-Caballud, Luis, and Marina Sitrin. 2013. 'Occupy Wall Street, Beyond Encampments.' *YES! Magazine*. Accessed July 29. http://www.yesmagazine.org/people-power/occupy-wall-street-beyond-encampments.

Muriel, Eduardo. 2012. 'El día en que la policía de Fraga disparó contra una asamblea.' *Público.es*, January. http://www.publico.es/espana/417425/el-dia-en-que-la-policia-de-fraga-disparo-contra-una-asamblea.

Nadal Oller, Jordi. 1978. *El fracaso de la revolución industrial en España, 1814–1913*. Barcelona: Ariel.

Nanclares, Silvia. 2009. *El Sur, instrucciones de uso 11 relatos 11*. Madrid: Ecobuk.

'NoLesVotes.com.' 2011. http://www.nolesvotes.com/.

No nos vamos – Comisión de Respeto. 2011. http://www.youtube.com/watch?v=3b8rGDVijbs&feature=youtube_gdata_player.

Nordmann, Charlotte. 2010. *Bourdieu/Rancière: la política entre sociología y filosofía*. Buenos Aires: Nueva Visión. http://blogs.unc.edu.ar/novedadesbm/2012/07/03/nordmann-charlotte/.

Oliveras, Jordi. 2013. 'Crisis, cultura, sector cultural y desobediencia.' *Nativa.cat*, June 10. http://www.nativa.cat/2013/06/crisis-cultura-sector-cultural-y-desobediencia/.

Ong, Walter J. 1982. *Orality and Literacy: The Technologizing of the Word*. London and New York: Methuen.

Padilla, Margarita. 2010. 'La Web 2.0 y el anonimato en primera persona.' *Barcelona Metrópolis*. http://w2.bcn.cat/bcnmetropolis/arxiu/es/page3baa.html?id=23&ui=420.

—. 2013. *El kit de la lucha en internet*. Madrid: Traficantes de Sueños.

País, Ediciones El. 1986. 'Medio centenar de intelectuales y artistas pide en un manifiesto el "sí" a la Alianza.' *El País*, February 18. http://elpais.com/diario/1986/02/18/espana/509065219_850215.html.

Papell, Antonio. 2011. 'Desaparecidos con poder en España (VII): José Mario Armero, servidor del Estado.' *El Economista.es*, September 27. http://ecodiario.eleconomista.es/interstitial/volver/ibjulag/sociedad/noticias/3406920/09/11/Desaparecidos-con-poder-en-Espana-VII-Jose-Mario-Armero-servidor-del-Estado.html#.Kku8fUtrtP6A71Y.

Peiró, Patricia. 2014. 'La cultura "okupa" Madrid.' *El País*, June 14. http://ccaa.elpais.com/ccaa/2014/06/13/madrid/1402677575_806851.html.

Peñamarín, Cristina. 2002. 'El humor gráfico del franquismo y la formación de un territorio translocal de identidad democrática.' *CIC: Cuadernos de información y comunicación* 7: 351–80.

Pérez Díaz, Víctor. 1987. *El retorno de la sociedad civil: respuestas sociales a la transición política, la crisis económica y los cambios culturales de España, 1975–1985*. Madrid: Instituto de Estudios Económicos.

Pérez Orozco, Amaia. 2014. *Subversión feminista de la economía. Aportes para un debate sobre el conflicto capital-vida*. Madrid: Traficantes de Sueños.

Picchio, Antonella. 2009. 'La economía política y la investigación de las condiciones de vida.' *Revista de Economía Crítica* 7: 27–54.

Piglia, Ricardo. 2000. *Crítica y ficción*. Buenos Aires: Seix Barral.

Piglia, Ricardo, and León Rozitchner. 2001. *Tres propuestas para el próximo milenio (y cinco dificultades*. Buenos Aires: Fondo de Cultura Económica.

Pino, Mario Espinoza. 2013. 'Politics of Indignation: Radical Democracy and Class Struggle beyond Postmodernity.' *Rethinking Marxism* 25 (2): 228–41.

Plataforma de Afectados por la Hipoteca. 2013. 'Modelo escrito para solicitar la nulidad de los procedimientos en trámite en base a la sentencia del TJUE.' http://afectadosporlahipoteca.com/documentos-utiles/.

'Poder en la sombra.' 2012. *Robo*. http://esunrobo.bandcamp.com/track/poder-en-la-sombra.

Precarias a la deriva. 2004. *A la deriva por los circuitos de la precariedad femenina: precarias a la deriva*. Madrid: Traficantes de Sueños.

Prego, Victoria. 1995. 'La Transición.' *RTVE*.

Público.es. 2011. 'El manifiesto "Una ilusión compartida" se propone movilizar a la izquierda.' *Público.es*, July 2. http://www.publico.es/espana/385049/el-manifiesto-una-ilusion-compartida-se-propone-movilizar-a-la-izquierda.

Publico.es. 2012. 'Educación subirá el precio de la matrícula universitaria a los alumnos.' *Público.es*, April 19. http://www.publico.es/espana/430067/educacion-subira-el-precio-de-la-matricula-universitaria-a-los-alumnos.

Qué pasó la noche del 23-F, según Carrillo. 2011. http://www.youtube.com/watch?v=h5W-oRp5-Ok&feature=youtube_gdata_player.

Ramírez Blanco, Julia. 2014. *Utopías artísticas de revuelta: Claremont Road, Reclaim the Streets, la Ciudad de Sol*. Madrid: Cátedra.

Ramonet, Ignacio. 2011. '¿En manos de quién estamos?' Conference paper, University of Heidelberg, June 8.

Rancière, Jacques. 1984. 'L'Ethique de la sociologie.' *Collectif Révoltes Logiques, L'Empire du sociologue*. Paris: Editions Découverte.

—. 2003. *El maestro ignorante: cinco lecciones sobre la emancipación intelectual*. Barcelona: Editorial Laertes.

—. 2004. *The Politics of Aesthetics: The Distribution of the Sensible*. London: Continuum.

Rancière, Jacques, and Amador Fernández-Savater. 2007. 'La democracia es el poder de cualquiera.' *El País*, February 3. http://elpais.com/diario/2007/02/03/babelia/1170461828_850215.html.

Reig, Rafael. 2012. 'Desde dentro de la burbuja.' *eldiario.es*, December 11. http://www.eldiario.es/Kafka/dentro-burbuja_0_78392198.html.

Rendueles, César. 2013. 'Contra la igualdad de oportunidades.' *espejismos digitales*, May 21. http://espejismosdigitales.wordpress.com/2013/05/21/contra-la-igualdad-de-oportunidades/.

Rendueles Menéndez de Llano, César. 2013. *Sociofobia: el cambio político en la era de la utopía digital*. Madrid: Capitán Swing.

Resina, Joan Ramon. *Del hispanismo a los estudios ibéricos: una propuesta federativa para el ámbito cultural*. Madrid: Biblioteca Nueva.

Richardson, Nathan E. 2002. *Postmodern Paletos: Immigration, Democracy, and Globalization in Spanish Narrative and Film, 1950–2000*. Lewisburg, Phil.: Bucknell University Press.

Robbins, Lionel. 1935. *An Essay on the Nature & Significance of Economic Science*. London: Macmillan.

Rodríguez, Emmanuel. 2013. *Hipótesis democracia: quince tesis para la revolución anunciada*. Madrid: Traficantes de Sueños.

Romanos, Eduardo. 2014a. 'Collective Learning Processes within Social Movements: Some Insights into the Spanish 15-M/Indignados Movement.' Accessed July 21. https://www.academia.edu/2298671/Collective_Learning_Processes_within_Social_Movements_Some_Insights_into_the_Spanish_15-M_Indignados_Movement.

—. 2014b. 'Humor in the Streets: The Spanish Indignados.' Accessed July 21. http://www.academia.edu/6099707/Humor_in_the_Streets_The_Spanish_Indignados.

—. 2014c. '"Esta revolución es muy copyleft". Entrevista a Stéphane M. Grueso a propósito del 15M.' Accessed July 21. http://www.academia.edu/1601448/_Esta_revolucion_es_muy_copyleft_._Entrevista_a_Stephane_M._Grueso_a_proposito_del_15M.

Ross, Kristin. 1997. 'The sociologist and the priest.' *Sites: The Journal of Twentieth-Century/Contemporary French Studies revue d'études françaises* 1 (1): 17–30.

Roubaud, Jacques. 1998. *Poesía, etcétera: puesta a punto*. Madrid: Ediciones Hiperión, S.L.

Rowan, Jaron. 2010. *Emprendizajes en cultura: discursos, instituciones y contradicciones de la empresarialidad cultural*. Madrid: Traficantes de Sueños.

—. 2011. 'El procomún como infraestructura.' Empresas del procomún. http://
   wiki.empresasdelprocomun.net/index.php?title=El_procom%C3%BAn_como_
   infraestructura.

—. 2013. 'Sé creativo, come mierda | Nativa.' *Nativa.cat*. http://www.nativa.cat/2013/12/
   se-creativo-come-mierda/.

Sainz Borgo, Karina. 2014. 'El 15M me parece un movimiento narcisista.'
   Interview. *Vox Populi*. Accessed April 30. http://vozpopuli.com/ocio-y-cultura/
   3507-felix-de-azua-el-15m-me-parece-un-movimiento-narcisista.

Salgado, María. 2012. 'no leo novelas.' *globo→rápido*. April 10. http://globorapido.
   blogspot.com.es/2012/04/no-leo-novelas.html.

—. 2014. *HACíA UN RUIDO frases para un film político // story board textual // FILM
   PROYECTO BORRADOR*. Madrid: La Lenta Editora.

Salvados. 2013. 'Salvados: ¿La vida sigue igual?' *Salvados*. La Sexta. http://www.
   lasexta.com/videos-online/programas/salvados/avances/salvados-vida-sigue-
   igual_2013102400095.html.

'Salvemos la princesa.' 2014. *salvemos la princesa*. Accessed July 28. http://
   salvemoslaprincesa.wordpress.com/.

Sánchez Criado, Tomás. 2013a. 'Ese conocimiento que la razón tecnocrática ignora
   (1): ¿Del doctor como el mejor gobernador?' Blog in a Digital Newspaper. *Fuera
   de clase*, September 2. https://www.diagonalperiodico.net/blogs/fuera-clase/ese-
   conocimiento-la-razon-tecnocratica-ignora-1-del-doctor-como-mejor-gobernador.

—. 2013b. 'Ese conocimiento que la razón tecnocrática ignora (2): ¿El estallido de
   comunidades epistémicas experimentales?' Blog in a Digital Newspaper. *Fuera
   de clase*. November 11. https://www.diagonalperiodico.net/blogs/fuera-clase/ese-
   conocimiento-la-razon-tecnocratica-ignora-2-estallido-comunidades-
   epistemicas.

—. 2014. 'Ese conocimiento que la razón tecnocrática ignora (y 3): Vulnerabilidad y
   mimo de la experimentación del cualquiera.' Blog in a Digital Newspaper. *Fuera
   de clase*. https://www.diagonalperiodico.net/blogs/fuera-clase/ese-conocimiento-
   la-razon-tecnocratica-ignora-3-vulnerabilidad-y-mimo-la.

Sánchez Dragó. 2011. 'El Circo de Sol.' *El Mundo*, June 17. http://www.caffereggio.
   net/2011/06/17/el-circo-de-sol-de-fernando-sanchez-drago-en-el-mundo/.

Sánchez Ferlosio, Rafael. 1984. 'La cultura, ese invento del Gobierno.' *El País*,
   November 22. http://elpais.com/diario/1984/11/22/opinion/469926007_850215.
   html.

Sánchez León, Pablo. 2004. 'Estigma y memoria de los jóvenes de la transición.' In
   La memoria de los olvidados: un debate sobre el silencio de la represión franquista, edited
   by Emilio Silva, Pancho Salvador, María Socorro Asunción Esteban Recio, and
   Javier Castán, 163–82. Valladolid: Ámbito.

—. 2010. 'Encerrados con un solo juguete. Cultura de clase media y metahistoria
   de la transición.' *Mombaça* VIII (Número Especial: 'Lo llamaban Transición'):
   11–17.

—. 2014. *Desclasamiento y desencanto. Representaciones sociales de clase media y poética de
   la participación democrática en la transición española*. Madrid: Contratiempo.

Sánchez Vidal, Agustín. 1990. *Sol y sombra*. Barcelona: Editorial Planeta.

Selci, Damián, and Violeta Kesselman. 2008. 'Juan Desiderio: delirios de juventud
   cultural.' *Planta*, February. http://plantarevista.blogspot.com/2008/02/nmero-3-
   subido.html

Seminario de Historia Política y Social de las Okupaciones en Madrid-Metrópolis. 2014. *Okupa Madrid (1985–2011). Memoria, reflexión, debate y autogestión colectiva del conocimiento*. Madrid: Seminario de Historia Política y Social de las Okupaciones en Madrid-Metrópolis.

Sitrin, Marina, and Dario Azzellini. 2014. *They Can't Represent Us! Reinventing Democracy from Greece to Occupy*. London and Brooklyn, NY: Verso.

Smith, Adam. 2013. *Lectures on Justice, Police, Revenue and Arms*. London: Forgotten Books.

Subirats, Eduardo. *Después de la lluvia: sobre la ambigua modernidad española*. Madrid: Temas de Hoy.

Teran Mantovani, Emiliano, and Raquel Gutiérrez Aguilar. 2014. "'Leo la historia reciente de América Latina desde las luchas protagonizadas desde abajo.'" Accessed December 27. http://anarquiacoronada.blogspot.com/2014/08/leo-la-historia-reciente-de-america.html.

Thompson, E. P. 2013. *The Making of the English Working Class*. London: Penguin.

Tilly, Charles. 2002. *Stories, Identities, and Political Change*. Lanham, Maryland: Rowman & Littlefield.

Toret, Javier, Arnau Monterde et al. 2013. 'Tecnopolítica: la potencia de las multitudes conectadas. El sistema red 15M, un nuevo paradigma de la política distribuida.' *IN3 Working Paper Series*. http://journals.uoc.edu/ojs/index.php/in3-working-paper-series/article/view/1878.

Traficantes de Sueños. '¿Quiénes somos?' http://traficantes.net/proyecto-traficantes-de-sue%C3%B1os.

Tudela de la Orden, José. 1966. *El hombre y la tierra*. Madrid: Instituto Nacional de Colonización.

Txarlie. 2012. 'La defensa de la red, el hacktivismo y otras contribuciones al código fuente de los nuevos movimientos.' Presented at the 'collective investigation' Tecnopolítica y 15m. La potencia de las multitudes conectadas. Sistema red #15m. Un nuevo paradigma de la política distribuida, Barcelona, October 24. http://dataanalysis15m.wordpress.com/2012/10/20/tecnopolitica-y-15m/.

'Un vecino corrige a un perdiodista de RNE que estaba mintiendo (Gamonal, Burgos).' 2014. http://www.youtube.com/watch?v=AxPWBLDFV9g&feature=youtube_gdata_player.

Uría, Jorge. 2003. *La cultura popular en la España contemporánea: doce estudios*. Madrid: Biblioteca Nueva.

Valera, D. 2012. 'La edad media de emancipación de los españoles se sitúa en los 29 años.' *Diario de León*, October 24. http://www.diariodeleon.es/noticias/sociedad/edad-media-emancipacion-espanoles-situa-29-anos_736643.html.

Vázquez Montalbán, Manuel. 1971. *Crónica sentimental de España*. Madrid: Lumen.

—. 1985. *El pianista*. Barcelona: Seix Barral.

—. 1986. *Crónica sentimental de España*. Madrid: Espasa-Calipe.

Vázquez Montalbán, Manuel. 1998. *La literatura en la construcción de la ciudad democrática*. Barcelona: Crítica.

Vicent, Manuel. 2009. 'El regalo.' *El País*, September 27. http://elpais.com/diario/2009/09/27/ultima/1254002401_850215.html.

Vila-Matas, Enrique. 2011. 'Empobrecimiento.' *El País*, May 24. http://elpais.com/diario/2011/05/24/cultura/1306188004_850215.html.

Wallerstein, Immanuel. 2002. 'New Revolts Against the System'. *New Left Review* 18: 29–39.

Yonomeaburro. 2008a. 'Subtitular series: entrevista integra a Marga, de Asia-Team.' *Yonomeaburro*, February 9. http://yonomeaburro.blogspot.com.es/2008/02/subtitular-series-entrevista-integra_09.html.

—. 2008b. 'Subtitular series: entrevista íntegra a Smalleye de Wikisubtitles.' *Yonomeaburro*. February 10. http://yonomeaburro.blogspot.com.es/2008/02/subtitular-series-entrevista-ntegra.html.

YProductions. 2009a. *Innovación en cultura. Una introducción a la genealogía y usos del concepto.* Madrid: Traficantes de Sueños.

—. 2009b. *Nuevas economías de la cultura.* Barcelona: YProductions. http://www.demasiadosuperavit.net/wp-content/uploads/2013/07/nuevas_economias_cultura_yproductions.pdf

Index